# Planning White Supremacy

the MODERN SOUTH

# PLANNING WHITE SUPREMACY

## Civil Rights and City Planning in Montgomery, Alabama, 1920–1970

REBECCA COLEEN RETZLAFF

THE UNIVERSITY OF ALABAMA PRESS
TUSCALOOSA

The University of Alabama Press
Tuscaloosa, Alabama 35487-0380
uapress.ua.edu



Typeface: Minion Pro

Cover image: City of Montgomery, Alabama, Land Use map, 1947, revised in 1948, 1949, 1950; courtesy of Special Collections & Archives, Auburn University Libraries
Cover design: Sandy Turner Jr.

Cataloging-in-Publication data is available from the Library of Congress.
ISBN: 978-0-8173-2254-0 (cloth)
ISBN: 978-0-8173-6234-8 (paper)
E-ISBN: 978-0-8173-9583-4

For Stuart Meck.
Thank you for your love and friendship.

# Contents

# Illustrations

## Figures



## Tables

# Acknowledgments

THE ORIGINS OF this book stem from a student project I was introduced to when teaching my historic preservation planning class at Auburn University in fall 2012. My friend and colleague in the Landscape Architecture program Charlene LeBleu and her class were working on a studio project in the historic Peacock Tract neighborhood in Montgomery, and she suggested that I incorporate a project in the neighborhood into my historic preservation planning class. I agreed and made the project central to my class that semester. I arranged for a tour of the neighborhood for my students with Gary Sharp—a city planner in Montgomery and Auburn alumnus. Gary met my class at the site with Charles P. Everett IV, a member of the historic Mount Zion A. M. E. Zion Church, for the tour. Although the congregation moved long ago to a new building, the historic building is still in the Peacock Tract neighborhood and is adjacent to the large I-65 and I-85 interchange. The church is where Rev. Dr. Martin Luther King Jr. was elected head of the Montgomery Improvement Association on the evening of the first mass meeting aimed at continuing the boycott. Later, the interstates plowed through the neighborhood, cutting it off from the rest of the city. On the tour, Mr. Everett mentioned that I-85 was routed to go through Rev. Ralph Abernathy's home in Centennial Hill. I was still relatively new to Alabama and found the idea that a major infrastructure project may have been designed to impact one individual to be a shocking possibility. While I knew that interstate highways were constructed through African American neighborhoods, I had never heard of one being intentionally routed for personal vengeance.

For several years I continued to think about what Mr. Everett told me. In 2018 my close friend and research partner Stuart Meck died unexpectedly. I was devastated by his death, and it was difficult to continue the same line of research on historic plans and legal decisions that Stuart and I had worked on together. As part of my healing process, I decided to start an entirely new line of research. I remembered the discussion with Mr. Everett years earlier and decided to find out if I-85 had indeed been routed through Rev. Ralph Abernathy's home. I was granted a semester leave from Auburn University and went to the National Archives II in College Park, Maryland. In those archives

I discovered the truth. Alabama Highway director, and extreme white supremacist, Sam Engelhardt rerouted I-85 to go through Rev. Abernathy's house just after the lunch counter sit-ins that students and faculty from Alabama State College were involved in. Although difficult to prove definitively, it is commonly understood locally that the highway was routed in retaliation for the community's civil rights activism, and I found evidence that activists believed this to be true. After writing an article on the routing of I-85, I published several more articles on city planning history in Montgomery. Even after his death, Stuart continues to have a major presence in my research and my life, and I think he would appreciate that I began this research because of his death. As he always did, Stuart would have told me that this book is the best thing that I have ever written if he were alive today.

First and foremost, I am grateful to my late dear friend and research partner, Stuart Meck, to whom this book is dedicated. I met Stuart when I was an intern working in a small closet in the research department of the American Planning Association (APA) in Chicago. Stuart was a senior research associate at the APA in an office with a beautiful view of Lake Michigan. Everyone at APA adored him and cherished his lovable exuberance and joy. I became friends with him when he asked me to work on a research project on affordable housing, which eventually became our first coauthored publication, and my first book. We continued to work together when I became a professor at Auburn University and when he moved to New Jersey for a faculty position at Rutgers University. I miss his presence in my life deeply and profoundly, including his loud laugh, warm hugs, strong opinions about furniture, and charisma. Stuart had a selfless devotion to helping young planners begin their careers and was generous with professional credit and coauthorship. His generosity helped me obtain my first academic position. If it were not for Stuart, I would probably be the slowest bicycle messenger in Chicago instead of the author of this book. I am grateful for every professional opportunity that he gave me, but I am even more grateful for his love and friendship.

The research for this book was aided by many librarians and archivists. The staff at the National Archives II in College Park, Maryland, was helpful during two extended research trips there. I am grateful for National Archives II librarian Amy Reytar, who made an exception to National Archives and Records Administration rules and allowed my son, Monty, to spend two weeks in the archives with me. At age nine, Monty spent part of his time at the national archives scanning archival documents, including the redlining map that was the basis for the map in chapter 1 (this is true!). Monty also accompanied me on many trips to the Alabama Department of Archives and History.

Archivists at the National Archives Atlanta, including librarian Shane Bell, assisted me in locating materials in Atlanta. I am also grateful for the assistance of librarians and archivists at the Alabama Department of Archives and History, Alabama State University, Montgomery County Archives, Birmingham Public Library, Archdiocese of Mobile Archives, Rev. Dr. Martin Luther King Jr. Archives, and the Montgomery Public Library. I am particularly grateful to the librarians at Trenholm State Community College in Montgomery, where Paul Blackmon and Joseph Trimble gave me access to their closed archives, which contain a treasure trove of materials from the honorable Rufus Lewis and others, all collected by the late Gwen Patton. The archivists at Auburn University Special Collections and Archives—Greg Schmidt, Kasia Leousis, and Tommy Brown—were invaluable in assisting my research and helping me find archival maps and plans.

My students and colleagues in the Auburn University Department of Political Science and the College of Liberal Arts were extremely helpful and supported my research and student service-learning projects in Montgomery for my classes. The staff at the Montgomery City Planning department, including Jocelyn Zanzot, Lois Cortell, Lynda Wool, Gary Sharp, Desmond Wilson, and Montgomery County commissioner Isaiah Sankey have hosted student projects in Montgomery. Those projects have helped me understand the city and have given my students and me the opportunity to learn more about planning outside the classroom.

I am also thankful for the editors and staff at the University of Alabama Press, especially Claire Lewis Evans and Daniel Waterman, whose wise advice and assistance helped the publication and peer-review process for this book go smoothly. Their help and advice on substantive content, particularly on broadening the focus of the book to include contextual issues beyond city planning, was invaluable. I am also grateful to two anonymous reviewers, whose advice and questions challenged me but greatly improved the manuscript. I am appreciative of Riley Dibble, who created most of the maps and edited the images in this book when she was working on her master's degree in the Community Planning program at Auburn University.

Finally, I am grateful to my family—Shannon, Monty, and Locklin, and our dear friend Meadows—for listening to me talk about racist city planning more than normal people should have to, and for their constant love and friendship. I am grateful to our pets, who were a welcome distraction from writing this book and whom I love very much: Carrot, Harry, Pearl, Maple, Clover, Juniper, many chickens, and about fifty thousand bees. I am also grateful to my grandparents, Marjorie and Albert Dudas, who paid for my college education and to my mom, Patricia Retzlaff, who encouraged me to major in urban and regional planning as an undergraduate at Michigan State University after it became clear that passing a chemistry class was not in the cards for me, thwarting my dreams of becoming a veterinarian.

# Planning White Supremacy

# Introduction

## City Planning for White Supremacy in Montgomery

MAXINE KIMBROUGH, AN African American mother of seven children ranging in age from two to twelve, lived in Montgomery's Centennial Hill neighborhood, a vibrant and inspiring community of doctors, teachers, and professionals, home to Alabama State College (ASC, now named Alabama State University, ASU, one of the historically Black colleges and universities, HBCUs), and the center of civil rights activism in the city.[1] Centennial Hill, or "The Hill," as locals called it, was home to leaders such as Rev. Dr. Martin Luther King Jr., Rev. Ralph Abernathy, Jo Ann Robinson, and Thelma Glass. Residents of the neighborhood were the driving force behind the direct action campaigns that made Montgomery the birthplace of the civil rights movement, including the bus boycott, lunch counter sit-ins, Freedom Rides, and the Selma-to-Montgomery march. The neighborhood and its longtime residents fostered activism and cultivated leadership in a new generation of young African American people, changing the course of American history, including nurturing and inspiring the young Rev. Dr. Martin Luther King Jr. in his first job out of college. As voting rights activist E. D. Nixon recalled, "Dr. King was not same man when he left as when he took over the boycott. . . . When he came here, he was humble, he didn't know his way around, hadn't been nowhere but to school and came out. We really pushed him a whole lot . . . it isn't what Reverend King did for the people of Montgomery, it's what the people of Montgomery did for Reverend King."[2]

Montgomery was—and still is—known as the "Cradle of the Confederacy" because it was in the city's senate chamber that delegates from six of the initial seven states that seceded from the United States met in 1861 to form a new government. Jefferson Davis was inaugurated as the new president of the seceded states on the portico of the Montgomery capitol building and maintained Montgomery as the seat of government until moving it to Virginia later in 1861. Montgomery is also a riverfront town, situated on the banks of the Alabama River. Although the city's location near the river helped it grow as the seat of government for the state and the Confederacy, the river was unnavigable for large ships, thwarting city leaders' aspirations to grow the city's industrial base to compete with the larger industrial city of Birmingham, located just an hour north. In addition to city leaders' white supremacist aspirations, rooted in Alabama's Confederate history, their aspirations for industrial growth propelled city planning.

In the mid-twentieth century, civil rights activists propelled the city beyond its roots of the Confederacy and its industrial aspirations, earning the city its second nickname, "Birthplace of the Civil Rights Movement," and setting the stage for the persistent resiliency of activists and the violent and sustained resistance from white supremacists. The irony that Montgomery was both the "Cradle of the Confederacy" and the "Birthplace of the Civil Rights Movement" was not lost on anyone. As Rev. Dr. Martin Luther King Jr. observed, "It is one of the ironies of our day that Montgomery, the Cradle of the Confederacy, is being transformed into Montgomery, the cradle of freedom and justice."[3] Alongside activists such as Rev. King, who thrust Montgomery into its new future, there were longtime residents such as Kimbrough, who struggled to pay for basic needs like housing amid the turmoil.

As a wife whose husband often worked out of town, Maxine Kimbrough struggled to pay rent in the deeply segregated neighborhood of Centennial Hill. Jobs for African American women did not pay much, and rent was expensive because the segregated neighborhoods in Montgomery were experiencing a massive housing shortage brought about by rural-to-urban migration, decades of discrimination, and unwavering residential segregation. Despite the population growth, segregated African American neighborhoods could not expand beyond the rigid neighborhood boundaries of segregation. Landlords and realtors took advantage of the housing crisis by raising rents and delaying or refusing maintenance of homes. Many white landlords also took advantage of and abused tenants, exemplifying the power imbalance that existed between landlord and tenant, white and Black, and rich and poor.[4]

Despite financial struggles, the Kimbrough family preferred to live in Centennial Hill instead of more affordable parts of town. Her home at 664C South Decatur Avenue was proximate to High Street, a thriving and vibrant business district of African American entrepreneurs and businesses, and close to her job dressing chickens at Poultry Products. By living in this walkable neighborhood, Maxine was able to avoid the indignity and violence endemic to Montgomery's segregated bus system and save money on bus fare. Mr. Kimbrough planned to rejoin the family permanently in April 1966 to study music at ASU under the GI Bill. The family's rented home in Centennial Hill was the perfect location for Mr. Kimbrough to complete his studies, for his wife to walk to work and do the daily shopping, and for their seven children to attend one of the best schools in the city that was available for African American children, located on the ASU campus.[5]

Many African American residents of Montgomery had recently moved into the city from rural areas in Alabama because of industrialization, mechanization of agriculture, the promise of better jobs, and the possibility of escaping the brutal conditions of sharecropping. City leaders welcomed this growth, as it better positioned them for industrial expansion, but they were also driven by racist ideology, so they ensured that the new African American residents stayed in segregated neighborhoods. Nonetheless, some neighborhoods were not entirely segregated because during the slavery era some African American people lived close to white residences in ramshackle homes called quarters. These former quarters were just a few blocks large and surrounded by more affluent homes for white residents.[6]

As rural transplants, many of the new urban residents had large families and low incomes, and struggled to find adequate housing.[7] City planning and residential segregation exacerbated the housing crisis. In 1957 members of the Montgomery City Commission, Mayor W. A. Gayle, Clyde Sellers, and Frank Parks, who all subscribed to varying degrees of white supremacist ideology, adopted a new housing code.[8] While the housing code had multiple objectives, including public health improvement, it targeted African American renters, like the Kimbrough family, by placing strict occupancy and building code requirements on city dwellings. While the city commissioners differed in their racial views and politics, they shared many common goals. They hoped that the new housing code would remove some of the former quarters and deepen segregation because white residents had long pressured city commissioners to address the quarters. Pressure on the city commissioners to pass a housing code intensified after a polio epidemic gripped the city in 1953; white residents believed the quarters were a public health threat.[9]

According to the new housing code, indoor plumbing, bathrooms, and windows in every room were required in every existing and new dwelling, and overcrowding of bedrooms was banned. The effects of the housing code targeted African American people because city officials refused to use tax dollars to pay for basic city services in some African American neighborhoods. Without sewerage and water infrastructure, it was impossible to comply with the new law in some neighborhoods, particularly on the Westside, where 43 percent of the homes lacked indoor plumbing in 1960.[10] Even in homes that had indoor plumbing, many large families squeezed into small spaces because housing was limited, violating the occupancy requirements of the code. In 1960 the median number of total rooms in nonwhite households was 3.7 (including the kitchen and living room), and the median number of persons per home was 3.1.[11] When the Kimbrough family moved into their home on South Decatur Avenue, they had no other choice but to violate the housing code and have all seven of their children share one small bedroom.[12]

Although developers were quickly building new homes in the city, many of these homes were available only to white families. Only 19 percent of the 12,179 housing units that were home to African American families in the city had been built between 1950 and 1960, while 41 percent of the homes for white people had been built during the same time period.[13] City leaders understood the need for more homes for African American people and advocated for developers to build more of them. Developers were motivated by profit, and while homes in segregated neighborhoods sold for less, they were in very high demand, which increased the profit. Some developers, therefore, sought to build new subdivisions for African American families despite the lower sales prices. However, it was also administratively difficult for developers to build new homes for African American families because many white residents opposed the construction, citing a loss of property value and increased crime, and racist home loan decisions made it difficult for white developers to build African American housing. As one newspaper article reported, "Plans for the construction of some Negro homes in Montgomery for sale to Negro veterans have stalled because of rough financing . . . at least three real estate men are trying to promote Negro subdivisions but they can't get satisfactory loan money. . . . Because of this situation the homes in Mobile Heights and Carver Homes, the main Negro subdivisions in Montgomery, are remaining at a high ownership maintenance level for its type of housing."[14]

As more rural to urban migrants moved into the segregated neighborhoods of Centennial Hill and the Westside, landlords raised rents, creating a housing shortage crisis. There was a lack of available housing in the city for African American families like the Kimbroughs, and what was available was expensive and poor quality. Intentional disinvestment in city services meant that African American neighborhoods often lacked paved streets, had no parks, had poor quality or missing infrastructure, flooded frequently, and suffered from community neglect. Even in neighborhoods that had infrastructure, the housing crisis led to haphazard and unplanned development. In white neighborhoods, on the other hand, taxpayer dollars were used to provide residents with beautiful parks, modern infrastructure, paved roads, street lighting, and public landscaping, and private developers were able to build more housing because they didn't face public outcry against the new developments, as they did when they proposed new African American housing.[15]

In 1966, Mrs. Kimbrough asked her white landlord, Thomas Tyson, to fix a broken light in the kitchen. Tyson, a prominent realtor, owned many rental properties in Montgomery's African American neighborhoods. Tyson was president of the Montgomery Real Estate Board and later served on the board of directors of the Montgomery Chamber of Commerce.[16] The superintendent who worked for Tyson, Archie Hassel, reacted violently to Mrs. Kimbrough's request, demanding that the Kimbrough family immediately move because too many people lived in the house, which was in violation of the housing code. According to Kimbrough, "I asked the superintendent . . . to fix the light in the kitchen, and he just blew up. . . . Every time someone complains to him, next thing they're asked to leave."[17] Because rental housing was in short supply, white landlords like Tyson could evict African American renters on a moment's notice for even the slightest inconvenience and be assured that there would be many potential new renters waiting to fill the vacancy. Superintendents like Hassel could treat African American renters poorly, with no threat of repercussions from the city's all-white police force, which made it clear over the years that they did not work to protect African American people and often inflicted and exacerbated violence.

Even if the Kimbrough family was not forced to move due to housing code violations, the home had already been declared blighted by the Montgomery Planning Commission one year earlier in the city's slum clearance plan, so they may have eventually needed to move because of demolition projects that multiple agencies, such as the Urban Renewal Agency (URA), Montgomery Housing Authority (MHA), and the Alabama Highway Department (AHD), were implementing in many African American neighborhoods. Despite the fact that she grew up poor, URA director Elizabeth Wright was unsympathetic to the Kimbroughs' struggles, using racist stereotypes to blame the Kimbrough family for the problems that were created because of these projects. She noted, "People with litters like this, they don't want her. That's what causes child delinquency, stacking them up on top of each other."[18] The Planning Commission, which was unable to approve more African American housing due to unrelenting public pressure from white citizens, was little help to people displaced by planning projects. Racist attitudes of MHA and URA staff also prevented the construction of more affordable housing. For example, Wright claimed that affordable housing for African American families was unfair to white families. She noted, "They wound up discriminating against the whites. They were trying to give the Negroes a better break."[19]

If the Kimbroughs' home was not demolished for slum clearance, or its tenants not evicted for violating the housing code, Interstate 85 would soon be constructed directly across the street. The AHD demolished large parts of the African American neighborhoods in town, and as the Kimbroughs' neighbor said, "The highway takes everything. The houses for low-income people are none. The town is going to be filled with just used car lots and service stations and highways in ten years, because they're tearing down all the houses."[20]

There were three major African American sections of Montgomery, and each area had very different socioeconomic levels. Low-income African American families lived north of downtown, which was interspersed with industrial development. Working-class and low-income African American families lived in West Montgomery (the Westside), which had the largest population of African American residents in town. The Centennial Hill neighborhood near ASU, southeast of downtown, was home to many African American families affiliated with ASU and other middle-class professionals with much higher incomes. The streets that were adjacent to but outside of these neighborhoods were also home to African American families. Outside of the three main segregated neighborhoods, some African American people also lived in quarters—small enclaves surrounded by large white neighborhoods. Likewise, white neighborhoods were separated by socioeconomics, with high-income white families living in and around Cloverdale and moderate- and lower-income white families living on the east side.[21]

The Westside and North Montgomery had fewer affluent residents than Centennial Hill and had worse neighborhood and housing conditions due to more disinvestment by city officials, poverty, and haphazard development. As civil rights attorney Fred Gray recalled, "I was born in a shotgun house in the Washington Park section of Montgomery [the Westside] . . . with no paved streets, no running water, and no inside sanitary facilities. There were no hospitals for African-American children to be born. . . . Religion and the church played a major role in my family life."[22] Many of Montgomery's civil rights leaders were middle class and lived near ASU, including Rev. Dr. Martin Luther King Jr., although there were also prominent civil rights activists in other neighborhoods.

Although some homes were in disrepair, Centennial Hill was vibrant and stable due to the socioeconomic status of many of the residents and the presence of ASU. The neighborhood's proximity to the wealthy white neighborhoods of Cloverdale, the Garden District, and downtown also meant better city services and infrastructure when compared with other segregated neighborhoods. As historian Mary Stanton describes, "Montgomery's Black middle class . . . consisted of educators, medical professionals, clergy and entrepreneurs. Many lived in or near the Centennial Hill district, just a few blocks from downtown Montgomery. The Hill was home to Alabama State College. A mecca for South Central Alabama's Black elite, South Jackson Street [Centennial Hill's main throughfare] boasted the Art Theatre, the Regal Café, the Ben Moore Hotel, Hale Infirmary, and the Episcopal Church of the Good Shephard. Many Hill residents attended Dexter Avenue Baptist Church [Rev. King's church] and supported the Women's Political Council, the NAACP, the Citizen's Coordinating Committee, and the Black interdenominational Ministerial Alliance."[23]

While Montgomery is a capital city, a center of business for central Alabama, and home to a large military presence, the centrality of ASU to the culture and lives of Centennial Hill residents made them describe Montgomery as a college town. The fact that white people, on the other hand, described Montgomery as a capital city is illustrative of the sociocultural separation of the races. Jo Ann Robinson, an activist and ASU professor who first called for and organized the bus boycott, believed that the presence of Centennial Hill and ASU created the conditions in which the bus boycott persevered, noting, "Dr. King and I often discussed the probability that Montgomery was the only city that a boycott could have thrived in. For Montgomery was a college town. Alabama State College was an institution of which the black masses took advantage. . . . They were well read. . . . The effect on attitudes was amazing: few inferiority complexes, no fear of 'whitey,' and great faith in self, in families, and people. A college town develops attitudes of defiance against discrimination, and people there are less prone to succumb to force. It also cultivates desires for learning and generates some philosophic depth."[24] The fact that the residents of Centennial Hill enjoyed better neighborhood conditions, less poverty, and more educational opportunities propelled their activism.

While middle-class African American culture centered around ASU, many white people were affiliated with the city's government and military presence. Montgomery is the capitol of Alabama and has a large military presence. The history of the aviation industry in Montgomery goes as far back as 1910, when Wilbur and Orville Wright opened a flying school on the site of what is now Maxwell Air Force Base. In 1918 the US military opened a repair facility on the site of the Wright brothers' flying school to aid with World War I. After the war, the War Department established a permanent military depot on the site in 1920, and later that year the base received its first flying units. In 1931 the US military established the Air Corps Tactical School on the site. The city of Montgomery, which would gain economically from the presence of the military, gave the military base seventy-five acres of land that it had taken through eminent domain from the small African American community of Douglasville, which, according to one military account, "had to be eradicated."[25] After playing a significant role in World War II, the flying school officially became Air University in 1945. The other major military presence in Montgomery is Gunter Annex, and together with Maxwell the two facilities are today Maxwell Air Force Base and Gunter Annex. Gunter's history dates to 1929, when the city of Montgomery established it as the municipal airport. In 1940 the land was leased to the federal government to build a pilot training facility for the war effort.[26]

Not only was the military presence important for the economy of the city; it was also important for development of civil rights activism. In 1948 President Harry Truman signed Executive Order 9981 mandating desegregation of the US military. By 1950 Maxwell was desegregated, including buses, dining, housing, and recreation. Because many African American civilians worked on the base, they were able to experience integration in the years before the civil rights movement. This includes Rosa Parks, when she worked there as a secretary in 1950. Parks noted that experiencing integration at Maxwell helped drive her activism. She said, "You might just say Maxwell opened my eyes up. . . . It was an alternative to the ugly policies of Jim Crow."[27]

After being evicted for violations of the housing code, the Kimbrough family searched for new housing in Centennial Hill, but none was available that they could afford, so the family moved to the Westside. Most of the houses that they found for rent outside of Centennial Hill or the Westside were in white neighborhoods, where landlords would not rent to African American families. Kimbrough said, "It burns you up. . . . On Hull St., I see a decent house, but I can't rent that house."[28] Idessa Williams, a civil rights activist and executive secretary of the Montgomery Improvement Association (MIA), the organization that led the bus boycott, sympathized with Kimbrough, noting, "You should be able to buy anywhere you can afford to buy, but that ain't true. You just can't do it. . . . And the prices they ask for these houses—I think that's awful. Most Negroes don't have decent jobs enough to make payments for this kind of houses."[29]

Although the Kimbroughs' new home on the Westside, at 751 Chilton Street, was larger than their previous home in Centennial Hill, it was far from family and friends, Mrs. Kimbrough's job, Mr. Kimbrough's university, and the children's school. Because school zones were drawn along racial neighborhood lines, some of the children changed schools when they moved to the Westside. But twelve-year-old Michael didn't want to leave his old school, so he continued to walk across town every day to school in Centennial Hill. Michael had to pass by all-white schools to get to his segregated school.

School segregation was an issue that drove city planning and tended to unite many white people with varying degrees of racist attitudes. Even many white racial moderates who did not participate in the violent protests over school integration were opposed to sending their children to integrated schools. School segregation, like parks and recreation segregation, intersected with many planning decisions, including the important decision by the Montgomery Planning Commission to use the neighborhood unit approach, which advocated placing schools at the center of neighborhoods, with most heavy traffic and commercial uses kept to the periphery. While this approach was motivated by multiple public goals, including neighborhood improvement, economic development, urban design, and traffic safety, it also facilitated school segregation by placing schools in the center of segregated neighborhoods. City leaders' placement of schools at the center of segregated neighborhoods and adoption of school zone policies that assigned children to schools in their own neighborhoods led to segregated schools.[30]

Within one year of moving to Chilton Street, the Kimbrough family was informed that they needed to move again. This time engineers working for the AHD were planning to run the path of I-65 straight through the Westside, demolishing all the homes on Chilton Street and removing the entire street. The route of the highway, planned under the close supervision of extreme white supremacist and AHD director Sam Engelhardt Jr.—during a time when the attitudes of many elected officials took a more racially extreme turn after the Montgomery bus boycott—would also demolish seventy-four businesses in the Westside business district and the homes of almost two thousand African American families that would struggle to find new homes. Maxine Kimbrough had dreams of attending college and making a better life for her family, but her housing insecurity and poverty made those dreams difficult to achieve. She expressed, "We don't like to live this way. . . . I'm dying to go to school, but you can't. You're just living from day to day. A piece of bread and a glass of water. I just want a decent place to live, close to work, and not always move, that's all."[31]

This book is an attempt to explain the complex history of midcentury Montgomery before, during, and after the civil rights movement. It explores the overall question of what the relationship between city planning (and city planners) and the civil rights movement (and activists) was, and it analyzes how planning was propelled by city leaders' industrial growth aspirations and the city's unique location as a capitol, military, and riverfront city that was also home to an active and progressive HBCU. This book also explores how race and city leaders' pursuit of white supremacy were prominent forces in decision-making and how those forces influenced the planning and improvement of neighborhoods, infrastructure, space, and place. It tells the story of how African American families, like the Kimbrough family, became victims to these complex and often contradictory forces as they struggled to find housing and rise out of poverty, all while being targeted for their civil rights activism and because of their race.

This book also explains how African American people fought back against residential segregation, racist city planning, and the forces of poverty. To do this, it puts the dramatic direct action civil rights campaigns, violent reactions from white people, and national headlines into the context of local city planning. It analyzes the work of the city planners, engineers, bureaucrats, and elected officials who sought to increase the city's industrial base, balance city budgets that were increasingly sparce as white flight to the suburbs accelerated, reverse outward growth trends, and maintain and strengthen residential segregation. As the civil rights movement accelerated and local racial attitudes became increasingly violent and extreme, some of these public officials also sought to punish African American people for their activism, keep them poor, and ensure that they remained politically disenfranchised. This mix of competing forces often resulted in planning that sacrificed important public goals and inflicted multigenerational and community trauma. These issues continue to affect the city and its residents today.

The direct action campaigns that began in Montgomery, such as the Montgomery bus boycott, Freedom Rides, lunch counter sit-ins, and the Selma-to-Montgomery march did not happen in a vacuum—they affected, and were affected by, the local, state, and national social and political contexts, including that of city planning. While the national, state, and local social and political contexts are well documented, the local context has not received the same amount of scholarly attention. Nonetheless, city planning, the focus of this book, shaped those actions and the people who shaped American history because they happened in the *place* and a *space* of Montgomery's segregated neighborhoods. Just as people shape neighborhoods, neighborhoods also shape people. Montgomery was not just a stage for civil rights direct action campaigns; it was a *space* of home, community, neighborhoods, citizenry, society, networks, friendships, brotherhood, sisterhood, culture, parks, schools, and heritage. The people who participated in civil rights activism were not just *activists*, they were mothers, fathers, children, home-makers, employees, business owners, friends, enemies, dreamers, teachers, and neighbors—the ones who called that *place* home. Residential segregation and systemic disinvestment in Montgomery's neighborhoods inadvertently helped fuel the civil rights movement because it gave activists a space to organize, it vividly demonstrated the systemic racial inequalities that residents faced, and it created shared experiences for residents to rally around.

City planning is a missing piece in the narrative of civil rights activism and the violent reactions to that activism from white residents in Montgomery, and this book fills that gap. In this book I examine issues of city planning and white supremacy, including economic development, neighborhood change, industrial growth, parks and recreation, school segregation, and white flight to the suburbs, prior to and throughout legal segregation, through the civil rights movement, and beyond.[32] I also examine the relationships between school segregation, parks and recreation segregation, residential segregation, and city planning. In examining this mix of competing and contradictory issues, I also examine the quality of plans and implementation strategies, including those that conflicted with the stated purposes of plans and the overall public goal, and those that used questionable analysis and methods.

Beginning with Arnold Hirsch's 1983 book, *Making the Second Ghetto*, planning historians began to broaden their understanding of the relationships between civil rights and city planning. Other planners and historians, such as Mark Rose, Raymond Mohl, Roger Biles, Eric Avila, Cliff Ellis, June Thomas, Eugenie Birch, and Chris Silver, continued this work, adding more detail and perspectives to the existing body of literature. This work was applied to Birmingham, Alabama, by Charles Connerly in his 2005 book, *"The Most Segregated City in America": City Planning and Civil Rights in Birmingham, 1920–1980*, and by Bobby Wilson in his two books, *Race and Place in Birmingham: The Civil Rights and Neighborhood Movements* and *America's Johannesburg: Industrialization and Racial Transformation in Birmingham*, both published in 2000. Historian J. Mills Thornton III focused on local politics and civil rights in Montgomery, Selma, and Birmingham, in his 2002 book, *Dividing Lines: Municipal Politics and the Struggle for Civil Rights in Montgomery, Birmingham, and Selma*. Glenn Eskew analyzed neighborhoods and the civil rights movement in his 1997 book, *But for Birmingham: The Local and National Movements in the Civil Rights Struggle*. Scholars such as Mia Bay, Richard Rothstein, Deborah Archer, Sarah Seo, Steven Higashide, and many others continue this work. This book extends that scholarship by analyzing city planning and civil rights activism in Montgomery.[33]

While white supremacists like Police Commissioner Bull Connor, who used water hoses on young African American protesters in Birmingham, and Alabama governor George Wallace, who stood in a schoolhouse door to resist desegregation at the University of Alabama, made national headlines, city planners, engineers, and other bureaucrats worked behind the scenes to form the massive white resistance to civil rights activism and activists. The aspirations of these individuals to maintain segregation sometimes conflicted with their other goals like industrial growth and combating white flight to the suburbs. Nonetheless, in the mid-twentieth century, instead of using city planning to improve the lives of vulnerable families, these bureaucrats solidified segregation, left poor African American people with inferior neighborhood conditions, attempted to keep them politically disenfranchised, denied them basic city services such as parks, sidewalks, and sewerage infrastructure, and demolished their homes.

City planning was used to maintain white supremacy long after attempts to preserve legal segregation failed. As Montgomery-based attorney and activist Bryan Stevenson of the Equal Justice Initiative explains when speaking of the progression from slavery to mass incarceration, "Slavery didn't end in 1865, it just evolved."[34] Likewise, so did the political disenfranchisement of African American people due to racist city planning, from racial zoning and redlining to slum clearance and gentrification. City planning became part of the evolution of efforts to maintain white supremacy, offering something that legal segregation did not: legitimacy in the court system. As segregationists amassed loses in federal courts in their efforts to continue legal segregation, they discovered that city planning—with its longstanding legitimacy drawn from the US Constitution through the tools of eminent domain and development regulation through police power—offered a solution to the goal that has existed since slavery and continued beyond: to maintain white supremacy.

# 1

# Building a System of Racial Planning and Zoning in Montgomery

When Alabama seceded from the United States in 1861 to protect the institution and economy of slavery, Montgomery was named the first capital of the Confederacy. The new Confederate government established a home for Jefferson Davis and his family on the east side of downtown. At the same time, the city was also the capital of the domestic trade of enslaved people in America—home to dozens of warehouses holding enslaved people along Commerce Street and what is now Dexter Avenue on the west side of downtown, and almost two hundred licensed traders of enslaved people.[1]

The small village of Montgomery grew into the city it is today largely because of the trade of enslaved people, the Alabama River, and its wharf, which connected cotton plantations in the region to national and international markets. Montgomery's ideal location for cotton trading and the presence of the river made it a strategic location for trading enslaved people before the Civil War. Enslaved people were transported to the city from eastern states along the Alabama River, walked up Commerce Street from the wharf, temporarily housed in warehouses, and then sold at the market at Court Square. Twenty years prior to the Civil War, the enslaved population of Montgomery grew by 80 percent, and compared with the earlier slave capitals of Natchez and New Orleans, almost double the number of enslaved people lived in and around Montgomery. By the start of the Civil War, Montgomery's enslaved population was almost equal to its white population, with 4,400 white and 4,341 enslaved people. However, those numbers are misleading because they don't reflect the large number of enslaved people who were temporarily housed in Montgomery's many slave warehouses and eventually sold and moved to large plantations outside the city and across central Alabama. The population of enslaved people in the region far exceeded that of white people, with 23,710 enslaved people and 12,124 white people in Montgomery County alone.[2]

One way of transporting all those enslaved people to Montgomery was on the Alabama River, which has a long and important history for the city.

The river connects to the Coosa and Tallapoosa Rivers in the east and north, where it rises steeply, and to the south it connects to the Tombigbee River toward Mobile Bay. The geography makes navigation on the river difficult and has also been a source of frustration for businesspeople and elected officials who seek to use it to grow the city's industrial base. One early idea to expand the city's industrial base was to make the Alabama River navigable from Mobile Bay into Georgia.[3] In pre–Civil War days, Rev. Peyton Dandridge Bibb, brother of Governor William Wyatt Bibb, proposed constructing a short canal at the top of the Alabama River peninsula because the city of Montgomery was charging plantation owners a wharf tax to load bales of cotton from wagons onto riverboats headed toward Mobile Bay. Bibb ordered enslaved people to begin digging a canal at the top of the peninsula, effectively turning it into an island, allowing plantation owners to load cotton onto boats on Bibb's property to bypass Montgomery and its wharf tax. However, Montgomery city commissioners quickly eliminated the wharf tax, and the canal was never completed.[4]

In 1823 the Alabama legislature passed a bill to connect the Coosa River to the Tennessee River. In 1828 surplus funds that Congress appropriated for the improvement of the Tennessee River were used to build a few narrow channels through shoals on the Coosa River to improve navigation. In 1876, at the end of the reconstruction era, Congress again appropriated funds to widen the Alabama River in some places; however, the entire project was not completed and large boats were not able to use the entire river system, so the state quickly stopped maintaining the widened channels.[5] These efforts were among the first of many trying to improve navigation of the Alabama River. They accelerated when the plantation economy collapsed and city officials pursued other means of industrial growth, and eventually took on an air of desperation, as city and state officials pursued impractical, unrealistic, and expensive navigation projects.[6]

The high number of enslaved people in the region before the war had a significant impact on postwar growth and demographics into the mid-twentieth century. It affected the economy of the city for many years, as the city struggled to sustain and increase economic growth and compete with the much larger industrial city of Birmingham. It also affected population shifts and, eventually, municipal politics and city planning. After the end of the Civil War and through Reconstruction, most African American people stayed in the South, including in and around Montgomery. At the beginning of the twentieth century, 90 percent of the African American people in the United States lived in the South, mostly in rural areas. While many formerly enslaved people stayed on plantations and became sharecroppers, others rejected the brutal conditions of sharecropping. Seeking to escape the harsh conditions, violence, and intimidation from white people—both in rural areas and in cities—a few people established their own towns on the edges of cities and in rural areas. Through these efforts, African American people sought control over local municipal politics in order to obtain better schools and more freedom to plan for urban amenities such as parks and open space. Montgomery residents were among the first in the South to establish new African American communities at the edge of town.[7]

Because of the city's military and government presence and rural-to-urban migration, Montgomery grew at a rate of about 30 percent each decade during the first half of the twentieth century. However, the white population grew faster as the Great Migration accelerated. In 1900 African American residents composed 57 percent of the population in the city and white residents composed 43 percent, but the proportion was nearly equal by 1910. By the end of the First World War, the city had become a majority-white city for the first time since the early days of slavery, with African American people composing 46 percent and white people composing 54 percent in 1920.[8] The shift from a majority–African American city to a majority-white city had significant city planning and political implications, as well as implications for the civic response from African American people to those political and city planning decisions and the responses to African American activism from white citizens through policy, violence, and terror.

Eli Madison, born enslaved in 1839, established Madison Park at the edge of Montgomery after the Civil War when he, Gadson Draw, Frank Felder, Killis Marshall, and their families purchased 560 acres of rural land outside Montgomery. The land was the former May Plantation, belonging to James and Molly May, who had fallen into financial ruin after the Civil War. Madison and the others were the first recorded group of formerly enslaved people to purchase land in Alabama. They established a church, gristmill, cotton gin, school, park, store, and farms, and they planted many of the oak trees that are still present in Madison Park. The community attracted African American residents, but despite its growth, Madison Park had no formal organized government, mayor, or city council.[9]

After Eli Madison's death in 1915, his son General Madison became the leader of the Madison Park community. Another one of Eli's twelve children, Arthur Madison, who attended college at Howard University, and later Bowdoin College in Maine, earned a law degree from Columbia University in 1923. Foreshadowing later voter registration efforts, before leaving for college Arthur Madison attempted to register to vote, and officials at the Montgomery County Board of Registrars told him to wait—they would contact him to come back to register. Years later Madison recalled being told to wait when he led Montgomery's first African American voter registration drive, noting, "Well, I have waited thirty years and have not yet been called back."[10]

While the field of city planning was in its infancy, activists such as Madison, as well as white city leaders, established themes that would follow city planning into the twentieth century: the desire to improve the city's industrial base and the navigation of the Alabama River through planning efforts that were impractical and contradictory, and the resilience and persistent activism of African American residents.

## CITY PLANNING ARRIVES IN MONTGOMERY

The first mention of a zoning ordinance for Montgomery was in 1922, when the Montgomery Chapter of the American Association of Engineers held their regular weekly meeting and invited Montgomery city engineer H. A. Washington to talk about a possible zoning ordinance, city planning commission, and a regional planning program.[11] Following national trends of zoning throughout the country, Washington and the group were motivated by the idea that zoning was needed to guide growth and ensure that there was enough industrial land to promote economic development and population growth. As Washington told the group, Montgomery would be unable to reach a population over forty thousand if there was not a planning commission and zoning ordinance to guide growth. One source of controversy that gave rise to the new ordinance was the common practice of placing fruit stands on sidewalks and the construction of sheds in the public right-of-way. Some downtown businesses owners viewed fruit stands in the public right-of-way as an antiquated practice, so they prodded city officials to restrict them through zoning. Industrial development, with the prospect of increasing navigation on the Alabama River, was also on the minds of the business leaders.[12] At the meeting, the association adopted a resolution calling for the establishment of a planning commission and a zoning ordinance.[13] Racial segregation was already accomplished though other Jim Crow laws and customs, violence, and intimidation, so it was not a major motivation for the group, although it was taken for granted that race would be included in the ordinance.

In 1924 the Montgomery City Commission asked New York land use attorney Edward Bassett to visit Montgomery to advise on a zoning ordinance. After Bassett's visit, Mayor Gunter appointed a commission to draft a zoning ordinance, chaired by businessperson Hartwell Douglas. Montgomery's first zoning ordinance was enacted on July 24, 1924. Although the ordinance did not use racial terms, racial boundaries were implied. The ordinance required the consent of all adjoining property owners and two-thirds of the property owners within three hundred feet for construction of a business in a white residential zoning district. Despite the inclusion of racial lines, racial segregation was not the main purpose of the ordinance—that was already accomplished through other means, except in African American quarters near white neighborhoods. The motivation of city officials was to establish industrial areas and prepare for population growth. About half the city was zoned for industrial uses. Those industrial areas, however, were also home to most of the African American families in the city.

City plans and ordinances of this era focused almost exclusively on nuisance issues and improving the physical environment, including infrastructure, housing quality and quantity, zoning, transportation, traffic congestion, population density, and civic beautification, which is now reflected in a planning theory called physical determinism. Public officials who created and implemented the first zoning ordinances in the United States in the early twentieth century were guided by the idea that physical space determines the behavior of people, and improvements to physical space alone could improve people's lives. Therefore, their focus was not on socioeconomics, history, and culture. These city leaders were instead motivated by the belief that improving a person's home or neighborhood could help alleviate poverty, health problems, and perceived poor morals. Many of these ideas were coupled with racist notions of what neighborhoods should look like, how people should look and behave, how city government should operate, and who was at fault for urban problems such as public health concerns. Finding a natural alliance with economic and business interests, the plans and ordinances largely targeted the homes and neighborhoods of African American families and other people of color who were blamed by the some of the public and elected officials for the urban ills that came from rapid growth, industrialization, neighborhood disinvestment, public health problems, and inequality. Additionally, colonial and racist notions of what a neighborhood and home should look like drove planning decisions.[14]

In the early years of zoning in Montgomery, the city commissioners, the city engineer, and the city building inspector, F. A. Gillette, implemented the ordinance. The fact that there was no planning commission meant that there was no legislative body that was responsible for the long-term planning of the city. In 1927 the Montgomery Chamber of Commerce called on city leaders to establish a planning commission for the purpose of improving Dexter Avenue using City Beautiful principles and increasing the availability of parking downtown.[15] City Beautiful, a planning movement that emphasized urban beautification with classical architecture and landscape design, was a popular movement throughout the world since the turn of the century, when the practice was adopted in the *Plan of Chicago*.[16] However, because of the economic downturn at the start of the Depression, it would not be until 1942 that a planning commission was established.

## THE NEW DEAL IN MONTGOMERY

Despite the establishment of zoning in Montgomery in 1924, city officials did not do much planning until the New Deal urban programs of the 1930s.

The zoning ordinance of 1924 was limited in scope, specifying only general uses and basic dimensional requirements. Prior to the New Deal, local governments in the United States did not do much planning because they were constrained by state legislative control over city charters, and cities, including Montgomery, did not have home rule powers. Around 1930 cities across the United States began completing city planning studies and enacting zoning ordinances with greater sophistication, although those early attempts bear little resemblance to modern planning and zoning.[17]

In 1933 federal agency staff associated with New Deal programs declared that 38 percent of the housing stock in the United States was substandard.[18] The following year, Congress created the Public Works Administration (PWA) and the Public Works Emergency Housing Corporation, which authorized and funded slum clearance and affordable housing programs, as part of the National Industrial Recovery Act. Congress also passed the 1934 National Housing Act, which created the Federal Housing Administration (FHA) and created federally insured loans and a mortgage insurance system (the Federal Savings and Loan Insurance Corporation) to stimulate new home construction.[19] Accompanying these housing programs were new mortgage policies and practices, including the creation of residential security maps that are now called redlining maps, that made it almost impossible for African American people in Montgomery and elsewhere to get home loans.

## Redlining in Montgomery

The Home Owners' Loan Corporation (HOLC), a New Deal agency established to prevent housing foreclosures, was created by Congress in 1933, during the first one hundred days of the New Deal. The agency would prevent housing foreclosures by refinancing failing mortgages using US government–insured bonds. The mortgages were immediately successful, and by 1935 some 40 percent of the country's homeowners applied for the loans. That year the Federal Home Loan Bank Board, a government agency, directed the HOLC to create residential security maps—now referred to as redlining maps—in large and midsize cities throughout the United States, including in Montgomery, for the purpose of determining the level of risk associated with real estate investment.

Just two years after it was created, the HOLC ended the "rescue" phase of its programs, which helped homeowners avoid foreclosure, and stopped accepting new loan applications. It then began to consolidate and sell off its real estate inventory. Many of the redlining maps were created during this phase, including of Montgomery. The maps used block-level data to rate neighborhoods from A (stable) to D (risky). The HOLC staff determined that neighborhoods classified as C and D were to be too risky for investment. Private banks and other lending institutions widely followed the HOLC's lead and adopted the maps and the practice of rejecting mortgages in neighborhoods that were considered risky. These neighborhoods tended to be in older central city locations, often home to African American families and other people of color and low-income residents. Thus, the practice of redlining, created by the HOLC, had the effect of making homeownership difficult to achieve for African American people, low-income people, and other people of color. Race, neighborhood conditions, and socioeconomics were at the heart of the classification of risk on HOLC maps.[20]

HOLC field agent Alec C. Morgan created the redlining map for Montgomery and rated the African American neighborhoods around downtown D, the lowest rating.[21] Those neighborhoods were where the bulk of African American residents lived: Centennial Hill, the Westside, and North Montgomery. This reflected not only race but also neighborhood conditions, which were often the result of the poverty of the residents in addition to disinvestment by city officials. The white neighborhoods in South Montgomery (Cloverdale and the surrounding area) were rated A and B. The middle- and working-class white neighborhoods in the east side were rated C. The neighborhoods south of downtown, west of downtown, near the Alabama River (outside Maxwell Air Force Base), and in the city's northeast corner (near Chisholm) were also rated D.

One of the most strikingly racial characteristics of Montgomery's redlining map is that vacant land near African American neighborhoods was ranked as a risky investment even when it had not yet been developed. However, land use planners generally agree that it is the *use* of land that gives land its value.[22] None of the A-ranked neighborhoods touched D-ranked neighborhoods. White neighborhoods adjacent to African American neighborhoods received a C rating.[23] For example, a small area of undeveloped land sandwiched between two African American neighborhoods in the southeast corner of the Westside was rated C, even though it was vacant. The largely vacant area outside Maxwell Field, which would later become the Riverside Heights public housing development, was ranked D, even though it had a beautiful location along the Alabama River and was proximate to jobs. It was, however, near the Westside and home to a small number of African American and white residents with low incomes. Additionally, a vast amount of vacant land surrounding the King Hill African American neighborhood was rated D.[24]

The HOLC map was based on an analysis of market and neighborhood conditions written by Morgan.[25] The analysis centered on the decline in industry, retail, and trade that occurred during the Depression, which was greater in Montgomery than it was in the rest United States. Morgan reported that nearly all the home sales and new homes constructed were in white neighborhoods

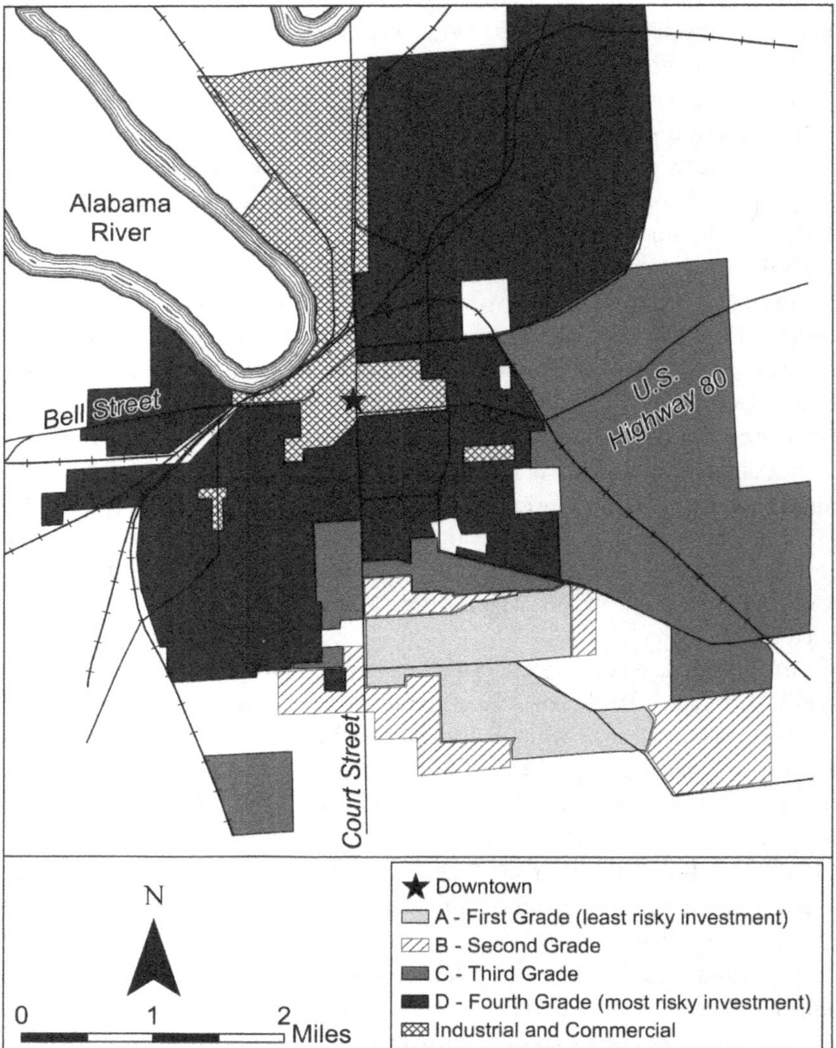


Figure 1.1. Home Owners' Loan Corporation analysts classified the African American neighborhoods in the city as grade D—a risky investment—setting the stage for mortgage discrimination and racial disparities for decades to come. (Map by Riley Dibble, based on Home Owners' Loan Corporation Appraisal Map, 1937, RG 195, National Archives II, College Park, Maryland.)

of Cloverdale and the east side, but even those were very low. In 1928 there were 2,096 homes sold, and by 1936 there were just 79 sold.

The racial composition of the city, and the poverty of the African American residents, was partially to blame for the lack of economic recovery from the Depression. Morgan wrote that the Depression hit African American people harder than white people, and African American–owned properties lost more value during the Depression and took longer to regain their value when compared with white-owned properties. Homes with an A rating retained 75 percent of their pre-Depression value, while homes of African American residents that received a D rating retained only 60 percent, and homes of white residents with a D rating retained 75 percent. Nonetheless, due to a shortage of affordable rental housing, the city had a 100 percent rental occupancy rate.

Demonstrating the effect of a lack of city services on property values—something that would be used by white city officials to justify the demolition of African American neighborhoods for the next four decades—Morgan wrote that a dearth of infrastructure, such as unpaved streets, was a principal detriment of property values. Morgan's report reflected racist attitudes of white people toward African American people, noting that unpaved streets and other infrastructure deficiencies did not affect African American residents as it did white residents. He wrote, "It should be borne in mind that an influence which is detrimental from a white residential standpoint is not detrimental from a negro standpoint."[26]

The ratings on the map partially reflected rates of homeownership. The areas that received an A rating had 90 percent homeownership rate. In the areas that were rated D—mostly African American neighborhoods—the homeownership rate was 20 to 35 percent. Racially mixed areas that were rated D had a homeownership rate of 25 to 75 percent. Not surprisingly, the report noted that the African American neighborhoods had the lowest property sales, with "no demand for residential property" and "virtually no sales activity."[27] About 90 percent of the home sales in 1936 were in four white neighborhoods—three neighborhoods around Cloverdale and one on the east side.

Morgan's report went beyond analyzing property, economics, and neighborhood characteristics, characterizing neighborhood values based on the race of residents themselves. In primarily white neighborhoods, Morgan determined that the presence of African American people and housing was detrimental to property values. Many Southern cities, including Montgomery, had separate blocks of African American housing within white neighborhoods, which were historically home to servants. These communities had existed since slavery times, and a few still existed in 1937. For example, the report noted that "B-1 [a white neighborhood at Carter Hill Road and Narrow Lane Road], which is affected to a small extent by the location of some negro property known as 'quarters' within the area; however, the occupants of these 'quarters' will eventually leave the area and, therefore, this factor cannot be considered a permanent detrimental influence."[28] That neighborhood was sandwiched between the Montgomery Country Club and the affluent Cloverdale neighborhood. Although the HOLC was a federal agency, local public officials, responding to public pressure from white residents and fears that that African American housing drove down property values, hindered economic development, and led to crime, also believed that African American people living in quarters near white neighborhoods should be relocated to more deeply segregated neighborhoods. In the decades that followed, many of these small African American enclaves within white neighborhoods transitioned to other uses, as elected officials and bureaucrats increased their efforts to deepen segregation.[29]

Near the Alabama River, a mostly vacant neighborhood with a few African American and white residents, was rated D because of its proximity to noxious land uses. The report noted, "In area D-2 the proximity to negro property and to city garbage disposal plant, encroachment of business, absence of restrictions, low percentage of home ownership, poor maintenance, heavy traffic conditions, and some vandalism all constitute detrimental influences."[30] In other neighborhoods, African American residents themselves were listed as detrimental influences to nearby white neighborhoods or in their own neighborhoods, along with tuberculosis sanitariums, slaughter houses, fertilizer plants, limited fire protection, industrial uses, overflowing open drainage ditches, surface toilets (outhouses), and gasoline storage tanks. The grouping indicates not only the degree of disregard that Morgan had for African American families but also the frequency of environmental justice problems.[31]

The lack of zoning in African American neighborhoods was listed as detrimental for both the neighborhood itself and nearby white neighborhoods, demonstrating the impact of city policies on Morgan's analysis. African American neighborhoods were zoned "B or unrestricted," which allowed for any land use, including toxic and noxious industrial land uses next to homes of African American families, greatly endangering the health of residents. The zoning revealed city officials' prioritization of economic development and industrial growth, because African American families lived near all the large locations for industrial growth in the city. Leaving North Montgomery unrestricted allowed existing and new industries to expand closer to the African American housing that was interspersed with industrial development in that area, and leaving Centennial Hill and the Westside unrestricted opened up the possibility of fostering new industrial development. By the 1950s city leaders proposed industrial development in all three neighborhoods.[32]

Accompanying the HOLC map and report were six letters from local real estate professionals attesting to the accuracy of the data. The letters focused on the favorable building and homeownership environment in white neighborhoods and made little mention of the African American neighborhoods. For example, Harry Douville mentioned new home construction near Capitol Heights, close to a new veteran's hospital there. Another reviewer, R. W. Chalker, noted that about one hundred new housing units had recently been constructed in East Montgomery. An appraiser, B. Frank Noble, wrote that because sewerage and water lines were being extended throughout the east side, construction was being stimulated in this area, with homes selling for $5,000 to $8,500.[33] At the same time, Morgan's report noted that African American neighborhoods lacked basic water and sewerage infrastructure and did not have paved streets.[34]

The impact of the redlining maps and their adoption by private banks and federal agencies would condemn African American people to segregation, neighborhood decline, and a lack of homeownership for generations, contributing to a wealth gap between African American people and white people that still exists. As the HOLC was targeting African American neighborhoods in Montgomery to deny them mortgages and the opportunity for homeownership, a new city agency, the Montgomery Housing Committee, was beginning to use New Deal funding to implement the city's first slum clearance program, with the goals of improving neighborhood conditions and deepening residential segregation.[35]

## New Deal Housing: Paterson Court and Riverside Heights

William B. Paterson Court, a 156-unit housing project for African American residents near ASU, and Riverside Heights, a one-hundred-unit housing project for white residents near Maxwell Air Force Base, were Montgomery's first federally funded public housing projects, funded by the New Deal's PWA. The two projects were among the first PWA low-income housing projects in the country. Both projects increased neighborhood density and replaced owner-occupied and rental single-family detached homes with denser apartment-style rental housing. Riverside Heights displaced about ten white and African American families but was largely on vacant land, while Paterson Court displaced eighty-two African American families.[36]

The two projects were planned and implemented by the Montgomery Housing Committee, a group of white businesspeople and civic leaders appointed by Mayor Gunter. The Housing Committee was chaired by William Nicrosi, an appraiser and realtor whose family had recently immigrated and who also worked as the housing manager. Members of the committee had strong ties to downtown economic interests and felt pressured to demolish slums and build better housing in order to improve property values and public health and deepen segregation. Members of the committee were city Police and Fire Commissioner William Screws, Chamber of Commerce director L. D. Rouse, publisher of the *Montgomery Advertiser* R. F. Hudson, and Daisy Thigpen, wife of a wealthy physician.[37] White-owned downtown business interests that wanted the economic development that went along with improved living conditions—including the Montgomery Chamber of Commerce, the Montgomery Real Estate Exchange, and the *Montgomery Advertiser*—adopted resolutions in support of the projects.[38]

Nicrosi and the Housing Committee applied for funding for the two projects in January 1934. The following month, the PWA sent Eugene Kabor, an architect, on a trip to investigate slum conditions throughout the South, including in Montgomery, where he met with the Housing Committee. Kabor and PWA staff were mainly interested in using New Deal funds for the African American part of the project due to the poor living conditions and poverty, but Nicrosi and local elected officials stressed the need for housing for white people, and Kabor agreed to study the feasibility of that project.[39]

The PWA's desire to fund only the African American project reflected the reality of the housing crisis in segregated neighborhoods, while the Housing Committee's preference for building both white and African American housing reflected their hope that improved living conditions for the poor would result in economic development, while also reflecting their desire to deepen segregation. They also relied on planning theories of physical determinism, believing that improvements in living conditions could improve socioeconomics and the perceived moral deficiencies of residents. Although 92 percent of African American residents lived in substandard homes, many without indoor plumbing, and only 31 percent of white residents lived in similar circumstances, powerful Montgomerians were more concerned with the housing conditions of white people than African American people and spent more public funding for infrastructure in white neighborhoods. Nonetheless, because of the presence of slums close to downtown and near white neighborhoods like Cloverdale, white residents prodded elected officials and members of the Housing Committee to do something to improve living conditions for African American people.

While white people justified these differences in neighborhood conditions by notions of racial difference and economic disparities, wealthy white people and city officials grew concerned about "race mixing" when poor white people began moving into African American neighborhoods during the Depression, drawn to more affordable housing.[40] The new presence of white people living among African American people was deeply disturbing to segregationists, who were particularly concerned that white children were being raised in the same neighborhoods as African American children. As one Montgomerian,

J. M. Harrison, wrote to Nicrosi, "It is true that the negro living conditions are bad and have been for many years, but in recent years some of our white citizens, in numbers since the depression, have been compelled through necessity to seek the simplest form of living . . . it is shocking to me to find white children being brought up in such environments."[41] Nicrosi wrote to the PWA regional office in Atlanta to impress on them the importance of the white project: "With reference to the white division, it is just as important and just as necessary for serving humanity as the negro low-cost housing. . . . With the depression we have had hundreds of our white citizens driven to the lowest level of existence through want. These people must be given opportunities of again recovering their former existence if our race is to remain intact. Opportunities for their reinstatement do not exist. Low cost housing for whites has never been considered a commercial enterprise in Montgomery. . . . Now these white people have been driven into negro quarters, attracted by low rents . . . the result is, that the white and negro children are living in the same squalor, and if this continues, it will lead to miscegenation and race decay."[42]

US representative from Alabama Lister Hill wrote to the PWA housing division head Horatio Hackett, urging him to take the white development seriously, arguing, "Please do not look upon the white development as a mere gesture to go hand in hand with the negro development. White low cost housing in the opinion of our leading citizens is more important than negro development."[43]

While Nicrosi did need to convince the PWA that funding for the white project was needed, he didn't need to convince the federal agency that the housing should be segregated. In other cities, PWA projects not only reinforced segregation but also introduced it to integrated neighborhoods. The PWA, under Secretary of the Interior Harold Ickes, established a "neighborhood composition guideline," requiring that new housing developments funded under the program reflect the previous racial composition of the neighborhood, although the PWA didn't always follow the rule. In African American neighborhoods, the PWA reinforced residential segregation by building housing only for African American people. However, PWA homes regularly established new patterns of segregation in previously integrated neighborhoods, such as Techwood Homes in Atlanta, the DeSoto-Carr neighborhood in St. Louis, and Outhwaite Homes and Cedar-Central Apartments in Cleveland, all of which were integrated before slum clearance but segregated afterward. Nonetheless, housing for white people was the priority for the PWA, and only one-third of funding under the federal program went toward housing for African American people.[44]

Nicrosi and members of the Housing Committee also justified the projects based on stereotypes of racial difference, as well as public health, crime reduction, and segregation. One reporter claimed that African American families had more children when they lived in crowded housing, and white families did the opposite—reproducing more when they lived in homes that were not crowded. Therefore, better housing would reduce the population of African American citizens and increase the population of white citizens. The article claimed, "Better housing with more room would serve, it seems, to reduce the number of the less desirable and also increase the numbers of the socially fit."[45] Although the new rental housing increased the density on both the sites, Nicrosi and the Housing Committee created the perception that the new public housing would decrease density. This theme would continue in housing programs for decades, with city officials advancing plans that failed to achieve their stated goals, claiming that African American neighborhoods were too dense and needed to be demolished—but the replacement housing was often even denser. This reflected geographic realities of segregated neighborhoods in the city, because white citizens refused to allow elected officials to expand the boundaries of African American neighborhoods.[46]

City officials were also motivated to redevelop African American neighborhoods due to concerns about public health and crime. Nicrosi linked housing conditions with crime and other social ills, noting, "It is generally known . . . that crowded conditions and unsanitary living conditions produce criminals and disease."[47] That sentiment was echoed by many white people, including in an editorial in the *Montgomery Advertiser* that linked slums with poor voting decisions, noting, "One who is reared in a filthy hovel is not likely to take a benign, tolerant view of his environment once he grows up. He becomes discontented and bitter, and thereafter votes in that spirit."[48] From the start, the two projects were characterized differently and reflected white supremacist notions of racial difference. The paperwork that the Housing Committee filed with the PWA when it applied for federal funding for the African American project was for "negro housing and slum clearing," while the application for the white project was for low-income housing. Nicrosi and members of the Housing Committee made the case that the housing project for white people would subsidize the project for African American people because higher rents could be charged to white families and their homes would be larger, even though in the early days of the program, management, rent levels, and ongoing funding for both projects had not yet been established.

Accompanying the application for PWA funding was a citywide survey that identified 350 "occupied negro hovels,"[49] which would be demolished off-site to compensate for the new housing units built. African American residents complained about the invasive questioning tactics of the surveyors. One reporter wrote, "The men ask housewives rather intimate questions about their finances, how much their homes cost, how much their husbands make. One such canvas man was broomed out of the house by an irate wife who resented the inference that she lived in a slum."[50]

Because PWA funding prioritized slum clearance and there was little clearance on the Riverside Heights site, the Housing Committee proposed demolishing these additional 350 African American homes elsewhere in the city to accomplish the slum clearance goals of the project. The owner of the demolished building would not be allowed to build a home on the land for two years after it was demolished to prevent an oversupply of housing. This was a major motivation for choosing vacant land for the white project; it allowed African American homes in white neighborhoods, such as the quarters near the Montgomery Country Club that were identified in the redlining map, to be demolished. Nicrosi wrote, "This has the added advantage that it will take from white neighborhoods negro hovels that are badly placed."[51] This plan reinforced the HOLC study for the redlining map, which claimed that the presence of African American residents in and near white neighborhoods had a detrimental effect on property values. It also provided elected officials with a political advantage, because it helped them demonstrate to white residents that they took their concerns about property values seriously.[52]

The *Montgomery Advertiser* reported that Montgomery had fewer vacant homes than any other midsize city in the South in 1935, and the HOLC study found that the city had a 100 percent rental occupancy rate. Despite the housing crisis and the fact that the Housing Committee planned to demolish an additional 350 homes, the two new developments were not available to very low-income people. Local officials were motivated by economic interests to house people who had jobs and who could contribute to their economic development aspirations. Nicrosi announced that the new housing would not be "a home for indigents, or a poor house" and that "the Government was not interested in sheltering those who cannot shelter themselves."[53]

After months of lobbying by Nicrosi and other powerful Montgomerians, including US representative Lister Hill, members of the Housing Committee, and Mayor Gunter, in May 1934, the PWA approved $600,000 for an 80-unit development for white families and a 140-unit development for African American families. Eventually, the sizes were increased to 156 units for African American people and 100 units for white people.[54]

Three sites were initially considered for the African American project, but two were quickly eliminated from consideration: the first was near the Five Points/Peacock Tract, west of downtown and adjacent to Loveless School, and the second was near Oak Park in Centennial Hill.[55] The PWA and Nicrosi quickly dismissed those options in favor of a site near ASU. Although there were areas of the city with worse housing conditions, PWA staff member Robert Mitchell favored the ASU site because it was adjacent to educational opportunities.[56] The site also appealed to white residents because it reinforced segregation and was not proximate to housing for white people. By choosing the site near ASU, the Housing Committee revealed that it was not tackling the city's worst housing and neighborhood conditions, nor did it provide homes for families who were the most in need; instead, they were motivated by residential segregation and pressure from white residents, a trend that would continue into the 1970s.[57]

The Housing Committee and PWA had lengthy discussions about the best location for the white project. The first potential site was at the end of Clay Street, which was "in the process of blight but is not a slum"[58] and was an "isolated negro settlement surrounded by whites."[59] Although the site would advance the Housing Committee's goals of improving housing conditions and residential segregation, and removing African American people from white neighborhoods, it was eliminated early on because the surrounding neighborhood was "rather shabby,"[60] and it would be difficult to get desirable tenants and high rents. The neighborhood was rated D on the redlining map due to its proximity to the Westside. PWA staff was motivated by making sure the new housing would be in areas where people would want to pay high rents because they needed the rent to fund ongoing management and maintenance of the buildings.

The second potential site was near whites-only Oak Park, the largest and loveliest park in the city. The neighborhood was home to African American families "living in the customary shacks"[61] and adjacent to a white neighborhood, where Centennial Hill met the white east side neighborhoods. Nicrosi and the Housing Committee initially favored the site because it would replace African American housing with white housing in an area that was adjacent to a white neighborhood and segregated park, thus strengthening segregation and protecting the property values of the white neighborhood. Nicrosi argued that the neighborhood was not located near an African American school for the existing residents, so children had to travel long distances and pass by white schools to get to school. He wrote, "The property is covered by a negro slum whose inhabitants are out of touch with their own people and with any negro schools or community activities. If this site is chosen, it will be for an income group higher than the industrial worker and at larger rentals. It is adjacent to an excellent white section, and I think that one reason why it is considered with favor locally is that it will improve the adjacent property."[62] Nicrosi's proposed use of slum clearance funds to demolish African American housing that was not proximate to an African American school (but was instead proximate to a white school) was a theme that would follow city planning in Montgomery for decades. PWA staff, driven by the practical needs of funding the long-term management of the projects, were concerned that the site would not attract white tenants who could afford to pay high rent, because although the project would demolish African American housing, it was still close to downtown, so it was near other African American neighborhoods, and white people with higher incomes preferred to live in much more racially homogeneous neighborhoods like Cloverdale and the east side. The Montgomery Real Estate and Insurance Board also opposed the site because they preferred single-family housing, which was favored by most middle-class white people, noting that it was in a dense part of town where apartments would be necessary because it was too small for single-family homes with individual yards.[63]

The third site, which was eventually recommended by the members of the Housing Committee and approved by the PWA, was near the Alabama River on Bell Street, on a large site containing a historic building. Nicrosi and members of the Housing Committee eventually changed their initial recommendation and lobbied for this site over the Oak Park site because it could be acquired easily, developed immediately, had historic interest, and had a beautiful setting along the river.[64] However, the site was problematic for the PWA because it was mostly vacant and could "hardly rate as slum clearance,"[65] according to the PWA staff architect Eunice Klaber. Although slum clearance was a primary purpose of PWA funding, Nicrosi successfully argued that the site was a good location because of its beautiful setting along the Alabama River. He told PWA head Horatio Hackett, "It is true that there are only a few houses which would come down but we believe that there are so many advantages with relation to housing and social work that the good done would be of greater magnitude than on another site with more slum clearance and less good housing and social uplift."[66] Because Nicrosi and other city officials were likely concerned with demolishing slums on a larger scale—beyond these two projects—a major motivation for Nicrosi and other city officials was that choosing a largely vacant site allowed them to complete slum clearance of an additional 350 homes off-site. This allowed elected officials and members of the Housing Committee to respond to concerns from the white public that was calling for the demolition of slums to strengthen residential segregation, improve housing and public health conditions for all races, and protect property values in white neighborhoods.[67]

The Alabama River site was favored by Montgomery's business leaders, including several large business owners and the boards of the Young Men's Christian Association (YMCA), the Montgomery Chamber of Commerce, the Montgomery County Medical Association, and the Montgomery Real Estate and Insurance Agency.[68] Circuit Court judge Walter B. Jones supported the site, noting that the west side of the city was home to many low-income white people who were living alongside African American people and working at the mills near the river. Poor white people began moving into the neighborhood during the Great Depression in search of more affordable housing. Jones wrote, "Many of the people now living in the West End are living in homes that are not suitable for them, but have been forced into these homes, homes not even suitable for Negroes, because they had nowhere else to go."[69] Despite their acknowledgement of the poor conditions of African American neighborhoods, slum clearance was the only solution Nicrosi and the Housing Committee offered for improving the neighborhood.

The Alabama River site was also advantageous for white people because it would improve the area near the entrance of Maxwell Air Force Base. The US military had built a new aviation school (now Air University) in Montgomery, and the commander of the new military installation, Colonel Curry, was concerned about housing conditions just outside the entrance. Klaber reported, "The field is a splendid modern layout with excellent quarters for officers and men. Colonel Curry is concerned about the existence of some eighteen or twenty shacks situated just outside of the entrance to the field. . . . Toilets are in outhouses which are not sewer connected. There is only a surface drainage ditch."[70] Although the proposed site would only demolish a few of the existing homes, Nicrosi told the PWA that the remaining homes could be acquired and demolished by the Housing Committee after the project was complete. The location would also drastically increase the number of white residents living in the northwest part of town, aiding economic development in the area around the base. The HOLC survey rated the neighborhood as D because of the proximity to African American families on the Westside and nearby industrial uses. Adding the large new white housing development would change the character of the area and entrench it as a white neighborhood, improving property values in an important location in the city.

To finalize the site selections, the Housing Committee completed land use surveys for the ASU and the Alabama River sites. Neither survey sought to determine the cause of neighborhood decline—they only documented problems. The survey for the African American project was accompanied by a series of photographs showing outhouses, wood-sided homes, and barnyard animals roaming in yards, which led to designation of the neighborhood as a slum.[71] The survey listed tenants who had family members that were incarcerated and their reasons for living in that home, with responses such as "low rent, near own race, near work, near transportation."[72] The survey reflected the racist biases of the surveyors, neighborhood disinvestment by city planners, and the poverty and rural lifestyle of the African American residents. Many of the residents had only recently left rural sharecropping to move to the city, so they were accustomed to home gardens and farming, which was lost when residents were relocated to denser apartments after the slum clearance projects, contributing to stress and trauma.[73] The surveys revealed not only the racial bias of planers but the crudeness of planning methods employed by Nicrosi and the Housing Committee.[74]

Because the projects were among the first PWA projects in the country, they received national attention, which Nicrosi was proud to publicize locally. The architectural drawings were displayed at the Whitney Museum of American Art in New York and replicated in PWA projects in four other cities. Construction of housing for African American residents began in June 1935, and the housing for white residents began four months later. After construction began, PWA housing director A. M. Clas informed Nicrosi and Mayor Gunter that zoning changes were needed to protect the developments from nearby incompatible land uses. While Montgomery's zoning ordinance was not explicitly racial, the racial basis was implied. The African American neighborhoods and commercial districts, including around Paterson Court and Riverside Heights, were zoned "nonrestricted or industrial," while the white neighborhoods were zoned "residential." Because of the scattered nature of the edges of the segregated neighborhoods, the zoning often resulted in a checkerboard pattern, where white blocks were zoned residential but adjacent African American blocks were unrestricted.[75]

Although the PWA preserved residential segregation throughout the country, staff members wanted to protect the housing investments from incompatible industrial development. Clas notified Nicrosi that the new developments and adjacent neighborhoods would need to be rezoned from unrestricted to residential to prevent incompatible land uses.[76] Nicrosi and Mayor Gunter argued that the presence of a box factory and Maxwell Air Force Base near Riverside Heights would make it difficult to enforce residential zoning. Although Riverside Heights was a white development, the area was formerly home to low-income families, so it was close to industrial development and the Air Force base. The area, therefore, presented a problem for the Housing Committee because changing the zoning to residential use would prevent industrial expansion in the neighborhood. However, because it was a white development, it would normally be zoned residential. Although the Housing Committee typically protected white neighborhoods from industrial development through zoning, Riverside Heights was located near some light industrial land uses, and the zoning ordinance was not yet sophisticated enough to make the distinction between classes of industry. Paterson Court also presented Nicrosi with a problem, because the neighborhood was African American, so zoning it as residential would mean deviating from the racial lines of the zoning ordinance.[77]

For both neighborhoods, therefore, Nicrosi and Mayor Gunter prioritized industrial growth over protecting federal housing investments and refused to rezone the neighborhoods. For Paterson Court, Nicrosi argued that zoning the

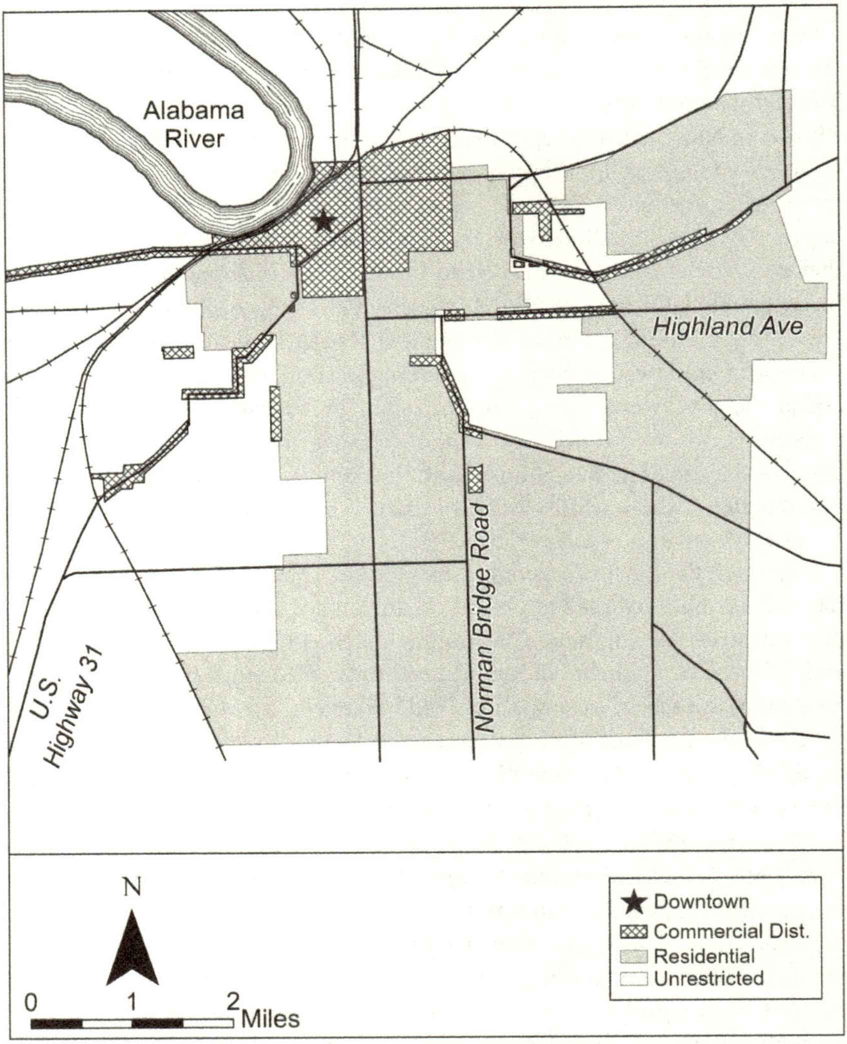


Figure 1.2. In the zoning ordinance of 1933, city planners classified white neighborhoods as residential, protecting those residents from industry, heavy traffic, and other land use conflicts. Planners classified African American neighborhoods as unrestricted, so any industrial or conflicting land use could be located near African American homes, leading to long-term environmental injustice and public health and environmental disparities. (Map by Riley Dibble, based on Montgomery City Commission, Zoning Map, 1929, corrected 1933, RG 196, National Archives II, College Park, Maryland.)

area residential was contrary to the presence of existing industrial and business uses in the neighborhood. He also noted that the city allowed any use in African American neighborhoods, so the residents could make a living, he wrote, "because of the policy of permitting Negroes in their own neighborhood to engage in such minor commercial occupations as they can aid in eking out a living."[78] Nicrosi told PWA director of housing H. A. Gray that the neighborhood around Paterson Court is the "most undesirable section of the city" and that there was "no possibility in the near future of any substantial betterment in the type of buildings or inhabitants."[79] The Montgomery city engineer's office recommended against rezoning, and Nicrosi informed the PWA that the city would not rezone the property.[80]

Nonetheless, hoping to protect their investment, the PWA continued to insist on the rezoning. By November 1937, after six months of negotiating, US Housing Authority administrator Nathan Straus sent zoning consultant and PWA staff member Jacob Crane to Montgomery to write a new zoning code and create a zoning map for the two neighborhoods, and asked Nicrosi to submit it to the City Commission for adoption.[81] Crane, who was from Michigan, was cautious about zoning African American neighborhoods, telling PWA staff Raymond Leonard, "I am not familiar with the attitudes of the public authorities in a town like Montgomery on questions of zoning in districts partially or wholly inhabited by Negroes."[82] However, Crane argued that without residential zoning, the area adjacent to Riverside Heights was "likely to go from bad to worse,"[83] and rezoning would "afford a larger degree of protection both to the project and to the neighborhood than is now present."[84] Mayor Gunter and Nicrosi resisted the rezoning, requesting that it be postponed until the buildings were occupied. After they were occupied, H. A. Gray again requested the rezoning, and Mayor Gunter refused.[85]

The differences between the two projects, once constructed, were substantial. Driven by beliefs in racial difference and the view that any new housing would be an improvement over the slums for African American families, the Housing Committee and their hired architect designed the two developments with significant differences. Riverside Heights had gas, electricity, laundry facilities, modern stoves, washing machines, refrigerators, a nursery school, and recreational facilities such as tennis courts and playground equipment. Paterson Court had electricity (no gas), wood or coal stoves, no laundry facilities, and ice boxes. The two developments had different annual budgets for painting, decorating, refrigeration, and community activities, and different levels of office, maintenance, and janitorial workers.[86] Nicrosi asked ASU president H. Councill Trenholm to provide recreation and social activities for the tenants of Paterson Court, while those activities were provided through PWA funding at the historic building in Riverside Heights.[87] The *Montgomery Advertiser* noted that although the two projects were similar, Riverside Heights would be nicer: "Plans are to make these bungalows slightly larger and more comfortable than those in the negro project."[88] The streets near Riverside Heights were widened and paved and a new bridge was constructed. In Paterson Court, a few streets were vacated to fit in additional housing units, and an open ditch was covered, but no streets were improved, despite the fact that poor-quality infrastructure was a reason for slum clearance in the first place.[89]

Condescending and racist views about the moral shortcomings of African American people also contributed to the design and management of Paterson Court. Some of the apartments included a small personal garden, despite PWA staff Robert Mitchell's claim that the African American residents would not maintain the gardens. Nicrosi, who was more familiar with the rural backgrounds of many of the residents, argued that the gardens should be

Figure 1.3. Riverside Heights was the first and only public housing development for white residents in Montgomery, built after many white people moved into segregated African American neighborhoods during the Depression. White supremacist city leaders believed that the presence of white people in African American neighborhoods would lead to "race decay." In this aerial view of Riverside Heights, with the expansion completed, Maxwell Field is in the foreground, and the Alabama River is in the background. (Maxwell Field Photographs Collection, 1943–44, file Q9005, Alabama Department of Archives and History, Montgomery, Alabama.)

Figure 1.4. Paterson Court, constructed near Alabama State University, was the first African American public housing project in Montgomery. (Alabama Writers Project Photograph Collection, 1930s–1941 circa, file Q1118, Alabama Department of Archives and History, Montgomery, Alabama.)

considered a social program. He noted, "I am a bit skeptical about the interest that the negroes may develop in these gardens, but I believe that it offers opportunities to teach them frugality along such lines and should be considered."[90] Nicrosi also told PWA staff that Southern African American people would prefer detached units with a small yard. He argued, "The negro, especially in the South, is accustomed to and prefers an individual home and yard, where washing can be done and a few vegetables raised. He would not object to rather crowded quarters indoors provided there was sufficient space outside for gossiping and gambling."[91] Four years after the first tenants had moved in, the press reported that the gardens were neat and attractive.[92]

Although Paterson Court was ready for occupancy a month before Riverside Heights, Nicrosi delayed the opening ceremony to avoid the perception that the city leaders were prioritizing African American people. Mayor Gunter, the Housing Committee, and Nicrosi were aware that white residents would be critical of any public spending for African American residents such as Paterson Court, especially if they gave the impression that African American people were getting more public benefits than white people were. Delaying the opening ceremony, Nicrosi noted, would "minimize the impression that the Negro Project is being pushed ahead of the white project."[93] The opening ceremony occurred after residents had already moved into Paterson Court and before residents began moving into Riverside Heights.[94]

Riverside Heights and Paterson Court were among the first PWA housing projects completed in the country, so PWA staff did not initially have a plan for how the new public housing developments would be managed, but, hoping to protect their investments, they determined that the developments would be federally owned and managed.[95] Mayor Gunter and the Housing Committee, hoping to maintain local control and residential segregation, wanted to purchase the projects and manage them locally. Nicrosi stressed that a local management plan was needed because projects in the South should be treated differently from how they would be treated in other parts of the United States where segregation was less rigid.[96] City officials were concerned that PWA housing managers would allow integration. Mayor Gunter wrote to Clas, "Local public race relations must be observed and the social order of the community must not be disturbed . . . we most strongly feel that these projects cannot serve to their capacity if they are not operated and directed locally. Any form of management or degree of managerial functions which would be detrimental to the social order of Montgomery, even if proposed or attempted by your organization, shall be opposed not only by my administration, but the whole citizenry of Montgomery."[97] Reflecting racist views about the ability of African American people to perform basic job functions, Nicrosi argued that African American staff would be unable to manage Paterson Court, and so local white leadership was needed, writing, "I do not believe that the negro is capable of dealing with the various issues that will arise at the beginning, and that he will not be able to coordinate the many agencies required for successful development."[98]

Although Clas preferred federal ownership and management, he agreed to follow the segregation rules established by the city of Montgomery. He wrote to Mayor Gunter, "I concur . . . that local public racial relations must be observed and that the local Advisory Committee should be consulted on all matters that affect the peculiarities of the local social order in establishing the policy for management of the two Montgomery projects."[99] H. A. Gray decided that resident managers would live in the projects once they were constructed—a white manager for Riverside Heights and an African American manager for Paterson Court. The managers would be in charge of social welfare and recreation in the respective projects, but the white manger, with a higher salary, would be responsible for the accounting and rent collection for both developments.[100]

Within a year of completing construction of Paterson Court, the Housing Committee began to have problems with federal management of the development, and the federal employees found it difficult to manage buildings that were located across the country. Nicrosi wrote to H. A. Gray, complaining of inadequate heating, leaky roofs, missing payments for workers, and rents for larger units that were unaffordable for low-income residents.[101] PWA staff had to apply for a variance from the local plumbing code because the kitchens in Paterson Court were not up to code.[102] Urban housing agencies throughout the country began to complain to the PWA that the rents were unaffordable for low-income residents.[103] At the same time, however, the PWA and the Housing Committee, who agreed that public housing should be for middle-class residents, were concerned that lowering rents would attract residents from lower classes. According to Nicrosi, "There are shiftless, low type negro that most people despair helping. . . . We assume that homes for indigents are not contemplated, nor glorified slave quarters, neither is it proposed to house people of a level that need no help."[104] Six years later, however, with the number of vacant units increasing, the rent was lowered for both developments to ensure that the developments were fully rented out.[105]

Despite questions about management, Paterson Court received praise from the press and public officials, aided by Nicrosi's publicity. The Housing Committee and PWA staff were anxious to get the apartments fully rented out and publicized the fact that most of the female residents were employed as domestic workers or teachers, and men were employed as porters or chauffeurs. The Housing Committee also publicized the various tenants' clubs, including a decoration club, a book lovers' club, and a thrift club, and provided the press with quotes from residents, such as, "I feel that I have never lived before. This is the most ideal community I have ever been privileged to live in,"[106] and "When the gods of a thousand fates seemed to be communicating and pronouncing our destiny, 'housing' came into existence, creating new opportunities and providing homes for the low-income groups."[107] The push for positive publicity was not only a marketing strategy; it was a political one because white residents were reluctant to support public housing for low-income people, especially African American residents. By 1937 the apartments were almost fully rented out.

Even before the two projects were completed, Montgomery officials sought to expand both, especially Riverside Heights. Supporters differentiated between the goals of the African American and white developments, just as they had when the two projects were initially developed. Nicrosi stressed the need for more housing for white residents and the need to clear slums in African American neighborhoods.[108] Local union leaders, the Housing Committee, and US representative Lister Hill wrote to President Roosevelt and PWA head Horatio Hackett to request funding for expansion of the white project.[109] Nicrosi told A. R. Clas that although "the negro problem is larger,"[110] it would be easier to expand the white project first because the City Commission already purchased the land to expand Riverside Heights.[111]

The Housing Committee applied for PWA funding to expand both projects by one hundred units each in 1935.[112] The Housing Committee's application for the African American expansion was on an entirely different site in West Montgomery, at Nash and Oak Streets. The new site was necessary because the Housing Committee would not be able to acquire land near ASU at an affordable price.[113] The reason for choosing a different site for the African American project was, again, blight removal. Aware of the zoning controversy of the previous projects, Nicrosi also argued, paradoxically, that approval of the funding would allow the City Commission to improve the zoning, writing, "The main argument is, that the influence of these projects will extend beyond the project its self and influence the existence of people in the particular neighborhood. It will also stop ingrowing rot and enhance the value of the areas and enable the city to improve the zoning of the neighborhood."[114] The PWA did not approve funding for either of the projects because some cities in the United States had not received any funding.[115]

In 1939 the State of Alabama established the MHA. While elected officials continued to have significant input in housing decisions, including the location of slum clearance and zoning of adjacent land uses, they were happy to distance themselves from the new projects because business leaders had begun pressuring city staff and elected officials to rely on private investment instead of federal dollars. Although businesspeople supported the first two developments because they advanced their segregation goals, improved public health, and improved neighborhood conditions, they were growing increasingly opposed to public housing, fearing competition with the private market and believing that economic development goals could be better accomplished with public investment in private development. Throughout the South, business leaders began to oppose public housing in the late 1930s and significantly increased their opposition after the World War II. The MHA took over local management and ownership of Riverside Heights and Paterson Court and received funds from the US Housing Authority to expand Riverside Heights and construct another African American development at a site that had not yet been selected. Because MHA staff wanted to get more white people out of African American neighborhoods, they proposed spending the entire amount to expand Riverside Heights, leaving no funds for the new African American project, but the US Housing Authority rejected the idea.[116]

At the same time, city officials were growing frustrated with the slow pace of federal funding and project approvals and began using municipal bonds to locally finance slum clearance, seeking to accelerate demolition of African American neighborhoods.[117] The MHA received approval to issue $1,176,000 in bonds for slum clearance near Riverside Heights for the construction of 136 dwelling units and a new 150-unit African American slum clearance project on the Westside—Cleveland Court, which led to the demolition of 62 dwellings that previously existed on the site, home to 80 African American families.[118] The US Housing Agency purchased 90 percent of the bonds, and the remaining 10 percent were sold by the MHA.[119]

With US involvement in World War II escalating, federal funds were directed toward defense housing and away from public housing for civilians. Following the precedent set by the housing programs of the New Deal, the defense housing was segregated and lower quality for African American residents. The MHA changed its expansion plans for Riverside Heights to 424 new apartments for white defense workers, while the new Cleveland Court development kept the name slum clearance.[120] The projects benefited the local economy, which was still recovering from the Depression. MHA director Charles Rogers, trying to encourage businessmen to support slum clearance, told the press that the slum clearance program led to increased real estate and construction profits in Montgomery and throughout the country because businesses such as demolition and building contractors, architects, and materials and equipment suppliers, were profiting from projects.[121]

The defense housing expansion of Riverside Heights was completed by December 1940—less than a year after starting construction. Cleveland Court opened in February 1941 and was the only project completed on the Westside for almost three decades. In the upcoming years, the MHA focused their attention on slum clearance in the more affluent African American neighborhood of Centennial Hill, which was the center of civil rights leadership and organizing and more proximate to white neighborhoods. Riverside Heights was the only housing project built for white people in Montgomery.

As the MHA completed construction of Cleveland Court and the Riverside Heights expansion, the agency applied for funding from the US Housing Agency for another large slum clearance project and sold another $113,000 in slum clearance bonds to finance the local cost-share requirement. By then, former Alabama governor and politician Col. Bibb Graves was chairman of the board of the MHA.[122] Later that fall, the MHA announced that the funds would be split into two projects to demolish African American neighborhoods. One of the locations would be an expansion of Paterson Court, and the other would be at an undecided location. Locating another project near ASU underscored the interest of the MHA to direct slum clearance to Centennial Hill, which was closer to affluent white neighborhoods, instead of neighborhoods with worse housing and neighborhood conditions. However, by December, with the Japanese bombing of Pearl Harbor and the United States entering the war, the US Housing Agency announced that new plans for slum clearance would be put on hold due to a shortage of construction materials and funding.[123]

Although Montgomery's prewar housing and slum clearance plans involved a relatively small number of housing units and demolished a small portion of African American neighborhoods, the projects were significant. The first efforts at slum clearance in Montgomery gave rise to much larger efforts for widespread clearance of African American neighborhoods and the relocation of African American people into denser rental units. It also reinforced the idea that public housing would be segregated in Montgomery and demonstrated the difficulty of breaking the established racial neighborhood patterns in the city. The refusal of city planners to deviate from the existing racial zoning ordinance to protect both Riverside Heights and Paterson Court, even with the urging of PWA staff, underscored city leaders' commitment to industrial growth. Also illuminating was the fact that the HOLC redlining map and study used a lack of infrastructure and city services to justify the conclusion that African American neighborhoods were a risky financial investment, noting that unpaved streets mattered more in white neighborhoods than they did in African American neighborhoods. As late as the 1960s, city staff and elected officials followed a similar tactic of adopting physical determinist ideology, using a lack of city services such as sewerage and water infrastructure, unpaved streets, and mixed land uses to justify the demolition of African American homes, and blaming disinvestment in African American neighborhoods on moral and personal failings of the residents, on crime, and on public health problems. Likewise, the questionable planning methods—even from the perspective of the 1930s—foreshadowed later practices.

Implementation of federal funding programs allowed city officials to demolish African American neighborhoods, relocate residents into denser and more concentrated rental apartments, and concentrate poverty. By doing so, city leaders reinforced the white power structure and used public funding to neglect infrastructure, streets, and other services in African American neighborhoods, blaming poor neighborhood conditions on moral failings of the residents. Prewar housing and slum clearance programs established and reinforced the idea that race would be the central factor in where slum clearance took place, where people would live, how public housing was designed, and who would benefit. It established the political coalitions that led to widespread slum clearance plans after the war. These plans were rooted in the concept that city planning was not a technical or economic exercise but a political one, with city planners and elected officials using rational planning methods as a subterfuge for these political goals.

Contrasting the efforts of public officials such as Nicrosi, members of the Housing Committee, and PWA staff to improve housing conditions while deepening segregation through slum clearance, however, were the organizing efforts of local civil rights activists. The idea that African American activists would begin to push harder to register to vote was on the minds of Montgomery public officials when a group of industrial workers in Birmingham formed the Right to Vote Club to increase African American voter registration in 1938, and the following year activists established similar organizations in Selma, Montgomery, Mobile, Gadsden, Tuscaloosa, and Tuskegee. In 1938, before Riverside Heights and Paterson Court were completed, Arthur Madison passed the Alabama bar exam and began trying to register African American voters in Montgomery. During what is now known as a pivotal time of organizing prior to the civil rights movement, the efforts of activists such as Madison to form organizations for voter registration in the 1930s demonstrated that the struggle for civil rights had found an institutional base.[124]

## BUILDING AN INTEGRATED CITY

In 1934 a white Catholic priest, Father Harold Purcell, arrived in Montgomery with the dream of building an integrated city. For Purcell, the purposes of the city were twofold: First, and most important to him, were religion and education. He wrote, "The first [purpose]—which is by far the most important—is the intellectual training and spiritual development of the Negro."[125] The second purpose was social justice. As Purcell wrote, "The second purpose . . . is to translate into positive action some of those fundamental principles of Social Justice."[126] For the next twenty years, Purcell worked to build his dream of an integrated city on the Westside. Although the dream of a functional city never materialized because St. Jude remained politically within Montgomery's city limits, it was a significant effort to create an integrated city and the first by a white priest. His support for African American issues stood out as a model for white civil rights activists in later decades. Purcell's work was consistent with patronizing charity ideas of the 1930s, and he did not approach community development with a focus on empowering people and building local capacity, but Purcell did approach his work with his own sense of biblical justice that was rarely, if ever, seen in 1930s Montgomery. Purcell was often credited for being one of the only white people to advocate for African American issues.

Before Purcell came to Montgomery from New Jersey, he worked as founder and editor of *The Sign*, a publication of the Catholic Passionists order. Purcell wrote in *The Sign* about his distress at the Catholic church's inadequate response to the living conditions of African American families and requested transfer to the Diocese of Mobile, which included Catholic churches in Montgomery, to establish a mission to help African American people.[127] Upon arriving in Montgomery, Purcell rented a small home in a mostly white neighborhood and immediately opened a health clinic for African American people with the assistance of two white nurses who volunteered to staff the clinic two days a week. Soon thereafter, Purcell and the clinic were evicted because the neighbors complained about the presence of African American patients in the neighborhood. Purcell then rented a house on the Westside and began providing health, social, economic, and religious services. Two white physicians, Dr. John Martin and Dr. Clarence Weil, joined the clinic full time, and later an African American physician, Dr. R. T. Adair, also began working there.[128] Adair was well known among African American people in Montgomery because he formed the Negro Civic and Improvement League in 1936, which sponsored bond drives during the war and a voter registration drive in 1946, held classes to help potential African American voters pass the voter registration test, and campaigned to improve African American parks.[129] The clinic was one of two medical clinics for African American people in the city, second to Hale Infirmary, which was opened in 1899 by Alabama's first African American physician, Dr. Cornelius Nathaniel Dorsette, with financial gifts from James and Anne Hale.

For the next few years while Purcell worked at the clinic and mission on Holt Street, he made frequent trips to the northeast to raise money for his dream of building an integrated city. By 1936 he raised enough money to buy forty acres off Fairview Avenue on the Westside. Bishop Thomas Toolen of the Diocese of Mobile dedicated Purcell's work in the name of St. Jude Thaddeus, the saint of difficult and impossible cases, and the land became known as the City of St. Jude.[130]

Development of the City of St. Jude began quickly after Purcell purchased the land. Father Purcell's first project, reflecting his religious mission, was to build a large church in 1938 with a white marble scene of the crucifixion. After its completion, Purcell arranged for a group of nuns from Chicago to move to Montgomery to establish an elementary school in the basement of the church. While the school was primarily for African American students, it also allowed white children to attend, making it among the first integrated schools in the South.[131] One year later, a new building was built nearby to house a health clinic and social center on the main floor, headed by Dr. Adair, with apartments for the staff above. By 1940 the basement school was overcrowded, and Purcell began constructing a much larger school building, but World War II delayed construction, so it was not completed until 1946. After construction, enrollment ballooned to nearly six hundred children, with at least two white children attending, and the school expanded into adult education for returning veterans.

As the war delayed construction of St. Jude and expansion of public housing and slum clearance came to a halt, activist organizing had only begun. In 1944 Rosa Parks and the Montgomery chapter of the National Association for the Advancement of Colored People (NAACP) investigated the rape of Recy Taylor, an African American woman who lived in Abbeville, in southeast Alabama, where Parks's father was from. Parks and others formed an organization, the Alabama Committee for Equal Justice for Mrs. Recy Taylor, and received national press coverage to support Taylor, gaining valuable experience at centering media attention on civil rights in the South and framing their activism as equal justice. The attention pressured elected officials to open a grand jury investigation, and although two grand juries predictably dismissed the case, it gave Parks, E. D. Nixon, and other local activists experience with civil rights organizing and the legal system, and, as historian Danielle McGuire notes, "The Recy Taylor case brought the building blocks of the Montgomery Bus Boycott together a decade [prior to the boycott]."[132]

While Parks, Nixon, and others were learning how to organize for civil rights, one of the city's first African American attorneys began working in Montgomery. After graduation from Columbia Law School, Arthur Madison established a law practice in Harlem and eventually became legal counsel for the NAACP. Every summer Arthur Madison traveled back to Madison Park to visit his family and run voter registration clinics called citizenship classes.[133] During his frequent visits to Madison Park, he also studied for the Alabama bar exam, and in 1938 he passed the exam and was admitted to the Alabama State Bar, becoming one of just two African American lawyers in the state.[134] Madison hoped to get enough people in the community registered to vote to qualify for establishing a municipal government for Madison Park, because state law required a petition from voters to establish a government. Establishing a municipal government had long been a dream of Madison Park residents, because as an unincorporated town, many services, including police, were under Montgomery County authority. Establishing Madison Park as a separate city meant African American control of such services and more autonomy from the white sheriff's department. A municipal government, and the autonomy it held, had been a longtime dream of the city's founders, but because the Board of Registrars and state legislation made registering to vote difficult for African American people, it was an elusive dream.

The number of African American registered voters in Montgomery before the war was just a fraction of the number of white voters—just 114 African American voters were registered in 1928 (0.24 percent of all registered voters). However, early activism shed light on the movement that would soon emerge. By 1938 the number of registered African American voters grew by 51 percent, to 165. In the coming years, Rufus Lewis would establish citizenship schools at St. Jude and across the city to educate African American citizens on how to register to vote, and he, E. D. Nixon, and others would spearhead massive voter registration efforts.[135] The seeds of activist organizing that had begun with the Madison family, the City of St. Jude, faculty and students from ASU, and other activists across the city before the war grew during the war. Those activists emerged after the war with more strength, resilience, and determination.

# 2

# Voter Registration, Demographic Changes, and the Planning Response in the Early Postwar Years

City officials in Montgomery emerged after the war with new ideas that would deepen residential segregation, increase economic and industrial development, advance the economic interests of downtown businesspeople, and use new federal funding to pay for it. They also continued to rely on physical determinist ideas, claiming that their efforts to demolish African American housing would improve the lives of the poor, improve public health, and remedy what they considered to be moral failings of slum residents. The Montgomery City Commission passed new laws to implement these goals. Following national trends and using new federal funding for slum clearance, city officials proposed massive new public works projects, wrote new comprehensive plans with growing sophistication, and used city tax revenues from the thriving postwar economy to invest in white neighborhoods while disinvesting in African American neighborhoods.

During the war, the city experienced an influx of new residents, with a 36 percent increase between 1940 and 1950 due to the expansion of Maxwell Air Force Base and state government staff expansion (see table 2.1). Although wartime rent control programs sought to minimize evictions, those programs ended with the end of the war, while the population kept growing. As solders returned home from World War II, the region expanded due to the baby boom, which fueled postwar suburban and urban growth and created a severe housing shortage throughout the country. The housing shortage was particularly acute in African American neighborhoods, where the boundaries of neighborhoods rarely expanded. Although many white families moved to newly built suburbs, most of those suburbs were segregated and were not available to African American people.[1]

The early years after the war were a transition period from the prewar planning model of demolishing selected African American neighborhoods and replacing them with federally funded rental public housing, to comprehensive approaches to slum clearance that relied on city plans and federal funding to

Table 2.1. Population of Montgomery, Alabama, 1880–2020

| Year | Total population | Percent white | Percent African American |
|---|---|---|---|
| 2020 | 200,603 | 28 | 60 |
| 2010 | 205,764 | 37 | 57 |
| 2000 | 201,568 | 47 | 49 |
| 1990 | 187,106 | 57 | 42 |
| 1980 | 177,857 | 60 | 39 |
| 1970 | 133,386 | 66 | 33 |
| 1960 | 134,393 | 65 | 35 |
| 1950 | 106,525 | 60 | 40 |
| 1940 | 78,084 | 56 | 44 |
| 1930 | 66,079 | 55 | 45 |
| 1920 | 43,464 | 54 | 46 |
| 1910 | 38,136 | 49 | 51 |
| 1900 | 30,346 | 43 | 57 |
| 1890 | 21,883 | 41 | 59 |
| 1880 | 16,713 | 41 | 59 |

*Source:* US Census of Population and Housing.

pave the way for large-scale clearance of African American neighborhoods, both relying on racist notions of physical determinism. The early postwar era saw new policies that disproportionately impacted and targeted African American families in Montgomery, including city codes for housing and sanitation, slum clearance programs that replaced African American neighborhoods with commercial and industrial buildings and parking lots, and clearance of middle-class African American neighborhoods.

Increased civil rights activism, especially from people associated with ASU, posed growing challenges for city officials in the early postwar years. The threat of civil rights activism, increased federal funding for local planning, and pressure from white citizens to improve neighborhood conditions and economic development were all major influences on city leaders. Due to these issues, city officials increased their programs for slum clearance, maintained plans to keep schools and other institutions segregated, and strengthened residential segregation. The relationship between schools and city planning is institutionally complex, but in the postwar years planners in Montgomery influenced school siting decisions through neighborhood planning. Increased incomes brought about by the postwar thriving economy reduced the need for low-income white Montgomerians to live in segregated African American neighborhoods as they had during and just after the Depression. Therefore, city planners in Montgomery no longer proposed public housing for white families, and Riverside Heights and its expansion was the last and only public housing development for white people. Instead, city officials focused on demolishing African American neighborhoods for nonresidential uses such as industrial or civic buildings and moving African American families into smaller and denser rental apartments in deeply segregated neighborhoods.

The postwar period also brought demographic changes to Montgomery. Before the war the white and African American populations of Montgomery were almost equal in number. However, in the postwar period, migration of African American families from the South to Northern states continued. At the same time, migration of rural African American and white families to Montgomery increased as the American economy became more urban, and the movement of white families to the suburbs began, in what is now called white flight. These forces accelerated the demographic shifts that began before the war, and the African American population in Montgomery increased by less than the white population did. In 1950 the city was 40 percent African American and 60 percent white, and by 1960 it was 35 percent African American and 65 percent white (see table 2.1).[2]

While the proportion of African American residents to white residents in Montgomery was shifting, the overall population of both races was growing. Between 1900 and 1940, the number of African American residents in the city doubled. White people moved to new subdivisions in East and southeast Montgomery. Between 1951 and 1954, sixty new subdivisions were built in East and southeast Montgomery, with another thirty-three in the planning stages by 1955.[3] Wealthy white families lived south of downtown, particularly in and around the Cloverdale neighborhood, while lower- and middle-class white people lived on the east side.

White residents also moved to suburbs outside Montgomery, and as they moved, so did businesses and employment. Between 1950 and 1960, employment in the construction industry increased 14 percent in Montgomery County, while it decreased 4 percent in the city. Manufacturing grew in both the city and the county, by 18 and 22 percent, respectively, but it grew faster in the county. Likewise, the areas of wholesale, retail, public administration, educational services, and other services grew faster in the county than in the city. Predictive of future growth of the suburbs, real estate, finance, and insurance grew by 145 percent in Montgomery County, and just 34 percent in the city (see table 2.2). In 1952 the Normandale Shopping Center was built three miles from downtown. Although it was within the city limits, it initiated new fears from downtown business owners about competition from outlying businesses.[4]

At the same time, there was minimal expansion of the segregated African American neighborhoods. The expansion that did occur was nowhere near large enough to meet the demand for housing, creating a tight housing market and housing crisis for African American families in the city. There was little action to solve the problem by city leaders, and in fact most city planning actions and laws passed by the City Commission made the crisis worse. While some developers proposed new African American subdivisions in the city, those proposals were usually rejected by the City Commission after nearby white residents complained that they would decrease property values and the safety of nearby white neighborhoods. Although city commissioners supported programs that claimed to improve living conditions in African American neighborhoods, they tended to defer to white residents' concerns.[5]

Along with demographic changes and segregation, many years of inattention and neglect to city services and infrastructure in African American neighborhoods, and improvements in infrastructure and services in white neighborhoods, resulted in extreme social and physical disparities between African American and white neighborhoods. In 1950 one-quarter of the homes in Montgomery did not have indoor flush toilets—most of these homes were serviced by outdoor pit privies and residents got (or "toted") water from common outdoor spigots. Eighty-nine percent of the homes in the city that lacked indoor flush toilets were home to African American families, and 75 percent of them were rentals, mostly owned by white landlords. The lack of sanitary facilities in African American neighborhoods was due to the fact that city officials neglected to use tax dollars to provide basic infrastructure and services; they didn't think African American neighborhoods were worth the costly improvements. Over one hundred streets in African American neighborhoods lacked basic sewerage and water infrastructure in 1950, which made indoor plumbing impossible. Even along streets that did have sewerage lines, many absentee white landlords refused to upgrade their homes to provide residents with indoor plumbing. City officials targeted these neighborhoods for slum clearance, claiming that the lack of public infrastructure—something that the city controlled—was the cause of blight.[6]

The expansion of housing for white families increased the spatial disparity between the white classes, which had implications for voting and politics. Prior to the war, the wealthy white elite controlled the city government, just as they did the state government. However, when low- and middle-class white people moved to East and southeast Montgomery in increasing numbers, they began to take leadership roles, and some of them eventually challenged the wealthy white power structure, called the "Big Mules," who had controlled the city's politics since the Antebellum period, for power in city government.[7]

Table 2.2. Employment in the city of Montgomery and Montgomery County, 1950–1960

| Labor category | 1950 | | 1960 | | Percent change, 1950–1960 | |
|---|---|---|---|---|---|---|
| | City of Montgomery | Montgomery County (excluding city of Montgomery) | City of Montgomery | Montgomery County (excluding city of Montgomery) | City of Montgomery | Montgomery County (excluding city of Montgomery) |
| Total employment | 41,595 | 10,140 | 47,250 | 9,855 | 14 | -3 |
| Agriculture, mining, and other | 362 | 4,389 | 368 | 2,277 | 2 | -48 |
| Construction | 3,334 | 674 | 3,205 | 768 | -4 | 14 |
| Manufacturing | 4,616 | 1,284 | 5,426 | 1,566 | 18 | 22 |
| Transportation | 3,620 | 472 | 3,212 | 428 | -11 | -9 |
| Wholesale and retail | 9,514 | 1,073 | 10,320 | 1,412 | 8 | 32 |
| Finance, insurance, and real estate | 1,914 | 86 | 2,573 | 211 | 34 | 145 |
| Public administration | 4,404 | 597 | 5,798 | 846 | 32 | 42 |
| Educational services and government | 1,757 | 150 | 3,011 | 283 | 71 | 89 |
| Private household | 5,160 | 782 | 4,912 | 1,131 | -5 | 45 |
| Misc. services | 6,914 | 688 | 8,425 | 933 | 22 | 36 |

*Source:* US Census of Population and Housing.

A parallel shift away from the wealthy elite power structure was occurring at the state level. Before the Civil War, wealth was unevenly distributed in Alabama, and as little as 10 percent of the white population owned nearly all the land and the enslaved people in some counties. A small number of these wealthy elite planters survived the economic ruin after the Civil War and eventually formed a political alliance that evolved into the Big Mule coalition of wealthy elites that controlled state and, in many cases, local politics. In 1947 that power structure was challenged when Jim Folsom was elected governor on a platform of changing the status quo. Folsom appealed to low- and middle-income white people by campaigning with a hillbilly band, and he won easily, beating Lyman Ward, a universalist minister.

As the white power structure and demographics of the city were changing, African American activism met a critical moment, with the first voter registration drive in the city led by Arthur Madison and E. D. Nixon. Establishing a city charter for Madison Park had long been a dream of the community's residents, but state law required a petition from registered voters in order to establish a charter. Therefore, Arthur Madison and other community leaders needed to get more African American citizens registered to vote. In 1943 Madison teamed up with Nixon, a voting activist from the Westside who also had experience in activism during the Recy Taylor case, to launch a massive voter registration campaign—the first in Montgomery—with the lofty goal of getting fifty thousand African American voters registered. When the Montgomery County Board of Registrars rejected the first two applications—from Ola Galloway and Willie Madison—Madison filed a lawsuit on their behalf and sent a letter to Alabama governor Chauncey Sparks requesting that the entire Montgomery County Board of Registrars be dismissed for violating election laws. The lawsuit soon grew to include thirteen others that were also rejected.[8]

Madison's lawsuit was the first voting rights lawsuit in Alabama and among the first of any kind filed by African American people. The backlash from segregationists was swift and harsh. The Montgomery County Sheriff's office sent deputies to threaten the parties to the lawsuit, warning them that if they refused to withdraw their lawsuit they would face violence and job loss and their homes would be destroyed.[9] The intimidation tactics worked, and eight of Madison's clients—including several of his family members—told the court that Madison never asked their permission to include them in the lawsuit and requested that their cases be withdrawn. The court agreed to drop the parties from the lawsuit but kept the court date for Madison's remaining clients.[10]

Two months later the US Supreme Court determined all-white primaries to be unconstitutional in the *Smith v. Allwright* decision.[11] The decision was a major win for African American voting rights activists because Southern states were essentially one-party states, so keeping primaries all-white meant that for African American citizens who did manage to register to vote, their votes were meaningless because the only elections that mattered were primaries. The all-white primary had long been on the mind of Madison. As he told the *Southern Watchman*, "The poll tax . . . is not your greatest obstacle. Your County Board of Registers and your white primary are the worst of the fascist-like stumbling blocks against progressive and democratic government in the South."[12]

The voter registration drive became a political issue because Alabama senator James Simpson was mounting a serious campaign against US senator Lister Hill and accused Hill of being weak on segregation because of his support for New Deal housing and economic policies. Madison's voter registration drive occurred one day before Hill's successful primary election over Simpson. Afterward, Hill was eager to demonstrate his commitment to segregation and volunteered the services of his family law firm—Hill, Hill, Whiting, and Rivers—to represent the Montgomery County Board of Registers in its lawsuit against Madison for representing clients without their permission.

With segregationists feeling the first public threats to white supremacist orthodoxy from African American organizing and activism, Madison was arrested and jailed for illegal representation on April 8, 1944, eleven days before he was scheduled to appear in court to represent his remaining clients who were denied registration. He was swiftly convicted, fined $2,500, and stripped of his Alabama law license the day before he was scheduled to argue the case in court. The cases for the remaining clients, including Nixon, this time with representation from African American attorney from Birmingham Arthur Shores, lost their cases after Judge Walter B. Jones determined that they were not filed within thirty days of the denial of their registration.[13]

Undeterred, two months later, with the opening of the Montgomery County Board of Registrar's office that June, Madison and Nixon accompanied fifty African American applicants to register to vote. The board allowed the group to apply in groups of two all day, but did not rule on the applications immediately because boards of registrars were allowed to take up to thirty days to make voting registration application decisions. Within thirty days, all the applications were rejected. Nixon, however, had learned important lessons about activist organizing and voter registration, and he immediately established one of the first statewide civil rights organizations in Alabama, the Alabama Voters League, with the purpose of getting African American citizens registered to vote.

Although the first efforts to register to vote and establish a city charter for Madison Park were unsuccessful, the voter registration drive was a success for activism and organizing. It was the first time many African American activists in Montgomery became acquainted with the process of registering to vote, and it allowed activists, like Nixon, to understand the process of registering to vote and the types of roadblocks that the boards of registrars would put in front of them. Nixon and others would later use the experience to establish an impressive voter registration network in Montgomery. By 1945 Nixon was registered to vote.[14] The voter registration drive capitalized on increased interest in registering to vote, and African American voter registration quickly increased from 165 registered voters in 1938 to 891 in 1949, an increase of 540 percent. Nixon would go on to challenge the white power structure of the city in the coming decades, registering African American voters and helping foster the emerging civil rights organizing that led to the bus boycott.[15] Other groups of African American activists began to form civil rights organizations, including in 1946 when Mary Fair Burks formed the Women's Political Council (WPC) after she was falsely accused of cursing at a white woman and later arrested. WPC members, including Jo Ann Robinson, later had a pivotal role in starting the Montgomery bus boycott following the arrest of Rosa Parks for violating the bus segregation ordinance.

While the first voter registration drive was occurring, Father Purcell was working to expand the City of St. Jude on the Westside and later established a voter registration clinic there. Although a hospital was not initially high on his plans when he arrived in Montgomery, Purcell quickly learned about the almost total lack of health-care facilities and services for African American people, resulting in high infant mortality rates and high rates of preventable adult deaths and diseases. Purcell turned his attention to raising funds for a large hospital for African American patients. The goal was big—he would need $1 million to build a 165-bed hospital. Donations for the ambitious project came from Purcell's contacts among wealthy white people in the northeast, a $1.5 million hospital grant from federal Hill-Burton funds, and many one- and two-dollar small donations from the poor. The hospital was completed in 1951 and was the first integrated hospital in the southeast.[16]

City officials responded to the growing activism by Nixon, Madison, Rufus Lewis, members of the WPC, and others with increasing sophistication of city laws and plans that targeted African American neighborhoods at the state, regional, and city levels. The State of Alabama and federal agencies assisted by strengthening aiding plans for industrial development in the city.

## INCREASING THE CAPACITY OF CITY PLANNING IN MONTGOMERY

Improving navigation on the Alabama River was a longtime dream of city leaders in Montgomery and central Alabama who were motivated by hopes of industrial growth for the city and the region. In 1937 Governor Bibb Graves asked

R. D. Jordan and Alabama Industrial Development Board assistant director Armstead Leake to prepare a request for funding to the US Army Corps of Engineers (COE) to expand navigation on the Alabama River.[17] In 1941, with Jordan and Leake's assistance, COE staff proposed an extensive dam and navigation project along the Alabama and Coosa Rivers, which would make the river system navigable from Mobile Bay to Rome, Georgia. The project had the support of the Coosa-Alabama River Development Association, a group of powerful businesspeople established in 1890 to increase navigation on the river system. While the project would lead to industrial expansion throughout the region, supporters noted that the city of Montgomery, the largest city along the waterway, would enjoy the most benefits. Backers of the project promised "unbelievable"[18] industrial and commercial growth. Boyce Christiansen, chief of the regional COE office, told supporters, "The economic stature of the Coosa-Alabama Basin will be so enhanced as to make it one of the leading industrial, commercial, and agricultural regions of the Southeast."[19]

While most of the major economic and political interests in the region supported the river navigation project, it did have some less-powerful detractors. Many of the rural landowners whose land would be flooded protested the project because, as one report noted, the land had been in their families for generations: "Many of the landowners objected to flooding the valley because it would mean moving cemeteries, displacing 'old persons,' and giving up their homes which have been in the families for generations."[20] Planning for the project continued despite the protests.[21]

The plan initially centered on six locks and dams along the Alabama River south of Montgomery that would create a nine-foot navigable channel from Mobile to Montgomery. The project was aided by the Alabama Power Company, which spent $120 million on other dams, leaving just three projects for the federal government to fund (Millers Ferry Dam, Claiborne Dam, and Jones Bluff Dam). The entire navigation project from Mobile to Rome was expected to dramatically increase industrial growth in Montgomery, and the city of Montgomery would later include the project in its comprehensive plan.[22]

While the project had support from local public officials and businesses interests, only a small fraction of the eventual cost had been authorized by Congress. The channel from Montgomery to Rome, Georgia, was still unfunded. National leaders questioned whether the economic gain would be worth the high cost of the project and whether river navigation was really needed because the region already had rail transportation to support industrial growth. Due to a lack of funding, the rest of the project was put on hold while the three lower locks and dams were completed.

In Montgomery the institutional structure for planning was aided when Mayor John Goodwin announced that the city would establish a planning commission to guide long-range development in the city in 1946. In 1947 Jack Knight, an engineer who worked with the Alabama Planning and Industrial Development Board, was hired as the city's first planning engineer.[23] Mayor Goodwin recognized the need to professionalize the structure of planning and was motivated by the hope that better planning would increase economic growth. With these two fundamental systems in place—professional staff and a planning commission—the city was able to add much more sophistication to planning in the coming decades. Chief among the targets of these planning efforts was economic development and improving housing and neighborhood conditions, both of which affected African American neighborhoods. The next year, Knight spearheaded an effort to update the ageing zoning ordinance, which hadn't had any significant updates since 1924. Knight and a zoning subcommittee chaired by Judge Alex Marks—an attorney and judge in the Montgomery County Court of Common Pleas who was well known to African American activists because he often used his court to punish activists—oversaw updating the ordinance. Other members of the committee were realtor Sloan Cassels and William Hunter, who were both appointed to the original planning commission in 1946 but had cycled off it, and city building inspector F. A. Gillette. The Alabama State Planning Board and director W. O. Dobbins assisted with preparation of the ordinance.[24]

The new zoning ordinance was more sophisticated than the former ordinance. Although race was not mentioned, white neighborhoods were zoned "Residential A" and "Residential B" and protected from industry, while African American districts were zoned "Residential C" and "Residential D" and interspersed with industrial development. In some cases, formerly African American neighborhoods were zoned completely industrial, making any residential use in those areas a nonconforming use, including residential use by the African American families already living there.[25] While the new ordinance did not leave African American districts unzoned as previous ordinances had, African American neighborhoods were less protected than white districts. In "Residential A" districts, only single-family dwellings and duplexes were allowed; in "Residential B, C, and D" districts, apartments for any number of families were allowed; and in "Residential C" districts, hotels and office buildings were allowed. In "Residential D" districts, the ordinance permitted commercial uses such as barber shops, public dining rooms, and signs. From today's perspective, some mixed-land uses are regarded as a good thing because they promote walkability and sustainability, but from the standpoint of 1948, the Planning Commission sought to protect white neighborhoods from undesirable land uses more than it did for African American neighborhoods.

The ordinance reflected the dual, and sometimes conflicting, goals of economic development and industrial growth while also seeking to improve neighborhoods. The Planning Commission recognized the need to improve segregated neighborhoods but also desired industrial growth in those same neighborhoods. With these dual goals, the commission had two options: first, to transition areas that already contained industrial uses and African American housing to one or the other, or second, to allow industrial uses to take place within African American neighborhoods. The Planning Commission pursued the second option and also added new industrial areas on sparsely developed land on the far Westside, but there was not enough land in the city that would allow them to add the industrial growth that they desired while avoiding the white neighborhoods on the south and east sides of the city.

The result of these conflicting goals, along with the new planning structure, was planning that was more professional but still maintained a degree of haphazardness, burdening African American neighborhoods with the city's industrial growth ambitions. The new zoning ordinance included industrial land uses spotted throughout African American neighborhoods, but it protected white neighborhoods from industrial development, setting the stage for environmental injustices in African American neighborhoods for generations. For example, the Five Points/Peacock Tract area at the intersection of Mobile Street, Grady Street, and Day Street was zoned industrial, surrounded by "Residential C" and "Residential D." In Centennial Hill, industrial development was planned along South Decatur Street near Carter Hill Road, adjacent to Paterson Court.[26]

Local and state public officials also continued to try to expand industry by completing the Alabama River navigation project. COE engineers and Alabama State Planning Board staff shared the same industrial growth ambitions, but COE engineers also had more realistic goals and analytical methods and determined that the shoals and topography of the river presented some real challenges for completing the project. Navigation was still difficult by anything but small boats because of the frequent gravel shoals in the river. For the river to be useful for industrial growth in Montgomery, the project had to be completed in entirety, because if large ships could not pass through even a small part of it, they would be unable to use the channel for shipping. Nonetheless, the 1941 river navigation plan had support from many of Alabama's most powerful individuals. Congress responded favorably to the proposal in 1945, lobbied by Alabama's congressional delegation, and included the project in the US Rivers and Harbors Act. The following year, Congress appropriated an initial $60 million for the first stages of the project, which was eventually expected to cost $450 million.[27]

In 1949, building on the improved structure of planning, Jack Knight, members of the Montgomery Planning Commission, and staff from the Alabama Planning Board started working on Montgomery's first modern plan—a parks and recreation plan.[28] The choice of a parks and recreation plan as the city's first formal plan reflected the pressures that elected officials felt from white residents about improving neighborhoods, particularly white neighborhoods, but also, to a lesser degree, African American neighborhoods, driven by concerns about public health, economic development, and property values. Reflecting these concerns, the analysis linked a lack of park space with crime, slums, and disease. However, implementation of the plan largely benefited white neighborhoods, because although white people desired improvements to African American neighborhoods, those pressures were contradictory; they also often criticized city commissioners for spending public funds for those improvements.[29]

The city had 156 acres of park space, and planners recommended increasing it to 1,227 acres, a drastic increase for a midsize city. While the planned increase was significant, even the existing parks were small and not always available to the public. Most of the 156 acres of park space were either small playgrounds nestled in white neighborhoods or at white schools. Coupling parks with segregated schools meant that African American children would not have any outdoor space either during school or during nonschool hours because African American schools were on small lots without space for parks, and there were few public parks for African American children. City ordinance 21–57, adopted in June 1957, formalized the decades-old informal segregation practices in the parks, making it a misdemeanor "for any white and colored persons to enter upon, visit, use or in any way occupy public parks or other public houses or public places, swimming pools, wading pools, beaches, lakes or ponds except those assigned to their respective races."[30] Montgomery had just one large municipal park, Oak Park, which was available only to white residents, and African American residents resented their exclusion from it. Park segregation was more obvious to all classes of African American people than other segregated facilities. While middle-class African American families could avoid segregated public transportation and send their children to the ASU elementary school, there were no options for parks and recreation for African American residents of any income level. Further, the placement of Oak Park, along the eastern edge of Centennial Hill and surrounded on three sides by African American neighborhoods made their exclusion ever more present.[31]

The Montgomery Parks and Recreation Department was not created until

1948, one year prior to adoption of the plan, so in the early twentieth century the Montgomery city commissioners and the city engineer developed Oak Park into a recreation area. A large pool, the H. A. Washington Memorial Adult Swimming Pool, named for city engineer H. A. Washington, opened in 1920. In 1940 the city commissioners hired the Olmsted Brothers, a well-known landscape architecture firm, to design Oak Park. The firm designed the meandering paths, trees, a lily pond, and a stream with a small bridge in their popular, picturesque style of landscape architecture.[32] By the time the comprehensive parks and recreation plan was completed in 1949, Oak Park contained a water wheel, monkey island, zoo, picnic areas, children's rides, and tennis courts. The zoo was eventually home to two bears, an alligator pool, ducks, geese, rabbits, three peacocks, twelve deer, and a lion named Melissa.[33]

Figure 2.1. One of the popular features in Oak Park, a whites-only park adjacent to the African American neighborhood of Centennial Hill, was the monkey island, shown in this photograph. (John Engelhardt Scott Collection, May 26, 1956, file Q81983, Alabama Department of Archives and History, Montgomery, Alabama.)

Figure 2.2. Swimming was an extremely sensitive issue for white supremacists, who did not want white women and girls swimming with African American men and boys. The pool in whites-only Oak Park was not available for African Americans, despite its proximity to Centennial Hill. African Americans had no swimming options in Montgomery. (Alabama Department of Archives and History Photographs Collection, no date, file Q5071, Alabama Department of Archives and History, Montgomery, Alabama.)

The 1949 plan covered a range of types of parks, from neighborhood play lots to large city parks and recreation centers. It established the minimum standard of one-eighth acre of playground space per one hundred people for the number of parks, and a minimum service area of one playground per square mile. Like later plans, it differentiated between twenty-three white and nine African American neighborhoods. While the authors of the plan conceded that there was more of a need for parks for African American people than for white people, noting that "parks for negroes are badly needed in Montgomery,"[34] and though the plan included vague statements about future needs for African American recreational facilities, it failed to follow through on those aspirations in the implementation sections of the plan, largely ignoring park needs for African American residents.

Although the plan proposed increases in park space for both races, it did not remedy the disparity. In 1948 there was 0.00138 acres of park space per white resident and 0.00043 acres of park space per African American resident—a 105 percent difference. The authors of the plan recommended increasing the acreage of park space for white neighborhoods by 110 percent, and African American neighborhoods by 207 percent; however, because there was such a dearth of park space for African American residents to begin with, the higher proposed increase in African American neighborhoods would bring their ratio up to only 0.00132—less than the original ratio in white neighborhoods before the proposed increases.

Driven by the cost efficiencies of combining parks with school playgrounds, and the desire to maintain segregation, planners encouraged a colocation strategy for parks and elementary schools because, as the authors noted, colocation avoided unnecessary duplication of parks, simplified supervision, and allowed children to use parks during school hours.[35] However, because African American schools were usually on very small lots and lacked any outdoor space, the only available land for new parks was next to white schools. Therefore, the practice of colocating parks and schools had the effect of increasing park and open space inequity because new parks would be located only next to white schools, and African American families would not have access to those spaces. To that end, the analysis identified thirteen parks that were already colocated with white schools (59.4 acres total), and only three parks that were colocated with African American schools (7.3 acres total). At the high school level, schools were situated on larger lots, with 85.6 acres for white junior high and high schools and 50 acres for African American junior high and high schools. However, athletic grounds at white schools were bolstered by city park facilities that were not available to African American students, including the whites-only city arena Cramton Bowl, which was 46 acres alone. The plan proposed that part of the athletic field at George Washington Carver School be used for an African American city park instead of a school athletic facility.[36] The result of the practice of combining parks with schools made them unavailable to African American children because schools remained entirely segregated.

Integrated sports and pools were a sensitive topic for segregationists in Montgomery. The idea of African American football teams winning against white teams, and African American men and boys sharing pools with white women and girls while wearing bathing suits, was deeply troubling to many white residents. To that end, pools and athletic fields were more unequal than other types of parks. White people had use of 151.5 acres of athletic fields, while African American people had use of forty acres, with another ten acres proposed in the plan. Most of the athletic fields for white people were well developed and included baseball diamonds, bleachers, tennis courts, and basketball courts. The forty acres of athletic fields available for African American people consisted of two vacant fields—one at George Washington Carver School and another on Deming Street. The plan proposed modest improvements in facilities at these two locations, but only a three-acre increase. Driven by the apprehension toward African American sports felt by many white citizens, the plan proposed a football field for African American people that could be used only for playing the game, with no area for spectators. The document did not include plans for public swimming pools or indoor gymnasiums for African American people.[37]

As the parks and recreation plan was being developed, the City Commission also began working on two health and sanitary ordinances in 1948, introduced by Mayor Goodwin, who was under increasing pressure from white homeowners to improve or demolish African American neighborhoods that were near the homes of white residents, because they were concerned about property values, crime, and public health. The sanitary ordinance allowed the city and county health officer, Dr. A. C. Graham, to require property owners to provide sewerage facilities in homes, to inspect homes, to declare houses to be unfit for human habitation, and to forbid homeowners from leasing or renting out such houses. The sanitary ordinance allowed the health officer to demolish homes with outhouses and outdoor communal water spigots and to prevent occupation of residences or offices if they were not properly ventilated, weatherproof, lighted, or if they lacked sanitary facilities or were smaller than 450 cubic feet of space. The ordinance targeted African American homes, which were most of the homes fitting that description in the city. Newspaper articles declared that the ordinance would allow "slum clearance on a major scale."[38]

Despite passing the two ordinances, the City Commission sometimes did not provide sewer or water infrastructure in African American neighborhoods. On the contrary, the Planning Commission continued to give building permits to developers to construct homes with outhouses along streets where there were no sewers.[39] The result of the new ordinances was less housing available in African American neighborhoods, squeezing the housing market. Another result was the removal of some former quarters near white neighborhoods and demolition of African American homes near downtown, as those places were the most subject to enforcement of the ordinance, with Dr. Graham receiving the most pressure from white residents and city officials.[40]

At the federal level, slum clearance was becoming the dominant force in US housing policy. The Housing Act of 1949, signed by President Truman, broadly expanded the federal role in housing, mortgage insurance, and public housing. It included financing for slum clearance in cities throughout the United States, funded by $1 billion in loans and $100 million every year for five years in grants. The federal government would pay for two-thirds of the cost of slum clearance, and cities would have to come up with the funding for the other one-third, although federal grants were available for the city's cost share. The act also allowed cities to pay for their one-third with in-kind construction of public facilities on the cleared land. The most controversial part of the act was the public housing component, which had widespread opposition from realtors, including realtors in Montgomery. The act established loans and grants to build 810,000 new public housing units over ten years and required that one slum unit be demolished for every new public housing unit built. To get the act passed in the Senate, an amendment prohibiting discrimination in public housing was rejected by both Southern segregationists and Northern liberals.[41]

Like prewar planning, the foundation of the Housing Act of 1949 was the notion that improving physical housing conditions would advance social goals. As city planner Alexander von Hoffman explains, "Title III of the Housing Act of 1949, however, had a fatal flaw: a naïve reliance on physical dwellings to carry out social goals. The planners and developers of postwar public housing . . . inherited from earlier generations a faith in the influence of physical environment on individual values."[42] Although the act was consistent with the theories of physical determinism they agreed with, local realtors wanted cities to invest in private development instead.

As slum clearance was advancing in Montgomery, city leaders continued to view improvement of navigation along the Alabama River as key to industrial growth in the city, despite the impracticability making the river navigable. Throughout the 1950s and early 60s, Alabama elected officials lobbied Congress to allocate funding to complete the Alabama River navigation project, with little success. Alabama senator Lister Hill, a member of the Senate Public Works Appropriation Subcommittee, succeeded three times at adding funding for the project to public works appropriation bills, but they were removed from each bill before passage by the US House of Representatives. Although there was not enough funding to complete the project, President Eisenhower mentioned the project as an example of effective federal-private partnerships in his 1955 State of the Union address, noting, "The Federal Government and local and private organizations have been encouraged to coordinate their developments . . . the Coosa River development in Alabama . . . already [has] the approval of the Congress."[43]

# 3

## Planning, Slum Clearance, and Activism Prior to the Bus Boycott

THE SEPARATION OF white Montgomerians into different neighborhoods by class—middle- and lower-income white residents moving to the east side and wealthy white residents living south of downtown—which began after the war, resulted in a split in voting patterns between the white socioeconomic classes. The split began to challenge the wealthy white power structure that existed in the city since Reconstruction. The implications of that shift became clear with Montgomery's 1953 election, when Representative Joe Dawkins, the candidate for city commissioner backed by wealthy white residents, lost to Dave Birmingham, who won with the support of lower- and middle-class white voters and African American voters.[1]

Adding to the increased independence of low- and middle-class white voters were increasing numbers of African American voters. In 1949 the Montgomery chapter of the NAACP began the "Operation 2,000" campaign to register two thousand African American voters, and in 1955 the Citizen's Coordinating Committee, with Rufus Lewis as chairperson, took over the campaign and renamed it "Operation 5,000."[2] In the early 1950s African American citizens registered to vote in increasing numbers, despite the many obstacles to and violence as a result of registering, due to the earlier voter registration efforts of Nixon and other activists like Lewis, who established an impressive and sophisticated voter registration infrastructure. In September 1954 Rev. Dr. Martin Luther King Jr. arrived in Montgomery to become the minister at Dexter Avenue Baptist Church. Although members of the church were politically active before King's arrival, his arrival and soon his leadership in the community catalyzed increased voter registration and activism. Within a month of King's arrival, members of Dexter Avenue Baptist Church formed a new political and social action committee, which sent out a voter registration questionnaire to members of the church, offering to help people get registered. They wrote, "Your committee is anxious to help every member of Dexter become a qualified voter. Please help us to help you!"[3]

The number of African American voters doubled in Montgomery between 1950 and 1955, from 813 to 1,678. Although the number of African American voters was small, it was not insignificant because of the new political division between low- and middle-class white people and wealthy white people. Due to residential segregation, African American voters in and around North Montgomery, the Westside, and Centennial Hill constituted a significant proportion of voters in some wards. African American voters made up as much as 31 percent of the voters in Ward 7A, which included Centennial Hill. With the increase in African American voting, African American activists found themselves with access to city government for the first time (albeit a small amount of access) and began to pressure city officials on a range of issues, including housing, parks, neighborhood conditions, infrastructure, and slum clearance. While the increased access to city government was a welcome change for African American activists, their power was limited by division among the socioeconomic classes and along geographic lines. Factions between socioeconomic classes, as well as personal rivalries between male community leaders, stymied the effectiveness of African American pressure on city officials because the activists did not speak with a united voice.

The divide between the African American neighborhoods and classes was most apparent in the rivalry between Rufus Lewis and E. D. Nixon. Nixon, who worked as a sleeping car porter but lacked a formal education, provided leadership to the working-class African American people on the Westside and had a long history of influence and activism from his early involvement in Madison's voter registration drive. He eventually became president of the Montgomery branch of the NAACP and later the statewide chapter. Lewis, a college graduate and businessperson, provided leadership to Centennial Hill and had a key role in voter registration efforts and later in the bus boycott. Lewis created the Citizen's Club in 1952, an exclusive nightclub that was available only to registered voters or those seeking to register to vote. Reflecting the growing interest in registering to vote, initial membership in the Citizen's Club in 1952 was 159, and by 1960 club membership grew to 341.[4] The divide between the neighborhoods and socioeconomic classes was a detriment to the activist's ability to use the newfound power of African American voters to create neighborhood and political change. White city leaders encouraged the division by emphasizing class differences among the African American people.[5]

One source of unity came from African American women associated with the WPC. While many of the members of the WPC were affiliated with ASU and were middle-class—Mary Fair Burks, Jo Ann Robinson, and Thelma Glass were professors, and Jule Clayton Lewis, Geraldine Nesbitt, Portia Trenholm, and Irene West were wives of prominent leaders—they generally did not get involved in power struggles. WPC membership included women of all income levels. Men were intentionally excluded from the organization because they would, according to Burks, "take it over and women wouldn't be able to do what they could do."[6] WPC members sought to overcome the fractious male leadership that split African American residents in the city and undercut their ability to create change. To that end, WPC members began a campaign to announce their preferred candidates for political offices after weekly church services. Although middle-class male religious leaders were much more conservative in their approach to gaining civil rights than women were, women had a slight advantage over African American men when dealing with white elected officials because they were perceived as less threatening to white power.[7]

Underscoring the concerns about the increasing number of African American registered voters was the fact that an African American woman, Jessie Guzman, announced her candidacy for one of the seats on the school board in nearby Macon County in 1954. Although she lost to a white candidate, her candidacy shocked white Montgomerians, who feared that the power of the political divide among the white citizens of Montgomery could potentially give rise to a successful local African American candidate for public office.

As African American organizing increased, planners completed increasingly sophisticated plans, following national trends in planning practice that relied on the rational planning model, which continued to promote physical determinism but used more sophisticated analysis, data, and city planning methods. The rational planning model is a method of city planning that is based on the scientific method, with a reliance on quantitative data and analysis as the basis for the planning process, claiming the utilization of a value-neutral lens. However, those increasingly sophisticated plans were often a subterfuge for elected officials' already desired ends, giving the impression that planning was done scientifically and impartially, when it was really a highly political act, often without genuine citizen participation and citizen power.[8]

To that end, city officials and staff in Montgomery, led by city planner Jack Knight, MHA director Charles Rogers, and the Montgomery Planning Commission, with an increasingly important role for engineers and politicians working for the AHD, created and implemented plans that reshaped the city, with much of the public benefit directed toward white neighborhoods and downtown, and much of the social costs directed toward African American neighborhoods. Those plans were implemented through ordinances and budgets that improved housing conditions, invested in neighborhoods, roads, infrastructure, and parks, and focused on economic development downtown, including increasing much-needed parking downtown and industrial growth throughout the city. Schools played an important role in comprehensive planning, and schools and neighborhoods were planned together with increasing sophistication, keeping schools segregated. At the same time, efforts to demolish African American neighborhoods through slum clearance programs increased, bolstered by increased federal funding and programs and the rational planning paradigm.

White citizens grew more concerned about the increase in African American voting and also wanted to expand the city's industrial base. City planners in Montgomery saw other Southern cities, such as Birmingham, which had a much larger industrial base prior to and during the war, increase their industrial growth. Montgomery planners sought to emulate their approach, but momentum toward industrial growth was never as strong. Some efforts, such as slum clearance aimed at demolishing African American neighborhoods and replacing them with industrial uses, resulted in only minor industrial growth and mostly expansion of existing Montgomery industries—not the new growth that planners hoped for. Other projects, such as the Alabama River navigation project, proved too impractical and expensive and never gained traction. Although these plans were completed with more sophistication than in the past, the planning overall was no more effective or practical.

## THE MONTGOMERY SLUM CLEARANCE ERA BEGINS

In 1950 the MHA received $938,210 from the FHA for slum clearance and redevelopment and $16,050 for a survey to determine the best areas for slum clearance in the city. FHA division director Nathaniel Keith toured potential slum clearance sites with MHA director Charles Rogers (former mayor Gunter's son-in-law) and Mayor Gayle in May 1951. Following the visit, the MHA established two new slum clearance sites, established a new redevelopment officer staff position, and hired retired World War II veteran Harwood Bowman for the job.[9]

The first slum clearance project was in North Montgomery on a fifty-one-acre site that was home to 222 African American families and twenty-two white families, adjacent to industrial development. The colocation of African American housing with industrial development was an outcome of decades of residential segregation, codified in the 1924 zoning ordinance that designated North Montgomery, as well as Centennial Hill and the Westside, as unrestricted and allowed housing near industrial uses. Although the area was designated as a slum, not every house that would be demolished was substandard, and city officials conceded that some of the houses that occupied the site were in good condition. Nonetheless, the Planning Commission and MHA staff, including Rogers, argued that any housing that was proximate to industrial development constituted a slum, regardless of the condition of the housing, claiming "the area is surrounded by heavy industry . . . and for that reason can be nothing but a slum where housing is concerned, even if the housing is 'gilt-edged.'"[10]

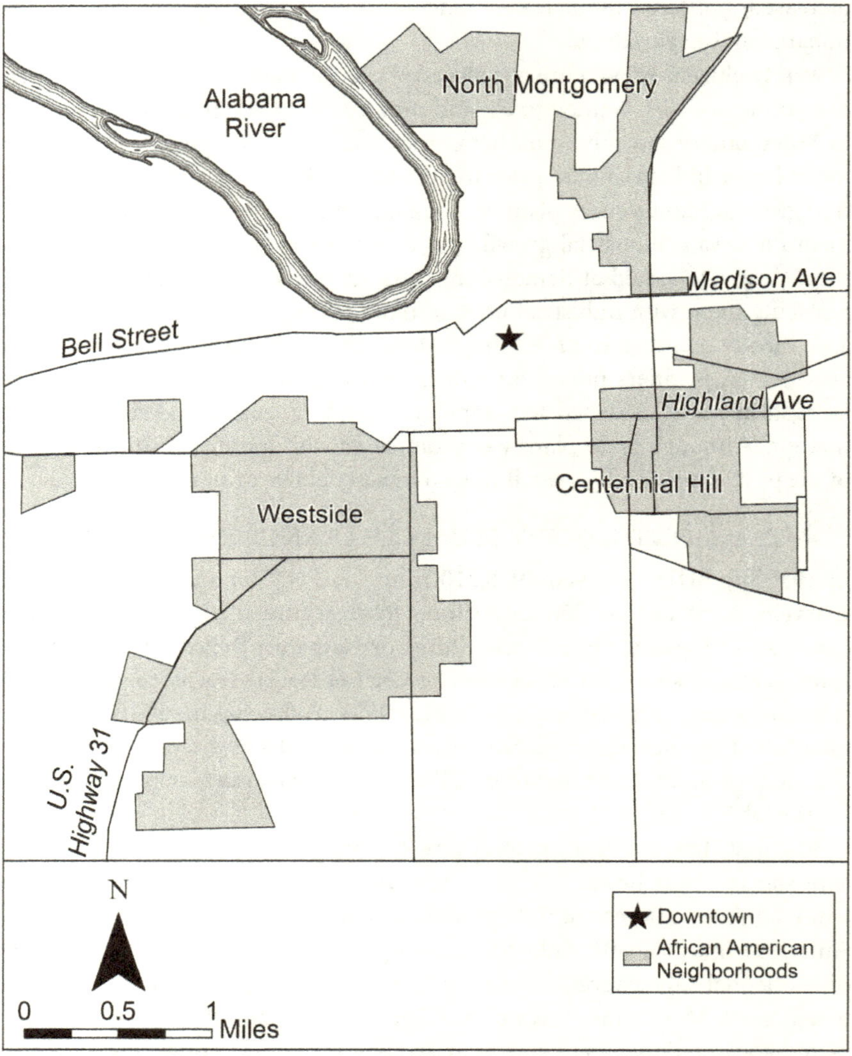


Figure 3.1. This map shows a simplified overview of neighborhood segregation in Montgomery. The neighborhood boundaries of the major African American neighborhoods of Centennial Hill, the Westside, and North Montgomery are shaded gray. However, there were also racially mixed neighborhoods that are not shaded on the map, including the area between Centennial Hill and the Westside. (Map by Riley Dibble, based on Montgomery City Planning Commission, 1950, Auburn University Archives Map Collection, Auburn, Alabama.)

The major motivation for the project was to increase industrial growth, and it represented a common cycle: first city leaders enacted policies and disinvested in neighborhoods that resulted in unfavorable conditions, then they began to view the area as having the potential for economic development, and then they declared those neighborhoods slums because of the deficient neighborhood conditions. They then relocated African American residents of slum clearance sites to newly developed rental public housing in denser African American neighborhoods with more concentrated poverty. To that end, the motivation of city officials was to increase industrial development, but the project was implemented at the expense of the African American residents, a common narrative in the city, even though it was done through increasingly sophisticated planning methods.[11]

MHA staff told the residents of North Montgomery that they could move to the new Trenholm Court public housing development, discussed later.[12] Moving African American residents of slum clearance sites to newly developed public rental housing on formerly cleared land, in more concentrated African American neighborhoods, eventually became a common theme in planning in mid-twentieth century Montgomery. Of course, not all the residents wanted to move into new apartments. Many of the residents of North Montgomery were descendants of families that had lived in the area since the end of the Civil War, and 25 percent of the families in the neighborhood owned their homes, which were situated on large lots with substantial yards.[13] While the neighborhood was close to industrial uses, it also had a rural quality because it was close to the Alabama River, which many residents used for fishing and recreation. Allen Rankin, a reporter for the *Montgomery Advertiser*, interviewed an elderly couple who preferred the rural atmosphere of North Montgomery, with space for farm animals and vegetable gardens, painting a picture of a rural lifestyle in North Montgomery that would be unattainable in a rental apartment closer to the city. He wrote, "Mark Twain, if he could be reincarnated at the river-end of Mammie Street [in North Montgomery], would find nothing changed since the days of Tom Sawyer. . . . A barefoot Negro dozes over three fishing poles. . . . A voice from the settlement on the bluff hails him, 'Hey Seafood, got any catfish today?'"[14]

Once the homes were demolished, the property was sold to private developers for industrial development.[15] City officials prioritized the needs of industrial expansion over the preservation of an African American neighborhood, noting that the increased taxes that the development would bring to the city would be significant. Kenon Francis, director of the city planning division for the Alabama Planning Board, reported that the area was an excellent location for industry because it was proximate to railroad lines, gas mains, and other facilities. Montgomery Chamber of Commerce representative Noble

Crump told the Planning Commission that the city's industrial development plans were hampered by a lack of good industrial sites, so the area was needed for industrial expansion.

While the project did not lead to much new industry, as city leaders had hoped, it did provide space for existing industries to expand. The area was already home to industries such as Alaga Syrup, W. W. Pickle and Canning Co, Texas Oil, and Alabama Power Company, which were given the first chance to purchase the land to expand. Taxes collected from the property rose from $2,000 per year in 1953 to $11,000 per year in 1963.[16]

While the North Montgomery slum clearance project was underway, the MHA began several slum clearance and affordable housing projects in and around Centennial Hill. In 1949 the US Public Housing Administration authorized construction of 1,300 new affordable public housing units in Montgomery. The first project was Victor Tulane Court, which had been planned before the war and resulted in 140 homes of African American families being demolished to make way for 216 new public housing units. The project was later expanded to house an additional 320 families as part of a plan to house almost 400 African American families displaced from another slum clearance project, Houston Hill, discussed later.[17] The project was aided by the Alabama legislature, which passed a law in 1949 allowing local governments to assume part of the cost of slum clearance and use eminent domain for slum clearance for either public or private use.[18]

Just three months after the MHA announced Tulane Court as a segregated African American housing development, the FHA banned the use of federal funds for racially restrictive properties, including slum clearance projects. Alabama congressional representatives and MHA staff predicted that slum clearance projects would be canceled throughout the South because the new housing could not be race restricted, but were quick to point out that Montgomery, unlike Birmingham, did not have a race restrictive zoning ordinance (although race was implied), and that the rule would not apply to "unwritten agreements." The day after the FHA issued the rule, after intense pressure from Southern elected representatives, it announced that the new rule would not be retroactive and later clarified that the new policy did not apply to housing projects that were planned by local housing authorities, even those using FHA funds.[19]

By 1952 another African American slum clearance and affordable housing development was underway in Centennial Hill—Trenholm Court, located northeast of downtown. The project demolished 295 homes of African American families and constructed 390 new apartments for African American families. Some of the residents of the site were relocated to the newly completed Tulane Court; however, strict minimum income requirements meant that many very low-income families were ineligible for the apartments, leaving some people less housing secure. The development also included new baseball and softball sports facilities for African American people.[20]

Although the new housing developments constructed more housing for African American families than what had been demolished, the new housing was smaller, denser, and apartment-style, and it had less access to outdoors. They were also all rental units, and although there were low homeownership rates in African American neighborhoods in the city, the projects did demolish some owner-occupied homes.

The motivation for these projects was to improve neighborhood conditions in the most visible locations in the city because white downtown business leaders, who were feeling the effects of white flight to the suburbs, complained that African American slums were driving away businesses. The MHA also needed housing for residents who had been displaced by other slum clearance projects that replaced housing with industrial and commercial development. However, the MHA was also heavily criticized for the projects by local developers and realtors who believed they competed with private real estate interests. Thus, the MHA, city planners, the Planning Commission, and elected officials felt dual pressure and criticism from white businesspeople—first, from downtown business owners to improve African American neighborhoods near downtown, and second, from realtors and developers who wanted slums demolished but preferred that it be accomplished with private funding in order to boost their profits.[21]

Responding to these dual pressures, the MHA began another slum clearance project, Houston Hill, located behind the Alabama capitol building and near the city sports arena, the Cramton Bowl, north of Centennial Hill and near downtown. Houston Hill also became a target of real estate interests who lobbied city leaders to scale back plans for new public housing construction in the project due to concern that it would compete with the private rental market. The project was originally planned to be a mixed-use development with drastically expanded parking for 1,800 cars for the Cramton Bowl; an African American playground, park, and swimming pool; space for the construction of a new city arena to replace the Cramton Bowl; and land for sale to commercial and industrial developers. The entire project was 185 acres, but the plan would demolish only the housing on the site, which was on 59 acres. The rest of the site was occupied by the Cramton Bowl, parking, and civic and commercial buildings, which would not be demolished. Although the neighborhood was almost entirely segregated, home to 20 white families and 365 African American families, white Montgomerians had longstanding fears of that specific neighborhood becoming integrated because it was close to the capitol building, downtown, and ASU. Demolishing all the homes and transitioning the area to civic and commercial development would prevent integration of the neighborhood, and moving the African American residents into more concentrated developments would deepen segregation.[22]

For over a decade, public officials sought to demolish the African American neighborhood near the Cramton Bowl, which many white people viewed as an unsightly and unflattering representation of Montgomery to out-of-town guests who visited the area to attend sporting events. To get downtown after attending an event at the Cramton Bowl, visitors had to walk or drive through the African American neighborhood, on streets that were unpaved and poor quality due to city disinvestment. In 1937 a *Montgomery Advertiser* editorial suggested slum clearance of the neighborhood after the Southeastern Conference intercollegiate football game. As editors wrote, "Slum clearance should have begun in the neighborhood of the Bowl with some kind of parking facilities and roads leading to the Bowl."[23]

Government and business leaders also had a strong economic incentive to redevelop the neighborhood because it was located close to downtown and the Alabama capitol building. However, African American families also found the area desirable because of the proximity to ASU and the High Street African American commercial district. An editorial in the *Montgomery Advertiser* noted, "The project's boundaries encompass some of the most potentially valuable land in the city . . . the property is considered valuable from a residential standpoint for Negroes. Its accessibility to Alabama State College for Negroes and the more affluent Negro residential areas make it particularly valuable."[24] After the land was cleared of African American residents, it would be even more valuable. The newspaper noted, "One of the most significant aspects of the redevelopment program is the project assessment value of the property compared to its past value."[25]

The Houston Hill project coincided with increased civil rights activism and the beginning of the Montgomery bus boycott. Although the idea of the project was announced several years before the boycott, the MHA initially had difficulty arranging funding for the project, and it was not until federal spending on slum clearance increased, which coincided with the bus boycott, that planning accelerated. The Planning Commission approved the project just one month after the start of the boycott. In the public hearing to approve the plan, city officials, including Fire Chief R. L. Lampley, Assistant Fire Marshall Tom Hall, MHA attorney Thomas Martin, and MHA executive director Charles Rogers described the area as a "veritable cesspool," a "fire hazard," and a "menace to the health and morals of the community."[26] On the same day that Dr. Martin Luther King Jr. announced that African American people in Montgomery had voted to continue the bus boycott at Day Street Baptist Church, the City Commission announced the allocation of $2.5 million from the city of Montgomery and $3,522,077 from the FHA to complete the project.[27]

Local realtors, hoping to avoid more public spending on public housing, argued that building public housing would not solve the housing crisis in Montgomery because it was African American people who were at fault for poor neighborhood and housing conditions. Shifting the goals of slum clearance away from public housing and toward the commercial interests of white businesspeople, MHA employee Eugene Ballard argued that the construction of public housing was not the solution to the housing crisis, blaming African American families: "The problem [is] one of 'city decency' and . . . public housing was not the answer. 'We need to encourage the people living in filth and squalor of our slums to help themselves by educating them to higher health and sanitary standards.'"[28] These racist arguments ignored the fact that it was decades of neighborhood disinvestment by public officials and employees that created the poor neighborhood conditions in the first place.

Responding to the concerns of both white realtors and white businesspeople, Mayor Gayle and the city commissioners announced their opposition to public housing for Houston Hill and convened more than fifty members of the Montgomery Real Estate Board and the Montgomery Home Builders Association to call on private developers to build three hundred new private homes to rent to African American families in order to comply with FHA relocation assistance requirements.[29] Gayle asked the developers to build more housing for African American residents so the MHA could demolish slums without having to build public housing. While this position was politically acceptable to both groups, it proved difficult to achieve because building African American housing outside of deeply segregated neighborhoods was rarely approved by the Planning Commission due to opposition from nearby white residents who opposed such developments.[30]

A few weeks later, Alabama senator John Sparkman supported a bill in Congress that would remove the FHA relocation assistance rule, which required relocation of every family living in demolished slum housing, because, as Senator Hubert Humphrey, who also supported the bill, said, "[It] involved such burdensome planning operations that many municipalities in need of new projects and slum clearance have found it impossible to qualify."[31]

Around the same time, "separate but equal" accommodations were effectively overturned by the US Supreme Court in the *Brown v. Board of Education* decision. Following the decision, Berchman Fitzpatrick, general counsel for the FHA, announced that the *Brown* decision did not apply to housing. The Eisenhower administration also abolished several meager policies that were enacted by the Truman administration to work toward more equity in FHA funding, including ending a rule requiring that African American people and white people receive equal funding for public housing (which was rarely enforced anyway) and another rule that the overall quantity of housing for African American residents in a city not be reduced by slum clearance projects.

Despite Mayor Gayle's request, private developers were largely unable to build replacement housing for the Houston Hill project. Most proposals for new African American subdivisions were rejected by the Planning Commission because they were too close to white neighborhoods and white residents feared decreases in their property values. White residents also claimed that police patrols would need to increase to protect white women when they were home alone if African American housing was built near white neighborhoods. Eventually, one developer was able to get a project approved in an undeveloped part of the city at the far northern edge of the city near the Chisholm neighborhood, but it was too small to meet the overall demand for African American housing or to comply with FHA relocation assistance requirements.[32]

Reluctant to build more public housing but unable to foster private development of affordable housing, MHA staff was presented with conflicting goals and began looking for new ideas for complying with FHA relocation assistance rules. One idea was to move displaced people to a property that was being foreclosed by the FHA, Jackson Heights, a 184-unit housing development that was originally constructed for African American occupancy. Jackson Heights was constructed by a private developer in 1951 using an FHA loan, and the terms of the loan required that the rents be set at nearly forty dollars per month, making the housing development unaffordable for many African American families. The project transitioned to housing for white residents before any African American families moved in. The high rents, however, also kept many white families from moving in because they could find larger homes for the same price in East and southeast Montgomery, so the development was never more than half occupied.

In 1955 the FHA foreclosed on Jackson Heights and tried to sell the development, and the MHA considered purchasing it to house the relocated families from Houston Hill. By then, however, the MHA had revised its plans to include a small public housing development for African American people in Houston Hill, and the FHA approved the relocation plan. The new Houston Hill public housing, combined with public housing at Tulane Court, would house the residents displaced by the project and allow the MHA to comply with the federal relocation assistance rules. The plan for new public housing in Houston Hill was immediately controversial, and the Montgomery Real Estate Board, the Montgomery Home Builders Association, and white developers and businesspeople, who did not want public housing built, especially in such a prominent location in the city, opposed the construction of any new public housing. By then there were two thousand African American applicants on waiting lists for public housing in the city.[33]

Ray Amos and Ed Watts, representing the Montgomery Real Estate Board, argued that the MHA should purchase Jackson Heights to rehouse the African American residents of Houston Hill instead of building new public housing.[34] Jackson Heights was at the edge of a segregated neighborhood, so while it would expand the boundaries of segregation, it advanced segregation goals because it was located far from downtown and was not in an economically important neighborhood. Houston Hill, on the other hand, was in an important location near downtown and the capitol, so segregationists did not want public housing to be part of the project. MHA chairman Paul Fuller opposed purchasing Jackson Heights because of the poor condition of the building, claiming, "Jackson Heights was a 'lemon the FHA has been trying to put off on Montgomery.'"[35] However, despite the fact that the building was probably a bad investment, it addressed the conflicting pressures from white businesspeople to both stop building public housing and allow slum clearance to continue. Therefore, the MHA agreed to purchase the property from the FHA, although it was not large enough to meet the housing needs of all of the residents displaced by the Houston Hill slum clearance project.[36]

The early post–World War II years were a transition period to the comprehensive slum clearance plans that would emerge after the bus boycott. The Houston Hill development spanned both periods, as we will see later—it began before the boycott but was completed afterward—and the plan evolved from one that included public housing to one that did not. Both the North Montgomery and Houston Hill projects added a new dimension to slum clearance—the idea that African American housing could be demolished and replaced with commercial, civic, and industrial uses that catered to the interests of white businesspeople. The enactment of the health and sanitary ordinances created an environment in which widespread city codes targeted African American residents after the bus boycott. Many issues remained constant during the postwar planning years, however, including the focus on Centennial Hill, with most slum clearance projects taking place in or around the largely middle-class neighborhood (Paterson Court, the expansion of Paterson Court, Tulane Court, Trenholm Court, Houston Hill, and the purchase of Jackson Heights). Just a few scattered projects were completed in the other African American neighborhoods (Cleveland Court and North Montgomery), despite worse housing conditions in the Westside and North Montgomery. After the bus boycott, public officials accelerated plans for economic development, industrial growth, and neighborhood improvement, resulting in demolition of African American homes, and they used increasingly sophisticated planning methods that resulted in impressive-looking plans but failed to accomplish many of their stated objectives.[37]

# 4

## City Planning and the Montgomery Bus Boycott

As the Planning Commission, City Commission, MHA, and agency staff advanced slum clearance plans—hoping to increase economic development, industrial growth, and neighborhood improvement, targeting African American neighborhoods, and using increasingly sophisticated planning methods—businesspeople and real estate developers continued to pressure local elected officials to rely on private investment rather than federal funds to build affordable housing. They also pressured elected officials to do more to clean up African American neighborhoods near downtown. The Montgomery Real Estate Board took out a large advertisement in the *Montgomery Advertiser* calling for a citywide referendum to ban new public housing in the city.[1] At the same time, white flight to the suburbs accelerated, city leaders' dreams of becoming an industrial center were no closer, and activists continued to push for civil rights.

Although the population of Montgomery was increasing, the 1950s brought new economic competition to downtown from eastern suburbs just outside the city limits. Montgomery County (excluding the city of Montgomery) experienced an 11 percent decline in population between 1940 and 1950, but had a 7 percent increase in population between 1950 to 1960. While the first hint of white flight from Montgomery was small, and primarily to the east, after 1960 an even larger increase in population occurred to the north of the city in Elmore County, with a 10 percent increase in population between 1960 and 1970, and in Autauga County, with a 28 percent increase. The city of Montgomery's population began to decline (see tables 4.1 and 4.2).

At the same time, city planning practices nationally were increasing the use of rational planning methods, developing new scientific-appearing methods that used technical models and quantitative data analysis to guide development and public expenditures. Emerging from these methods was the idea that comprehensive planning could accomplish economic development and industrial growth goals better than the case-by-case incremental approach used during previous decades.[2] In these comprehensive plans, planners eventually

Table 4.1. Total population, Montgomery region, 1940–1970

| | City of Montgomery | Montgomery County (excluding city of Montgomery) | Elmore County | Autauga County |
|---|---|---|---|---|
| 1940 | 78,084 | 36,336 | 34,546 | 20,977 |
| 1950 | 106,525 | 32,414 | 31,649 | 18,180 |
| 1960 | 134,393 | 34,817 | 30,524 | 18,739 |
| 1970 | 133,386 | 34,404 | 33,535 | 23,990 |

*Source:* US Census of Population and Housing.

Table 4.2. Population change, Montgomery region, 1940–1970

| | City of Montgomery | Montgomery County (excluding city of Montgomery) | Elmore County | Autauga County |
|---|---|---|---|---|
| 1940–1950 | 36 | -11 | -8 | -13 |
| 1950–1960 | 26 | 7 | -4 | 3 |
| 1960–1970 | -1 | -1 | 10 | 28 |

*Source:* US Census of Population and Housing.

proposed demolishing the entirety of the African American neighborhoods in the city by using the full force of urban policies: comprehensive planning, transportation planning, parks and recreation planning, zoning, budgeting, infrastructure, and housing codes. Federal funding programs increased and aided this approach by requiring comprehensive plans for slum clearance, increasing funding for slum clearance, and establishing massive new programs such as the Interstate Highway System.

As in previous decades, white people continued to blame African American people for a range of urban problems, including disease, moral failings, crime, fires, urban density, poor-quality infrastructure, and a lack of economic development. By the 1950s city officials added more issues to the list of grievances, including traffic congestion, white flight to the suburbs, and a lagging urban economy. City officials implemented comprehensive plans to improve urban issues and the economy, using these false arguments to justify the demolition of African American neighborhoods. Linking blight with traffic congestion and white flight to the suburbs, and arguing that the presence of African American slums was the reason white people moved to the suburbs, allowed city officials to easily couple slum clearance plans with new major investments in urban expressways, parking for downtown, and other economic development strategies.[3]

Schools also became a focus of planning, as the comprehensiveness of plans increased through improvements in the rational basis for planning. Adding school location decisions to the purview of planners allowed them to cover a more complete set of issues and consider the location of schools when planning for neighborhoods and transportation. While these would normally be considered improvements to planning practice, in Montgomery in the mid-twentieth century, school segregation was a major goal of elected officials, so school segregation was added to the increasingly long list of planning goals that more acutely affected African American people than white people.

As Montgomery's comprehensive plans for economic development, transportation, neighborhood improvement, industrial growth, schools, and other issues were developed, slum clearance and public housing became major implementing strategies for multiple programs. At the same time, African American people became increasingly opposed to demolition of their homes and resettlement into smaller and denser rental apartments in deeply segregated neighborhoods. Further, efforts to desegregate public institutions accelerated after the *Brown v. Board of Education* decision.[4] In response to these and other political pressures, the local political environment grew more volatile and the violent responses from white people grew more extreme and dangerous.

## MONTGOMERY'S SCHOOL AND PARK DESEGREGATION EFFORTS

Montgomery, which had a unified city and county school system that included rural and urban schools, was the first city in Alabama to have a school desegregation effort and the last big city to achieve school desegregation. After the US Supreme Court's 1954 school desegregation decision, *Brown v. Board of Education*, African American activists in Montgomery began to organize to integrate the public schools. In January 1954 Thurgood Marshall, director of and attorney for the NAACP, who had represented the *Brown* case at the US Supreme Court in 1952 and 1953, gave speeches at ASU, Tuskegee University, and in Anniston urging African American activists to take action to desegregate schools. Marshall's visits, which occurred before the *Brown* decision was announced by the US Supreme Court, were accompanied by a fundraising campaign to support school integration lawsuits.[5] Marshall was confident about the forthcoming *Brown* decision and urged African American people and white people to cooperate with the decision, noting, optimistically, that he foresaw "complete cooperation—not upheaval."[6]

When schools opened in Montgomery in September 1954, the Montgomery chapter of the NAACP submitted a desegregation petition to the Montgomery County Board of Education. On the first day of school, twenty-three African American children from the small and underfunded all-African American Vineyard Elementary School sought admission to the all-white Harrison Elementary School. The group was accompanied by Rev. Horace Bell, who served as their spokesperson and represented the Montgomery chapter of the NAACP; white attorney Nesbitt Elmore; white liberal activist Aubrey Williams Jr.; and E. D. Nixon. Bell's son, William Bell, had earlier applied for admission to the all-white Auburn University in 1948 but withdrew his application because of the threats he received and bullying he endured.[7]

Vineyard Elementary School was at the edge of Abraham's Vineyard, a low-income neighborhood at the southern edge of Montgomery, which city planners designated a slum.[8] The neighborhood was formerly quarters—home to African American residents who worked in the homes of nearby white residents as enslaved laborers before the Civil War and as low-paid servants after. The school sat at the far corner of the large lot that all-white Harrison Elementary School occupied, past the playgrounds and sports fields that were available only to students attending the white school. The two schools, which were located just two hundred yards away from each other, epitomized the concept of *separate and unequal*. Some of the African American families in the neighborhood lived closer to Harrison Elementary School than they did to Vineyard School because the schools were surrounded by an African American neighborhood on three sides, with a white neighborhood to the north. Many of the homes of African American families were in disrepair but were largely owner-occupied. Because the neighborhood was at one time a rural part of the city, some African American families had lived there for generations.

Before the start of the school year in 1954, the Montgomery County School Board proposed closing Vineyard School and busing children across town due to the poor condition of the school. Even by the school board's low standards for African American schools, members of the board felt it was best to simply abandon the school. Parents, however, wanted a walkable school in their neighborhood and asked the board to make improvements instead of busing their children across town. The board agreed to make a few minor improvements, including the addition of a third classroom, running water, and indoor toilets and hiring a third teacher. The building was also relocated farther to the back of the lot—away from the white school. Despite the proposed improvements, the school was still merely a shack, with no gas, electricity, or dining facilities.[9] Harrison Elementary School, on the other hand, was a modern twenty-room brick building that accommodated 650 students.[10] School board chairman T. L. Bear and Superintendent C. M. Dannelly promised the parents that the board would install gas, electricity, and landscaping improvements at

Vineyard School, but because African American schools were not a priority for funding or attention from the school board, the board failed to complete the improvements prior to the beginning of the school year.

When the activists arrived at Harrison Elementary School on the day of the integration attempt, Principal Robert Anderson denied the students admission, citing the school boundary lines that were drawn along residential segregation lines, and he told the group that he had no power to admit the students under Alabama law.

Parents and activists felt conflicting tensions between the desire to increase activism and the fear that the school board would simply close schools if they pushed for school desegregation. The Vineyard School Parent Teacher Association and R. L. Matthews, president of the Montgomery chapter of the NAACP, told newspapers that they had nothing to do with the attempt to enroll the children at Harrison School, although Matthews did admit that NAACP members accompanied the group as observers. So it was with some trepidation that the NAACP presented a petition to the school board two weeks later, signed by twenty-three parents, attorney Peter Hall, and E. D. Nixon, requesting a hearing before the board to discuss desegregation of the public schools.[11]

The petition cited the *Brown v. Board of Education* decision, requesting reorganization of the school boundary lines. The group wrote, "We . . . call upon you to take immediate steps to reorganize the public schools under your jurisdiction in accordance with the constitutional principles enunciated by the Supreme Court. . . . As we understand these principles, children of public school age attending and entitled to attend public schools cannot be denied admission to any school or be required to attend any school solely because of race and color."[12] School superintendent Clarence Dannelly scheduled a meeting with the parents and activists, and five parents showed up. However, when a journalist walked into the meeting, Dannelly immediately canceled it, telling reporters that he did not want the meeting publicized because it was not important enough to merit attention.[13]

By the next school board meeting, the activists, feeling pressure from their neighbors who feared that the board would close the schools, and also fearing violence and intimidation from white parents, announced that they would not pursue integration. Matthews told newspapers that anyone attending the school board meeting was doing so on their own—not as a representative of the NAACP. Attorney Nesbitt Elmore did not attend the meeting and told reporters that he was unaware of any activists planning to attend.[14] African American activists faced violence and intimidation when seeking to integrate schools throughout the South. On the day of the next Montgomery school board meeting, the *Alabama Citizen* ran a story describing how a similar integration attempt in Brewton, Alabama, was eliminated, noting, "The school board gave the name of the petitioners to the . . . local white weekly [newspaper] which ran a long story giving the names of all the signers. . . . Pressure was immediately applied either from a physical or economic source which caused some to withdraw their names and support from the project."[15] Similarly, the *Montgomery Advertiser* published the names and home addresses of all the signatories of the effort to desegregate Harrison Elementary School.[16]

At the end of the school year, as Marshall predicted, the *Brown v. Board of Education* decision was announced by the US Supreme Court, declaring school segregation unconstitutional. After the *Brown* decision, Alabama legislators, prodded by the white supremacists, lobbied for adoption of numerous reactionary bills, including one that urged Congress to study "what part, if any, the Communist Party had in writing the U.S. Supreme Court school decisions,"[17] and bills calling for impeachment of the US Supreme Court justices who voted in favor of the *Brown* decision.

School desegregation didn't just threaten white supremacy in terms of power and privilege; it also threatened to take funding away from white schools, at least according to segregationists. In 1955, 29,000 children in Alabama attended schools with no electricity, 27,000 children attended schools with no toilets, and 222,000 children attended schools with only outdoor privies. School funding was lower in Alabama than in any other state. Desegregating schools would almost certainly not result in white children attending formerly African American schools, which were far inferior—most of them were mere shacks; instead, it meant the opposite. If African American children began attending formerly all-white schools, limited school funding would be stretched, necessitating the construction of new schools.[18]

State Representative Sam Engelhardt Jr., who later became the director of the AHD, anticipating the decision, had a bill waiting that would eliminate the public schools entirely and set up funds for private schools, which could maintain segregation. Engelhardt proposed such a law twice previously—in 1951 and 1953.[19] After the *Brown* decision, Senator Albert Boutwell, a white supremacist from Birmingham who represented the "Big Mules," chaired a committee that included Engelhardt to propose a solution to keep schools segregated. In an unlikely partnership of wealthy business interests, represented by Boutwell, and Black Belt farmers, represented by Englehardt, the committee found common ground in the desire to keep schools segregated.

The Boutwell committee modeled their recommendations on Engelhardt's previous two bills, proposing to abolish the public school system and eliminate the words "public school" from the Alabama constitution. In its place, they proposed a system of private schools funded by grants from the state. Seeing the abolition of public schools as a last resort, however, the committee also proposed a pupil placement bill, which allowed placement boards to assign students to public schools based on existing school facilities, the student's abilities, home life, social environment, and phycological ability. There would be a lengthy process for appealing the board's decisions.[20] The law would serve segregation by allowing local school boards to use any number of subjective and racist criteria for placing children in schools.

The pupil placement bill passed in the Alabama Senate and House with a combined vote of 132–1. The legislature also passed a companion bill, approved by voters in 1955, which removed compulsory education from the Alabama constitution, gave the legislature the power to abolish public schools, and made school employees judicial officers so they would be immune from lawsuits.[21] As a backup, if the courts overturned the pupil placement law, the legislature could quickly abolish public schools, because that law had already been approved by voters. Local school boards immediately began implementing the pupil placement law to make sure African American students remained in segregated schools.[22]

Aware of the threat of closing the schools, African American activists turned their attention to park desegregation, putting schools on hold. In January 1955 a WPC delegation, including Jo Ann Robinson, Irene West, Mary Fair Burks, and Mrs. J. E. Pierce, asked the City Commission to appoint an African American representative to the Parks and Recreation Board, recommending Irene West for the position. Trying to appeal to the members of the commission's racist ideas, the women argued that adding an African American to the board would help curtail child delinquency. One city commissioner, Dave Birmingham, seeking to make good on a campaign promise, proposed that the next board vacancy go to an African American, but withdrew the motion because there was no vacancy at the time. Mayor Gayle told the group that the commissioners would consider an African American board member at the next vacancy.[23]

The proposal for an African American member of the Parks and Recreation Board became a major issue in the 1955 election, just before the bus boycott. Commissioner Birmingham proposed expanding the board from five to seven members to add two new African American members. Gayle and Commissioner Cleere voted against the proposal, responding to political pressure from white people, but said that they would use bond funds to improve and increase parks in African American neighborhoods. In August, Rufus Lewis encouraged the Citizen's Coordinating Committee to sponsor a federal lawsuit to desegregate parks, but most of the committee voted instead to try to use their political connections to increase and improve parks. In September, Fred Gray and others requested—and were granted—a hearing of the Parks and Recreation Board to demand better African American park facilities. The board granted the hearing after Gray attended a City Commission meeting and threatened court action if parks were not improved. The city commissioners, hoping to avoid a desegregation lawsuit, promised Gray that a future bond issue would fund the park improvements. Nonetheless, activists planned to make parks a major focus of civil rights activism in the coming year.[24]

Earlier that November, US Supreme Court decisions ordered desegregation of parks and public golf courses in Baltimore and Atlanta, and the Alabama Council on Human Relations urged activists in Montgomery and across the state to follow suit.[25] Plans to increase activism for parks were sidelined, however, in December, with the arrest of Rosa Parks and the start of the bus boycott, and all civil rights organizing shifted to the boycott. It would be a few more years before activists returned to the issue of parks. However, African American activists would emerge at the end of the bus boycott stronger, more organized, unified, and determined, while segregationists emerged more dangerous, extreme, and violent.

## RACIAL PLANNING AND THE MONTGOMERY BUS BOYCOTT

The quality of African American homes and neighborhoods, including sewerage and water extensions into those neighborhoods, became a political issue in the 1955 city elections, in addition to parks. Incumbent city commissioner Dave Birmingham, who won his seat on the City Commission with the support of African American voters in 1953, voted against extending sewerage and water infrastructure to a new south Montgomery white neighborhood and demanded that the homeowners pay for the utilities. Birmingham hoped to again align himself with a coalition of low-income white voters and African American voters, who were usually told they needed to pay for basic city services. Frank Parks, who was challenging City Commissioner George Cleere, also aligned himself with this position and hoped to win the election with the same coalition of voters.[26]

Slum clearance also became central to political campaigns. Candidates walked a fine line between trying to appeal to African American voters and appealing to white voters. Other candidates used racist attacks to try to create a larger coalition of white voters without relying on African American voters. Mayor Gayle pledged to Montgomerians that if reelected, he would finish the North Montgomery and Houston Hill slum clearance projects (which had stalled) and make sure Montgomerians had good neighborhood conditions. Cleere pledged to continue to expand the slum clearance program in the city.

At the same time, African American voters and residents became more vocal about the impacts of slum clearance on their neighborhoods. Although many African American leaders supported slum clearance in earlier decades because they believed it would lead to improvements in neighborhood and housing conditions, by the 1950s many began to realize that slum clearance meant the destruction of African American neighborhoods, not improvement of them. African American residents also realized that slum clearance, failing to accomplish the program's stated goals, had increased density and residential segregation. African American leaders hoped to capitalize on the divide between the white classes by trying to get promises from elected officials for improvements: better conditions on segregated busses; better housing and neighborhood conditions; improved public services in African American neighborhoods, including sewer extensions, street widening, curbs, and fire services; more African American representation on the Parks and Recreation Board; and employment of African American people in city government.[27]

E. D. Nixon arranged a public forum at the Ben Moore Hotel with the mayoral and City Commission candidates, a significant change from earlier decades when candidates for elected office would not consider attending a forum for African American voters. The candidates' responses to questions from the African American attendees differed widely depending on their individual strategy of either trying to win African American votes or trying to appear the most racist to win the votes of racial extremists. Moderate candidates promised to appoint an African American Parks and Recreation Board member, while others, like Clyde Sellers, increased their racist attacks. Sellers said that slum clearance—not neighborhood improvement—was the answer to conditions in African American neighborhoods, noting that he intended to continue the slum clearance program, because "I will not compromise my principles nor violate my Southern birthright to promise something I do not intend to do. I will not be intimidated for the sake of a block of negro voters."[28] After Gayle won reelection as mayor, and Sellers and Parks won seats on the City Commission, the political lesson learned from the election, according to historian J. Mills Thornton III, was that in order to win an election in Montgomery, a candidate needed to either exploit the city's racial tensions through racist attacks or build a coalition of low- to middle-income white voters and African American voters. It was in this election that it became clear that the most racially volatile and white supremacist candidates were the ones who would likely win an election for local public office.[29]

As the 1955 elections were occurring in Montgomery, the federal Bureau of Public Roads (BPR) was working on a new interstate highway system that would drastically reshape cities across the United States. A US interstate highway system had been debated for many years, with federal officials recognizing the need for such a system but disagreeing on how to pay for it. The BPR released a comprehensive report outlining the urban locations of a national interstate highway system, *General Location of National System of Interstate*

*Highways* (i.e., the *Yellow Book*) in September 1955, but had not yet determined how to pay for the massive infrastructure program. In the book, engineers routed the highways around most midsize cities with a small spur into their downtowns. Highway engineers tried to route interstates only through urban areas in large cities, and typically not in small and midsize cities, because they were aware that building urban interstates would be very expensive owing to high land acquisition costs, so they tried to avoid routing interstates through cities when it could be avoided. Therefore, federal highway engineers planned bypass routes around most cities in Alabama, including for Montgomery.[30]

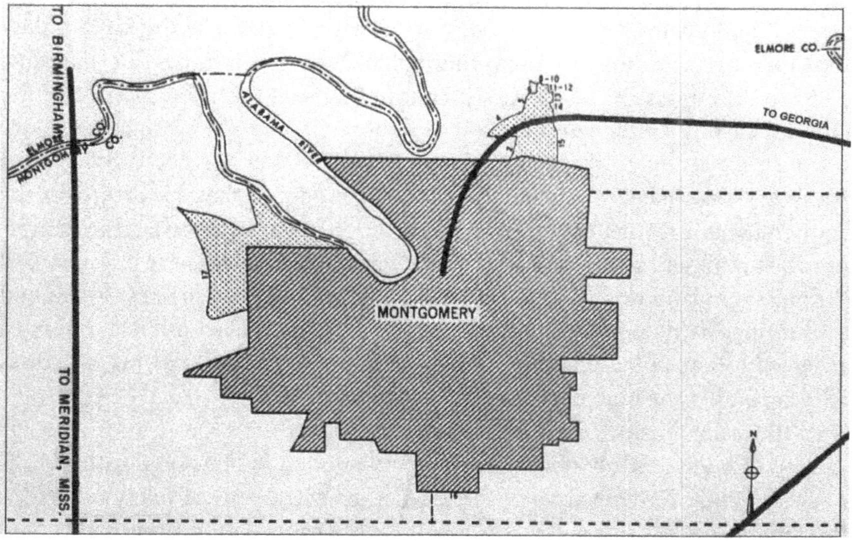


Figure 4.1. Engineers and planners working for the US Federal Bureau of Public Roads initially planned to route I-85 and I-65 outside Montgomery with a spur from I-85 through North Montgomery into downtown. This proposal would have been much less expensive than an urban interstate route, would have disturbed fewer homes and residents, and would have been closer to emerging suburban growth centers. (US Department of Commerce, General Location of National System of Interstate Highways, 1955, RG 406, National Archives II, College Park, Maryland. Modified by Riley Dibble.)

After the BPR released the *Yellow Book*, President Eisenhower signed the Federal-Aid Highway Act and the Highway Revenue Act, authorizing construction of the Interstate Highway System. The funding would come from the gas tax, which would feed into a highway trust fund, and states would pay 10 percent of the cost, while the federal government paid 90 percent.[31] With funding secured, the BPR began working more closely with state highway departments, including the AHD, to finalize routing decisions.

Early in the interstate routing process, AHD engineers agreed that a bypass route with a spur connector into downtown was the best option for Montgomery because traffic was not heavy, and a bypass route would be closer to Maxwell Air Force Base. In July 1955, four months before the start of the bus boycott, the AHD was working with the BPR to design the 13.5-mile spur through North Montgomery to connect a bypass route for I-85 into the city, and the BPR generally supported the design. The spur for I-85 would connect to Columbus Street at North Ripley Street, avoiding the white neighborhoods on the east side, and cutting through the African American neighborhoods north of downtown, including Newtown and King Hill. It would also provide access to the industrial area north of downtown and advance the city's industrial growth aspirations by providing better access to the area for shipping. I-65 would bypass the city entirely, running outside the western edge of the city just east of Antioch and cross into Elmore County along Highway 31, allowing easy access to the new highway from Maxwell Air Force Base and a planned industrial expansion on the far western edge of the city. Except for the spur connector through the North Montgomery African American neighborhoods and industrial district, all the interstates would bypass the city, running through rural and undeveloped land, avoiding a costly urban expressway, and preventing the demolition of many homes.[32] The proposed interstate designs reflected rational planning ideas, seeking to go near major economic activities while avoiding the high cost of an urban route.[33]

With racial tensions on the rise, just days before the 1955 election, fifteen-year-old Claudette Colvin was arrested for violating the bus segregation ordinance.[34] While Colvin's arrest was preceded by the arrests of many others for the same violation, her arrest was significant because she pled not guilty, and she was represented by African American civil rights attorney Fred Gray, who had just passed the Alabama bar exam. Judge Wiley Hill Jr., brother of Senator Lister Hill, heard the case and found Colvin guilty of violating the bus segregation ordinance and of assault and battery of the officer who arrested her.[35]

There was also a growing resistance to civil rights activism from all factions of segregationists. The Ku Klux Klan (KKK) saw a revival and growth in Montgomery, and white middle-class professionals established the Montgomery chapter of the White Citizens' Council (WCC), a hate group. The Citizens' Council, led by white ministers and businesspeople, was promoted as a "more refined version of the Ku Klux Klan,"[36] and although the group was less publicly violent than the KKK, the Citizens' Council was just as dangerous. It sought to prevent desegregation through economic pressure, denial of credit, and loss of jobs and housing for African American residents. The Montgomery chapter of the WCC was led by Sam Engelhardt Jr., a state congressperson who worked on school segregation and who was later appointed state highway director.[37]

African American people were aware of the threat posed by the WCC, and Rufus Lewis sent a letter to ministers, African American groups, and other civil rights leaders, inviting them to a meeting at the Citizen's Club to strategize resistance against the Citizens' Council. As Lewis told the group, the growth of the council posed a real threat to the well-being of African American people. He wrote, "The White Citizens Council has threaten the rights, freedom and even the very life of every Negro in the South. Any Negro who has the courage to speak up for his own rights is threaten and denied a job, credit, or the privilege to mortgage or remortgage his own property. We have practically no voice in the operation of our government. Our elected officials turn a deaf ear to our plea for justice."[38]

After the 1955 election, the Montgomery Real Estate Board and the Home Builders Association, frustrated by the new public housing developments that were constructed in and around Centennial Hill, increased pressure on city officials to rely on private construction of housing instead of public housing. At the same time, white businesspeople pressured city officials to increase clearance of African American neighborhoods. The Montgomery Real Estate Board proposed a "Build Montgomery Better" program, which would create a new city agency to facilitate slum clearance by private developers.[39] Like slum clearance programs, the new program was promoted as one that would foster neighborhood and housing improvement and economic development, demolishing older African American homes and neighborhoods to make way for private investment. The City Commission agreed to sponsor the program and the Montgomery Chamber of Commerce supported it, with a focus on updating local housing and health and sanitation codes, broadening the city's condemnation authority, and allowing the City Commission to demolish buildings that were "undesirable from health and community safety standpoints."[40]

Despite the program's powerful supporters, who were motivated by their own economic interests as well as a concern for public health and property values, the Build Montgomery Better program was slow to start because Mayor Gayle preferred more aggressive slum clearance programs with federal support and financing. As Chairman E. S. Watts noted, "It has been lagging lately due to the racial difficulties in the city and Mayor W. A. Gayle's opinion that the program should be put aside in view of this problem."[41]

The "racial difficulties" began in December 1955 when Rosa Parks was arrested for refusing an order from bus driver Fred Blake to give up her seat to a white man on her way home from her job as a seamstress at the Montgomery Fair, a department store downtown, to her home at Cleveland Court. E. D. Nixon posted bail for Parks, along with white attorney Clifford Durr and his civil rights activist wife, Virginia Durr.[42] After the arrest of Parks, African American leaders, including Jo Ann Robinson and Nixon and members of the WPC, called for a bus boycott on the day of her trial. Robinson mimeographed flyers at ASU calling for a boycott and, along with other WPC leaders including Johnnie Rebecca Carr and Irene West, distributed them to African American households and churches.[43]

The initial one-day boycott was a huge success due to the organizing efforts of the WPC and the previous decades of learning, organizing, and activism. Neighborhood segregation also made it easy to spread the word about the boycott. On the afternoon of the boycott, African American leaders met at Mount Zion African Methodist Episcopal Zion Church and formed a new organization to manage continuation of the boycott—the MIA. They elected Rev. Dr. Martin Luther King Jr. to head the organization, and although Rev. King was a newcomer to the city and relatively unknown to the activists, by the end of the boycott he became the national voice for civil rights. Rev. Ralph Abernathy headed a committee to draft a resolution to continue the boycott. That evening, the MIA held a mass meeting at Holt Street Baptist Church, and with a crowd of some five thousand people that spilled out onto the street in front of the church, the community voted to continue the boycott.[44]

In February 1956, when the bus boycott was in its third month, eighty-nine MIA leaders, including twenty-four ministers, were arrested for violating Alabama's anti-boycott law and brought before a grand jury. It was then that Mayor Gayle proposed pausing the Build Montgomery Better program to pursue more comprehensive slum clearance using federal funds.[45] Two weeks later, Mayor Gayle announced a broad expansion of slum clearance in the city, with a program of incentives and regulations for privately funded rehabilitation and a new housing code that appeased the Real Estate Board and the Homebuilders Association. Gayle also announced the newly created city position of urban renewal coordinator and an Urban Renewal Board to advise the Planning Commission on slum clearance.[46] With these strategies, Gayle was responding to intense pressure from white residents to do more to punish the African American activists. He and the professional planners who would implement these programs were also responding to pressure from white businesspeople to both increase slum clearance and pay private businesspeople to do it.

Plans for three new slum clearance projects for which the city would seek federal assistance were also announced, all of them in African American neighborhoods—Washington Park on the Westside, King Hill/Dixie Drive in North Montgomery, and Abraham's Vineyard in south Montgomery. With increasing pressure from the federal court system to desegregate parks, city officials included improvements to King Hill Park and Washington Park in these plans because Mayor Gayle, city commissioners, and members of the Parks and Recreation Board hoped that by improving the parks they might be able to prove that the doctrine of "separate but equal" was working, allowing them to avoid desegregation.[47]

The shift in slum clearance plans from projects in and around Centennial Hill to projects in neighborhoods that were not close to downtown represented a significant shift toward more comprehensive plans covering the entire city. Nonetheless, all three neighborhoods had ties to activism. The first, King Hill, north of downtown, was home to Claudette Colvin and other activists. The second, the Westside, was home to many working-class activists who were boycotting buses, including Rosa Parks, E. D. Nixon, and Lucille Times. The third, Abraham's Vineyard, south of downtown, was the location of the integration attempt at William Harrison Elementary School in 1954.[48]

Targeting Abraham's Vineyard for slum clearance underscored the practice of using slum clearance to deepen residential segregation and reinforce segregated school boundary lines, removing former quarters near white neighborhoods. This accomplished multiple goals, because it allowed city commissioners to respond to white citizens' concerns that nearby African American housing was driving down property values and increasing crime, and it functioned as a punishment for the activism of African American residents. It also allowed city officials to argue that school segregation was based on residential patterns and was not a school segregation policy.[49] Abraham's Vineyard was surrounded by white neighborhoods to the north, so if the neighborhoods were demolished and the residents relocated to more deeply segregated neighborhoods, the school could be closed, and William Harrison Elementary School would be situated within an entirely white neighborhood.

Mayor Gayle used divisive language to describe the new projects, hoping to find allies in white residents: "It's an old story. . . . A story you have seen before and will see again in newspapers, hospital records, and fire reports. It is the story of slums with its killing disease, vicious crimes and juvenile delinquency, charred bodies in tinderbox frame shacks, infants assaulted by rats and vermin, the story of shattered lives."[50] Because the plan also included incentives for private development and did not propose new public housing, it was endorsed by the Jaycees, the Montgomery Real Estate Board, the Montgomery Association of Homebuilders, and the Montgomery Chamber of Commerce. However, implementing the slum clearance plans with only private investment for the three neighborhoods never came to fruition, and the city did not receive federal funding for them.

As the bus boycott dragged on and statements from public officials grew tougher, the local mood grew increasingly violent against African American people. The discussions on political issues, including slum clearance, became more racially divisive. In January, Gayle announced that the City Commission would no longer negotiate with African American leaders of the boycott, referring to "negro radicals" who wanted to "stir up racial strife."[51] Reflecting the more racially radical tone of the city that was emerging, Gayle and the city commissioners received hundreds of congratulatory calls, telegrams, and messages of personal gratitude following the announcement. Later that month, white extremists threw dynamite onto the front porch of Rev. Dr. King's home, with his wife, baby, and a visitor present; and Nixon's home was bombed. Across the state in Tuscaloosa, violent white mobs protested the admission of Autherine Lucy to the University of Alabama. The WCC, led by Senator Sam Engelhardt Jr., grew exponentially and became a major political force. At a WCC rally in Montgomery in February, which filled the fifteen-thousand-capacity space at the city's Garrett Coliseum, standing ovations were given to Senator James Eastland, Mayor Gayle, and City Commissioner Sellers after they joined the WCC and delivered racist speeches. In May a bomb went off at the home of Rev. Robert and Jean Graetz. White moderates received threats for voicing any support of African American causes or the boycott, including for driving their African American maids to work. However, while the violence increased, so did the resolve and unity of the boycotters.[52]

At the federal level, while the bus boycott continued, Congress passed the 1956 Housing Act, which authorized funding for the creation of comprehensive urban renewal plans and surveys of blighted areas. The act allowed projects to be completed in stages and authorized new grants and loans for public housing, requiring that any city receiving such funds must have a comprehensive program for preventing and eliminating slums approved by the FHA, all but amounting to a federal requirement for rational comprehensive planning.[53]

In December 1956, just fifteen days before the US Supreme Court issued the decision that integrated the buses and ended the boycott, a group of white businesspeople organized an independent "war on city slum areas" and named the new organization "Forward Inc."[54] The group criticized Mayor Gayle for not doing enough to spur private investment in slum clearance and for not following through on the Build Montgomery Better program, announced earlier that year. Despite the announcement by Gayle that slum clearance would increase, implementation of the plans stalled as the bus boycott dragged on, and no federal funding was forthcoming for the projects. With the boycott ending and integration of the buses imminent, white leaders pressured Gayle to do more to demolish African American housing in the city and, motivated by their own economic interests, insisted that the new programs rely on private investment.

The end of the boycott quickly gave rise to more racial extremism in the city. The reaction from city planners to this new racial environment was equally quick and extreme, and they immediately began to broaden their focus on demolishing African American neighborhoods with renewed vigor and new tools. By the end of the bus boycott, city officials were starting to develop a comprehensive vision of demolishing the home of nearly every African American in the city, fueled by new federal funding programs that required such a comprehensive approach, in the next decade. While concerns about white flight to the suburbs increased and slum clearance plans accelerated, plans for public housing became more modest due to pressure from white businesspeople to rely on the private market, and the political environment in the city grew more racially extreme.

# 5

## Emergence of Comprehensive Citywide Slum Clearance after the Bus Boycott

THE CITY THAT arose after the bus boycott bore little resemblance to the city when it began. White people were more polarized, more violent, and more racially extreme, and African American people were more united and committed, putting an end to the rivalry for leadership with the uniting presence of Rev. Dr. Martin Luther King Jr. and the success of the bus boycott. The sophistication and planning that went into the bus boycott, including arranging transportation for the boycotters, insurance for cars, and fundraising, propelled activism in the city to a new level.

One of the outcomes of the increased sophistication of organizing was a rise in the number of African American voters, which grew by 256 percent, from 891 voters in 1949 to 2,285 voters in 1958.[1] Two months after the end of the boycott, the MIA formed a committee on countywide registration and voting, hoping to capitalize on the increased momentum from the success of the boycott, and appointed Rufus Lewis as chairperson. At the following MIA meeting, Lewis outlined an extensive plan for getting every qualified African American person in Montgomery registered to vote. The plan involved a detailed precinct and ward system, with captains for every precinct and ward, five block workers in each precinct, and extensive recordkeeping and follow-up visits to ensure African American citizens were qualified to vote, prepared to register, successfully registered, and knowledgeable about candidates, and that they voted on election day. Block captains and workers kept detailed records of every voter and potential voter, including when and how they were contacted by block workers, what their response was, if they attended a voter education class (called citizenship classes), and when they voted. The organization included a speaker's bureau and a facts-and-figures chairperson to educate voters and send out sample ballots with recommended candidates. On election day the committee organized transportation and childcare, block workers to help people vote, and a headquarters staffed by an attorney and others to advise on any voting problems.[2]

Women and members of the WPC were at the heart of the voting activism infrastructure. Lewis recruited African American women to be block captains and workers throughout the city, telling them that their role in politics was just as important as male leaders'. As he told block leaders, "Women have just as much stake in politics as men. Each year more and more women, working mothers and homemakers, are bringing their influence to bear on the political scene. . . . They have discovered that politics is their baby, too."[3] The WPC also worked with increasing sophistication to register voters. They distributed a pamphlet across the city, describing in detail how and when different officers are elected—from tax assessors and board of education members to judges. It told people where, when, and how to vote, and defined terms such as "initiative," "referendum," "recall," "absentee voting," and "ballot."[4]

One way for white supremacists to counteract the efforts of activists, however, was to terrorize them by demolishing their homes, as evidenced by the bombings during the boycott. City planners and elected officials also believed that slum clearance accomplished important public goals of increasing economic development and industrial growth, provided space for new transportation infrastructure, improved neighborhoods, and kept schools segregated. Members of Forward Inc. immediately began lobbying elected officials to accelerate slum clearance by adopting a new housing code for existing buildings. The proposed housing code would supplement the city's building code because, as secretary of the group Arthur Stewart (who was a home builder) argued, a building code dealt only with new construction, but the new housing code addressed conditions in existing buildings. The new ordinance would strengthen the 1948 health and sanitary ordinances. Realtor Edward Watts, elected chairman of the group, blamed the presence of slums on moral deficiencies of African American families, arguing, "People don't live in slum areas because they can't afford better housing. . . . The common laborer makes at least a dollar an hour."[5]

Mayor Gayle was motivated to respond quickly and favorably to the new group because he came from a weakened political position at the end of the bus boycott. Gayle directed the Water Works and Sanitary Sewer Board to complete a comprehensive survey of city streets to determine which streets needed sewerage lines, formed a committee to develop a new housing code, and directed the Planning Commission to prepare a land use map to determine the location of blighted areas. All three of these strategies followed theories and methods of comprehensive rational planning. Gayle told Forward Inc. that he and the city commissioners were in favor of private industry accomplishing the task of clearing slums and would resort to federal funding and public housing only if it were necessary.[6]

The violence against African American people in the wake of the bus boycott, like the city's slum clearance plans, was unrelenting. In January 1957

Figure 5.1. An African American woman stands on a street corner while going door-to-door to register voters. Women activists were a crucial part of the African American voter registration infrastructure in Montgomery. (John Engelhardt Scott Collection, March 16, 1959, file Q74131, Alabama Department of Archives and History, Montgomery, Alabama.)

four African American churches and two homes of civil rights leaders were bombed: Bell Street Baptist Church, Mount Olive Baptist Church, Hutchinson Street Baptist Church, First Baptist Church, and the homes of Rev. Ralph Abernathy and Rev. Robert Graetz. Bombs at Rev. Dr. King's home and church were defused, but another bomb destroyed his neighbor's home. Willie Edwards Jr. was murdered when KKK members mistook him for a different person whom they planned to murder. For white moderates, any hint of support of African American people led to ostracism, threats, and violence.

City staff prepared the new housing code and a local planning consultant, Urban Consultants Inc. began drafting a new land use plan financed by the Montgomery Planning Commission. Urban Consultants Inc. would go on to play a major role in planning during the next decade, assisting the Planning Commission with many plans and policies and even staffing the URA. Urban Consultants Inc., which also went by the firm name Urban Consultant Associates, was cofounded in 1958 by Eugene C. Brock, a landscape architect, and H. K. Francis, an engineer. By 1970 the firm had a staff of twenty-six and was headquartered in Montgomery at 908 South Hull Street.[7]

Although the plan was not adopted as policy, it provided important documentation of slum clearance, seven years before the City Commission adopted the city's first comprehensive plan, at a crucial political time—the end of the bus boycott.[8] The plan contains many of the same goals reflected in the 1963–1965 comprehensive plan, including concerns about white flight, slum clearance, expansion of downtown, demolition of African American neighborhood commercial districts and replacing them with strip commercial development, and industrial development. It also reflected a strategic shift toward targeting the homes of African American residents on a more comprehensive level, including the homes of civil rights leaders and middle-class families. Although the plan contained analysis (albeit fuzzy analysis) and documentation of inadequate conditions in African American neighborhoods, it was not geared toward improving those conditions, other than demolishing homes.

The analysis by the consultant determined that one-quarter of the homes in the city did not have indoor flush toilets, and 89 percent were home to African American families. The main reason the homes lacked indoor plumbing was that there were no sanitary sewers in some neighborhoods. Nonetheless, the consultant recommended adoption of a housing code to aid in remedying blight.[9]

The consultant recommended a neighborhood unit theory of city planning. The neighborhood unit theory, developed in 1929 by city planner Clarence Perry, proposed a physical arrangement of neighborhoods in which the needs of families were central to design. Key principles of the neighborhood unit theory include streets with little traffic; centrally located elementary schools, parks, and community buildings; and shopping centers that are within walking distance. Heavy traffic would be kept on the outskirts, and neighborhoods would be no larger than what could support a small community elementary school.[10]

The plan redefined neighborhoods in the city based on the concept of neighborhood planning, where each neighborhood would be a distinct unit centered on a neighborhood school. Each neighborhood would contain four thousand to five thousand people, a school, a playground, public buildings, and a shopping area. High-density neighborhoods would contain more than one school and a park.[11] Adoption of the neighborhood planning concept advanced segregationist goals because locating schools within distinct neighborhoods, and keeping those neighborhoods segregated, meant that school zones that were drawn along neighborhood boundary lines would result in segregated schools without an official school segregation policy.

The plan also included a neighborhood-by-neighborhood analysis of blighted areas, splitting up the city into fifty-one different sections, which the plan referred to as "neighborhoods." This approach followed the neighborhood unit theory by splitting up existing large neighborhoods into smaller sections. Actual neighborhoods in the city, such as the Westside and Centennial Hill, each contained several of these sections. Twelve of the sections were primarily African American and the rest were primarily white. The plan identified seven African American sections and one older white section as "badly blighted."[12] All but five of the twelve African American sections contained over 50 percent blight, while none of the thirty-eight white sections were over 50 percent blighted. The plan identified the sections in the large African American neighborhoods of the Westside and Centennial Hill as blighted. The only African American neighborhoods that were not declared blighted were newly built and very small.[13]

The plan was full of contradictions and revealed the priorities of elected officials, which were often at odds with data and urban conditions. City officials, hoping to attract new industrial growth to the city and reverse or halt white flight to the suburbs, and realizing that population growth was essential to their industrial aspirations, proposed increases in density in both white and African American sections. At the same time, the plan contended that density was a cause of blight but proposed large increases in population and density in some sections. For example, the plan proposed density increases of 5,614 percent and 2,528 percent in two sections at the far western edge of the city. The plan proposed large population increases in sections that were designated as blighted, including one near the southwest edge of the city that had a proposed 2,841 percent population increase, even though it was 50 percent blighted. And another in North Montgomery near King Hill had a proposed

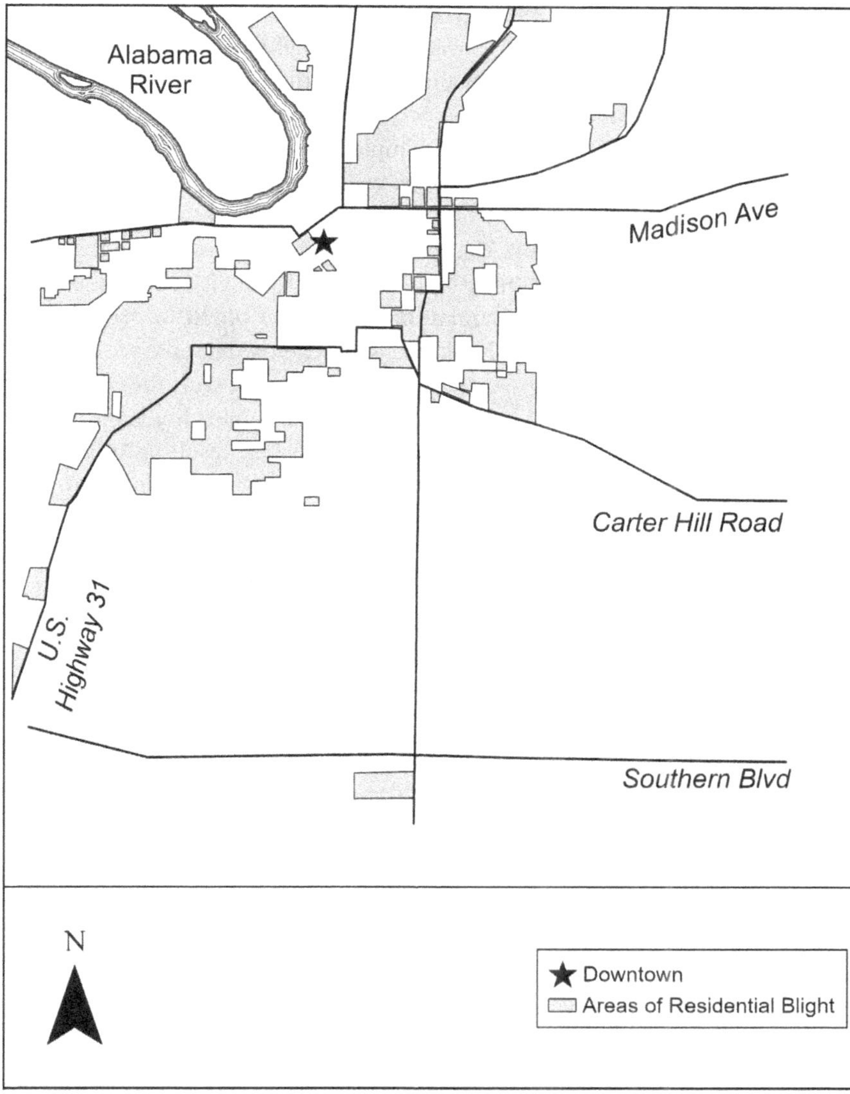


Figure 5.2. This map shows the neighborhoods that were declared blighted in the 1957 draft land use plan, shaded in gray. (Map by Riley Dibble, based on Urban Consultant Associates, Land Use Plan Draft [Montgomery: Montgomery Planning Commission, 1957], 9.)

271 percent population increase, even though it was 90 percent blighted.[14] Through these contradictions, the consultant bent their analysis to fit desired goals but failed to specify the realistic implementation strategies, beyond slum clearance, that would meet those goals.

Almost every African American person in the city lived in one of the blighted areas. The plan noted, "Seven of the [blighted] neighborhoods are Negro neighborhoods and in which almost the entire Negro population in the city lives."[15] The consultant recommended slum clearance and redevelopment as the solution for blighted areas, so full implementation of the plan would result in demolition of the homes of almost every African American person in Montgomery.

Demolishing the homes of African American families meant that they would have fewer options for housing in the segregated city of Montgomery. New housing for African American families—whether public or private—was not being built at the same rate that housing was being demolished. New private housing was more expensive and was not consistent with the prices paid to people who were displaced by slum clearance.[16] The new housing that was constructed by private developers was for-sale housing, resulting in a lack of affordable rental housing in the city. Over half of the people displaced by slum clearance sought rental homes, the *Southern Courier* reported, "but even if the houses were cheaper, more than half of the people moving out still wouldn't buy them. Many are renters now, and they don't want the responsibility of owning a home. . . . So, in the next year and a half, hundreds of families will be looking for the kind of homes they won't find."[17] African American people displaced by slum clearance would either have to leave the city, pay more for housing in the city, or relocate to housing that was in worse condition. One report noted, "People who can't get credit to buy a new home—or who don't want to go into debt—will probably end up in worse homes than they had before. They will, as one lady put it, 'trade a shack for a shack.' The others will have to take the leap into more expensive housing."[18]

The plan singled out the Five Points/Peacock Tract area near downtown for slum clearance, setting the stage for proposals in the 1963 plan, the 1965 neighborhood analysis, and plans for the Interstate Highway System, which all targeted the same neighborhood that was close to downtown. The proposed demolition of the Five Points area is notable because it included the demolition of two important meeting places for the Montgomery bus boycott—Mount Zion A. M. E. Zion Church and Holt Street Baptist Church.[19] The proposed demolition of the neighborhood, along with the two churches, supported the interests of downtown business owners who wanted to enlarge the size of downtown, increase parking, and make it more accessible to the proposed I-85 and I-65 interchange. Without demolition of the neighborhood, visitors exiting the expressway at the interchange would have to travel through several blocks of African American housing to get downtown.[20] Therefore, targeting Five Points/Peacock Tract advanced multiple goals for economic development while also punishing activists with demolition of important landmarks in their community.

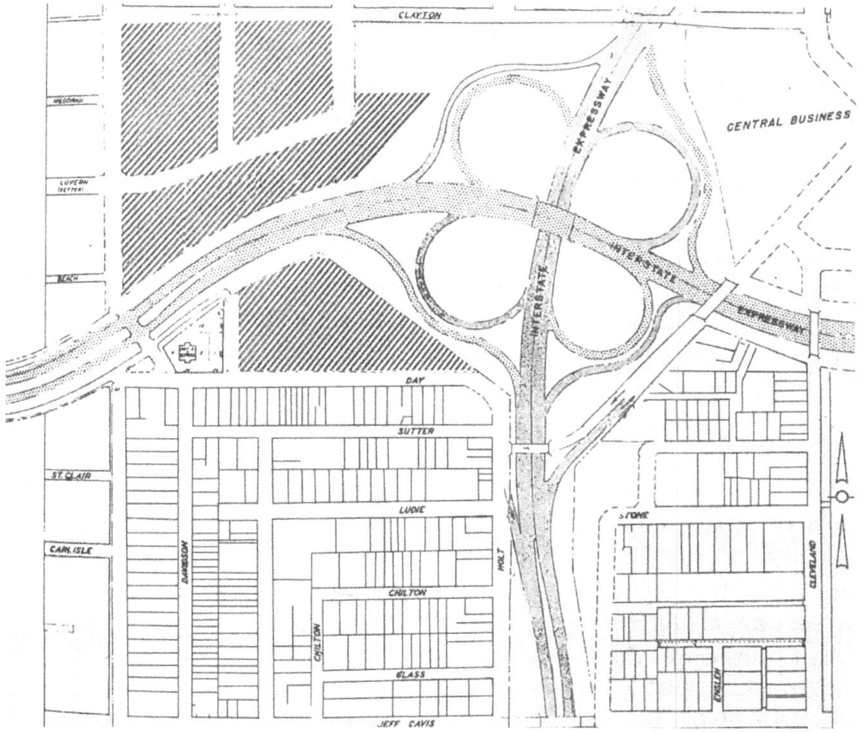


Figure 5.3. In 1957 planners proposed demolishing the African American Five Points/Peacock Tract neighborhood adjacent to downtown, which included Mount Zion A. M. E. Zion Church and Holt Street Baptist Church, both important meeting places for civil rights activists. The interstate was eventually shifted to avoid a curve in the highway, saving the two churches. (Urban Consultant Associates, Land Use Plan Draft [Montgomery: Montgomery Planning Commission, 1957], 46. Modified by Riley Dibble.)

Seeking to increase economic development, planners also proposed demolition of African American neighborhood shopping areas. With suburban expansion of Montgomery and the development of new suburban shopping centers in the 1950s, downtown Montgomery businesses lost sales, and city leaders and white downtown business owners viewed the destruction of African American retail districts, along with expansion of downtown into the Day Street/Five Points neighborhood, as a potential way to boost business revenue. Between 1954 and 1958 downtown business saw a decline of about 5 percent of their sales, and the downward trend was expected to continue. At the same time, retail sales in the region increased by 26 percent because of new suburban shopping centers. The demolition of African American business districts would leave African American people with fewer shopping options in their neighborhoods.[21] The strategy of demolishing African American business districts would also fail to achieve the objective of facilitating economic development and counteracting white flight and business growth in the suburbs; public officials failed to realize that neighborhood shopping districts were important for the vitality of the city and that the forces of suburbanization were stronger than anything public officials could do for the core city.[22]

The 1957 land use plan draft provided city leaders with a basis of knowledge about the general location of slum areas and which streets lacked sewerage and water infrastructure. However, based on decades of policies targeting the same neighborhoods and hoping to accomplish the same major public goals, the plan came to conclusions that had already been reached. To implement the plan, the City Commission adopted a new housing code that would immediately apply to new construction. Existing homes would be required to comply within two years of passage of the law.

The new housing code put more responsibility on renters (who were largely African American) and less responsibility on homeowners (who were largely white) to maintain homes, with the requirement that renters—not homeowners—keep structures clean and free from infestation. One window with screens in each room, heat, and reasonable weatherproofing were required in each residential structure. The ordinance required a kitchen sink, indoor toilet, bathroom sink, and shower or bathtub inside every dwelling, even though city commissioners knew that many city streets did not have water or sewerage mains. The lack of infrastructure in some African American neighborhoods made it impossible to comply with the code, similar to the problems that arose when the City Commission adopted the 1948 housing and sanitation ordinances.[23] Nonetheless, the city commissioners hoped that it would facilitate private funding of neighborhood improvement or demolition, allowing them to appease the increasingly vocal white business community that pushed for such goals.

Within one year, at least 110 homes were demolished for violations of the new housing code, and there were 61 additional cases in which homeowners had been notified that their homes had to be either brought up to code or demolished. City officials used the housing code to advance the interests of white businesspeople—65 of the homes that were demolished were replaced by doctor's offices, parking, motels, and office buildings downtown. Between October 1960 and October 1961, another 92 homes were demolished, 274 homes with pit outhouses were notified that they needed to connect to new city sewerage, and 59 homes were pending demolition if they did not come into compliance with the code. In 1965, 300 families were notified that their homes would be demolished because of noncompliance. The *Southern Courier* reported in 1966 that almost 1,000 people would need to move: "People are on the move in Montgomery, whether they like it or not . . . 950 [people] will be moved over the next three years as a result of . . . stepped-up enforcement of the Montgomery housing code."[24] Despite the need for new water and sewerage lines along some streets to comply with the new housing code, in 1957 there were still 1,500 pit outhouses in the city, and by 1960 the number grew to 1,700 due to increased housing pressure and contradictory policies that allowed building permits to be issued for such developments, as more African American neighborhoods were demolished for slum clearance and interstate highway construction.[25] Enforcement of the housing code meant that African American families often had to pay more for housing that was farther away from work and school, and families were often shuffled from one home to the next because of multiple land condemnations.

In 1959 the local political environment took an even more racially radical turn, with the election of Governor John Patterson, who won with the support of the KKK and WCC.[26] In the municipal election that year, Mayor Gayle faced three serious challengers: East Montgomery resident Earl James, who criticized Gayle for negotiating with the MIA to end the bus boycott; Dave Birmingham, a former city commissioner; and extreme white supremacist John Crommelin. With these candidates, African American voters were faced with a bad set of options, and all the candidates sought to appear the most racially extreme to get white votes. Eventually, reflecting both the political naiveties of some new African American voters and the poor set of options available to them, the MIA endorsed Sullivan for city commissioner and James for mayor. An editorial in the *Montgomery Advertiser*, citing analysis by the WCC, predicted that African American voters could decide the outcome of the election due to the political divide among white voters, writing, "All evidence is absolutely conclusive that in Monday's election the Negro voters will decide who will be mayor of Montgomery unless the white voters wake up, fight Negro bloc voting with white bloc voting, get behind one of the two candidates and take the balance of power out of the control of the agitators."[27]

In a runoff, the more radical candidates won, and Earl James defeated Mayor Gayle, while Clyde Sellers lost his City Commission seat to L. B. Sullivan.[28] The MIA claimed victory that their preferred candidates won, noting "the relentless efforts on the part of Negroes to get qualified as voters bore some fruit in the election."[29] Thus, the city elections reflected the extreme racial environment that emerged from the bus boycott and also the emerging power of African American voters.

## SHIFTING THE INTERSTATE HIGHWAYS THROUGH MONTGOMERY

Two months after the bus boycott ended, AHD director Herman Nelson sent a memo to the BPR proposing an urban route for I-65 through the Westside, significantly modifying the proposed route that ran west of the city through rural land. One year later, in March 1958, Nelson also proposed changing I-85 from a bypass route through rural land with a spur into North Montgomery to an urban route through central Montgomery.[30] The shift from bypass routes to urban interstates was a reflection of national highway politics and also the racially radical turn of state and local decision-making. As plans for the Interstate Highway System moved from the draft schemes headed by BPR engineers to clearer route proposals by state highway departments, mayors and governors began to get involved in highway routing decisions and tried to use highway routing to increase urban economic development.[31] Despite these national trends, the specific routing through the Westside and Centennial Hill was also an important reflection of the racially radical shift in state and city politics at the end of the bus boycott, as both routes directly affected two of the large African American neighborhoods in the city but avoided much of the negative impact to white neighborhoods. Although the goals of the new highway routes were to increase economic development downtown, African American residents would bear a far greater burden for urban interstate routes across the country, including in Montgomery. Many civil rights activist's homes would be in the path of the highways, including Rev. Ralph Abernathy's, Jo Ann Robinson's, Mary Fair Burks's, and Irene West's.

AHD engineers considered four alternative locations for I-65. The first, the peninsula route (alternative coordinate A), the one eventually chosen, entered Montgomery parallel to US-31, and then shifted to the east, cutting through the Westside before crossing the Alabama River and exiting the city through the middle of the undeveloped Alabama River peninsula. The second route option, the downtown route (alternative coordinate B), followed the same route into the city and through the Westside, but veered to the east next to the Alabama River, close to downtown, and then curved north along the eastern shore of the river. The third proposed route, the bypass route (alternative coordinate C), bypassed the city through rural land west of Maxwell Air Force Base. The fourth route, alternative coordinate No. 2, was similar to route A, but veered about ten more blocks to the west, toward the less developed edge of the neighborhood, an area where planners had long hoped to locate new industrial development.

For I-85, AHD engineers proposed three alternative coordinates. All the routes except the bypass route entered the city near Mount Meigs and shifted north at Ann Street. The three urban route options varied only as they went past Oak Park near ASU. The first ran north of Oak Park, the second went south of Oak Park, and the third went through the park. The fourth alternate coordinate was a bypass route, closely following the southern bypass.

Of all the route options, federal highway engineers were most concerned with the peninsula route of I-65, which would involve the construction of a

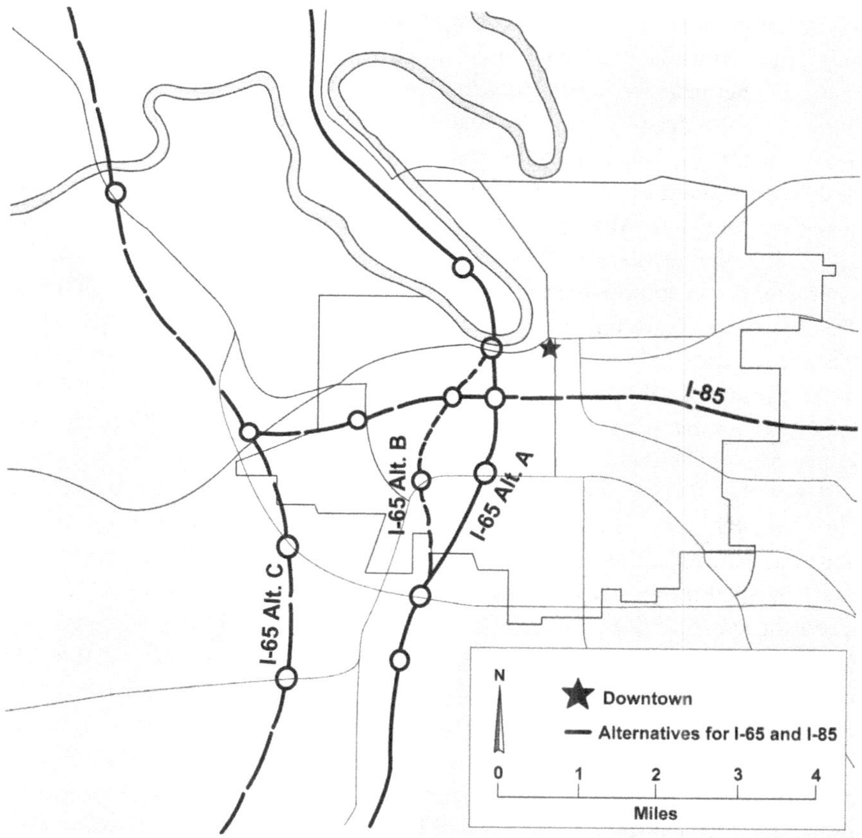


Figure 5.4. Planners considered multiple options for I-65 through the Westside, as shown on this map. The bypass route, Alt. C, would have done the least damage to residents and ran closer to Maxwell Air Force Base. Alt. B, running through the city but bypassing the heavily populated part of the Westside, would have done less damage to the homes and businesses than the route that was eventually chosen by the AHD, Alt. A, which ran directly through the Westside. The proposed location of I-85 connecting to all three route proposals for I-65 is also shown on the map. (Map by Riley Dibble, based on Wilbur Smith and Associates, Major Route Plan: Montgomery Metropolitan Area, Vol. 2 [Montgomery: Alabama State Highway Department and City of Montgomery, 1960], 2.)

large bridge over the Alabama River peninsula—a wetland. BPR engineers asked the US Geological Survey (USGS) to complete a study of the proposed peninsula route, and the analysis concluded that the route could present environmental concerns for the floodplain, which extended two miles up the peninsula, due to potential flooding and distribution of flood flows at the river crossing. USGS engineers noted that the peninsula was composed of river silt because the river frequently changed course, and the silt was deposited all along the peninsula, resulting in inadequate material for bridge fill.[32]

AHD engineers, however, were motivated not by environmental engineering but by the desire to run the highways close to downtown for economic development. Responding to the analysis, AHD engineers proposed a series of dykes upstream to protect the bridge and fill, but USGS engineers were unsure that the dykes would provide enough protection for such a large bridge, noting that the northern part of the bridge would change the hydraulics of the river, and it was impossible to forecast the full implications of those changes. The high-water mark for the river was 152 feet, and the US Army Corps of Engineers required bridges to be 36.3 feet above the highwater mark, so the interstate bridge would need to be 199.3 feet tall. Engineers were concerned that the silt under the bridge would provide inadequate support, so BPR bridge engineer Murrell Wilburn recommended rejection of the route.[33]

Once the AHD proposed the urban interstate routes, the analysis for the route of I-85 centered entirely on whether the interstate would run north or south of Oak Park. The BPR estimated that the route south of the park would cost $565,000 more than the north route and quickly approved the AHD's request for approval of the route running north of Oak Park. The Montgomery City Commission unanimously passed a resolution, approving the north route in March 1958.[34] Despite the approval of the route north of Oak Park by the AHD, BPR, and Montgomery City Commission, within two years AHD engineers, working with local planners, would reroute I-85 through the middle-class neighborhood south of the park and through Rev. Ralph Abernathy's home. In the meantime, activists would set their sights on desegregating Oak Park, and the AHD would briefly consider—and ultimately reject—another proposal for the highway though the park.

## DESEGREGATION ACTIVISM FOR PARKS

Facing increased activism for desegregation and losses in the court system with the end of the bus boycott, state and local officials were anxious to prove that the doctrine of "separate but equal" was working, particularly in the most sensitive areas of segregation—parks and schools. So in 1957, the Alabama legislature appropriated funding for two new state parks for African American people. One would be located in central Alabama and one in South Alabama, although there was no clear plan for acquiring specific sites for the parks. Eventually, the Alabama Department of Conservation reallocated the funds, and the parks were never created. By the end of the 1950s Alabama still had just one state park for African American people and no historic sites, fishing lakes, or other facilities.[35]

The lack of park space continued to be a major issue for African American people across the state, especially in urban areas like Montgomery. Many

Montgomery residents were former sharecroppers and were accustomed to rural lifestyles and natural surroundings. As densities increased in cities due to increased residential segregation and population growth, many people sought refuge from the harsh segregated conditions of Montgomery by spending time in nearby rural counties, but there were few public or private green spaces available to them. In 1959 three separate incidents of racial violence shed light on the issue.

On Saturday, May 23, Rev. Horace Bell and several other men went fishing at a Dallas County public lake. After fishing for some time, the other men returned home and left Rev. Bell to continue fishing. Rev. Bell was murdered, and his body was discovered a week later. Bell was an activist and a member of the MIA. His wife was a teacher in the county school system, and they had five children. He was one of the parents who tried to enroll his child in Harrison Elementary School in 1954. A day before his body was found at the lake, Rev. Dr. King, Rev. Abernathy, and Rev. Solomon Seay Sr. wrote to Governor Patterson and US attorney general William Rogers asking for help in locating Rev. Bell. In another incident of racial violence the next day, Quintus Hooten and his two sisters, who lived on Boliver Street, next door to Rufus Lewis, went fishing at a rural lake in Dallas County. As they approached the lake, they encountered a group of white men, who severely beat Hooten. In the third incident, on the same day, E. L. Carl, Fannie Foster, and her son, Johnny Foster, were fishing at another spot on the same lake and were attacked by another group of white men, who severely beat them.[36]

Racial violence at urban parks was also common. In October 1957 Mark Gilmore, an African American teenager who lived west of whites-only Oak Park, took a shortcut through the park to his job at Jackson Hospital, just east of the park, and was arrested and beaten by police. Hoping to avoid a repeat of the court loss they sustained when they charged Rosa Parks with violating a segregation ordinance, the prosecutor charged Gilmore with disorderly conduct instead of violating the park segregation ordinance.[37] Gillmore was levied a fifty-dollar fine. In court, Gilmore and attorney Fred Gray claimed that his arrest was illegal because the park should not be segregated, and although Gilmore lost his initial case in a segregation-friendly court, the charges were later dropped on appeal to the circuit court because city attorneys were afraid that it would lead to an integration order.

After the bus boycott, city attorneys avoided charging African American people with violating segregation laws and instead charged them with crimes like disorderly conduct or disturbing the peace. Gilmore's arrest was preceded by two other arrests for violating the park segregation ordnance the previous summer.[38] After other incidents, white supremacists painted KKK signs on the sidewalks in and around the parks, but police did not make any arrests.[39]

Mark Gilmore was no stranger to civil rights activism. His mother was Georgia Theresa Gilmore, a member of the MIA and the Montgomery chapter of the NAACP. Georgia Gilmore was a well-known cook and midwife who raised funds for the carpools during the bus boycott by selling food at the weekly mass meetings. She was fired from her job as a cook at the whites-only National Café after testifying in court on behalf of the boycotters. After she was fired from her job, Rev. Dr. King, who gave her the nickname "tiny," suggested that she open her home as a restaurant, which would provide the activists with a safe place to strategize. The MIA gave her some initial funds to start the restaurant and Rev. Dr. King was one of its regular customers. She called the restaurant and her efforts to raise funds for the boycott the Club from Nowhere and kept the identities of her customers secret so the money she raised could not be traced back to supporters of the boycott. Over the years, many well-known people ate at the restaurant, including President Lyndon Johnson, Attorney General Robert Kennedy, and Alabama governor George Wallace.[40]

The issue of park desegregation often went together with school desegregation, just as planning for schools and parks were often coupled. In June 1958 Rev. Dr. King, who had just returned from an integration retreat at the Highlander Folk School with other activists, including Rosa Parks, attended a meeting on school integration in Washington, DC, with President Eisenhower. The group proposed a school integration plan with federal support when the school year began in September.[41] Although that meeting did not get the federal support that activists hoped for, it did lead to school integration efforts later that year. And at the end of 1958, Rev. Dr. King and the MIA announced that they would help African American children apply to attend white schools at the beginning of the school year.[42] King noted that he hoped to work with white school leaders to develop a voluntary school desegregation plan, and if they resisted voluntary integration, the MIA would have no choice but to file a school desegregation lawsuit to show that the pupil placement law was being used to segregate schools.[43]

Cautious because of the previous failed effort to desegregate schools, fearing violence and intimidation and hoping to avoid the closure of schools by the school board, but also aware that school desegregation was a top priority for civil rights leaders nationally and locally, Rev. Dr. King walked a fine line between Montgomery residents who feared school closings and those who wanted school desegregation to progress faster. King asked the Montgomery School Board to voluntarily desegregate schools, as he announced, "First we will try to get community support and then we will go to the Board of Education. There will be no attempts to register individual Negro students in any school and we will go to the courts only as a last resort."[44] If the community support plan failed, King noted that the MIA would file several integration lawsuits in the city to establish a pattern of using the pupil placement law to avoid integration.

Despite the timidity of the proposal, King's announcement frightened both African American and white families. White racial extremists threatened violence, and white politicians vowed to resist integration by any means possible. Montgomery School Board attorney Vaughn Hill Robison announced that the board would fight any effort to integrate schools, noting, "I don't feel that we'll take integration in the public school system lying down."[45] Robert Shelton, grand dragon of the KKK, announced that the KKK would use any means possible, including violence, to prevent integration of schools. He told the *Montgomery Advertiser*, "The Klan would take whatever steps are necessary to prevent school integration. . . . We are warning the Negroes and white manipulators who have no regard for either race that if Martin Luther King's statement and announced plans of last week are carried out it will bring bloodshed to Alabama."[46]

Montgomery city commissioners Parks and Sellers and Mayor Gayle, along with the Montgomery chapter of the WCC, called for a grand jury investigation into the plans to integrate schools for ill-defined "violations."[47] Both the City Commission and the Montgomery County Board of Revenue pledged to assist the school board in fighting integration and the lawsuits.[48]

Many African American activists were reluctant to support the school integration plans due to fears that the board of education would close schools to avoid integration. That fear became further substantiated within the African American middle class because the MIA soon filed another desegregation lawsuit—this time for parks.

In response to Mark Gilmore's arrest and beating, forty-eight African American activists, including Gilmore, Rev. Dr. King, Rev. Abernathy, and Rev. Seay Sr. sent a petition to the Parks and Recreation Board asking them to desegregate the city parks. The petition noted that Oak Park, with its location in Centennial Hill, was more accessible than the African American parks in the city, and those parks were poorly equipped and substandard and requested that the Parks and Recreation Board adopt a policy of nondiscrimination for park facilities. They wrote, "The denial of Oak Park facilities to Negroes does not accord with fundamental and inherent principles of justice and equality."[49]

The petition was addressed to Mrs. James Fitts Hill, the chairperson of the Montgomery Parks and Recreation Board, and requested a hearing on the issue of desegregating the parks. The board, however, hoping to avoid making the issue a political win for the activists, responded that they had no authority to alter the city park segregation laws and rejected the request. The activists immediately sent the petition to the city commissioners and asked for a hearing and for the parks to be desegregated.

Mayor Gayle and City Commissioners Parks and Sellers, anxious to demonstrate to the increasingly racially volatile white public that they were firm on segregation, announced bluntly, "In order that there be no misunderstanding as to the attitude of the City Commissioners, we state that we have no intention of operating any integrated parks in the city of Montgomery." Gayle, Parks, and Sellers argued that African American people were not entitled to use the parks because they didn't pay enough taxes, a theme that would follow the issues of park and school desegregation for many years. The statement continued, "The commission has in the past sought to provide excellent facilities for Negroes despite the fact that Negroes have contributed comparatively little to the taxes and virtually nothing in the way of personal gifts."[50] The statement included a list of the parks that African American people could use in the city to support the claim that the doctrine of "separate but equal" was working: Washington Park, King Hill Park, Mobile Heights Park, the park in the Trenholm Court housing project, and the proposed park in the North Montgomery slum clearance project, which was planned but not yet under construction, and was never built.

The white press published names and addresses of some petitioners, including Rev. Dr. King, Rev. Abernathy, and S. S. Seay Jr. Days after the petition, Rev. Abernathy was attacked and beaten near his church. The attacker, an African American man, was reportedly driven by rumors of an affair between Rev. Abernathy and the attacker's wife. At a hearing a few days later, Rev. Dr. King was arrested for loitering, after police choked and assaulted him.[51]

On December 22, 1958, a group of eight activists, with support of the MIA, filed a case with Judge Frank Johnson Jr.'s district court to integrate the parks. The parties in the lawsuit were Georgia Theresa Gilmore; J. C. Smith, a carpool driver during the bus boycott; Fred Harris, a registered voter; Gussie Carlton; Sylvia Johnson; Mattie Cargill; George Stephens; and Elizabeth Brown, represented by attorney Solomon Seay Jr. Eight days after the lawsuit was filed, the city commissioners permanently closed all the parks, and large signs were posted at each of the city's fourteen parks—four for African American people and ten for white people—to announce their closure. The Parks and Recreation Department was renamed the Recreation Department. Seventy African American park maintenance workers, making a combined $101,134, were fired.[52]

Closing parks was a common response to integration attempts in the South. In Birmingham, Rev. Fred Shuttlesworth sent a petition to desegregate the parks just two months later. Bull Conner threatened to close all the parks after a desegregation case was filed in federal district court in October 1959, and eventually closed the parks in 1961, after the deadline for the desegregation order passed.[53]

The park desegregation case made it to Judge Johnson's district court in

September 1959. In the pretrial motions, Johnson rejected three requests: first, a motion from the activists to order the city to reopen the parks; second, a motion from the city to postpone the case indefinitely, after city attorneys argued unsuccessfully that the case was moot because the parks were closed and would not reopen; and third, a motion from the activists, requesting an immediate integration order because the parties did not dispute the facts of the case.[54]

At the trial, two African American women—Gussie Carlton and Georgia Gilmore—testified for the activists. Georgia Gilmore, who had also testified at the bus boycott trial, told the court that she entered white-only parks to take white children to the park when she was working as a maid, but could not take her own children to the park and had never tried to do so. Gilmore testified that she would like to be able to take her children to Oak Park because she did not have a car, making it difficult to get to an African American park. Carlton echoed Gilmore's testimony, telling the court that she lived two miles from an African American park but three blocks away from Oak Park.[55]

Judge Johnson determined that segregation of the parks in Montgomery violated the Fourteenth Amendment of the US Constitution and that if the parks were ever reopened, they must do so on an integrated basis. Johnson did not order the parks to be reopened because the city was not required to operate parks.[56]

The news that the parks, if reopened, had to be desegregated was met with mixed reactions from city officials but all of them motivated by public pressure to affirm segregation and vowing to never integrate the parks. Mayor Gayle, appealing to white citizens who wanted to maintain segregation, immediately announced that the city would appeal, noting, "We'll fight to the last to preserve segregation."[57] City Commissioner Parks, on the other hand, had a more restrained reaction, announcing that it would not be "worth the time and effort"[58] to appeal the decision. Incoming mayor James announced that he would try to reach a settlement that would maintain segregation, announcing, "Integrated parks will not be operated by the city. However, it is my intention to work toward a settlement of this problem that will be beneficial and fair to all citizens of Montgomery."[59] Foreshadowing park management in the decade ahead, the city commissioners considered leasing parks to private groups to maintain segregation. With some degree of skepticism, one reporter wrote, "Officials here are of the opinion that the city cannot successfully circumvent the court's ruling by leasing parks to private owners. However, the properties can be sold by resolutions of the City Commission."[60] The city did appeal the decision, and the appeals court upheld the desegregation order.

At the end of 1959, the Recreation Board announced that the parks would remain closed permanently and followed through to assure the public that they meant what they said. They sold the animals in the zoo, dismantled the rides, and shattered the bottom of the pool. The only activity remaining in Oak Park was in the administration building.[61]

White people denounced closure of the parks as an atrocity, blaming the African American activists. An editorial in the *Montgomery Advertiser* noted, paradoxically, that it was the first time that Montgomerians were denied access to the park: "The gates were barred as a result of the filing of a racial integration suit and for the first time in 60 years, the people of Montgomery were denied use of the most beautiful and unspoiled recreation spot in the city."[62] Newspapers referred to African American activists as "vindictive,"[63] and City Commissioner Sellers announced, "I would rather see them [the parks] plowed up and planted in corn, rather than see them integrated."[64] Some white Montgomerians suspected that the activists sought to integrate the parks not because they wanted access to them, but because they wanted them closed. As an editorial in the *Montgomery Advertiser* noted, "A park is not a bus system or a school. It is something that can be dispensed with. Oak Park might simply be closed down. . . . We suspect that the colored petitioners know this. Perhaps their motive is to prod city officials to move faster and on a larger scale to provide truly separate but equal parks in Montgomery. . . . Even a visionary like Dr. King must know perfectly well that race mixing in Oak Park is not to be. Probably he does."[65]

While closure of the parks was inconvenient for white people, they were still motivated to support closing them because they still had access to private recreation options, including country clubs and the YMCA. Closure of the parks was acutely felt by African American people, however, who has much less access to green spaces and also feared that the city commissioners would close other public accommodations, including schools, if they filed more desegregation lawsuits. The issue began to splinter the African American communities that had been united over the bus boycott.

Despite closure of the parks, most of the leaders of the MIA, however, wanted to press on with school desegregation, and one week before school began in 1959, the MIA sent a letter to the Montgomery County Board of Education asking about their plans for school integration. Rev. Dr. King told the press that he did not expect those plans to be forthcoming, saying that he was "realistic enough to know [that] this will have to end up in court."[66] The letter—addressed to school board chairperson Harold Harris and signed by MIA executive committee members Rev. Robert DuBose Jr., Rev. H. J. Palmer, Rev. Ralph Abernathy, Rev. H. H. Hubbard, Rev. Solomon Seay, and Rev. Dr. King—said that the MIA was working on plans to enroll African American children in all-white schools. It noted that "Negro parents and students are making inquiries . . . and several of them are already prepared to apply for admission to all-white schools."[67] School superintendent Walter McKee, hoping to avoid publicizing the issue, replied to the group that he would not hold a special meeting to discuss the letter, nor would the school board discuss the letter at their next regularly scheduled meeting.[68]

With school integration lawsuits filed across the South, white people rushed to organize private schools, and two months later a group of white people, with funding from the WCC, announced a new whites-only private school, The Montgomery Academy, and hired G. Orum Hammer as the headmaster. As a private school, it would avoid integration. Governor Patterson sold the former governor's mansion to the school at a deeply discounted price of $27,505, half of its original 1906 purchase price of $46,500.[69] Also in 1959, another whites-only school, St. James School, which opened in 1955, announced plans to expand through the sixth grade.

Governor Patterson announced that while he hoped that schools would open without integration attempts, he was prepared to prevent African American students from enrolling in all-white schools. He asked the Alabama legislature to pass a bill that would give him the authority to close any school faced with integration, although local school boards already had that authority under the pupil placement act.[70] Patterson used his weekly radio address to warn African American activists to not seek school integration, warning, "Now this fellow here in Montgomery, Martin Luther King came out the other day and indicated that they were going to start some agitation here about integrating our public schools. I would like to caution the Negro citizens of this state again, as I have many times in the past, that if you follow a man like Martin Luther King, it is only going to lead to chaos and disorder and violence and the destruction of our public school system."[71] Based on his observation of school integration elsewhere, Rev. Dr. King was optimistic that Governor Patterson would not close public schools, and he tried to convince concerned African American activists in Montgomery that they could safely integrate schools. He told them, "What we now see in both Little Rock and Virginia is something very revealing. Two powerful institutions have collided in the South—the institution of segregation and the institution of public schools. And the people, on the whole, have made it palpably clear that when the final moment of choice comes, they will choose public schools rather than segregation. People are gradually coming to see the futility of attempting to close the schools. The price to be paid by schools closing is too high. Business suffers. Children receive an inferior education. Many responsible persons move away. The cultural life of a community lags."[72]

Although many activists were publicly defiant about the governor's speech, including Rev. Shuttlesworth, who told the press that the speech "gives many people the impression of a desperate man,"[73] many African American people feared that the governor would follow through on plans to close schools if they attempted integration, especially in light of the closed parks.

Despite Rev. Dr. King's assurances, responding to pressure to back off from school integration attempts from families and teachers, two days after sending the letter, the MIA and King told the press that they would not seek to enroll any African American children in all-white schools and instead would encourage voluntary desegregation: "We would like to see good faith, now, in this direction."[74] When school opened that week, no African American students tried to enroll in white schools. Nonetheless, the city of Montgomery assembled the entire police force, including off-duty officers, as well as the Alabama National Guard around the schools.[75]

School integration and the potential closure of schools became a contentious issue within MIA leadership and eventually contributed to Rev. Dr. King's decision to leave Montgomery. Rev. Dr. King announced that he would leave Montgomery to move to Atlanta by February 1960. He described the intense pressure that Montgomery's African American families felt because of a potential school desegregation lawsuit and the possibility of closure of the schools and told friends that if he left Montgomery, the pressure on African American families in the city would lessen.[76]

At one of Rev. Dr. King's farewell celebrations, at Bethel Baptist Church, King remained confident about school integration, announcing that the school board did not reply to the MIA's letter requesting integration, so they had no choice but to pursue integration through the courts. Aware of the reluctance of many parents who feared the dismantling of the school system, King added that Governor Patterson's threats to close the schools "will not in the least deter us from our righteous efforts."[77]

Rev. Dr. King's, and later Rev. Abernathy's, departures for Atlanta left a leadership void in Montgomery that was difficult to fill. While there were many strong African American leaders in the city, none was as powerful or charismatic as Rev. Dr. King, and his departure was felt deeply in all areas of activism in the city. Adding to the leadership void was the fact that activists did not have the single uniting force of the bus boycott to get behind. King's departure and the leadership void it created threatened to split open the deep class divisions that healed during the bus boycott, particularly over the issue of school integration.[78] At the same time as Rev. Dr. King departed Montgomery, city officials continued to try to improve economic development, neighborhood planning, and industrial growth through plans and policies that benefited white residents to the determent of African American residents. Engineers working for the AHD accelerated plans for routing the new interstate highways through Centennial Hill and the Westside, while the Planning Commission, staff at the MHA and URA, and other city staff advanced the city's comprehensive plans for economic development through slum clearance, kept the parks closed, and deepened school segregation through neighborhood planning.[79]

# 6

# Interstate Highway Routing as a Racial Planning Tool

When Governor Patterson was elected in 1959, he appointed Sam Engelhardt Jr., a white supremacist politician with almost no transportation experience, as director of the AHD. Engelhardt was known as the "leading segregationist of the South,"[1] a nickname given to him as an insult by African American member of Congress from New York Adam Clayton Powell, but Engelhardt adopted the slogan in his campaign literature. Powell said of Engelhardt, "No one man has done more to destroy democracy for Negroes in Alabama than this man."[2]

Within two weeks of taking office, Governor Patterson called the legislature into a special session, proposing a new $60 million revenue bond issue that would provide matching funds for federal highway grants and accelerate highway building. Patterson's motivation for accelerating the highway program was to make good on campaign promises and provide himself with some leverage with legislators in their home districts. After the legislature unanimously approved the bonds, within one month of taking office, Patterson and Engelhardt had secured most of the match funding that was needed to complete the interstate highways in the state.[3]

Patterson's desire to accelerate highway building led to more serious consideration of the interstate route options for Montgomery, and the AHD quickly completed an initial analysis of alternate routes for I-65 and I-85, including cost estimates, engineering, and local land use and transportation connections. The AHD's initial cost estimates for I-65 supported the peninsula route through the Westside and the Alabama River peninsula, but the BPR was skeptical of the AHD's conclusions. BPR engineer G. M. Williams expressed concerns to regional director Rex Anderson about the cost estimates, expected benefits, and hydrologic conditions of the Alabama River peninsula crossing, concerned that the AHD's analysis underestimated the severity of the environmental and engineering problems with the bridge over the Alabama River. Williams wrote that the AHD's cost estimates were too low and their traffic estimates too high, resulting in an inflated benefits analysis favoring the

AHD's preferred peninsula route and disfavoring the bypass route, which was preferred by the BPR.[4]

The BPR also favored the bypass route for I-65 because it would better serve Maxwell Air Force Base.[5] The BPR was also motivated by the cost savings of the bypass route because it would avoid acquiring expensive urban land. BPR engineer B. A. Scott argued that there was a lot of potential interstate traffic that was not dependent on the central business district, including from the Air Force base, other federal government activities, and some state government activities. Many state and federal employees did not work downtown, Scott argued, and thus an expressway route through downtown would not be needed. Moreover, Scott pointed out that a bypass expressway closer to the Air Force base would be more effectively meet traffic needs for the base.[6] Although politics was never completely removed from highway routing, BPR engineers were often more motivated by cost and technical considerations than state highway departments were. State highway departments often favored urban interstate routes regardless of their high economic and social cost because they believed that running the highways near downtowns would boost economic development. The highways were mostly run through areas that local officials had already targeted for slum clearance, accomplishing the dual goals of economic development and slum clearance. These priorities were often supported by urban mayors.[7]

Scott told Anderson that downtown Montgomery was not expected to experience the growth that would necessitate an urban route and the traffic estimates assigned to the downtown route in the AHD analysis were too high.[8] Scott added that many businesses were relocating to the suburbs for easier parking. He wrote, "Doctors and lawyers . . . have been migrating, not by normal expansion of the C. B. D., but by jumping fringe areas into many small centers. Insurance companies are fast following to the suburbs for parking relief. Lack of parking space downtown has caused two very large suburban shopping centers to spring up and prosper."[9]

The motivations of Montgomery's public officials and the motivations of the BPR for highway routing differed drastically. Scott argued that it was not the role of the Interstate Highway System to encourage a city's aspirations to expand downtown or expand its industrial base: "This raises questions as to how far we should go in using interstate highway funds to perpetuate and expand present business and industrial areas in small cities like Montgomery when cheaper locations for the interstate might encourage decentralization of the business and industrial areas. . . . In other words, it is my opinion that expressways are not vitally needed to handle traffic in and out of Montgomery unless we assume that the present industrial and business areas are to expand so as to result in about three times the present industrial and traffic volumes into and out of these districts."[10]

AHD engineers, as well as the city officials who they worked with, were largely motivated by the promise of downtown development, industrial growth, and slum clearance in African American neighborhoods. The AHD responded to Scott and Anderson's criticism defiantly. Jordan wrote, "We would also like to advise that in the event our request for the route through Montgomery is not approved we shall vigorously urge reconsideration and approval of the route through Montgomery since it is our opinion that the facts in the case warrant such routing."[11] Scott asked Engelhardt to hire an engineering consultant to prepare an economic analysis and a user-benefit analysis of the route options for I-65.[12] Although common practice was to prepare comprehensive cost estimates for just one route, the AHD agreed to prepare them for both routes. The AHD insisted on the peninsula route. Anderson wrote, "It was the State's contention that this alternative location [the peninsula route] was the only location which well served the traffic of the interstate route. Both your office [division BPR office in Montgomery] and this office [BPR regional office in Atlanta] were of the opinion that the estimate should be made along Alternate Line C [the bypass route] because this was the least costly alternate lines being considered on this section of Interstate 65."[13] The AHD executed an agreement with a consultant to prepare cost estimates for both route options.[14]

Even after the new analysis was complete, BPR engineers were still skeptical about the consultant's cost estimates. Scott pointed out many inaccuracies and continued to favor the bypass route.[15] The BPR sent one of their highway engineers, R. H. Talley, to AHD offices in Montgomery to go over the analysis for four days in the fall of 1960, just as ASU students' lunch counter sit-ins were taking place downtown. He found a few discrepancies in the data but nothing significant enough to change the results. As a result of the BPR's review, the proposed route of I-65 through the Westside had to be shifted to the west, away from Holt Street, which avoided demolition of Holt Street Baptist Church and Mount Zion A. M. E. Zion Church.[16] The shift resulted in a cost savings of $1,611,000, a significant difference favored by the BPR. Local city officials, on the other hand, had been targeting the neighborhood for many years in plans and policies, hoping to dislodge the African American neighborhood that was proximate to downtown because the space would allow them to build parking lots for downtown businesses and improve the neighborhood in an economically important area.

While Engelhardt and AHD engineers maintained their insistence on the peninsula route for I-65, they also changed their recommendation for the route of I-85 to run south of Oak Park instead of north of it, as their previous proposals recommended. With the change, AHD engineers claimed that they initially supported the north route to avoid a planned expansion of ASU, which had been canceled. The motivations behind rerouting I-85 south of Oak Park were seemingly entirely racial, unlike the motivations behind I-65, which were perhaps only partially racial. Although it is difficult to prove that the routing of I-85 was due to racist intent, the historical record provides some planning, engineering, and cost justifications for the route north of Oak Park. The historical record also provides some hints that the route south of the park was planned with racist intent and was designed to dislodge the best middle-class African American neighborhood in the city. Historian Raymond Mohl reached the same conclusion in 2002, writing, "[Rev. Ralph] Abernathy's home stood in the path of the highway project [I-85], obviously targeted by Alabama Highway officials. A notorious racist, Alabama's state highway director, Samuel Engelhardt, served simultaneously as a high level officer of the Alabama Ku Klux Klan and of the White citizen's Council, which organized against school integration."[17]

Mohl reached the same conclusion for highways in Birmingham, also routed by engineers working for Sam Engelhardt Jr., writing, "In the early days of the interstates, the racial routing of the Birmingham expressway . . . was rather typical. So was the response from Federal Highway Administrator Whitton to Senator Sparkman. The route had been chosen by the Alabama Highway Department and approved by the Bureau of Public Roads, Whitton wrote, 'Based on a thorough evaluation of all engineering, economic, and sociological factors involved.' If that was the case, then it would seem that the destruction of the Birmingham black community was indeed a planned event."[18]

The news of the shift of I-85 from north of Oak Park to south of the park immediately raised concerns from middle-class African American residents who lived south of the park, including Rev. Abernathy.[19] With the route of I-65 at a standstill due to the disagreement between the BPR's preference for the bypass route and the AHD's preference for the peninsula route, and the route of I-85 uncertain because of the proposed shift to the south of Oak Park, the BPR provided funding to the AHD and the Montgomery City Commission to complete a transportation study to determine the interstate routes and local street linkages. The first volume of the two-volume study, written by planning consultant Wilbur Smith and Associates, was a quantitative analysis of transportation issues in the city, prioritizing the needs of motorists, who were mostly white, and downplaying public transportation riders, who were mostly African American. Prioritizing cars over public transportation reflected transportation planning practices at the time that, like in many other cities, were almost entirely centered on facilitating automobile transportation. Nonetheless, the plan reflected racial biases because although the data revealed a need to improve public transportation, the recommendations focused on improvements for motor vehicle users. For example, 47 percent of the homes in Centennial Hill and 44 percent of homes on the Westside had access to a car, while every home had access to a car in the white Cloverdale neighborhood; so with such a low car ownership rate in some neighborhoods, the data suggests a need to improve public transportation, but instead the study focused solely on road and highway improvements.

The consultant noted that the bus boycott was the reason for the decline in bus ridership. The analysis used ridership data from just after the end of the boycott, which likely skewed the analysis. Prior to the boycott, bus ridership was about 9,680,000 trips per day, which declined to two million trips per day during the boycott. Although planners estimated that had the boycott not occurred ridership would have increased 8 percent by 1957, they pointed to a national decline in public transportation use as justification for the focus on road improvements for private automobiles.

The land use and transportation connections for the AHD's preferred proposed routes included many inconsistencies, such as not providing any connections to the industrial area north of downtown despite the city's industrial growth aspirations. Trucks from I-65 would need to drive through downtown or take rural roads through Elmore County to get to the North Montgomery industrial area. Likewise, the city's land use plan recommended a large expansion of industrial uses on the Westside, which had no direct connections to the interstate because there were no exits provided for the neighborhood.

With the priority of running the interstates close to downtown and through African American neighborhoods, the resulting plan was filled with contradictions. Planners today can learn important lessons from many midcentury plans, because even with multiple objectives including economic development, much of the planning was not only racist but conflicted with overall public goals. To that end, the report proposed an unusual series of interchanges that would have the effect of disconnecting African American residents from the rest of the city. The plan did not provide any exits or underpasses to downtown from I-65, and instead motorists on I-65 would need to drive to I-85 and use the Court Street exit to access downtown, and pedestrians from the Westside would be largely unable to access anything east of the interstate on foot.[20] I-85 south of Oak Park disconnected ASU from its historic residential neighborhood of Centennial Hill. Revealing the difficulty of accomplishing the contradictory goals of economic development, industrial growth, slum clearance, and racial targeting of the middle-class African American neighborhood, the plan failed to accomplish some of its key objectives.

Despite the lack of many connections between the city and the interstates, Jordan argued that the interstate needed to be close to downtown for economic development. Engineers failed to provide a direct connection from Maxwell Air Force Base to the interstate highways even though Maxwell, along with state government institutions, was the driving force of the local economy.[21] The plan also failed to make important transportation connections for industrial uses in North Montgomery, where city officials had long hoped to increase industrial development. Despite these problems, the study concluded that the routes of I-85 south of Oak Park, and I-65 through the Westside and the Alabama River peninsula were optimal.

Like interstate highway routing in other places, the interstates in Montgomery were designed to cater to multiple interests. Suburban residents and elected officials wanted them to foster suburban growth, and urban mayors wanted them routed near downtowns to provide economic development. None of these interests favored routing the new highways through white neighborhoods, and instead engineers and politicians believed that routing them through African American neighborhoods would achieve multiple goals. AHD engineer R. D. Jordan said in 1958, "This road definitely will hurt some people. . . . It will mean they may have to travel five or six miles to get to the other side of the road."[22] Jordan also noted that the AHD sought to run highways through substandard homes, as he told the *Alabama Journal* in 1960, "Whenever possible . . . the route goes through areas where housing is substandard."

However, these multiple objectives again were contradictory, because city planners also expressed concerns about economic competition from increased suburban growth. Competition from development of suburban shopping centers was a major focus of Montgomery's 1957 land use plan draft, where the consultants noted, "In the last few years, Montgomery has been considered a city with a fast growing retail trade. No doubt some of this increase can be contributed to the new successful shopping areas. The central business area is feeling the competition presented by the suburban areas."[23]

As Jordan and other AHD engineers were working on approval of the Westside route of I-65, plans for the I-85 route south of Oak Park were progressing quickly. Despite the higher economic and social costs and major objections from the middle-class African American residents, the AHD wanted the south route approved by the BPR quickly, without an analysis of alternatives or consideration for relocation of the residents, many of whom had incomes that were too high to qualify for public housing.[24] The AHD's desire for a quick approval, however, was stalled by a lengthy freeway revolt that included many civil rights activists and ASU faculty.

## THE I-85 FREEWAY REVOLT

The freeway revolt began with a public hearing on the proposed route of I-85 on April 19, 1960, with seven hundred people in attendance at the city auditorium.[25] About five hundred people were opposed to the south route, fifty were in favor of it, and the rest didn't make their opinions known. Many people questioned why the highway should be routed through the urban center and not located on the periphery of the city along the bypass roads. Jordan told attendees that the interstate should be built where people want to go, but the location was contrary to existing city plans, such as the 1957 land use plan draft, that indicated stronger residential and commercial growth in the eastern and southeastern suburbs than in downtown.[26]

At the public hearing, residents questioned the routing of the interstate south of Oak Park rather than to the north. One newspaper account of the meeting reported, "Air Force Sgt. Morris Cox said he had heard the cost would run $560,000 for the route to go [south] rather than [north]." With this, W. F. Land, assistant chief of the AHD's interstate bureau, agreed: "Land said that the additional cost is figured at nearly $300,000, or 5 per cent more, for the route south, rather than north, of Oak Park."[27] Although the south route was 170 feet shorter than the north route, the property value was higher ($4,151,000 for the south route and $3,586,000 for the north route).[28] In terms of the number of people affected, the routes were identical—both routes would demolish 14 to 15 businesses, 245 African American residences, 135 white residences, and four African American churches.[29]

Both routes would take a portion of land from Oak Park, which was then permanently closed due to the integration court order, and the city of Montgomery was looking for new uses for the closed parks. However, the south route would destroy one of the best neighborhoods available for African American families in a key location next to ASU, and many civil rights leaders' homes, including that of Rev. Abernathy, who was Rev. Dr. King's closest advisor, Jo Ann Robinson, who played a crucial role in starting the bus boycott, and many others. The south route was also more expensive.

After the public hearing, Engelhardt obtained preliminary approval from the BPR for the south route and began purchasing rights-of-way.[30] Residents affected by the south route increased their efforts to fight against it, starting with a telegram from Rev. Abernathy to President Kennedy, which read as follows:

> "Mr. President if this route is approved it will destroy one of the best negro neighborhoods in the south and make for a hazardous condition near the local negro college, a high school, and an elementary school . . . my home will almost be in the center of this route. . . . But my concern is mainly for the large number of negroes who have sacrificed across the years and from inferior wages built comfortable homes. These families will not have decent neighborhoods in which they can relocate their homes, businesses, churches, etc. You are familiar, I am sure, with the restrictions placed upon negroes in a southern city such as ours. The vast majority of the home owners in this area are professional and business people. They constitute to a great degree the few negro voters in this community. The destruction of this neighborhood will only aid the segregationist in their attempt to make the negro vote as ineffective as possible."[31]

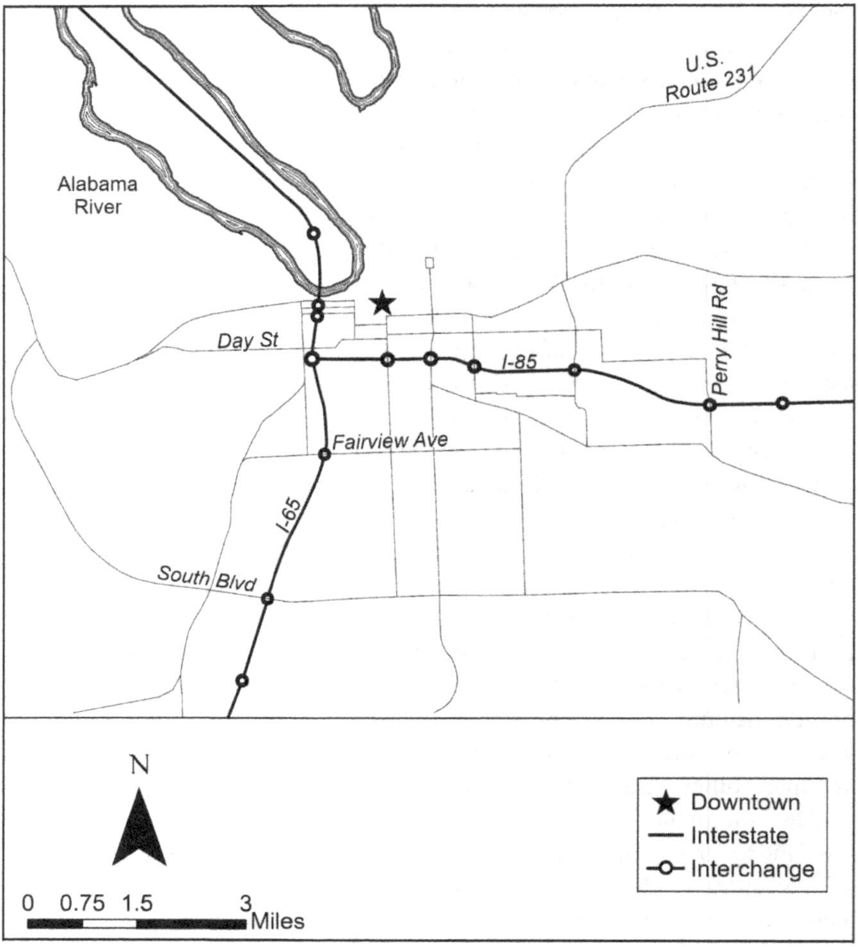


Figure 6.1. The routes for I-85 and I-65, as shown in this map, did the most damage to African American neighborhoods and prevented as much damage as possible to white neighborhoods, while going close to downtown. (Map by Riley Dibble, based on Wilbur Smith and Associates, Major Route Plan: Montgomery Metropolitan Area, Vol. 2 [Montgomery: Alabama State Highway Department and City of Montgomery, 1960], 5.)

After Abernathy's telegram to President Kennedy, news of the controversy spread quickly throughout Washington, DC, as more activists pressured their political contacts to move the highway away from the south route. Individual homeowners began writing letters to members of Congress. Another anti-freeway activist, Rev. George Curry, whose house also would be demolished because of the highway routing, met with BPR chief

Rex Whitton in Washington, DC. After the meeting, Rev. Curry and Rev. Abernathy wrote to former first lady Eleanor Roosevelt to request her help in getting the interstate rerouted. Upon receiving the letter, Eleanor Roosevelt then asked her son, US representative James Roosevelt, for assistance. Representative Roosevelt assisted by asking President Kennedy to intervene, and the president asked the Department of Commerce and the BPR about the route.[32]

Rev. Curry, J. Garrick Hardy, and C. R. Williams, who all lived within the proposed interstate route, circulated a petition to oppose the expressway and gathered over one thousand signatures, including signatures from many prominent civil rights activists who would be affected by the routes of I-85 and I-65, such as Rufus Lewis, Robert Nesbitt, and Thelma Glass. The petitioners were concerned about the loss of equity in their homes and the fact that the expressway would demolish the only middle-class neighborhood in the city.[33] The petition also mentioned that there were families along the route who had already been forced to move multiple times over the years due to slum clearance, and that there were between three hundred and four hundred schoolchildren and ASU students living in the area who needed to be within walking distance to their schools.[34]

The residents identified two alternative routes in the petition: the first, to the north side of Oak Park and away from the middle-class neighborhood, which "includes more sub-standard and vacant property . . . rather than the occupied property of a much higher value,"[35] and the second, a route bypassing the city near the southern bypass. The bypass route, the petitioners wrote, was cheaper, disrupted fewer communities, and would make more sense for long-term planning because of the high rate of growth in the south and east. The residents wrote, "The cost of this alternate plan will occasion less expense in acquiring properties along the route and could be constructed within a shorter period of time . . . it would perhaps be nearer the center of heavy traffic some fifteen years hence."[36]

Although their motivations were to save the middle-class neighborhood, the activists' bypass proposal was also arguably *more* grounded in the realities of suburban growth than AHD's urban interstate route proposal, which served multiple and conflicting goals. The bypass proposal recognized the decline of downtown, the growth of suburban shopping centers, urban growth to the south and east of the city, and the human toll that the expressway would have on urban residents. Even in the early days of the white flight period, by the 1960s shopping centers were already constructed on the periphery of the city, including Eastbrook Shopping Center on the eastern edge of town and Cloverdale and Normandale Shopping centers near the southern bypass. The bypass proposal would run the interstate through mostly vacant land and would not have the social or economic costs of the proposed urban route. However, the bypass proposal was not near downtown, so it would not increase downtown economic development, it did not advance the goal of demolishing the middle-class neighborhood of civil rights activists, and it did not cut off ASU from its residential neighborhood. The proposal was ignored by Engelhardt and AHD engineers.

## THE LUNCH COUNTER SIT-INS AND ACTIVISM AT ALABAMA STATE UNIVERSITY

In 1960, as civil rights activists were staging lunch counter sit-ins throughout the South, Bernard Lee and thirty-five other ASU students staged a sit-in after they were refused service at the segregated Courthouse Grill in downtown Montgomery. The response from police was quick and violent. After the sit-in was violently dispersed, a KKK rally near downtown ended with a mob of Klansmen roaming through downtown with baseball bats, threatening and beating African American people. Governor Patterson demanded that ASU president H. Councill Trenholm expel all students who participated in the demonstration. Later, after ASU students marched to the capitol to protest the expulsion, nine more students who participated in the protest were expelled and twenty others were placed on probation.[37]

African American leaders and ministers scheduled a mass prayer meeting outside the Alabama capitol on Sunday, March 6, in response to the student's expulsion. When a large crowd of African American activists gathered at Dexter Avenue Baptist Church located near the capitol building, another even larger crowd of white people surrounded the church and violently assaulted the activists. State and local police used fire hoses to disperse the crowd. Later that month, Engelhardt wrote to a colleague in Atlanta, R. G. Underwood, saying that he enjoyed seeing the activists running from police: "I believe that the near race riot we had here on Sunday, the 6th, and the quick action by State and local law enforcement people have the coons on the run. One of the most joyful sights I have seen was Abernathy and a group of his cohorts running like hell with their ecclesiastical robes up over their butts. It was really a sight to see."[38]

Montgomery Chamber of Commerce president Carl Bear, a supporter of slum clearance, went on NBC's *Today Show* to argue that the protests following the lunch counter sit-in were led by "outside agitators" who wanted to "provoke the Southern white man to the very limits of his patience and endurance."[39] That June an investigation of ASU faculty led to the firing of seventeen faculty members, including Lawrence Reddick, Jo Ann Robinson, and Mary Fair Burks, and the forced resignation of President H. Councill Trenholm. Many of the faculty thereafter left Montgomery for other jobs, but activists who remained soon found their homes demolished for I-85 or for slum clearance projects.[40]

## INTERSTATE ROUTING ADJACENT TO ASU

After the events surrounding the lunch counter sit-ins, many of the activists that remained in the city continued to fight the routing of I-85. AHD engineer R. D. Jordan met with Rev. Curry and other property owners on February 2, 1961, to discuss the route of I-85. Jordan agreed that the residents would have a difficult time finding new homes, writing, "We agree that the real problem is the availability of suitable residential lots or dwellings to which the people in the residences within the right-of-way will be able to move."[41] Jordan recognized that the expressway location posed a greater problem to the residents south of Oak Park than to residents located any other place along the interstate because it would demolish the best middle-class African American neighborhood in the city: "We do realize that the southern route presents a problem to the people involved [that is] substantially more difficult than that which will face most of the other people along the freeway right-of-way."[42] Nonetheless, relying on rational planning methods that gave the appearance that engineering was solely a technical exercise, Jordan and the AHD maintained that the south route was preferable because it allowed more space for the Hall Street exit into downtown. Later, however, the Hall Street exit was eliminated from the plan, but the AHD continued to insist on the south route.[43] Jordan told the activists that the public benefit was worth the personal cost to the residents, writing, "It is thought that this long range benefit of the southern route over the northern more than offsets the problem of people along the southern route arranging suitable relocation."[44]

Rev. Curry and his attorney, Roy Ellis, met with representatives from the US Civil Rights Commission[45] and filed a complaint against the interstate route:

> The routing of this highway will uproot a Negro community, which has no place to relocate, and two Negro churches. It is claimed that there is a nearby alternate route which would cost $300,000 less. Rev. Curry charges that the proposed routing of the highway is designed by State and local officials to purposely dislodge this Negro community where many of the leaders of the fight for desegregation in Montgomery reside. Rev. Curry said that in a recent conversation with a Mr. Sam Engelhardt, Alabama's Highway Director, Mr. Engelhardt stated that it was his intention to get Rev. Abernathy's church [*sic*, possibly his home]. (Rev. Abernathy was Rev. Martin Luther King's lieutenant in the 1956 bus boycott and has since been active in the "freedom riders.")[46]

Two months later, activists, AHD staff, and federal agency staff attended a high-level meeting in Washington, DC, to discuss the highway route.[47] The meeting was rare because the issue of highway routing rarely advanced above the level of state highway departments and the BPR; however, the middle-class activists had unique access to national elected officials due to their prominence in the civil rights movement, and the White House was sometimes sympathetic to their struggles. White House Cabinet Secretary Fred Dutton, Civil Rights Commission staff William Taylor, BPR administrator Rex Whitton, AHD engineer R. D. Jordan, BPR engineer George Williams, Secretary of Commerce representative Hyman Bookbinder, Department of Commerce Transportation Bureau representative Byron Nupp, and attorneys Belford Lawson and Marjorie Lawson, who attended the meeting to represent the residents, were all in attendance.[48] At the warning of BPR administrator Rex Whitton, Engelhardt determined that it would be unwise to attend the meeting to avoid giving the perception that the routing was a political decision. Nonetheless, Whitton told Engelhardt that the BPR was on the AHD's side in the controversy. Engelhardt told Governor Patterson, "He advised me that he also wanted it clearly understood that he was on our side."[49]

At the meeting, Jordan insisted that the south route was based only on engineering data—not politics: "At no time had any of the political heads of the Department, or State Government, taken any part or manifested any concern or given any instructions in regard to the matter . . . they simply had nothing to do with it, but left it to the engineers."[50] However, given the hundreds of memos between department staff, Engelhardt, and Governor Patterson discussing the route, the contention that it was strictly a technical act is suspect, and the historical record of highway routing indicates that similar decisions were highly political acts.[51] Hoping to avoid a controversy involving the leaders of the civil rights movement, which usually brought national press attention with it, the White House staff asked for a different route. As the *Montgomery Advertiser* reported, "The White House did not care where the Montgomery road went so long as it does not go through that particular negro section."[52] William Taylor, the representative from the US Commission on Civil Rights, stressed the importance of the decision. Jordan recalled, "Mr. Taylor . . . stated that not all problems like this could be decided on an engineering basis, that people had to be considered, and that on the south line we were disturbing some of the most able and best educated people in the negro race and they were important not only in the south but also in the north."[53]

Multiple newspapers reported the meeting with conflicting information. The *Birmingham Post-Herald* reported that "a few-block section of the high-priced highway construction is being rerouted out of a Negro section in Montgomery, Ala. on orders of the White House."[54] On the same day, the *Alabama Journal* reported that Engelhardt and Patterson could not confirm that the highway had been rerouted by the White House.[55] The *Birmingham*

*Post-Herald* later reported that the decision was made by the Bureau of Public Roads to "delay work on the route until the matter is mostly forgotten and then can move as it desires at that time."[56] Reports also indicated that the White House wanted the route moved away from the south side of Oak Park because "the proposed route would go through a section of residential homes owned by faculty members of the all-Negro Alabama State College."[57]

Concerned about the perception of political interference with highway routing, which was supposed to be a technical, nonpolitical, rational planning activity, Pierre Salinger, White House press secretary, denied that anybody from the White House ordered the rerouting.[58] Eleanor Roosevelt also denied intervening. Her spokesperson told the press, "Mrs. Roosevelt . . . said she can't recall any part in the Alabama highway case, but that if she interceded at all it was on a basis of—in her opinion—simple justice and not race."[59]

Despite the White House's denial, Governor Patterson, motivated by local racial politics, held a press conference to protest its involvement: "Patterson Tuesday accused Dutton [secretary of the cabinet] and an employee of the Civil Rights Commission of 'finagling' to get the Montgomery segment of the highway relocated to save the property of Negro leaders."[60] Patterson announced that he would rather abandon that section of the interstate than reroute it, telling the press, "We're going ahead with the highway whether the White House wants it or not."[61] Patterson warned, paradoxically, that "political manipulation of highways by the White House could wreck the interstate program" and added, "We must have some knuckleheads in the White House who know nothing about what they are doing meddling in the Interstate Highway Program."[62]

Patterson claimed he was unaware that the activists lived in the path of the proposed interstate route, announcing that he "'had no idea' who lived in the area to be covered by the new road at the time it was planned, and still didn't know the exact route."[63] This is difficult to believe because newspapers regularly published the addresses of civil rights leaders—Rev. Abernathy's home was in the news after it was firebombed it in 1957, and the governor's mansion was located nearby. Relying on the rational planning model, Patterson claimed that highway routing was an apolitical engineering exercise, announcing, "I am not concerned with that—that's none of my business. We have experts in the field who handle such matters, and they set the route through the most practical approach. That's where it's going."[64]

Patterson and Engelhardt maintained that the route was chosen using technical engineering factors, not politics, and accused the White House of inserting politics into the decision. Later, Patterson and Engelhardt met with Whitton, and Patterson warned him that "it would be very unwise to move this road for political or personal reasons, that such had never been done in this state before and if ordered moved, we could not build it."[65] Whitton told Engelhardt that he could continue with the project after a while, noting, "Let the dust settle for about six months and then proceed with construction of the project."[66]

While the decision over the route of I-85 was on hold, and after years of negotiating with the AHD, the BPR reluctantly approved the peninsula route for I-65 despite the fact that it was more expensive than the bypass route and BPR engineers had significant environmental and engineering concerns about the route. The peninsula route was endorsed by the Montgomery Chamber of Commerce, which adopted a resolution predicting that it would improve the downtown economy and draw more industry and tourism to the city.[67] Members of the all-white Montgomery Downtown Business Association also adopted a resolution recommending the peninsula route and sent copies of the resolution to BPR administrator Rex Whitton, all of Alabama's senators and representatives, Engelhardt, and Mayor James.[68] The association, motivated by their own financial interests, argued incorrectly that route A was less expensive than route C, provided more direct access to downtown Montgomery and the capitol, and would increase tax revenue for the city. Senators John Sparkman and Lister Hill both forwarded the resolution to federal highway administrator Rex Whitton and indicated their support for the peninsula route.[69]

The AHD held a public hearing on November 21, 1961, to discuss two proposed route options for I-65—the peninsula route and the bypass route. About six hundred people attended the meeting, which was a significant number for the time, and about 110 of the attendees were African American and were required to sit in segregated seating. While the effort to oppose the route of I-65 was less organized than the I-85 freeway revolt because residents of the Westside did not have powerful connections in Washington, DC, many were not in favor of the route.[70] Letters and newspaper accounts of the meeting suggest that most of the people in attendance favored the bypass route. As one resident told the *Montgomery Advertiser*, "It seemed to some of us that this was a 'cut and dried' affair and that the hearing was a joke on all of us who opposed the Route 'A' [the peninsula route]. . . . The majority present were for Route 'C' [the bypass route]."[71] Another report noted, "If applause is an indicator, most of them opposed the eastern route [Route A, the peninsula route]."[72] Among the issues that attendees at the public hearing were concerned about was cost of the project and potential flooding and environmental issues, and they doubted that the peninsula route would cost only an estimated $5 million more than the bypass route. At least one attendee spoke against the peninsula route for humanitarian reasons, when attorney Sol Brinsfield pointed out that the route through the Westside would affect over two thousand people. One attendee, L. C. Pinson, wrote to the BPR that if the interstate was to be used by Maxwell Air Force Base, it would make more sense to approve the bypass route over the peninsula route.[73]

Two weeks after the public hearing, the BPR approved the peninsula route advanced by Engelhardt, AHD engineers, and the downtown business owners, despite the preferences of federal and regional BPR engineers, and most of the attendees at the public hearing for the bypass route.[74]

With the peninsula route of I-65 approved through the Westside, Engelhardt and AHD engineers turned their attention back to the route of I-85. In November 1961, Engelhardt spoke to Whitton at a conference and reported to Governor Patterson that the route for I-85 was still on hold: "Mr. Rex Whitton . . . was awfully nice to me and relayed a message to me to 'still lay low,' so to speak, concerning the East-West route on Interstate [I-85]."[75] Nonetheless, Engelhardt considered the route certain and told the press, "We have orders to proceed with the construction of this section of Interstate Route 85. We are going along with plans to bring the new highway along the south line route."[76] In November Patterson announced that the White House "backed down" and approved the south route.[77] In February 1961 Engelhardt announced that appraisals to purchase the homes along the south route would begin that week[78] and set a target date of mid-April to award a construction contract for the route.[79] In October 1961 the AHD purchased some homes along the contested south route.

Figure 6.2. This image shows the demolition of homes between Centennial Hill and the Westside for construction of I-85. (John Engelhardt Scott Collection, August 28, 1964, file Q79326, Alabama Department of Archives and History, Montgomery, Alabama.)

Figure 6.3. This image shows I-85 under construction with downtown and the Alabama River in the background. (John Engelhardt Scott Collection, May 20, 1968, file Q79195, Alabama Department of Archives and History, Montgomery, Alabama.)

Figure 6.4. Before planners and engineers routed I-65 through the Westside, the neighborhood was a thriving African American community of homes and businesses. Although all African American neighborhoods in the city suffered from disinvestment, this Westside street, Holt Street near Columbia Street, shows a well-kept and thriving community. The white-frame building on the right with the sign in front is Cooper's School, a segregated African American school. The Holt Street Washateria is across the street on the left. Most of the businesses closed, and the homes were demolished in the years following the construction of the highway. The street has a lot of vacancy today. (John Engelhardt Scott Collection, July 22, 1964, file Q77824, Alabama Department of Archives and History, Montgomery, Alabama.)

## KKK SIGNS ALONG THE INTERSTATE HIGHWAYS

With the interstate routes approved, activists sought to ensure that public displays of hate would not be part of the Interstate Highway System, as they had been on roads throughout the South. Public displays from groups such as the KKK and the WCC were long used by hate groups to instill fear in African American people. KKK signs had long been present along state, local, and federal roads, particularly near the entrances of cities. Just before the interstate highways were constructed through Montgomery, prominent civil rights activists from the north wrote to BPR officials, complaining about KKK signs along Highway 80, which connects Selma to Montgomery, and asking them to ban KKK signs from all federal roads, including the new interstate highways.

The issue quickly reached President Kennedy's office, when Kennedy and Special Assistant to the President Frank Reeves received a series of separate letters and communications from American Veterans Committee executive director J. Arnold Feldman, NAACP attorney J. Francis Pohlhaus, general counsel for the American Jewish Committee Edwin Lukas, and secretary of the US Department of Commerce Luther Hodges.[80] One week after the complaints, BPR regional administrator Rex Anderson asked Engelhardt to remove the KKK signs from federal roads. That day Governor Patterson, trying to appeal to the racial extremists who supported his candidacy, held a press conference questioning the BPR's authority in the matter, telling the press that there was no federal law that gave the BPR the power to determine which organizations were in the public interest and could have signs on the right-of-way.[81]

However, federal regulations for highways prohibited most encroachments on federal highways, including signs that were not related to traffic, operation, or maintenance.[82] Other signs, such as signs for civic organizations and advertising, were allowed along a federal rights-of-way only if the BPR determined that they did not interfere with the free and safe flow of traffic and were in the public interest.[83] The BPR typically deferred to state highway departments to determine which signs were in the public interest. The AHD allowed hate group signs along federal highways, referring to the groups as "civic organizations," like churches, Lions Clubs, and women's clubs, which also placed signs near entrances to cities. Determining what signs could be allowed on highways and expressing those rules in a way that maintained content-neutrality proved difficult for the BPR.[84]

The BPR drafted a temporary instructional memorandum banning all nonhighway encroachments in public rights-of-way. Nonetheless, eight months after issuance of the instructional memorandum, KKK signs remained on federal roads in Alabama, including at on least three federal roads in Montgomery.[85] In August 1961, just as I-65 was beginning construction through the

Westside, the BPR issued another instructional memorandum banning signs on federal rights-of-way from about 250 hate groups.[86] Although neither the Montgomery KKK nor the Alabama KKK were on the list, the AHD reluctantly removed the signs due to fear of losing federal funding. Within days, members of the KKK used permanent paint to paint KKK slogans directly on four main roadways in the city, and the KKK burned crosses and painted KKK symbols on the roadways.[87] When KKK members criticized Engelhardt for removing the signs, his assistant, Walter Craig, responded that Engelhardt had defended to KKK signs for many years: "We had argued this for three and one-half years. We have made an effort to leave them all up and frankly Sam [Engelhardt] has made three trips to Washington and the Bureau of Roads has sent men to Montgomery twice because of the Klan signs. . . . I am sorry that this came up but I can assure you that you do not have a single Klan member that has stood and face the fire from Federal pressure that Sam Englehart has stood."[88]

## REDEVELOPMENT OF OAK PARK

As the highways were beginning construction, the parks were still under an integration court order, and members of the City Commission and Recreation Board vowed that they would never reopen the parks on an integrated basis. The City Commission could sell or give away the parks because of an amendment to the Alabama constitution in the wake of the bus boycott that allowed cities to sell or give away parks, housing projects, swimming pools, and other facilities to evade court-ordered desegregation.[89] The amendment paved the way for Montgomery and other cities in Alabama to give parks to private organizations, such as the YMCA, which could maintain segregated private facilities.[90]

With the parks lying idle and overgrown, businesspeople began to pressure elected officials to sell the parks for private economic gain. Although elected officials, reflecting the views of many white citizens, preferred to keep public ownership of the parks in hopes that the integration order was reversed, they did sell or give away parks for civic uses and entertained ideas of selling them for private development. Yancey Park, with a pavilion and a swimming pool, was sold to the Montgomery Spastic Children's School. Hamner Hall Park was reused as a fire and police station, Perry Street Park was donated to the YMCA, Civic Park was sold to the Children's Center of Montgomery, Bear Park was sold to the East Montgomery Exchange Club, and Kiwanis Park became a fire station.[91]

Oak Park, with its prime location near downtown and the Alabama capitol building, became a sought-after development opportunity. City commissioners considered other ideas for using Oak Park, although they were also motivated by public pressure and nostalgia to keep the park in public ownership.[92] A factory and a large residential subdivision for white people were first proposed for the park. Because it was at the eastern edge of Centennial Hill, transitioning the park to housing for white residents would allow city planners to maintain a clear border between the adjacent African American and white neighborhoods. Routing I-85 through the park was briefly considered, which would avoid the demolishing of African American neighborhoods on either side of the park. However, city officials rejected that proposal, perhaps because demolition of the neighborhood was a goal of the highway route. Other proposed uses were a hospital and a trade school.[93]

The Montgomery Recreation Department preserved Oak Park, hoping that the integration order would be overturned in court. In the meantime, the Recreation Board entered into a secret agreement with the Montgomery branch of the YMCA to provide segregated recreation in the city. The agreement allowed the YMCA to offer the entire recreation programming for the city on a segregated basis, including athletic programs, clubs, educational classes, and community centers.[94] Under the agreement, each elementary school in the city was assigned to a YMCA branch that would supervise and administer segregated athletic and swimming programs. YMCA branch managers met with Recreation Department employees on a regular basis to coordinate their efforts, but the agreement was unknown outside a small number of city and YMCA staff.

# 7

## The Freedom Riders and Neighborhood Planning for School Segregation

In May 1961 the Freedom Riders—groups of young African American and white students—began riding segregated buses throughout the South to desegregate interstate travel. After one of the rides encountered mob violence in Anniston and Birmingham, President Kennedy intervened and managed to get Governor Patterson to guarantee the riders' safety to Montgomery. Once the bus arrived at the Montgomery city limits, however, it was abandoned by police escorts and turned over to Public Safety Commissioner Sullivan. Sullivan told members of the KKK of the bus's arrival, and the riders were met by an angry white mob at the downtown Montgomery bus station. The mob attacked the protesters, beating many of them unconscious, including future member of Congress John Lewis.

The next day Rev. Dr. King returned to Montgomery to deliver a speech at a rally for the protesters at Rev. Abernathy's First Baptist church. Another violent white mob circled the church and threatened to burn it down, despite efforts by US Marshals to keep them at bay, and some one thousand African American people were trapped inside the church. Police and US Marshals eventually managed to disperse the crowd, which were then left to roam throughout African American neighborhoods in the city—shooting into homes, overturning cars, assaulting people, and setting homes on fire.

Despite the violence, civil rights activists were starting to see consistent success when their battles were waged in the federal court system, especially in the US District Court for the Middle District of Alabama under Judge Frank Johnson Jr. Johnson, who was appointed to the court by President Eisenhower in 1955. Judge Johnson Jr. was well known to activists but had a reputation as a conservative judge before 1962 because he declined to intervene when Montgomery city officials wanted to shut down the carpools during the bus boycott in 1955, when the city commissioners closed all the public parks to avoid desegregation in 1959, and when the Alabama Board of Education expelled the ASU students involved in the lunch counter sit-ins in 1960. However,

Johnson's decisions shifted in 1961 when he began handing down specific and sweeping desegregation orders for issues such as voter registration, school desegregation, transportation, and library integration.[1]

By 1962, the efforts of civil rights activists to dismantle legal segregation had begun to show real progress, particularly in Judge Johnson's court. Bus and train stations in Montgomery were desegregated in 1961, the city's airport terminal, libraries, and museums were desegregated in 1962, and the city's private bus contractor hired its first African American bus drivers in 1962. In 1962 President Kennedy signed Executive Order 11063, directing all federal departments and agencies to take action to prevent discrimination in public housing. However, enforcement of the order was lax, and it affected only new—not existing—public housing, so many Southern cities, including Montgomery, continued to maintain segregated public housing.[2] Driven by this progress and their successes at organizing, African American activists initiated more sophisticated and bold campaigns. The MIA began a new voter registration campaign in October 1961.[3] In November 1962 African American activists won a major victory in Judge Johnson Jr.'s court when the federal Justice Department won a lawsuit against the Montgomery County Board of Registrars, barring racial discrimination in voter registration. Following the order, African American voter registration increased rapidly.

Another political shift came to Alabama in January 1962, when George Wallace, also a segregationist, was elected governor of Alabama with the support of the KKK after Governor Patterson was prevented by term limits from running again and Engelhardt's time as highway director ended.[4] By then, AHD staff, including incoming AHD director Ed Rogers, were considering the route of I-85 south of Oak Park certain, even though it had not yet been officially approved by the BPR. An editorial in the *Alabama Journal* announced, "It has been generally understood for some time that the southern route, okayed by the U.S. Bureau of Public Roads, was definite."[5]

As legal segregation was gradually dismantled by federal courts, city leaders, motivated by public opinion and their individual and varying racist beliefs, began to focus on other ways to maintain segregation. One such way to accomplish racial objectives, as well as other city goals such as economic development, industrial growth, school segregation, and infrastructure improvement, was through city planning, including slum clearance, transportation planning, selective code enforcement, neighborhood disinvestment, and residential segregation. Comprehensive planning and local development regulation had longstanding legitimacy in the courts, with their foundation in nuisance law, which was weighted toward local government, so activists seeking to protest city planning activities had a much tougher fight than those protesting legal segregation through the court system.[6]

Slum clearance reemerged as a political issue as planners more aggressively pursued the Houston Hill project, which had been delayed for six years due to slow federal funding and approvals, property acquisition delays, the use of eminent domain, relocation assistance delays, and a stalemate between the MHA and white businesspeople over the public housing portion of the project. After acquisition of Jackson Heights in 1955, the MHA removed the planned public housing for Houston Hill but left in the fifty-four vacant lots to be sold for market rate construction to make up the difference of relocation units available for displaced people. Segregationists remained concerned that the lots might be sold to both white people and African American people, resulting in an integrated neighborhood. Many white businesspeople were opposed to public housing. Some white residents on the east side were also concerned that African American housing in that location would drive down property values and increase crime.

In January 1962 white businessperson George Rivers presented Mayor James with a petition signed by six hundred people, requesting that the entire Houston Hill area be zoned for commercial or industrial use out of fear that "the races might become mixed in that area."[7] The petitioners were concerned that housing for both white residents and African American residents would be built on the site because it was close to the white neighborhoods of Oak Park and Capitol Heights, as well as the African American neighborhood of Centennial Hill. The area was also close to the African American High Street commercial district, the Alabama Capitol Complex, and downtown Montgomery. Even if only African American housing was built, white residents from neighborhoods east of Houston Hill would need to travel through the neighborhood to get downtown, which would, as Rivers told the press, "impose a threat to the people of the eastern section of the city, and is unjust, unfair and displays prejudice to our section of the city, by placing Negroes near our neighborhood."[8] Because FHA rules prohibited segregated housing using federal funds, petitioners noted, there was a possibility that it would become integrated: "It has been contemplated that the lots will be used for high class residences for Negroes, but actually anyone can bid on them and build on them. There are no race restrictions in zoning."[9]

At the same time, African American residents also presented the City Commission with a petition requesting that the homes be set aside for African American residents. Although FHA rules prevented race-restricted housing, the homes would be sold by the MHA, which unofficially maintained segregation in all their developments. As single-family residences, the homes would be attractive to middle-class African American people because of their proximity to ASU and Centennial Hill. Middle-class homes for African American people were in high demand and short supply because of the housing crisis, a decade of slum clearance, and the planned construction of I-85 south of Oak Park.[10]

Charles Rogers, director of the MHA, told both sets of petitioners that people who lost their homes due to interstate highway construction and slum clearance would be given priority to purchase the new houses.[11] Rogers walked a thin political line, reassuring white residents that segregation would be maintained, while pledging to white businesspeople that no new public housing would be built. Nonetheless, the white residents who were concerned about property values and crime were not pleased with the outcome. In 1963 the MHA sold all but two of the fifty-four lots to a single developer who resold them to African American families.[12] The lots were sold to one developer so that the private developer could maintain segregation. The rest of the Houston Hill project was developed as civic buildings, including a school, community center, a parking lot for the nearby auditorium, two churches, sixteen commercial lots, and a clinic. The swimming pool, which was proposed in the original plan, was never constructed because by then all the parks were closed due to the integration order. Like other slum clearance projects, the Houston Hill project increased profits for white businesspeople. Ten years later, a new hotel was under construction on the last vacant lot on the site. The project drastically increased the taxable value of the land. Prior to demolition of the neighborhood in 1953, the city received about $5,000 annually in taxes, and after redevelopment in 1963, it received over $49,000 per year.[13]

In 1962 Downtown Unlimited, an organization of white businesspeople, asked the Montgomery City Commission to complete a comprehensive plan for downtown revitalization and renewal. This request followed national trends toward comprehensive planning and away from demolishing neighborhoods on a case-by-case basis. The following year the City Commission hired local planning consultants Urban Consultants Inc. to complete the study. Downtown business interest groups, including Downtown Unlimited and the Chamber of Commerce, supported the plan. Studies for the plan are contained in six lengthy volumes published between 1963 and 1965.[14]

While the plan followed the general framework of the 1957 draft land use plan and contained many of the same overall goals, it was a more sophisticated document. It followed the rational planning model, included a comprehensive set of issues, analyzed quantitative data, and effectively linked the analysis with major goals. Nonetheless, the general idea of the plan remained the same: demolition of African American neighborhoods and commercial districts, expansion of downtown, economic development, and industrial growth.

The 1963–1965 comprehensive plan responded to the concerns about the national attention to civil rights activism that white business people had expressed to city officials. According to many white businesspeople, civil rights violence was impeding business growth because out-of-state firms were unwilling to locate in Montgomery. Although many businesspeople were unsympathetic to the struggles of African American activists and some were active perpetrators of the violence, they were unwilling to allow national attention to the violence that followed protests such as the Freedom Rides and lunch counter sit-ins affect them economically. Further, moderate white Montgomerians had increasingly begun to denounce the violence and extreme tactics, albeit modestly—a position that had not been articulated since before the bus boycott.[15] This motivated city officials to pay more attention to planning because comprehensive planning could accomplish some of the goals of white supremacy, but it was not something that normally resulted in violence and national press attention. It also accomplished other economic goals and often resulted in increased profits for businesspeople.

The plan focused on economic growth and slum clearance, often combining the two, to demolish African American homes for new commercial and industrial uses and downtown parking. The plan expressed concerns that growth in the region was being directed toward the suburbs and away from downtown. Although expansions of Maxwell and Gunter Air Force Bases added new families to the region, these families often chose to live in the suburbs. After 1960 the largest population growth in the region was in Autauga and Elmore Counties, which had a 28 and 10 percent growth rate between 1960 to 1970, respectively, while the city of Montgomery lost 1 percent of its population (see tables 4.1 and 4.2). Near Maxwell Air Force Base in Autauga County, the city of Prattville almost doubled in population, with a 96 percent increase between 1960 and 1970.[16]

Likewise, suburban shopping centers were gaining a larger share of economic activity due to downtown's lack of parking, traffic congestion, older buildings, and commercial blight, the plan noted. While retail sales continued to decrease in downtown Montgomery, sales in the suburbs expanded, and retail sales projections for 1970 showed a 6 percent drop downtown and a 38 percent gain in the rest of the metropolitan area.

Although downtown businesses were losing customers to the suburbs, the plan projected an optimistic, and perhaps unrealistic, increased demand for downtown office and retail space due to the anticipated population growth, justifying the need for more parking and new strip commercial development. With a 4 percent vacancy rate, one-third of that projected new space could be accommodated in existing buildings, so new space adjacent to downtown would be needed to accommodate the expected growth.[17] Planners proposed a large expansion of downtown into adjacent African American neighborhoods, including the Five Points/Peacock Tract area. As the consultant wrote, this was key to supplying the much-needed parking and space for construction of new suburban-style shopping centers, which would allow downtown businesses to compete with suburban shopping centers. Revealing their racist motivations, planners focused solely on the Five Points/Peacock Tract area, which had been the subject of slum clearance and highway routing plans for decades, instead of white neighborhoods near downtown such as Cottage Hill.

In addition to expanding downtown, the plan sought to expand and reshape neighborhood commercial areas, proposing widespread demolition of neighborhood commercial buildings and replacement with strip commercial buildings with large parking lots.[18] The notion that older, walkable commercial districts should be replaced with automobile-oriented strip commercial development was consistent with planning practice nationally, which prioritized and highly valued automobile-dependent development.[19] The consultant recommended demolition of most of the remaining African American commercial districts in the city, including the entire High Street commercial district in Centennial Hill and the portion of the Westside commercial district that would remain after the construction of I-65.[20]

The plan included aggressive expansion goals for manufacturing, responding to pressure from businesspeople who had been lobbying elected officials for years to increase industrial growth. In 1962 there were 803 acres of industrial land, and the consultant optimistically, and also perhaps unrealistically, projected an increase to 3,450 acres by 1980. The plan proposed no new industry in white neighborhoods but strategically placed new industrial uses near African American homes. For the African American neighborhoods, the plan noted, "it is desirable to have industry grouped in several areas that are strategically located with regard to the residential, business, and transportation elements of the City."[21] In Centennial Hill, new industry would be located on both sides of the proposed I-85 and across the street from Paterson Court, surrounded by residential development. Beyond the Westside, a vast amount of new industrial space would occupy the area from the railroad tracks to the city limits, on largely undeveloped land adjacent to low-income and working-class neighborhoods. The existing homes on the far west side near the city limits, which was sparsely developed, would remain but would be surrounded by new industrial development.[22] Placing new industrial development next to residential uses was contrary to the longstanding principle of separating such uses, established as far back as 1950 when city planners claimed they were demolishing homes in the North Montgomery slum clearance project because they were close to industry. To that end, the consultant shifted their analysis and goals to fit their desired ends. The result was also planning that failed to achieve its stated goals of neighborhood improvement.

The plan projected a population increase of 45,000 people by 1980, which would involve an increase of 30,399 dwelling units and 17,800 acres of residential land.[23] Accommodating that growth would be a challenge, the consultant noted, because the ideal density of residential areas was seven to ten persons per acre in order to effectively provide public services and improvements. However, some African American neighborhoods far exceeded the recommended density: the Westside had twenty-five persons per acre—the highest in the city, Five Points/Peacock Tract had eighteen persons per acre, and Centennial Hill had fifteen to twenty-one persons per acre.[24] While the African American neighborhoods were among the densest in the city, there were also some dense white neighborhoods. However, revealing their contradictory treatment of segregated neighborhoods in plans, the consultant defined density as a negative trait only for African American neighborhoods, justifying slum clearance. Dense white neighborhoods—such as tract 22, located in South Montgomery, which had ten persons per acre and was at the high end of the city's ideal density—were defined as stable and thriving.

To implement the plan, the Planning Commission again hired Urban Consultant Associates to write a new zoning code and map, taking into consideration the growth of the city, proposed highways, the new comprehensive plan, and the proposed development of the Coosa-Alabama River system, which had again emerged in political discourse. The changes increased the number of residential zoning districts from thirteen to thirty-one, adding more specificity for things like density, minimum off-street parking, and allowable nonresidential uses. The controversial part of the zoning update was an increase in strip commercial development zoning along major roads outside of downtown, such as along Mount Meigs Road, Atlanta Highway, the southern bypass, and Upper Wetumpka Road. These proposals drew intense criticism from downtown business owners who did not want more competition from increased strip commercial development.[25] However, the consultant proposed changes that were consistent with national trends toward strip commercial development.

In Centennial Hill, the new zoning ordinance increased residential densities and added more strip commercial and industrial zoning, especially to the northwest of ASU, adjacent to Paterson Court, and to the north and south of the proposed route of I-85, consistent with the proposals in the comprehensive plan. Providing a sharp contrast to the African American neighborhoods next to I-85, the area around the all-white Huntingdon College and the white neighborhoods on the east side remained residential.

In addition to opposition from downtown business owners, city planner Jack Knight and the Planning Commission encountered stiff opposition from many of the residents whose residential zoning would be changed to business and commercial, and other nearby property owners. Some two hundred residents who lived near the southern bypass attended a meeting and complained about new business zoning in that area, pointing out that the area that would be zoned for business uses along the southern bypass was much larger than the area zoned for businesses downtown. Landowners also objected to the designation of 2,300 acres of land along Highway 31 as a flood hazard district.[26]

While newspapers reported no significant protests over the zoning changes from African American residents, that doesn't mean they agreed with them, because the white press rarely reported on their concerns. Additionally, in June 1963, while the consultant was updating the zoning ordinance, activists were busy with integration efforts, including responding to Governor Wallace's "stand in the schoolhouse door" protest on the campus of the University of Alabama to prevent the entrance of Vivian Malone and James Hood. Activists were also involved with the Children's Crusade in Birmingham and a whirlwind of school integration efforts across the state.

Demonstrating the important link between planning and school segregation, the plan followed the neighborhood planning approach. While this approach had multiple goals, including neighborhood improvement, traffic safety, and walkability, it would also keep schools segregated, an idea that was first established in the 1957 draft plan. The plan established a population limit goal of about 2,500 people for each neighborhood, although some African American neighborhoods had much larger population goals. Each neighborhood was bounded by major streets and centered on an elementary school. The neighborhoods were segregated by race, so by using the neighborhood planning approach, lawyers for the Montgomery County School Board could argue that school segregation was due to neighborhood segregation—not an official school policy.

The plan also relied on the neighborhood planning approach to enforce segregation of parks. The consultants wrote, "Because of Montgomery's present situation [the park desegregation order], it is felt that future recreation needs must be met by providing neighborhood type recreational facilities for both races, such as school playgrounds, recreation buildings (probably school oriented) and neighborhood parks (not necessarily city owned)."[27] The consultant proposed colocating future recreational sites with schools, further engraining the fact that neighborhood planning would maintain school and park segregation. Because schools were segregated, colocated parks would also be segregated, whether it be unofficially or officially. The YMCA would share oversight of the park facilities placed at schools. The plan noted, "The city Recreation Department will implement parts of this program; the School Board and the Y.M.C.A. will provide other parts. The supervision of these facilities will basically be provided by the schools during the school months, and by the City Recreation Department and by the Y.M.C.A. during the summer months."[28]

Another way that the plan aided school segregation was by channeling funding and resources to schools for white children in the eastern and southeastern neighborhoods, which were already served by large new schools, instead of improving African American schools. Many African American schools were older (one school was constructed in 1911), had fewer classrooms (one school had just three classrooms and two others had just six), were on smaller sites (as small as two acres for one school), and had less space for playgrounds and athletics (two schools had just 0.2 acres of playground and athletic space).[29] In just a few years from the plan's adoption, the landmark school desegregation case *Carr v. Montgomery County Board of Education* would be making its way to Judge Johnson Jr.'s court, and lawyers for the Montgomery County School Board argued that school segregation resulted from the personal preferences people had to live near their own race, underscoring the importance of the neighborhood planning approach.[30]

## SCHOOL INTEGRATION ACTIVISM IN ALABAMA

As the Planning Commission was initiating zoning changes, Alabama saw a whirlwind of activism to integrate schools, along with the predictable violent reactions from white students and parents. In fall 1963 African American students sought admission to public schools in most cities in Alabama, with the notable exception of Montgomery. African American attorney Fred Gray served as the lawyer for many of the cases, which, he wrote, had similarities: each was a class-action lawsuit in Judge Frank Johnson Jr.'s court, each included briefs in support of the activists from the United States as amicus curiae, the plaintiffs were African American parents who had a history of activism and filed the lawsuits on behalf of their children, and all were denied admission to all-white schools. All the cases resulted in court-ordered school integration.[31] Montgomery, as the sole big city in Alabama without a major school integration effort that fall, stood out in contrast to its leadership by local activists in past years.

In nearby Macon County, Judge Johnson ordered the school board to admit African American students, and within days the Macon County School Board received almost fifty applications to transfer African American children to white schools. That September the all-white Tuskegee Public High School was scheduled to admit twelve African American students, all of whom passed the rigorous and unreasonable testing by the school board. In Birmingham, the day before schools were scheduled to open, KKK grand dragon Robert Shelton held a rally at the Graymont National Guard Armory with thousands in attendance. The home of school desegregation activist Arthur Shores was bombed three times in three weeks. In Mobile the school board accepted two African American applicants to the all-white Murphy High School, and white racial extremists gathered, calling for civil war. In Huntsville, school superintendent

Raymond Christian accepted four African American children into formerly all-white schools. Colleges also began accepting African American students, with Florence State College registering Wendell Wilkie Gunn and Auburn University admitting Harold Franklin. The University of Alabama had already accepted two African American students during Governor Wallace's infamous "stand in the schoolhouse door" theatrics that June.

In Birmingham, on September 4, 1963, almost a decade after the *Brown v. Board of Education* decision, Dwight and Floyd Armstrong became the first African American children to enroll in a formerly all-white public school in Alabama when they entered Graymont Elementary School. The backlash from white supremacists was immediate and vicious. As angry white mobs filled the streets in cities across Alabama, assaulting African American people, Governor Wallace closed the schools in Birmingham before the Armstrong boys were able to attend classes, and subsequently also closed schools in Mobile and Tuskegee. He did not, however, close schools in Huntsville, where liberal white citizens had a strong presence thanks to the already-desegregated Redstone Arsenal military base there, so Sonny Hereford became the first African American child in Alabama to attend class at a formerly all-white public school at Fifth Avenue Elementary School. Huntsville already held the record for having the first private school with an official desegregation policy, when the all–African American St. Joseph's Catholic school enrolled its first twelve white students a few days earlier (although some Catholic schools, including Montgomery's City of St. Jude, unofficially enrolled white students in all–African American schools as early as the 1940s).[32]

As violence spread throughout cities and state officials sought to delay integrating schools, Robert Chambliss (a.k.a. Dynamite Bob) and other KKK members drove to the north side of downtown Birmingham under the cover of night and planted a bomb under the steps leading to the side entrance of the 16th Street Baptist Church. As two hundred African American people were about to fill the church for Sunday service that morning, the bomb exploded, killing four girls—Cynthia Wesley, Addie Mae Collins, Carole Robertson, and Denise McNair.

The 16th Street Baptist Church bombing made national and international headlines and tempered further white violence over school integration. Alabamians, including Governor George Wallace, and major newspapers pleaded for "law and order," although there was no racial reckoning for most white residents in the state. Into the fall semester, the violent demonstrations eased, although Governor Wallace and school boards continued to fight school integration in court. Notably absent from the school integration chaos was Montgomery, where activists were reluctant to seek school integration over fears of being left with no schools at all. Even some rural areas of the state begun desegregation in the fall of 1963, and during the fall school semesters that followed over the next few years, rural and urban schools began token desegregation. Even schools in Lowndes County and other counties throughout the Black Belt, where African American residents risked their homes and jobs for enrolling their children in white schools, achieved token desegregation.[33]

## CITY PLANNERS COMPLETE LONG-DELAYED INTERSTATE AND RIVER PROJECTS

After years of delays, the BPR quietly approved the route of I-85 south of Oak Park in January 1965. Nelson and AHD staff held another public hearing announcing that the BPR had approved the route. With the south route approved, the purpose of the hearing was to gather public comment on the removal of the interchange at Hall Street—the location of Rev. Abernathy's home, although Rev. Abernathy and his family had moved to Atlanta by then.[34] The removal of the interchange at Hall Street was significant because during the initial routing decision almost a decade earlier, the AHD claimed that the highway was rerouted from north of Oak Park to south of the park to provide more room between the interchange at Hall Street and downtown. The changes also scaled-down the interchanges at Forest and Mulberry Streets at the east side of Oak Park. At the hearing, African American residents continued to protest the route, even though it had already received final approval from the BPR and discussing the overall route was not the purpose of the public hearing. The *Alabama Journal* reported, "This routing immediately drew protests from Negro residents in that area. . . . Rev. George W. Curry, 1110 Tuscaloosa St., said the middle route through Oak Park wouldn't affect 11 city streets and would also cut down on the number of homes to be razed."[35] Curry also argued that middle-class residents of the neighborhood would have nowhere in Montgomery to live. The press reported, "He pointed out that it is much more difficult for Negro families in Montgomery to relocate because the subdivisions aren't available." Furthermore, Curry said the "residential subdivisions are inferior . . . and displaced persons are exploited by the real estate dealers and contractors."[36]

Construction of I-65 through the Westside had begun years earlier in 1961, and construction of I-85 through Centennial Hill along the route south of Oak Park began in 1965. Progress on construction of both the interstates was slow, particularly for I-85, where many residents refused to sell their homes. In April 1967 the State of Alabama sued a group of Centennial Hill residents, including Rufus and Jule Lewis, who refused to sell their property. Although the interstate did not affect their home on Bolivar Drive, located north of the interstate, the Lewis family also owned property in the Bel Air neighborhood that would be demolished for the interstate. The Lewis family had refused to sell their land to the AHD, so the AHD initiated condemnation proceedings to acquire the property.[37]

Both highways tore through the heart of the African American neighborhoods in the city, leaving residents with fewer options during the housing crisis and displacing thousands of people. The interstates also set the course for auto dependency in Montgomery, as city officials had disinvested in public transit in the wake of the bus boycott, and the federal government spent millions on auto-oriented infrastructure.[38] I-65 disconnected the Westside from the rest of the city and decimated the African American business district. I-85 disconnected ASU from its residential neighborhood. The routes of the interstates were also arguably bad planning, and ignored industrial uses, the Air Force base, the needs of vulnerable residents, the fast-growing and high-traffic areas of east and south Montgomery, and the need for public transit. The interstate highways also facilitated residential segregation and worsened housing, public health, and neighborhood conditions for many people.[39]

With the highways under construction, another long-delayed project—the Alabama River navigation project—also began to make progress. By the mid 1960s the three dams—Millers Ferry Dam, Claiborne Dam, and Jones Bluff Dam—that were initially proposed in 1941 were nearing completion. The Army Corps of Engineers funded $13 million for the project in 1964, and in 1965 Congress appropriated $28,740,000 to finally complete construction of the three dams.[40] The Jones Bluff Dam opened in 1966, the Claiborne Lock and Dam opened in 1969, and the Millers Ferry Dam opened in 1974. Completion of the three dams made river navigation from Mobile to Montgomery possible, but the northern portion of the project—from Montgomery to Rome, Georgia—was far from completion and more complicated and expensive because the terrain rises steeply as it nears the Appalachian Mountains. Therefore, the project had little impact on industrial development in Montgomery.[41]

# 8

## Urban Renewal and the Selma-to-Montgomery March

By 1964 African American activists across the South had made significant gains. Congress passed the Civil Rights Act in July 1964, and public and private institutions throughout the South, including in Montgomery, began desegregation, including in hotels, theatres, and restaurants. The Civil Rights Act gave the US Department of Housing and Urban Development (HUD) the authority to investigate segregation of public housing and prohibited local governments from discriminating when they chose new public housing sites.[1] Although much of the progress emerged from federal court–ordered desegregation and federal legislation, the MIA and local activists also continued to exert their increasingly important political pressure on city officials as African American voting grew. The responses from white racial extremists to the gains of African American people were predictably violent.

After the bombing at the 16th Street Baptist Church in Birmingham, James Bevel and the Southern Christian Leadership Conference (SCLC) proposed a series of coordinated civil rights demonstrations, including sit-ins, marches, and boycotts throughout Alabama, centered in Montgomery, called the Alabama Project. The plan called for twenty thousand to forty thousand African American activists to take to the streets to demand the removal of Governor George Wallace and the immediate voter registration of every citizen in Alabama of legal voting age. The plan included strategies like blocking roads and airports and a march on the state capitol—the first seeds of the idea of the Selma-to-Montgomery march.[2]

Rev. Dr. King and Rev. Abernathy supported the proposal, particularly the march on the Alabama capitol, with some reservations about things like blocking roads and airports, which were considered civil disobedience. Despite the support of King and Abernathy, not all local activists supported the plan. The proposal exposed a major rift between the local MIA leadership and the national civil rights leadership, because some of the leadership of the MIA was against the proposal, including the group's president, Solomon Seay, who preferred deliberate negotiation and dialogue, which, as Seay argued, was starting to show results. One example of that dialogue was the Biracial Committee on Community Affairs, established by the Montgomery City Commission in 1964.[3]

## THE BIRACIAL COMMITTEE ON COMMUNITY AFFAIRS

As testimony to the increasing political power of African American voters, the City Commission created the Biracial Committee on Community Affairs—one African American committee and one white committee, each with forty-five members that functioned as two separate committees. In addition to realizing the increasing political strength of African American voters and a genuine desire to solve problems without violence, the city commissioners were also motivated to create the committees due to by pressure from white businesspeople to avoid major civil disobedience in the city because they believed it was driving away business. The idea was supported by MIA leadership, including Seay. The job of the committees was to study urban problems in the city, including slum clearance and housing, according to the City Commission resolution, which noted, "It is a time when thoughtful leadership from respective white and Negro communities must come together in an atmosphere of trust and understanding to resolve mutual problems . . . among the areas which will be studied by these groups are problems of youth, housing, industrial growth, job opportunities, law enforcement, slum clearance, paving, and sewerage."[4]

Biracial committees were becoming a popular solution by white elected officials to racial conflict across the country. However, many of the committees bore out a deep disconnect between white people who cautioned against rapid changes to the racial status-quo and African American activists, who sought an immediate end to segregation. As parks were a visible form of segregation, and one that many white citizens held onto dearly, many of the committees were charged with tackling issues concerning parks and recreation segregation, without much success.[5] Rev. Dr. King, a skeptic of biracial committees, told MIA leadership that such committees didn't have a record of producing real results, arguing, "Too often they are window dressing committees."[6]

At a speech in Montgomery during the MIA's annual founder's day celebration, Rev. Abernathy called for more direct action for civil rights in the city, accusing African American residents of becoming complacent and criticizing them for not desegregating schools as other big cities in Alabama had already done. The city commissioners, capitalizing on the discontent between MIA and SCLC leadership and hoping to avoid the activities proposed in the Alabama Project, announced the day after Rev. Abernathy's speech that they would reopen the parks, and they began working on a plan for the Biracial Committee on Community Affairs to ensure peaceful integration.[7]

## SCHOOL INTEGRATION IN MONTGOMERY

Prodded by the dispute between the SCLC and MIA leadership over the proposed Alabama Project, MIA leadership decided to file Montgomery's first school desegregation case. MIA leadership, including Seay, wanted to show—particularly to the critics who pushed for more aggressive action—that their tactics could achieve results. Attorney Fred Gray filed the lawsuit in a matter of weeks on behalf of Johnnie and Arlam Carr and their son, Arlam Jr. Arlam Jr. had long wished to attend a white school, and when he drove by a white school, which were far nicer than the African American schools, Johnnie later recalled, "He'd say, 'Oh mama, I sure would like to go to that school.'"[8] Johnnie Carr was one of the organizers of the bus boycott, helped integrate the parks, and served in leadership positions in the MIA.[9]

Although there were two segregated committees on community affairs, the City Commission did not allow the African American committee to have a chairperson, so Winton Blount, a white businessperson, acted as chairperson of both. Blount was a trustee of the University of Alabama when Governor Wallace famously blocked integration efforts by standing in a schoolhouse door. Although Blount opposed civil rights legislation, including the Civil Rights Act, he worked with the administration of President Kennedy to end the crisis and integrate the university.[10] R. D. Nesbitt, a longtime civil rights activist who was on the MIA board and who was responsible for recruiting Dr. Martin Luther King Jr. to become pastor at Dexter Avenue Baptist Church, was secretary of the African American committee, the highest position available for an African American member.

As the Biracial Committee on Community Affairs began working, the *Carr* school integration case moved quickly through the court system because there were already school desegregation cases filed in many cities throughout Alabama. In July, after refusing the Montgomery County Board of Education's request to dismiss the case, Judge Johnson's court issued its decision, determining that the Montgomery County Board of Education was operating a dual racial school system for students, teachers, staff, and bus transportation. The decision provides evidence that neighborhood planning was used to keep schools segregated. The schools in Montgomery were using a feeder system in which the elementary school that a student attended determined the upper-level schools they attended. African American elementary schools were assigned to upper-level African American schools, and the same was true for white schools. By keeping elementary schools segregated, the Board of Education was keeping all the upper-level schools segregated. The court determined that school zone lines were drawn along the racial lines of neighborhoods, and because the neighborhoods in the city were almost entirely segregated, so where schools. Neighborhoods had been planned around elementary schools.

Teachers, staff, and substitute teachers were entirely segregated by race, and the racial composition of a school was a strong consideration in disbursement of funds for maintenance, operation, and construction.[11]

With multiple school desegregation cases filed throughout the state that summer and fall, courts began to seek uniformity in school desegregation plans, and in June 1964 Judge Johnson's court ordered a desegregation plan for the Montgomery City-County School District that conformed to other Black Belt plans and the school desegregation plan for Birmingham. The court required the Montgomery County School Board to draft a desegregation plan for the upcoming academic year, starting in September, that integrated first, tenth, eleventh, and twelfth grades. Skeptical of whether the board of education would inform African American families of the plan, the court required that the desegregation plan be widely advertised in major newspapers at least twice a week for two weeks, with applications for school transfers to be accepted at a central location. The next step in the plan would require the board of education to file a desegregation plan for complete desegregation of all grades by January 1965, with implementation beginning in the 1965–1966 academic year.[12] A month later, in response to the Macon County school desegregation case, *Lee v. Macon*, a three-judge panel that included Judge Johnson ordered another sweeping desegregation order. While the court stopped short of issuing a statewide desegregation order, many agreed that it amounted to as much.[13]

That September eight African American children enrolled in and attended class at formerly all-white schools in Montgomery, the last big city in Alabama to desegregate, at Sidney Lanier and Robert E. Lee High Schools and Harrison Elementary School. By then, the major uproar over school desegregation in the state had calmed down slightly, as more schools desegregated and more white families removed their children from the public schools altogether. On the first day that the eight children attended class, protesters gathered outside Robert E. Lee High School, led by Atlanta attorney and violent white supremacist Jesse Stoner, who was later convicted for the bombing of Bethel Baptist Church in Birmingham and suspected in at least a dozen other bombings. However, the protest did not amount to the wide-scale violence that other cities in Alabama saw in 1963. Nonetheless, school board officials rejected the majority of the twenty-nine applications from African American children to transfer to white schools, and it had only begun to desegregate a few grades. Arlam Carr could not attend a desegregated school because the ninth grade was not one of the four grades that was desegregated, so he moved to Connecticut to live with family and attend an integrated school to prepare him to enter Sidney Lanier High School the following year.[14]

The Biracial Committee on Community Affairs worked on the sidelines of school integration, trying to ensure calm and peaceful protests. The African American committee encouraged the city commissioners to hire more African American police officers and probation officers for the family court. Although seven African American police officers had been hired in 1954, they all resigned by 1959 because of the election of L. B. Sullivan to the City Commission, and they were not replaced. Another priority for the African American committee was to work with city leaders to ensure peaceful use of the newly reopened and desegregated parks.[15]

## CITY PLANNING AND THE SELMA-TO-MONTGOMERY MARCH

Despite the initial priorities of integrated parks and police, two months after the committees were created and ten days after the parks were reopened the Biracial Committee on Community Affairs took a significantly different path. On the morning of March 7, 1965, SCLC chairperson John Lewis and Rev. Hosea Williams led demonstrators in Selma in the first of three attempts to march for voting rights from Selma to Montgomery. The group was violently attacked by Alabama state troopers, Selma police, a group assembled by the Dallas county sheriff, and white citizens on the Edmund Pettus Bridge in front of national television audiences. Lewis suffered a fractured skull, Amelia Boynton was beaten unconscious, and many others were seriously injured. President Lyndon Johnson released a statement condemning the violence and promised to send the proposed Voting Rights Act to Congress.

On March 9, activists made a second attempt to march from Selma to Montgomery but turned around near the Edmund Pettus Bridge to comply with an order from Judge Johnson's court prohibiting the march until additional court proceedings could take place later that week. Protesters were attacked later that night by members of the KKK, and one—white Unitarian Universalist minister Rev. James Reeb—was killed.

On March 11, at the federal courthouse in Montgomery, Judge Johnson heard a petition for an injunction from SCLC to permit the peaceful march. That day, the Student Nonviolent Coordinating Committee (SNCC) began daily demonstrations outside the courthouse. On March 16, during the hearing in Judge Johnson's court, a demonstration of nearly six hundred people was stopped by police near the state capitol, and a group assembled by the sheriff and white bystanders beat the demonstrators and advanced on them on horseback. The next day, SCLC obtained the injunction to allow the Selma-to-Montgomery march, and Rev. Dr. King led a large group of protestors to the Montgomery County courthouse to protest the violent reactions from white people the day before.[16]

The Selma-to-Montgomery march began at Brown Chapel AME Church in Selma on March 21, and by the time marchers arrived on the Westside of Montgomery on the evening of March 24, the crowd had grown to thousands.

On the last day of the march, some ten thousand participants slept at the City of St. Jude on the Westside, in a neighborhood that had just been declared a slum in the 1963–1965 comprehensive plan. Marchers were treated to a live concert with singers such as Pete Seeger, Sammy Davis Jr., Nina Simone, Tony Bennett, and Harry Belafonte the night before they marched to the Alabama capitol building. Thousands more joined the final march to the capitol on March 25, and the line of marchers grew to some twenty-five thousand participants, stretching from the City of St. Jude to the Alabama capitol building.

Figure 8.1. This aerial view shows the route of the Selma-to-Montgomery march as it passes through Five Points/Peacock Tract on the Westside. The homes at the top of the photograph would soon be demolished for I-85, and the homes at the top right would soon be demolished for the I-65/I-85 interchange. (John Engelhardt Scott Collection, March 25, 1965, file Q82176, Alabama Department of Archives and History, Montgomery, Alabama. Modified by Riley Dibble.)

On the morning of the final day of the march, both the white and African American sides of the Biracial Committee on Community Affairs published a large advertisement in the *Montgomery Advertiser* urging calm and asking children to stay in school that day. Both sides of the committee were motivated to help ensure peaceful protest because of the public attention to the march and the negative publicity from the previous attempts. Clergy and members of the committee, aware of the media attention that followed the first attempt to march, reminded citizens that the march would get national attention, writing, "Those who observe from many sections of the world will have varied and different concerns. The behavior of Negroes will be of interest to many millions around the world. Others will be looking for evidence of brutality among law enforcement offices, now and after the march."[17] Many of the white members of the committee were businesspeople and were concerned that negative publicity would be bad for business, as they had learned after the violent reactions to the lunch counter sit-ins and Freedom Rides. Also on the minds of clergy and committee members was how to move forward after the march. They wrote, "The vital question that should be the concern of every citizen of Montgomery is—where do we begin when the march ends? It is our fondest hope that we will not be forced to begin trying to overcome a bitter climate by irresponsible conduct on the part of anyone."[18]

Police and activists succeeded in maintaining relative calm the day of the march and avoided much of the violence that was featured on national television during the first attempt in Selma. When marchers arrived at the Alabama capitol, Rev. Dr. King delivered a speech calling for voting rights, linking voting to segregated housing and slum clearance. He announced, "Let us therefore continue our triumphant march to the realization of the American dream. Let us march on segregated housing until every ghetto or social and economic depression dissolves, and Negroes and whites live side by side in decent, safe, and sanitary housing."[19]

Despite the relative calm of the march when it ended in Montgomery, that evening members of the KKK attacked and terrorized marchers being shuttled back to Selma. A white volunteer from Detroit, Viola Liuzzo, was fatally shot by four Klansmen along US-80, the main route between the two cities through a rural area. St. Jude's Hospital admitted her after other hospitals refused to admit a white supporter of the march, but it was too late for doctors to save her life.

The backlash for supporting the march was a turning point for the City of St. Jude, which saw an immediate and drastic drop in donations. Many of the white people who supported St. Jude and claimed to support issues of African American economic, social, and health improvement said that they did not support Rev. Dr. King or the "outside agitators," and they withdrew their contributions. Some white hospital staff quit their jobs to protest St. Jude's support of the march, and African American staff quit due to threats they received. The 165-bed hospital, which was typically full prior to the march, dropped to a regular capacity of fifty to eighty patients.[20]

After the Selma-to-Montgomery march there was a lull of activity in the committee on community affairs, and it met infrequently. Because one of the main priorities of the committees was to ensure calm and peaceful protest, city commissioners saw no need to put much effort into the committees after the Selma-to-Montgomery march. African American members of the committee, however, desired more active engagement of the committees because they hoped it would lead to peaceful integration. In the meantime, city officials also continued their comprehensive plans, resulting in the largest, most comprehensive, and most actionable plan for slum clearance yet—the 1965 neighborhood analysis.

## THE 1965 NEIGHBORHOOD ANALYSIS

After the Selma-to-Montgomery march, the notion that white people might win the battle for legal segregation began to erode due to their consistent losses in federal courts. While the court losses proved that legal segregation was failing, city planning proved effective at maintaining residential segregation, with the goal of strengthening white supremacy. City planning also accomplished other public goals, including economic development, industrial growth, and neighborhood improvement. At the same time, the US Housing and Urban Development Act of 1965 expanded funding for public housing and slum clearance and set a goal of twenty-six million new public housing units over the following four years.

With new federal funding available for slum clearance through the 1965 act, city officials sought to develop a new comprehensive plan for slum clearance that would provide the legal basis to demolish almost every African American neighborhood in Montgomery. While the 1963–1965 comprehensive plan provided the general justification for slum clearance in African American and older white neighborhoods, it did not label individual homes as blighted, so it did not provide a legal basis for the use of eminent domain to demolish specific homes. Aside from completing long-delayed slum clearance projects in Houston Hill and North Montgomery and the construction of public housing, the slum clearance program in the city had stalled, giving way to comprehensive rational planning and policy implementation of those plans.

To qualify for the new federal funding, and to provide the legal justification for the use of eminent domain, planners needed a detailed house-by-house analysis of blight. To that end, in 1965, the City Commission hired Urban Consultants Inc. to complete a comprehensive assessment of blight in the city. The assessment analyzed crime, traffic, and land use, and vaguely defined blight factors, identified individual homes that were blighted, and provided the legal justification for the use of eminent domain for slum clearance.[21]

Like previous slum clearance programs, the motivations for the new plan were economic development, the reversal of suburban growth trends, neighborhood improvement, white supremacy, and race. The consultant wrote that downtown businesses would suffer if customers had to pass through blighted neighborhoods on shopping trips, resulting in a negative opinion of the city by out-of-town guests, which could curtail the city's aspirations for industrial and economic growth. The consultant wrote, "A negative opinion is particularly damaging in the case of industrialists interested in bringing new firms to the city. Slums are decidedly 'bad business' both socially and economically."[22]

The consultant's conclusion that the negative opinions of out-of-town guests were curtailing economic development had long been a concern of the city commissioners. Concerns about the negative opinions of out-of-town investors had previously surrounded the violent reactions of white Montgomerians to civil rights activism, including the Freedom Rides, and was one of the reasons behind the Houston Hill slum clearance project. After the peaceful African American protesters were met with violent reactions from a white mob and the absence of police protection, and it was televised on national news, business interests expressed concerns about potential negative reactions from out-of-town industrial investors. The Montgomery Chamber of Commerce, Rotary Club, Kiwanis Club, Montgomery County Ministerial Association, Junior Chamber of Commerce, and Alabama State Chamber of Commerce all passed resolutions decrying the mob violence, as well as the Freedom Riders' "provocation" of the violence.[23] Likewise, white businesspeople were concerned that violence during the Selma-to-Montgomery march might hurt business. By 1965 white businesspeople were concerned that the very presence of African American neighborhoods, regardless of their condition, would deter investors.[24]

The neighborhood analysis declared most of the homes belonging to African American families in the city as blighted and proposed a massive new comprehensive demolition program. The blighted neighborhoods were home to about 75 percent of the African American people in the city, about 10,900 people. The consultant wrote, "It is estimated that only a very small part of the housing for white persons was in these categories [blighted], while most of the non-white housing was substandard."[25] The plan linked income with blight and pointed out that the white population in the city had much higher incomes than the African American population did. Solutions to those economic disparities, such as education, job training, and social equity programs, were absent in the plan because city leaders were not motivated by social justice. Instead, the plan focused entirely on housing demolition, which would exacerbate the income and wealth disparities.

Like earlier plans, the neighborhood analysis revealed many contradictions. Many of the conditions of blight in Montgomery that the consultant identified were deficiencies of city public services. In the data and analysis, the consultant claimed that issues like poor street layout, parcel layout, inadequate size and shape of parcels, excessive population density, and a lack of paved streets, sanitary storm sewers, curb and gutter sections, and other public facilities were determinants of blight. The survey revealed that the strategies of disinvestment targeting African American neighborhoods in the previous decades were now considered blighting influences in the neighborhood analysis. Therefore, the consultant defined neighborhood blight partially by identifying deficient public infrastructure and treated those conditions with housing demolition. The appropriate remedy for deficiencies in public infrastructure should have been improved land use controls and more funding for public infrastructure, such as providing storm sewers, paving streets, and density restrictions. Ironically, consultants wrote that the high cost of municipal services in blighted areas, such as police and fire protection, was an outcome of blight.[26]

By then, residents of some African American neighborhoods had been lobbying the Sanitation Department to install sewerage and water mains along streets for decades. One resident of North Montgomery, Sylvia Johnson, a party in the park desegregation case, asked the Sanitation Department to install sewers on her street, Jackson Ferry Road, in 1960 and then again in 1963. Her neighbor, Rachel Fenison, asked the Sanitation Department for sewers in 1966 and was told by city officials to submit a petition from the property owners in the neighborhood. After she formed a neighborhood committee and got signatures on a petition, Sanitation Department employees told the residents of the neighborhood that the city would need to build a disposal plant if they were to install sewers, which was too expensive, and they denied the request. Despite the denial, much of the residential land along Jackson Ferry Road was designated as blighted in the plan. Fenison noted that the white neighborhoods in the city did not have similar problems. She told the *Southern Courier*, "If it had been white folks they would have put a sewer in, but since we are Negroes they just won't do it."[27]

Some of the streets in African American neighborhoods were in such disrepair that the US Postal Service (USPS) informed mail carriers that it was impossible to deliver mail because the streets were impassable. A USPS memo noted, "Streets are in very poor condition. All are dirt with numerous holes in them and are difficult to travel even in dry weather. It is my opinion that they would be practically impassable after a long period of rain . . . [postal] carriers simply cannot safely serve this area in its present condition."[28] E. D. Nixon wrote to USPS to inquire about mail delivery in the area, and David Dunn, the postmaster of Montgomery, told him that it was the responsibility of the city to fix the streets, and until that happened, USPS would not deliver the mail.[29]

City planner Jack Knight told the *Southern Courier* that it was not the responsibility of the city to pay for things like sewers and roads, noting, "the city wants the people who live in a neighborhood to help pay for improvements . . . the city can't use its own money to pave roads and put in sewers. 'Why should my tax dollar pay for someone else's improvement.'"[30] However, while city commissioners and city staff denied requests to construct sewerage and other infrastructure from African American residents, they regularly funded the same improvements in white neighborhoods.[31]

In the 1965 neighborhood analysis, Urban Consultants Inc. proposed neighborhood demolition as the solution for these infrastructure deficiencies. The consultant noted that I-65 and land clearance would amount to removal of a significant portion of the African American families in the Westside, writing, "Approximately one-fourth of the negro families in Montgomery live in this neighborhood . . . the junction of the two interstates will cause a large loss of houses in this neighborhood. In fact about one-third of the houses will have to be torn down . . . there will be a decrease in population of about 4,000 persons by 1980."[32] In Centennial Hill, also designated as blighted, the consultant noted, "The area south of High Street extending to the Oak Park area is almost completely blighted. Some of the blocks surrounding Alabama State College are only slightly blighted but the area east of the college is deteriorating rapidly."[33] The plan called for demolition of the entire neighborhood and new residential and industrial development.[34]

The plan also declared the African American neighborhoods of North Montgomery and King Hill blighted. As in other neighborhoods, the consultant's analysis pointed to infrastructure deficiencies as the cause of blight. The remedy for the blight, according to the plan, was clearance of the entire neighborhood, except the public housing, and the construction of new rental public housing. Contradicting itself within the same few paragraphs, the plan listed density as a blight factor but recommended the construction of public housing at higher densities. The demolition of housing in North Montgomery would allow more room for industrial expansion. One of the most strikingly racial factors in the plan was the consultant's treatment of racially mixed neighborhoods, where the homes of white people were declared stable, and homes of African American people, some of which were former "quarters," were declared blighted.[35]

Another neighborhood that was home to both races living in close proximity to each other was Five Points/Peacock Tract (an African American neighborhood) and Cottage Hill (a white neighborhood), and part of downtown. City leaders had targeted Five Points/Peacock Tract for downtown expansion since at least 1957. They wanted to use the area for parking to follow trends in auto-oriented development that they believed may allow downtown to compete with suburban shopping centers. The homes that were designated blighted were at the south and west sides of the neighborhood, close to the Westside and a small enclave of African American residents north of downtown, home to forty-eight families. According to the analysis, the reason for the blight was a lack of downtown parking and future expansion plans for downtown, which were unrelated to blight. The downtown expansion, however, entirely skipped over the Cottage Hill neighborhood, which was home to white families and closer to downtown.[36]

The 1965 neighborhood analysis, therefore, followed the pattern of racist city planning that was established as early as the 1924 zoning ordinance, targeting African American neighborhoods, including the homes of middle-class civil rights activists, proposing demolition of those homes because of vaguely defined "blight factors," and reshaping land uses near downtown for the purposes of economic development, neighborhood improvement, and industrial growth. It blamed African American residents for blight that was often caused by the failure of city officials to provide adequate public infrastructure and development regulations in segregated neighborhoods, and for economic circumstances that African American people were faced with from living with systemic and institutional racism. Demolishing neighborhood commercial districts in favor of strip commercial development and demolishing the homes of African American families close to downtown reflected the interests of white businesspeople and the white political elite in the city. The plan also used rational planning practices that relied on data and analysis, which often proved to be incomplete and came at a high social and cultural cost. The plan provided the legal basis for demolition of African American neighborhoods on a comprehensive basis and represented a major escalation in racist planning in response to civil rights activism, though it also had other objectives, including economic development, neighborhood improvement, and industrial development. The plan eventually helped maintain residential segregation and influenced school integration plans.

The plan was adopted, but like all plans, it was not fully implemented. However, it provided the justification for the use of eminent domain to demolish the home of almost every African American resident in the city. This reflected city decisionmakers' long-term goal to control African American residential patterns, socioeconomics, and spatial mobility, while hoping to increase economic development, industrial growth, and white supremacy.[37] These goals were also propelled by white fears of the growing power of African American voters, underscored in 1966 when Lucius Amerson, an African American man, was elected sheriff in Macon County. Suburban growth was also on the minds of city planners, with much of the metropolitan commercial and residential growth in the prior decade taking place in the suburbs. Planners pursued downtown improvement to better position the city to compete with suburban shopping centers.[38]

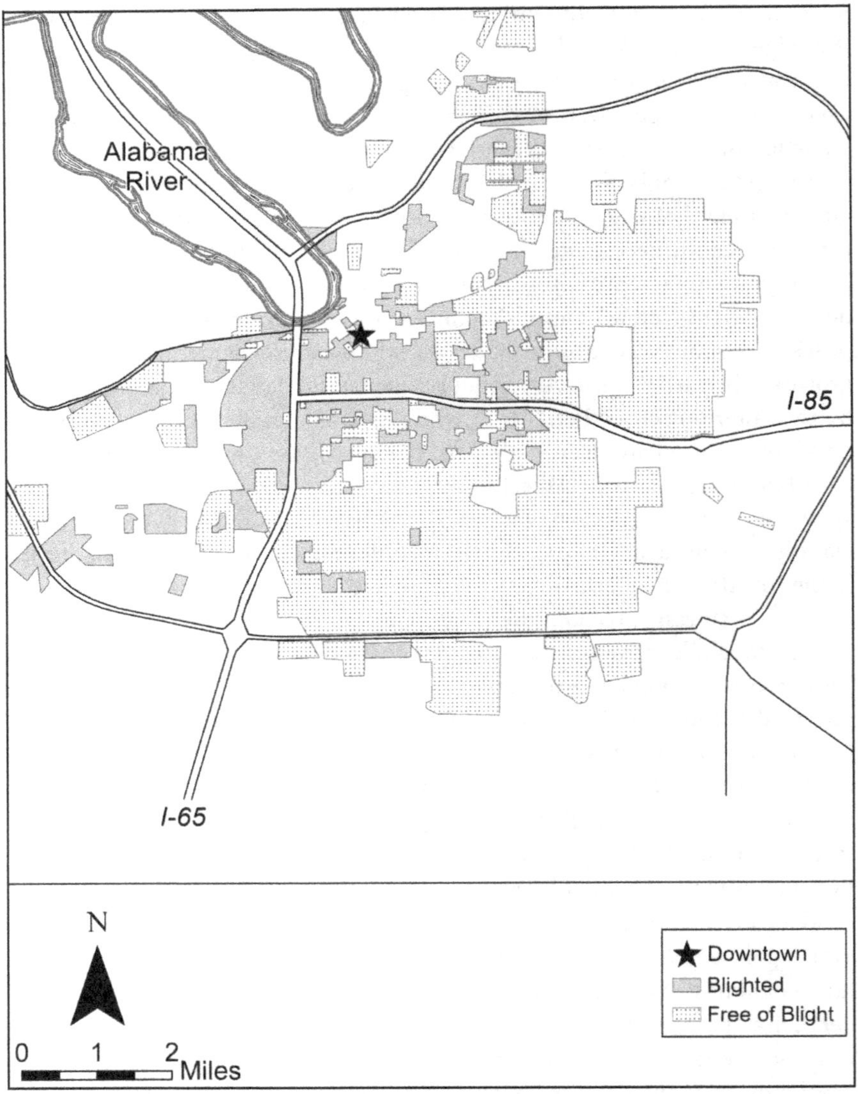


Figure 8.2. This map from the 1965 neighborhood analysis shows the neighborhoods that city planners declared blighted, shaded dark gray on the map. (Map by Riley Dibble, based on Urban Consultant Associates, Neighborhood Analysis for Montgomery, Alabama [Montgomery: Montgomery Planning Commission, 1965], 11.)

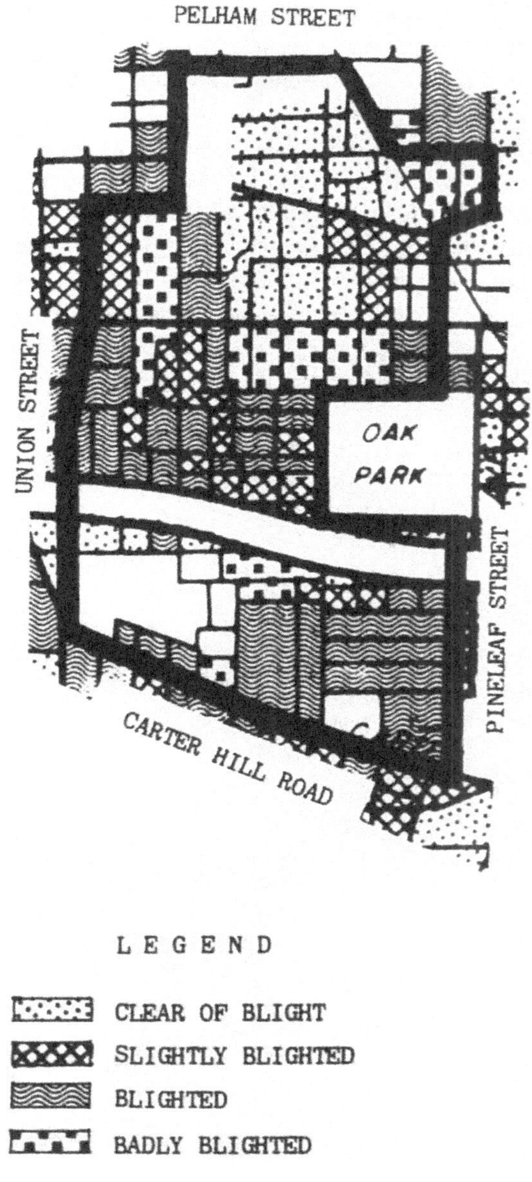


Figure 8.3. The 1965 neighborhood analysis included a neighborhood-by-neighborhood analysis of blight. This map of Centennial Hill is one example of such an analysis, where the homes of Rev. Ralph Abernathy, Johnnie Rebecca Carr, Dr. Richard Harris, and Rev. Martin Luther King's former home were designated blighted. (Urban Consultant Associates, Neighborhood Analysis for Montgomery, Alabama [Montgomery: Montgomery Planning Commission, 1965], 49. Modified by Riley Dibble.)

Implementation of the plan relied on the federal urban renewal and interstate highway programs to provide a comprehensive redevelopment strategy for economic development at the expense of African American residents, mostly funded by the federal government.[39] To carry out the plan, the City Commission created a new Urban Renewal Agency (URA) to implement slum clearance and downtown revitalization using federal urban renewal funds. Elizabeth Wright, a businesswoman and realtor who came from a meager upbringing, was appointed director of the agency. Wright viewed slum clearance as the principal solution to the problems of low-income families but left social services to other (unspecified) agencies. She said, "These low-income groups face problems which are quite complex. . . . I try to help by clearing slums, but social workers and all types of public agencies are necessary in working with low-income people."[40]

# 9

# City Planning in the School Desegregation Era

IN MARCH 1966, after years of delays and minor token desegregation, Judge Johnson Jr.'s court ordered a new "Freedom of Choice" school desegregation plan for the Montgomery County Board of Education. The plan required the Montgomery County Board of Education to fully desegregate first through fourth grades and ninth through twelfth grades by September 1966, with all grade levels desegregated the following school year. The plan also applied to teachers, staff, principals, and funding for school buildings and maintenance. It eliminated the feeder school system, which had been aided by the implementation of neighborhood plans, and required that no preference be given to any student for prior attendance at any school. Judge Johnson's court also addressed the inadequate and poorly maintained African American schools, ordering the closure of seven elementary schools by fall 1966 and another seven elementary schools the following year.[1]

The Alabama Council on Human Relations sponsored workshops on school integration to help African American children transfer to formerly all-white schools.[2] With desegregation of more grade levels, Arlam Carr and thirteen other African American students attended class at Sidney Lanier High School. Lanier was one of the best schools in the state and the children of Governors George and Lurleen Wallace were also students at the school.[3]

Nonetheless, by the start of the 1967 school year, public schools in Montgomery had still achieved only minor token desegregation, and athletics was almost entirely segregated. The State of Alabama operated two segregated school athletic associations—one for white and formerly white schools and one for African American schools. Only the white athletic association was recognized nationally, and thus only students from white and formerly white schools could attend state championships, hold records, and become eligible for college athletic scholarships. However, because there were some African American children attending formerly white schools, the white athletic association also achieved token desegregation because a few African American students began playing sports at formerly white schools. Nonetheless, aside from these few students, school athletics remained entirely segregated. Maintaining segregated sports, like maintaining park segregation, was important to segregationists because they feared that that integration would lead to racially mixed relationships and that African American boys would defeat white boys in the football program. In 1967 Judge Johnson's court ordered the Montgomery County School Board to integrate the school athletic system, and in 1968 the court ordered the two athletic associations to merge.[4]

Desegregation of school faculty was another big issue in Montgomery and statewide, which Judge Johnson's court addressed. School boards throughout the state claimed that African American teachers were not fit to teach in formerly white schools, a convoluted position given the claims by the school board that white schools were equal to African American schools in previous decades. In 1967 there were seven white teachers at formerly all-African American schools, and no African American teachers at formerly all-white schools in Montgomery.

Also in 1967, after a two-year absence, Montgomery again saw a resurgence of direct action for civil rights. Marches returned to the city after the fire and police chief in nearby Prattville, officer Kenneth Hill, shot and killed an African American man, Charles Raspberry.[5] The shooting occurred during a meeting between SCLC leaders and local activists, after police entered a home and arrested SCLC activists. Before killing Raspberry, police also beat activist Dan Houser until his skull, nose, and jaw were fractured and his eyesight nearly lost. In response to the violence, the MIA sponsored a series of marches that summer in Montgomery.[6]

## IMPLEMENTATION OF URBAN RENEWAL

As the demonstrations were taking place, Wright and URA staff began working on the first three urban renewal projects to implement the 1965 neighborhood analysis—Court Square, Western Hills, and ASU/Centennial Hill. The neighborhood analysis proved to be effective at providing the legal justification for the use of eminent domain. The three projects reflected the priorities of white public officials and businesspeople: economic development, automobile-oriented commercial redevelopment, and neighborhood improvement. Had the URA wanted to focus on improving the lives of people living in the worst housing conditions and with the lowest incomes, Wright would have perhaps chosen to improve sewerage and water infrastructure along city streets or to improve the housing conditions of the low-income African American families in North Montgomery. Instead, Wright and URA staff chose to demolish an African American neighborhood to make room for civic buildings adjacent to I-85, downtown economic development, and just one project that would demolish African American homes for replacement with improved housing.[7]

None of the projects included public housing because the URA and Wright sought to respond to concerns from businesspeople, who pressured the City Commission to stop building public housing because it competed with private real estate interests. The position to stop building new public housing followed trends in planning practice nationally toward slum clearance without public housing, and federal legislation made it possible.[8] Implementation of urban renewal in Montgomery followed a pattern that city officials had long before established, complemented by planning practice nationally. City planner Lawrence Vale describes, "Much of the history of public housing in the United States has followed the cyclical practice of displacement and neighborhood renewal, frequently directed at purging the poorest from communities being redeveloped."[9]

Alabama congressional representatives, while voting against national civil rights legislation, were well positioned to politically influence federal decision-making for slum clearance. Alabama senator John Sparkman was the chairperson of the Senate Housing Committee and Representative Albert Rains was the chairperson of the House Subcommittee on Housing. Sparkman claimed that slum clearance would ease racial tensions in the South. As one report noted, "Senator Sparkman has always maintained that better economic conditions for all our people instead of federal legislation will ease racial tensions. He has therefore voted 24 times against civil rights legislation, and in favor of such legislation as decent housing, slum clearance."[10]

Even though the projects did not contain public housing, some white businesspeople were still skeptical of any of federal housing programs. Announcement of the urban renewal projects revived the tension between white businesspeople who preferred private investment, and city officials who believed that the use of federal funds was the only viable option for implementing their plans.[11] Although city officials were in favor of the economic development that came with private investment, they were skeptical of the ability of private developers to demolish the slums on a large scale. Wright sent letters to businesspeople to try to convince them to support the urban renewal program, writing, "It is time that the Montgomery businessman recognized that the federal-local urban renewal program is, above all, a program for him."[12]

Despite the skeptics, many other business interests, however, supported urban renewal as long as it didn't involve public housing, because they expected the clearance of African American neighborhoods to improve property values and tax revenues. As an *Alabama Journal* editorial noted, "Private investors stand to gain. . . . They are guaranteed proper public facilities and land with demonstrated marketability. The program maintains property values and keeps the flow of tax revenues from declining. Moreover it arrests deterioration before it gets out of hand."[13] Downtown Unlimited president H. O. Davis said that the plan had the "unqualified support" of the group.[14]

Wright, however, told businesspeople at a public forum that the URA would need to relocate 1,295 families who would be displaced by interstate highway construction and slum clearance projects.[15] By then, the African American housing shortage had become even more acute due to decades of slum clearance, highway construction, neighborhood disinvestment, and segregation. The crisis was also worsened by the reluctance of the Montgomery Planning Commission to permit any new African American housing developments, because they drew considerable opposition from white neighbors.[16]

Large African American families that were displaced by slum clearance and interstate highways found it particularly difficult to find new housing due to racial discrimination. The public housing built in the previous decade contained a few units for large families, but it was in short supply. Wright used racist language to describe the needs of large African American families, blaming large families for social problems. She told an African American newspaper, “People with litters like this, they don’t want her. . . . That’s what causes child delinquency, stacking them up on top of each other.”[17]

Revealing the intentions of white businesspeople and city officials to prioritize their own economic interests over solving the housing shortage for African American people, the first URA project was the Court Square downtown urban renewal project, which had no housing component. The project focused on rehabilitation and conservation, instead of demolition, and did not significantly affect African American people. The plan, which was not fully implemented, covered 639 acres of downtown, including 64 acres of slum clearance and 568 acres of building conservation and rehabilitation. The plan would affect the homes of 400 families, totaling 777 individuals, including 695 white residents and 82 African American people. However, most of those families would not be displaced because the plan did not call for large-scale demolition.[18]

The downtown project was split into ten phases, but only the first phase—Court Square, on seventy acres of land—was completed. This project created a cultural center around Court Square, the city’s center of civic life and the former auction site for enslaved people before the Civil War. The URA demolished thirty-three buildings on ten acres and rehabilitated thirty-three buildings on sixty acres. After demolition, the URA sold or gave away the land to private businesspeople to build parking structures and a new department store, and to expand existing businesses. The project eliminated several major streets, created a pedestrian shopping mall, increased parking, installed canopies on buildings, erected new streetlights, and narrowed Dexter Avenue from six lanes to four.[19] Although the plan included some incentives for building rehabilitation such as low-interest loans, most of the funding was used for improvements in traffic circulation and parking.[20]

Wright and other city leaders had long hoped to increase parking downtown to be able to compete with auto-oriented suburban shopping centers. They hoped that the increase in parking would spur economic growth downtown because, despite over a decade of planning for economic development, downtown continued to lose retail sales to the suburbs. Between 1954 and 1958, downtown retail sales fell slightly (by $200,000), but sales in the suburbs grew by a significant amount (by $16,470,000). By 1963 there were over sixty vacant storefronts downtown.[21] Mayor James, Wright, and other city officials hoped that the project would turn around the downward trend in business growth and enlisted powerful champions in Congress to help secure federal funding for the project. Alabama senators John J. Sparkman and J. Lister Hill worked with the HUD to secure most of the funding for the project, and the city of Montgomery, led by Mayor James, provided the remaining one-third. Wright wrote to the MIA to ask them to support the project and was careful to not mention the other two urban renewal projects in the letter, both of which focused on slum clearance of African American neighborhoods.[22]

In June 1967 the Montgomery City Commission created two new city boards—the Montgomery Historic Development Commission, an eleven-member board for historic preservation, and the Architectural Review Board, a five-member board that would review the design of development proposals for the downtown urban renewal project.[23] Consistent with preservation planning practice nationally, the new boards used a racially biased definition of historic preservation and considered only the buildings that were important to white people as having historic value.[24] Later, the URA announced that some buildings in the Court Square urban renewal area would be preserved because of their historic value, including the Confederate post office, the law offices of secessionists William Yancey and John Archer Elmore, a bank that was one of the principal agents of the Confederacy, and the building from which the telegram was sent to Confederate troops to fire on Fort Sumter and begin the Civil War.[25] Downtown buildings important to African American people were not protected, including the Montgomery Fair building, where Rosa Parks worked as a seamstress; the corner of Moulton and Montgomery Streets, where Rosa Parks was arrested; the E. L. Posey parking lot, a transportation hub of the bus boycott; and any of the warehouses for enslaved people.[26]

With the Court Square project underway, the URA announced the second urban renewal project—Western Hills—an ambitious plan to demolish 639 acres of housing on the Westside, home to 1,800 African American families, 12 white families, and 86 commercial buildings (mostly African American–owned businesses). Nationally, the goal of plans such as this was neighborhood improvement, but as sociologist Herbert Gans argues, this was true only for the "deserving poor"—those with jobs—and not for the "underserving poor"—very low-income African American people, whom many white people viewed as being unworthy of assistance.[27] The plan, if fully implemented as city officials hoped it would be, would demolish the entire working-class African American Westside neighborhood in order to improve the neighborhood and, as some white city officials believed, improve perceived moral deficiencies of the residents. Also hoping to appeal to white realtors and businesspeople, the URA agreed that the land would be sold to private developers to construct better housing for African American people with higher incomes.[28] The project would be completed in eight phases, but only the first phase was completed—the demolition of 111-acres of housing west of Hill Street, which displaced 175 African American families. After demolishing the homes, the URA sold 320 vacant lots for $15,000 each to African American families to construct new homes. A new park—Western Hills Park—was included in the middle of the site.[29] Although the neighborhood analysis and other city plans claimed density was a cause of blight, the project ironically almost doubled the density of the neighborhood. The motivation for choosing to sell vacant lots was to avoid building public housing due to increased pressure from white businesspeople. Although the project provided essential infrastructure that was lacking prior to slum clearance, it increased housing costs for African American people, and many of the people who were displaced could not afford to build homes on the lots.[30]

The third urban renewal project was located in Centennial Hill on both sides of I-85. Originally, Wright announced that the URA would demolish 126 acres of African American homes, but the project was later scaled back to 40 acres. The neighborhood contained 624 buildings, home to 535 families—all of them African American. Four hundred ninety-two of those buildings (77 percent) were declared blighted and slated for demolition, while the rest would be improved through increased code enforcement.[31] If implemented fully, the plan would also include demolition of buildings south of ASU along Carter Hill Road, most of the African American commercial district along High Street, and several civil rights activists' homes north of I-85, including Rufus Lewis's home.[32]

The plan was not fully implemented, but approximately two hundred homes were demolished, and new public housing for the elderly, who were also defined locally as the "deserving poor," was constructed at Hall and Adams Streets. The project followed the neighborhood analysis, which declared some of the homes in the area blighted, and others stable, resulting in a patchwork pattern for implementation. Part of the land was used to expand Booker T. Washington High School, and about twenty acres was used to expand ASU.[33] The project exacerbated the housing crisis because it demolished homes but built schools and civic buildings.

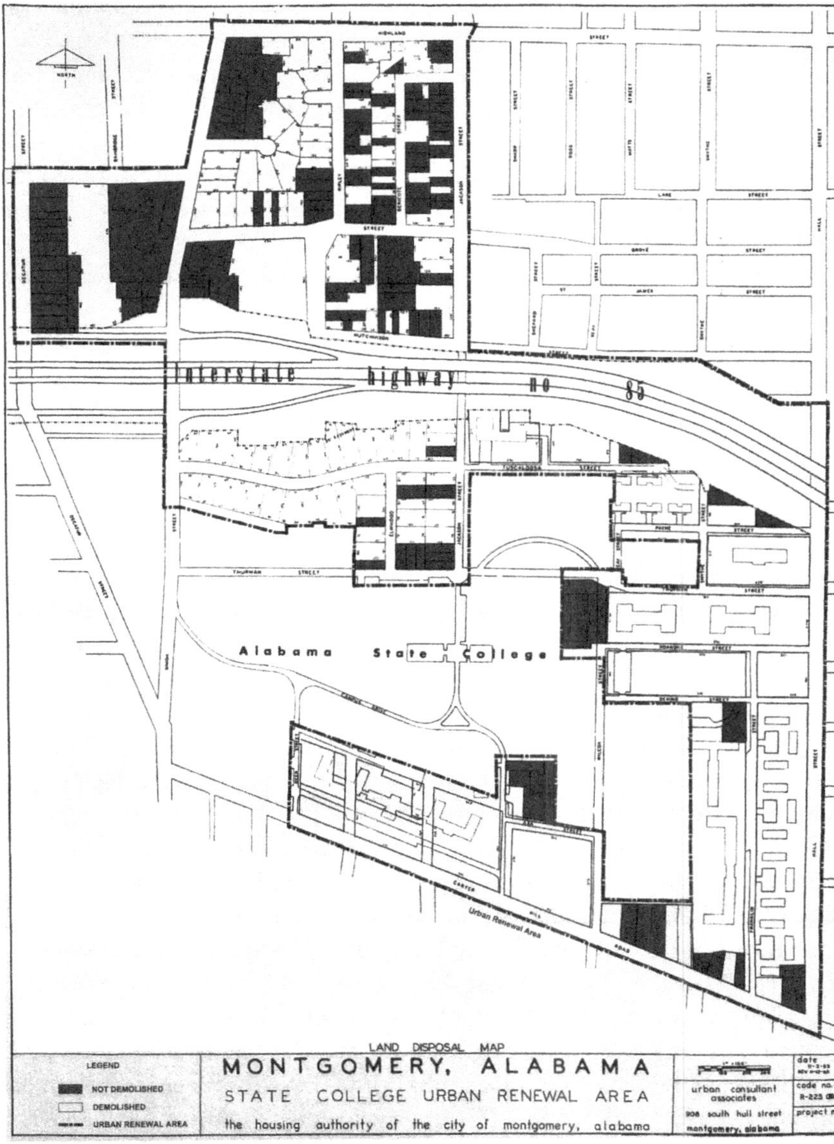


Figure 9.1. In the Alabama State University Urban Renewal Project, planners proposed the demolition of selected homes in Centennial Hill, which are unshaded on the map. (Urban Consultant Associates, State College Urban Renewal Area, November 3, 1965, Governor Patterson Files, Alabama Department of Archives and History, Montgomery, Alabama. Modified by Riley Dibble.)

Contrary to city plans that indicated a need for slum clearance in the African American neighborhoods with the worst housing and neighborhood conditions, the neighborhoods near Centennial Hill were comparatively in good condition. While the houses that were demolished for the construction of I-85 were some of the best-quality homes in the neighborhood, the homes in the ASU urban renewal project were still in better condition than many homes in other African American neighborhoods.[34] The MIA and SCLC opposed the Westside and the ASU urban renewal projects, but there were some African American supporters, including URA staff member Robert Nesbitt, whom Wright hired to try to win support for the project. Johnnie Carr, representing the MIA, and Rev. R. C. Boone, representing SCLC, wrote to Governor Wallace requesting a meeting to advocate for stopping both projects because they would perpetuate segregation.[35]

In a meeting with activists, Wright told the group that if they did not like the location of the projects, they should propose alternative locations. In October 1967, residents began receiving notices that their homes had been purchased by the URA and that they were being offered $200 in relocation expenses. The notices included the warning that a housing code for existing buildings was in effect, and if they moved into a substandard housing unit and were displaced again, they would not receive any more relocation funding. The notices also informed residents that if they had low incomes, they might be eligible for public housing, without mentioning that such housing was in short supply in the city.[36]

While the URA was working on slum clearance, the MHA continued to seek federal funding for public housing for displaced residents. Despite the continued protests from white businesspeople, public housing was often the only way to comply with federal relocation assistance requirements. The MHA received $6 million in federal funding for Gibbs Village, with a total of five hundred new housing units. Mayor James announced that the project was needed because urban renewal, the interstate highways, and enforcement of the housing code would necessitate the relocation of 2,966 families citywide in the coming years.[37] In May 1967 the MHA proposed a new four-hundred-unit public housing development, Highland Gardens, at Lower Wetumpka Road near Kansas Street, but the project was withdrawn from consideration after city engineers determined that the proposed site was entirely a wetland.[38] In 1968 Richardson Terrace was built in Centennial Hill, and in 1969 the HUD approved $2.49 million in funding for Young Forte Village and Smiley Court.[39] Although white businessmen continued to protest the construction of public housing, the MHA argued that it was necessary in order to advance important economic development goals of slum clearance and infrastructure improvement in the city.

While the MHA increased development of affordable housing, activists made gains in representation on city boards and commissions. In 1968 Mayor Earl James selected Dr. Moses Jones to become the first African American person appointed to the MHA board. Dr. Jones was also a member of the Biracial Committee on Community Affairs, which pressured city officials for the appointment.[40] That year Elizabeth Wright hired five more African American employees to URA staff positions.[41] Progress toward political representation for African American people and increased communication were the two major accomplishments of the Biracial Committee on Community Affairs.[42] By then, the two committees were holding joint meetings, largely consisting of addressing reports from committees and department staff, including Wright.[43] Despite the increasing representation, African American people did not make up a majority of any of the boards, so white members maintained the balance of power.

Despite the approval of Gibbs Village, Smiley Court, and Young Forte public housing developments, white businesspeople continued to pressure the MHA to not build affordable housing. At the same time, the new developments were still not enough to house those displaced by slum clearance and interstate highway construction. In order to continue implementing these programs and accomplish the economic development that city leaders hoped the projects would bring, while avoiding building more public housing, the MHA started to enter into agreements with private developers to construct high-density, affordable housing for African American families. This would allow the MHA and URA to meet federal relocation assistance requirements so they could continue the slum clearance program. After the private developments were constructed, the MHA entered into long-term lease agreements with developers, allowing the private developers to manage the buildings. The plan essentially privatized public housing construction and management and appeased white businesspeople, because they would benefit from the lucrative long-term contracts. [44]

Although it was still not enough to meet the demand for affordable African American housing, the new private housing was constructed cheaply and quickly and did not meet the requirements of the housing code, which had been passed at the request of white developers in 1957. Discrepancies between the housing and zoning codes were also problematic for the new developments. The issue gained political attention when residents were unable to move into a newly constructed building that was built by a private developer and funded by the MHA on the Westside because it exceeded the maximum density allowed under the housing code.[45]

Although African American activists gained some political power through the appointment of Dr. Jones to the MHA board, he was still just one member.

Activists criticized the MHA for the density of the new housing and the small spaces of the individual units. As civil rights activist Rev. Solomon Seay Sr. told the City Commission, "You can't find a playground near any of these projects. When we build we should think of the children and where they play."[46] African American people were also concerned that most of the new developments were located on the Westside. Civil rights attorney Fred Gray argued, "The west side of Montgomery is going to become the worst black ghetto in the nation. We should give consideration regarding the number of units, or provide a play space."[47] Local newspapers referred to the new housing developments as "instant slums"[48] and reported that developers were "putting up chicken coops and calling them apartments."[49] Despite this criticism, developers asked the City Commission for another revision of the housing code, and in 1968 the code was combined with the zoning ordinance to allow more density. The increase in density reveals that the analysis used in many city plans to justify slum clearance was largely subterfuge, given the fact that city officials used density as justification for demolishing African American housing for decades to pursue their economic development and other planning goals.[50]

Although Wright and the URA hoped that the urban renewal program would fund the neighborhood analysis plans for comprehensive redevelopment of nearly every African American neighborhood in the city, by the time the three first phases of Montgomery's urban renewal projects were completed, the federal program was coming under increasing fire. In 1968 the National Commission on Urban Problems issued a report criticizing the urban renewal program. Many of the projects took a long time to complete, and some projects halted at the demolition stage, leaving large areas of vacant urban space. The report criticized projects that demolished buildings that were in relatively good condition to build highly profitable buildings such as stadiums and theaters. The commission determined that 67 percent of projects in the urban renewal program were residential before demolition and only 43 percent were residential afterward, and most of those residential areas were unaffordable for the former residents who were displaced. Critics of urban renewal nicknamed the program "negro removal," due to the frequency of demolishing homes of African American people.[51] Thus, the major funding stream that allowed the URA to implement their neighborhood redevelopment plans came to an end, and the remaining plans for urban renewal in the city were never realized.

## RESTORATION OF OAK PARK

Following the construction of I-85 south of Oak Park, city officials returned their attention to parks, with the intention to restore them to keep people of different races from interacting. Although reopened, the remaining parks, including Oak Park, were in disrepair after years of being closed. The sidewalks were overgrown, the goldfish in the ponds had died, and the surfaces of the sports courts were distorted by vegetation. The most popular features in the park had been removed, such as the zoo, playground structures, and pool. Although Oak Park was reopened on an integrated basis, the Parks and Recreation Board did not encourage African American residents to use the park and instead tried to ensure that the races would have little opportunity to interact with each other. Picnicking was banned in the parks, and all the picnic tables and benches were removed so that people of different races could not sit together.[52] The Parks and Recreation Department erected a six-foot-high fence around Oak Park—the longest fence in the city—and hired additional security guards. The only entrance to the park was in the white neighborhood on the east side, preventing easy access into the park for the African American people who lived on the other three sides.[53]

Several months after the parks reopened, the Parks and Recreation Board began working on a plan to restore Oak Park. The board initially proposed a botanical garden, supported by the Montgomery Audubon Society, which would help prevent the races from interacting because it would have no areas for picnicking, playground structures, or pool. However, many white Montgomerians were nostalgic about the previous design of the park, particularly the amusement rides, the zoo, and the playgrounds. Some citizens and groups, including the Montgomery League of Women Voters, pressured the Parks and Recreation Board to restore the park to its former design, but without the tennis courts or swimming pool. Integrated swimming was an extremely sensitive topic because segregationists feared that the races together in a pool, wearing bathing suits, would lead to racially mixed relationships. So even those who advocated restoration of the original design of the park were opposed to reopening the swimming pool.[54]

Once Oak Park reopened, the Parks and Recreation Board began a significant effort to create new parks in African American neighborhoods, perhaps motivated by the desire to keep African American people from using the formerly white parks, most of which were in white neighborhoods. The park in the Western Hills urban renewal project was part of this effort to increase park space within African American neighborhoods. In 1969 the City Commission applied for $500,000 from the HUD to purchase a new 714-acre park on US 80, across from the city airport.[55] Mayor James, feeling pressure to also improve white neighborhoods, voted against the application because he favored a site in East Montgomery, but City Commissioners Cliff Evans and Jack Rucker preferred the airport site, which was accessible to African American residents on that side of the city. HUD staff rejected the funding because of public comments that Mayor James made against the site and because the city lacked a long-term plan for open space. They told the board to apply for funding for neighborhood parks serving low-income areas. Mayor James asked director of advanced planning J. Aronstein to apply for funding for twelve new neighborhood parks.[56]

In 1970 Aronstein hired planning consultant Urban Consultants Inc. to prepare a new parks and recreation plan. The top priorities, according to the plan, were to upgrade the parks that were in the worst condition.[57] Despite claiming that African American parks were equal to white parks just a few years earlier, in order to support the doctrine of "separate but equal," all the parks that were listed as most in need of improvement were formerly African American parks. Also in 1970, the city applied for federal funding to purchase five new neighborhood parks—all of them in African American neighborhoods—at Billingslea School, an African American school in North Montgomery near the Alabama River; Hale School, an African American school in North Montgomery; Hayneville Road on the Westside; Westwood-Westgate on the Westside; and the G. W. Smiley public housing project. While the Parks and Recreation Department upgraded playground equipment and built new parks for African American people, they also made a major investment in what would later become the Montgomery Zoo at the formerly whites-only Chisholm Park. City commissioners believed it was necessary to avoid being perceived by the white public as doing more for African American residents than they were for white residents, so improvements for things like parks in African American neighborhoods usually accompanied similar improvements for white people.[58]

Despite the desire to keep the races separate, the Parks and Recreation Board eventually determined that some of the measures for doing so were extreme. In 1970 the picnic tables were returned and the signs prohibiting picnics were removed from Oak Park. Nonetheless, the general racial motivations of the design and management of the parks remained. The parks still had no signs indicating that they were open to the public and desegregated. As a local news editorial said in 1970, "The development of present and planned parks are still too much motivated by racial reasons. . . . We consider it nothing less than deplorable that some city-owned playgrounds . . . including Oak Park and the big Cloverdale Park . . . still are not labeled with large signs indicating that they are public parks."[59]

## I-65 THROUGH THE ALABAMA RIVER PENINSULA

In 1968, after I-65 through the Westside and the Alabama River peninsula was approved, the AHD announced plans to acquire the entire 2,600-acre Alabama River peninsula north of the city, arguing that it needed to acquire the land to build the highway through it, because "a peninsula formed thousands of years ago is subject to flooding and, therefore, needs the protection of the State Highway Department."[60] The portion of the peninsula that was needed for construction of I-65 was just a fraction of the land that the AHD sought to acquire. After the interstate was constructed, only three hundred acres of land was needed on the peninsula for the highway right-of-way, but the AHD sought to acquire an additional 2,300 acres.[61]

The property owners, who were mostly white, didn't want to sell the land, arguing that the AHD wanted to acquire the peninsula to profit off it when the Alabama River became navigable. Landowners pointed out that if the AHD really wanted to protect the interstate, they could do so through easements, leaving the land in private ownership. Property owners believed that land values of the peninsula would increase when the river became navigable because it could be used for docks, recreation, or industry.[62] Belle Monsky, one of the property owners, told the *Montgomery Independent* that the proposal to acquire the entire peninsula was an illegal use of eminent domain and was, she noted, "nothing more than land grabbing, socialism, and political favoritism."[63] BPR documentation noted that acquisition of the entire peninsula was the AHD's decision—not the BPR's.[64]

Montgomery probate court judge Perry Hooper ruled against the use of eminent domain by the AHD to acquire the entire peninsula because the AHD failed to prove that it needed the land.[65] Several months later, the AHD acquired through eminent domain about 250 acres of the right-of-way for the interstate—not the entire peninsula.[66] At the same time, Alabama business leaders and congressional representatives pressured the BPR to build more exits from I-65 on the peninsula to encourage business development. Three government bodies—the Montgomery City Commission, the Montgomery County Board of Revenue, and the Central Alabama Regional Planning Commission—passed resolutions encouraging the BPR to provide more access to the peninsula to promote development of the wetland, revealing their interests in economic development at the expense of protecting the sensitive environment. The Montgomery County Board of Revenue's resolution noted that development of the land for industrial uses, recreation, docks, and storage would contribute to the tax revenue of the city and county.[67] The pressure from business leaders to develop the peninsula, just months after the unsuccessful effort by the AHD to purchase the land, may have substantiated the property owners' suspicions about the AHD's motives. It also reveals that planning for economic development was contrary to other public goals, in this case protection of a sensitive environment, and that public officials had not yet given up on their dreams of industrial development of the riverfront.

In September 1969 the AHD filed another court action against some of the property owners, including Belle Monsky, who owned much of the southern half of the peninsula, to acquire the entire peninsula to protect the highway from flooding. Judge Hooper again dismissed the lawsuit, noting that the case was almost identical to the previous attempt to acquire the land. Attorneys for the AHD did not appeal the decision, and the next month construction was underway for the I-65 bridge across the Alabama River onto the peninsula.[68]

## SCHOOL SEGREGATION RETURNS TO COURT

By 1968 only 550 African American students (out of about fifteen thousand) were attending formerly all-white schools in Montgomery, and no white students attended African American schools. Fifteen out of 1,365 teachers were teaching students of a different race, and almost all of them were at the high school level. The Montgomery Planning Department, under planning director J. Aronstein Jr., continued to use neighborhood planning to keep schools segregated. The school board assisted this neighborhood planning approach by improving and expanding only the schools in deeply segregated neighborhoods (white and African American) and did not improve any schools in racially mixed neighborhoods or near the edges of segregated neighborhoods.[69]

Newly constructed Jefferson Davis High School and Peter Crump and Southlawn elementary schools were in the middle of all-white neighborhoods and served only white children. At the same time, the school board expanded Hayneville Road Elementary School and Carver High School, located in deeply African American neighborhoods, which both served only African American children. Instead of building schools at the edges of segregated neighborhoods that would serve children from both races, the school board only expanded or built new schools that reinforced segregation and capitalized on the city's legacy of residential segregation.[70] Judge Johnson was aware of this practice, writing in a 1968 court decision, "One of the most aggravating courses of conduct on the part of the defendants and their agents and employees relates to the new Jefferson Davis High School. . . . The defendants in locating this school placed it in a predominantly white section of Montgomery. The evidence reflects that in determining the capacity of the school they approximated the number of white students residing in the general vicinity and constructed the school accordingly."[71]

To reinforce school segregation, the school board designated some all-white schools as "nontransported" when they were in walkable neighborhoods and could be accessed without using school bus services. Bus service was not available at the "nontransported" schools. These walkable neighborhoods, of course, were the result of decades of neighborhood segregation and planning the followed the neighborhood unit approach, which recommended keeping all heavy traffic out of neighborhoods that were built around a school. This reinforced school segregation because African American children did not live close enough to walk to schools that were located in the center of all-white neighborhoods.[72]

Because the school board failed to fully desegregate schools, and in fact increased the likelihood that schools would continue to be segregated in the future by constructing and expanding segregated neighborhood schools and removing bus services to some schools, Judge Johnson's court added more specificity to the 1966 desegregation plan. In 1968 the court added requirements regarding the number of faculty whose race was different from the majority in each school and a mandatory ratio of substitute teachers to teach in schools of both races, and other issues like night schools, student teachers, and integrated bus routes.

For the three newly constructed white schools, Judge Johnson Jr.'s court required that the school board send a letter to every parent of a child who was eligible to attend those schools with an application form for attendance. The court also determined that the construction of Jefferson Davis High School perpetuated the dual athletic system, so Johnson also required the school board to mail schedules of football practices to all male students. The school board was also required to provide transportation for anyone in the city to attend any school. The court wrote that the school board would be required to honor the school choice of every African American person unless there was a compelling circumstance provided to the court proving that they should not attend the school.[73]

The school board appealed the decision, focusing on the required five-to-one ratio for teachers of different races and the preference given to African American students to attend the newly constructed Jefferson Davis High School. Lawyers for the school board argued that teachers should not be required to take an assignment that they did not volunteer for. The appeals court disagreed, determining that it was the board's responsibility to desegregate—not the teachers'—so requiring teachers to take different assignments to achieve desegregation was acceptable. In regard to the issue of the numerical ratio of faculty of different races, however, the court agreed with the school board that the ratio of five-to-one white to African American faculty was too rigid and inflexible. The court modified the numerical ratio from five-to-one to "substantially" or "approximately" five-to-one to give the board more flexibility.[74]

The *Carr* parties appealed the weakening of the numerical ratio of teachers to the US Supreme Court, which reversed the decision back to Judge Johnson's original ratio of five-to-one.[75] Despite the specificity of Judge Johnson Jr.'s decision, in 1969 the district court determined that the 1966 freedom of choice plan—with the 1968 revisions—had not been effective in eliminating the racial dual school system in Montgomery, and it had no promise of eliminating segregation in the near future. The court ordered the US Department of Health, Education, and Welfare (HEW) to formulate a school desegregation plan for Montgomery by the beginning of 1970.

After the HEW plan was submitted to the court, the board of education proposed modifying it to establish neighborhood-based school zones to allow children to attend schools in their own neighborhoods and use a transportation system to bus kids from rural areas that were far from schools. The board also proposed closing several schools, including three all–African American schools—Hale Elementary, McDavid Elementary, and Booker T. Washington High School. The board's proposed modifications would result in no all-white schools and one all-African American school, Loveless Elementary School, in the heart of the Westside, in a deeply segregated neighborhood. The court accepted the modifications to the plan, and the *Carr* parties appealed.[76]

The appeals court determined that the plan was workable, writing that it was reluctant to modify the details of a desegregation plan. Attorneys for Carr argued that the school board sought to close three all–African American schools because the board wanted to avoid operating schools where white children were in the minority, and it wanted to place the burden of desegregation on African American children, making them travel to formerly all-white schools rather than making white children to do the opposite. However, the court determined that the school closures were proposed on a non-racial basis and approved the school closure plan.[77]

Thus, by the end of the 1960s, most schools had achieved minor desegregation, urban renewal was mostly over, the parks were open again, the interstate highways were mostly constructed, and activists had won most major desegregation lawsuits. City decisionmakers, however, continued to pursue segregation and white supremacy by other means. In 1967 the Alabama State Teachers Association (ASTA) lost a lawsuit to prevent Auburn University from opening a branch campus in Montgomery (Auburn University at Montgomery, AUM). The ASTA argued that the new branch campus would prevent ASU from becoming desegregated because white students in the region would attend AUM instead of ASU. ASTA lawyers argued that the new branch would also duplicate many classes and programs and consume state funding for higher education that could otherwise go to ASU. After the ASTA's loss in court, AUM opened the following year on Montgomery's eastern edge, providing an educational alternative for white college students in the city.[78]

# 10

## Planning in the Post–Civil Rights Era

DURING THE FIRST week of June 1969, two African American sisters, Annie Ruth Smith and Mary Louise Smith, tried to enroll their two children, Vincent and Edward Smith, in the YMCA's Camp Belser, a day camp located just outside Montgomery. Executive director William Chandler refused to accept their applications, telling the sisters that he did not have the authority to accept African American children and had never admitted an African American child to the camp. Chandler told the Smith sisters that he would confer with the YMCA Board of Directors and mail an enrollment decision to them within ten days.[1]

The Smith sisters had experience with civil rights activism. In 1955, two months before the start of the Montgomery bus boycott, Mary Louise Smith was arrested for refusing to give up her seat to a white passenger on a bus. After the arrest of Rosa Parks and the Montgomery bus boycott, Smith was one of the parties in the lawsuit that eventually desegregated the buses, *Browder v. Gayle*. She also participated in the March on Washington in 1963 and the Selma-to-Montgomery march in 1965.[2]

Bill Schultz, head of the Montgomery Council on Human Relations, who accompanied the Smith sisters when they tried to enroll their children in the camp, approached attorney Morris Dees at the Unitarian Universalist Fellowship of Montgomery, the only integrated church in the city, and asked him to represent the Smith sisters in a desegregation lawsuit against the YMCA. The case was significant because it challenged segregation in a private establishment. It also challenged the notion that upper-class white Montgomerians could maintain segregation by keeping private establishments segregated. Most of the desegregation battles to date had been waged over issues that were not proximate to wealthy white people, such as public transportation. Wealthy white citizens sent their children to private schools, so the issue of school integration did not affect them personally. When parks were closed and then integrated, they began recreating at private country clubs and the YMCA, which were both still segregated. Previous desegregation battles involved issues that were closer to the lives of lower-class white people, who composed the bulk of the KKK membership in the city. However, as Dees recalled, challenging wealthy white people was just as dangerous as challenging the KKK: "I knew a lawsuit against the Y would not sit well with most of the white folks in Montgomery, but I hadn't reckoned just how it would anger the country club set, the leading businessmen, and big landowners, many of whom sat on the YMCA's board. The case wasn't even three weeks old when these movers and shakers starting moving and shaking. And when they did, they quickly proved they could be just as dangerous and destructive as the Ku Klux Klan when they targeted an enemy."[3]

Because many of Montgomery's public institutions had begun desegregation, forced by federal court orders, wealthy white people fled to private institutions, including the YMCA and private schools, which they believed could maintain segregation. They also moved in increasing numbers to all-white suburbs. The YMCA was the last hope of preserving segregation for these wealthy white citizens, which included many elected officials. Dees recalled, "The Montgomery Y was an important symbol, an impenetrable fortress in the battle to hold on to the old, cherished Southern way; an educational, recreational, and most important, social institution that had managed to maintain segregation while many other institutions were forcibly integrated by Congress and the courts. Most whites reasoned that if the federal government could dictate how the Y—a private organization—operated, there would be no safe haven but the costly Montgomery Country Club and a handful of private dining clubs, and maybe those would fall next."[4] Despite integration of the parks, maintaining segregation of the YMCA allowed white members to swim in segregated pools and play on segregated sports teams, both of which were particularly sensitive issues for white people.

On June 11, 1969, the Smiths, represented by Dees, filed a case in Judge Johnson's court, asking it to prohibit the YMCA from operating segregated recreation programs. Ten days later, their children were accepted into the camp. Despite their acceptance, Judge Johnson allowed the case to proceed because other African American people could find themselves unable to go to the camp. The court wrote, "This post-suit change of heart, which is even more suspect in light of . . . [the YMCA of Montgomery's] showing of a long-standing practice of racial discrimination, strongly militates against a finding of mootness."[5]

During the legal process of exchanging information between parties ("discovery"), Dees uncovered the existence of a secret cooperative agreement that was established soon after the parks were closed, which gave the YMCA the authority to provide recreation for the city. The agreement established the YMCA as a quasi-governmental agency, meaning it constituted a place of public accommodation under the Civil Rights Act of 1964. The cooperative agreement was created and reviewed by a group of community center managers—the Community Center Council—in 1959 and reviewed again in 1965, and it was still in effect in 1970, after the parks reopened. The motivation of the cooperative agreement was obviously racial, as evidenced by a letter to the YMCA and Recreation Department employees in 1965 from Mayor James, calling for a meeting to discuss the agreement and reminding them not to invite African American people. He wrote, "I suggest that we do not include the Negro staff members or board members."[6]

In the years since the parks were closed and the cooperative agreement signed, the YMCA grew substantially. Although the Montgomery YMCA initially opened in 1869 and was segregated since then, there was just one small branch downtown with about one thousand members before the closure of the city parks and establishment of the cooperative agreement. Within two years of the agreement, it operated five branches and five swimming pools. By 1970 the YMCA of Montgomery operated six branches with eighteen thousand members. Four branches were in white neighborhoods with a white-only membership of a combined eight thousand members, one branch was in a racially mixed neighborhood with an all-white membership, and the Cleveland Avenue branch on the Westside had two thousand African American members and just fifteen white members. While the YMCA provided the funds for construction of the white branches, the African American community and the MIA donated $20,000 to construct the Cleveland Avenue branch, using donated funds that were leftover at the end of the bus boycott.[7] Outside the city, the YMCA operated the Prattville branch, located between African American and white neighborhoods, which had an all-white membership, and the camp branch, which consisted of Camp Rotary and Camp Belser, which had never had any African American members until the Smith children were accepted after the lawsuit was filed.[8]

Because the YMCA branches were almost entirely segregated, recreation within them was also segregated. The swimming program at the Cleveland Avenue branch had never had a white participant, and the swimming programs at the white branches had never had an African American participant. Programs with multiple YMCA branches participating from around the city, such as the Alabama Youth Legislature, maintained segregation and did not have any African American participants. All the participants in the citywide swim meet were white because the Cleveland Avenue branch was excluded from the meet. Segregation of the branches was amplified by the cooperative agreement between the YMCA and the Recreation Board because the agreement resulted in the YMCA's monopoly on recreation in the city when the parks were closed.

The YMCA's first argument to Judge Johnson's court was that their recreation facilities and educational activities were not purposefully segregated;

rather, they were segregated because of residential patterns in the city—the same argument used in school desegregation cases. Lawyers for the YMCA also argued that segregation was due to the personal preferences of individuals to recreate with members of their own race. Neighborhood planning and its implementation through policies for transportation, parks, public housing, infrastructure investment, and slum clearance had by then been working for decades to deepen segregation and ensure that boundaries for school zones and YMCA branches could be drawn along racial lines.

Despite city plans that established clear racial neighborhood boundaries, the facts of residential patterns in the city did not match up to YMCA's claims, because there was just one YMCA branch for African American people and three large (and some smaller) African American neighborhoods throughout the city, meaning the YMCA disinvested in African American neighborhoods just as city planners and other public officials did. Both the central branch and the Prattville branch, which were whites-only branches, had nearby African American neighborhoods to draw from, but the African American residents of those neighborhoods were members of the Cleveland Avenue branch located on the other side of town.[9]

Under the cooperative agreement, the Montgomery City Commission provided the YMCA with free water for its pools, and city employees paved YMCA parking lots with city-owned equipment and materials. After the parks were closed, the City Commission donated a park on Perry Street to the YMCA with the stipulation that the YMCA construct a recreation facility on the site within three years, which later became the central branch of the YMCA. Every elementary school was assigned to a YMCA branch for its recreation programming, and every predominantly white school was assigned to a white YMCA branch and every predominately African American school was assigned to the Cleveland Avenue branch, regardless of their location. Children from some African American schools had to pass by white branches to reach the Cleveland Avenue branch for school recreation. The court determined that the staff of the YMCA camps recruited only the children from predominately white schools.[10] Football was a sensitive issue for segregationists because they did not want to see African American football players beat white players in games, so each YMCA branch had an entirely segregated football team. White football teams played their playoff games at the city sports arena, the Cramton Bowl, and players from the Cleveland Avenue branch played at ASU.

Lawyers for the YMCA argued that even if their activities did amount to discrimination, they did not violate the Fourteenth Amendment's Equal Protection Clause, because it does not apply to private organizations such as the YMCA. Judge Johnson's court disagreed because the YMCA's activities had become so intertwined with governmental activities through the cooperative agreement that it was performing a "public function" and thus was subject to the constitutional limits of the Equal Protection Clause. The court also determined that the agreement was a direct effort to circumvent the court's earlier desegregation order for public parks.[11]

The decision of the court was comprehensive, similar to Judge Johnson Jr.'s other desegregation orders. The court forbade YMCA branches from excluding African American people from membership or participation, required construction of new branches in African American neighborhoods, required recruiting for YMCA programs in African American schools, and forbade the organization from excluding African American people from its board of directors or other governing bodies. A desegregation plan was required within thirty days, which would reassign schools to non-racially segregated branches, reassign at least one thousand members to integrated branches, and appoint African American representatives to the board of directors.

The YMCA immediately appealed, but the appeals court disagreed with all of the YMCA's contentions, except it did remove the requirement that the YMCA Board of Directors have a fixed ratio of African American members that corresponded with the racial composition of the city. By the time Judge Johnson Jr. decided the case, the YMCA Board of Directors had seventy African American members out of 285 voting members, a ratio that the appeals court determined was high enough for the possibility of more African American representatives to be elected to the board.[12]

## PARK DESEGREGATION RETURNS TO COURT

In 1970 attorneys Morris Dees and Solomon Seay Jr. were back in Judge Johnson's US District Court arguing that the City Commission and the Parks and Recreation Board failed to end racial segregation in parks and recreation when they reopened the parks. Dees and Seay argued that the public swimming pools in the city were available only to white residents and that parks had been reopened in a manner that avoided integration. At issue was $300,000 in federal funding for parks and $300,000 in matching funds from the Parks and Recreation Board, which activists wanted used for African American parks. The lawsuit claimed that while the board had created some new parks in African American neighborhoods, most of the new parks were planned and built "for white people's taste,"[13] with amenities such as tennis courts, softball fields, and golf courses. For example, the plan for Bruce Field, a new park that was under construction in Centennial Hill, was mostly tennis courts. Chisholm Park, on the north side, would include a golf course.

In the new court proceedings, pools and swimming were again a major issue. Like the YMCA desegregation case, many wealthy white people held segregated swimming close to their hearts and resisted desegregation longer than they did other issues like public transportation and public housing, which were less central to their lives. Integrated swimming pools also raised longstanding racist fears of white women and girls interacting with African American men and boys while wearing bathing suits. Accordingly, the activists claimed that the pools at Oak Park were closed and never reopened because white city officials did not want African American people sharing pools with white people, and no pools were planned for the new parks. The attorneys requested that the pools be reopened in Oak Park and a new pool constructed at Bruce Field instead of the planned tennis courts.[14] The case was settled with an agreement between the parties that would provide equal access to parks and recreation facilities, and it outlined new facilities and improvements to existing facilities.[15]

A few months later, the Montgomery Parks and Recreation Department asked Roger Brown, southeast regional director of the National Recreation and Park Association, to prepare a report on reorganizing the department, prior to the expansion of the board from five members to seven and the appointment of the first two African American members, Rufus Lewis and James Hall. The report detailed an odd organizational structure, which may have been designed to maintain segregation, with almost all staff—the maintenance superintendent, office staff, planetarium director, community center directors, and park supervisors—reporting directly to Harry Andrews, the superintendent of parks, instead of the heads of departments, which is the more typical structure. Not only was the organizational structure odd, but it was also cumbersome and inefficient, as Brown noted. The organizational structure allowed Andrews to maintain complete control of hiring, staffing, programing, and funding decisions across all units. The board also had a significant role in daily administrative functions of the Parks and Recreation Department.[16]

Brown recommended a diminished role for the board in the daily functions of the department and reorganization as a parks and recreation advisory board, with a policy-making and advisory function only, and no administrative functions. Only the chairperson the board would be allowed to communicate with staff. Brown recommended that the parks and recreation superintendent have full responsibility for hiring, dismissing, and programing (to which Rufus Lewis hand wrote in the margins of the report, "Not true"), with a diminished role for the board.[17] While the proposed changes may not have been racially motivated because they were more consistent with the role of other parks and recreation boards and would improve the efficiency and effectiveness of staff, the timing at the end of a decades-long desegregation struggle and just before the first African American members were appointed is curious.

Brown recommended uncoupling the school athletic program from the parks and recreation program. Because of the tie between school segregation and park segregation, the athletic programs of the schools were deeply intertwined with the parks and recreation program. The two agencies even had some joint staff, with school physical education teachers and coaches also working as Parks and Recreation Department coaches. This arrangement allowed the Parks and Recreation Department to keep athletics segregated as long as schools were largely segregated.[18] The board ignored this recommendation, and the two agencies remained connected until after a desegregation lawsuit was filed later that year.

On September 8, 1971, the original *Gilmore* group filed another lawsuit, asking Judge Johnson's court to prevent segregated private schools and other segregated groups from using city parks and recreation facilities. By then, Montgomery public schools were struggling with a major exodus of white students to suburban schools and private schools in the city. Private school enrollment in the city increased by 72 percent after school desegregation, from 39,524 during the 1968–1969 academic year to 68,123 during the 1970–1971 academic year. City commissioners hoped that making private schools in the city a viable and attractive alternative to integrated schools would prevent white families from moving to the suburbs.[19]

With the parks open again, the Parks and Recreation Board allowed whites-only private schools to use public sports facilities, pools, and parks, which undermined school and park desegregation orders because it made private segregated schools an attractive alternative to public schools. Allowing the segregated private schools to use parks and recreation facilities also generated financial savings for the private schools because they did not have to pay for the facilities. The *Gilmore* group also claimed that opening some of the parks avoided full integration because of a few reasons: their locations were not equally distributed among white and African American neighborhoods, the city discriminated in its employment practices, and the Parks and Recreation Board conspired with the YMCA of Montgomery to keep swimming and recreation programs segregated, referencing the *Smith* case.

On January 18, 1972, Judge Johnson Jr.'s district court issued its decision prohibiting the Parks and Recreation Board from allowing segregated schools, schools with discriminatory admissions policies, and other segregated groups from using parks and recreation facilities. Judge Johnson Jr. wrote that the Parks and Recreation Board provided aid to private segregated schools by giving them access to parks and recreation facilities, resulting in considerable financial savings because they didn't have to pay for football fields, gymnasiums, and other facilities. These facilities, provided by the city, made the segregated schools more attractive.[20]

On appeal, however, the US Fifth Circuit Court of Appeals reversed part of the decision, noting that the Parks and Recreation Board could allow segregated schools and other segregated groups to use its facilities if their use was nonexclusive.[21] That decision meant that as long as the Parks and Recreation Department allowed all private schools and groups to use park facilities, it could allow segregated schools to use them.

With the last vestiges of legal segregation coming undone, city officials still sought ways to avoid full integration of parks. Just a few months later, the YMCA and the Parks and Recreation Board initiated a program aimed at encouraging low-income youth to attend YMCA summer camp programs. In March 1972, YMCA of Montgomery director William Chandler proposed to Parks and Recreation Board chairman Jim Vice a revision of the summer camp and recreation program that YMCA provided for the Parks and Recreation Department. Chandler proposed a new affordable summer residential program subsidized by the Parks and Recreation Department, with increased staff, free transportation, reduced registration and craft fees, and free equipment such as sleeping bags, clothing, bathing suits, and towels. Chandler proposed recruiting for the program at schools, community centers, and public housing, which were still almost entirely segregated, and suggested that the program be used as a reward for good behavior and scholastics. He also proposed a similar subsidized day camp program for younger children, which would include free lunch and transportation and reduced craft fees, and a third subsidized day camp program at Cleveland Avenue YMCA, the African American branch.[22] While the new program was an expansion of youth programing, with the YMCA desegregated Chandler and Vice might have been hoping that African American children would attend the more affordable program, leaving the traditional programs for white children.

At the same time, the two new African American members of the Parks and Recreation Board, aided by the desegregation orders, were beginning have an impact on parks for African American people. Board minutes regularly included reports of efforts to comply with court orders. Following the 1971 settlement and Brown's report on reorganization, the board began to establish more community centers, starting with King Hill and Newtown Community Centers, both in African American neighborhoods, and expanded recreation programs, including a ceramics program at Loveless Community Center and a senior choral group at Carver.[23] Lewis and Hall visited community centers in African American neighborhoods across the city and established advisory councils in each one.[24]

Nonetheless, continued disinvestment in African American parks and recreation was significant, and desegregation was severely limited by the persistence of neighborhood segregation. Even with the increase in funding for parks and recreation facilities in African American neighborhoods, decades of past disinvestment had taken a toll on programming and facilities. At the

Newtown Community Center, for example, the building was in such disrepair that the recreation program could include only outdoor activities. The facility had no bathrooms, no water, and no female staff, so the programs were available only to boys. Likewise, there was no indoor space at McIntyre Community Center, near McIntyre Junior High School, which Judge Johnson's court had earlier determined was impossible to desegregate because it was located at the center of a deeply segregated neighborhood. Kiwanis Park was too small to accommodate many children, so Head Start programs had to use the park on alternate days.[25]

On October 15, 1973, the US Supreme Court noted the toll that decades of disinvestment had on parks and recreation facilities in African American neighborhoods when the *Gilmore* group petitioned the court for review of the decision allowing segregated groups to use parks. The Supreme Court agreed with the *Gilmore* parties that the policy of allowing segregated private schools to use parks and recreation facilities deprived the *Gilmore* group and other African American people of equal access to those facilities, when considered within the context of the 1958 park desegregation order, because the city had an obligation to provide affirmative remedies to past park segregation policies and practices. Affirmative remedies are actions that not only refrain from doing something but also take actions to rectify a situation. The court examined the legal history of both the *Gilmore* and *Smith* cases and determined that the actions of the city commissioners and the Parks and Recreation Board were an elaborate guise to undermine the desegregation order. The court's decision noted, "The city of Montgomery engaged in an elaborate subterfuge to anticipate and circumvent the court's order. Segregated recreational programs continued to be presented through the conveniently cooperating private agency of the local YMCA. All public swimming pools were closed allegedly to prevent the mixing of races. Facilities in Negro neighborhoods were not maintained equally with those in white neighborhoods . . . the exclusive use and control of city recreational facilities . . . by private segregated schools were little different from the city's agreement with the YMCA to run a 'coordinated' but, in effect, segregated recreational program. Such use and control carried the brand of 'separate but equal.'"[26]

Recognizing the important link between park segregation and school segregation, the court wrote that permitting private segregated schools to use parks and recreation facilities increased the attractiveness of those schools; allowed them to offer complete athletic programs, save money on athletics, and put those funds toward educational programs; and generated funding from concessions and ticket sales at public facilities. Those actions undermined the school desegregation order. The court wrote, "The city's actions significantly enhances the attractiveness of segregated private schools, formed in reaction against the federal court school order . . . this assistance significantly tended to undermine the federal court order."[27] In a five-to-four decision, the US Supreme Court prohibited the exclusive use of parks and recreation facilities by segregated schools.[28]

Three years later, in June 1976, the Montgomery Parks and Recreation Board asked Judge Johnson Jr.'s district court to dismiss the court desegregation order that had been in effect since 1958. The attorneys for the Parks and Recreation Board argued that the board exceeded the requirements of the court order when it built parks at Sheridan Heights, Hayneville Road, Newtown, and Twin Gates.[29] However, they still had not restored the pools at Oak Park, and integrated swimming remained a racially sensitive issue. A 1976 editorial in the *Montgomery Advertiser* speculated that the city's refusal to restore pools in Oak Park was because African American people would use them.[30] Nonetheless, the court agreed to end the desegregation order.[31]

## THE SLUM CLEARANCE ERA ENDS IN MONTGOMERY

As segregation of private and public parks and recreation facilities was coming to an end, the slum clearance era was also ending. After the city's three urban renewal projects were underway, Elizabeth Wright and the URA tried to pursue the subsequent stages of all three projects, but increasing criticism of the federal urban renewal program curtailed local plans for more comprehensive slum clearance. Although Congress tried to reform the program with the Housing Act of 1968, the reforms did little to improve the program. In 1972 the St. Louis Housing Authority began demolishing the large Pruitt-Igoe housing project that was built less than two decades earlier, and the failed project became an icon for the failed policy of urban renewal, marking the symbolic end of the urban renewal era. The program was formally terminated by President Nixon in 1973, and by that time planners in Montgomery were able to complete only the first phases of all three projects.[32]

Although city leaders, including staff at the MHA and URA, pursued slum clearance for decades to advance multiple goals, including economic development, downtown redevelopment, industrial development, neighborhood improvement, white supremacy, and racial targeting, those efforts were not strong enough to reverse urban decline in the face of suburban growth. The white population of Montgomery decreased from 66 percent to 60 percent between 1970 and 1980 (see table 2.1). Residential development also slowed, and between 1972 and 1976 Montgomery had an increase in occupied housing units of 13 percent, while nearby suburb Pike Road had an increase of 245 percent, and Mitylene had an increase of 616 percent.[33] Throughout the 1960s and '70s, employment in every nonmanufacturing category except government declined annually in the city.[34]

A major result of urban renewal and the decades that preceded it was not economic development, as city officials hoped. However, city officials' goals of increasing residential segregation of African American neighborhoods were accomplished. The goals of neighborhood improvement were also not successful, although from a physical determinist perspective, some of the buildings that were built were an improvement over the former development. However, urban renewal had a destabilizing effect on Centennial Hill and the Westside, with the economic condition of residents trending downward, leaving a social legacy of loss and community trauma.[35] As white people moved to the suburbs, African American neighborhoods expanded into formerly white areas in east and central Montgomery. Low-income African American people were pushed to live in and near public housing, and separate neighborhoods for middle-class African American people developed with little public housing, while white neighborhoods for all income levels developed without public housing.[36]

At the end of the urban renewal program, the city saw another pause in local civil rights marches, contributing to an end of the Biracial Committee on Community Affairs. In 1971 Carl Bear, the head of the white committee, concluded that it was not needed anymore, announcing, "Race relations are good enough locally that the committee isn't needed anymore." The head of the African American committee, W. E. Thompson, disagreed, arguing, "Meetings haven't been called due to a lack of initiative, not a lack of need . . . it was good to the extent that it really helped cool things off."[37] In 1972 the City Commission stopped requesting meetings of the Biracial Committee on Community Affairs and the executive secretary was cut from the city's payroll.[38]

As the urban renewal era ended, a renewed interest in the riverfront, focused on the river's economic development potential, emerged in Montgomery. In 1972 the Montgomery City Commission established a Riverfront Commission to develop a comprehensive plan for the riverfront. The major goals of the riverfront plan underscored the dual interests of developing industry along the river, improving recreation, and establishing the riverfront as a major landmark and civic center. Planners recommended the expansion of industrial uses in North Montgomery, improvements in the design of Riverfront Park, and better connections between the parks along the river and downtown. They also recommended the acquisition of other spaces for parks, including a proposed scenic overlook on Bell Street and a new river trail system. A proposal for designation of the entire riverfront as a historic district was also included in the plan.[39]

The plan designated most of the riverfront as blighted, except the developed area of downtown, including the African American residential neighborhoods that were surrounded by industrial uses north of downtown, which had been racially zoned decades earlier. Those homes, around the intersection of Leonora Street and Shady Street in what was then called the Riverview neighborhood, are what remained after the planners completed the North Montgomery slum clearance project. The effect of these combined projects, along with decades of disinvestment, drastically reshaped the neighborhood and led to its decline. By the time the neighborhood was designated blighted in the 1975 riverfront plan, it was surrounded by noxious land uses and a ramp to I-65 from the northern bypass. Nonetheless, it was one of the few residential locations in the city where people could live near the river. The plan recommended demolition of the neighborhood and its replacement with industrial uses, accompanied by increased code enforcement. Using code enforcement to implement the riverfront plan reflected planners' use of these basic laws, which were supposed to promote public health and safety, to advance their racial motivations and political agenda.[40]

## SCHOOL INTEGRATION PLANS IN QUESTION

The Montgomery County Board of Education's modifications of HEW's plan in 1970 remained in place until 1974—the longest stretch of time the case remained out of the court system—when Judge Johnson Jr.'s court ordered a new plan that focused on desegregating elementary schools because of changes in residential patterns, as more white families moved to the suburbs and African American families moved into formerly white neighborhoods. This neighborhood change resulted in increased residential segregation and thus the resegregation of elementary schools that had formerly begun to integrate. Three separate plans were proposed to the court. The first, proposed by the *Carr* parties, most effectively desegregated, but it was the most administratively complex because it would reassign the largest number of children to new schools and require extensive busing. The *Carr* plan paired white and African American elementary schools into clusters across the city, resulting in increased transportation for all but three schools, with many students traveling across town to attend school. Despite the shortcomings of the plan, it would create a system in which between 35 percent and 63 percent of the student body of each school would be composed of African American children.[41]

The second plan, proposed by the National Education Association, one of the parties in the case, and written by Dr. Larry Winecoff, a professor at the University of South Carolina, split the elementary grades into two schools and zoned schools in long strips from east to west through the city that were just four to six blocks wide but many miles long. It required extensive busing and reassignment of 70 percent of the children to different schools. The third plan, proposed by the school board, proposed closing many African American schools and building new schools, and avoided extensive busing. That plan, however, would result in higher levels of segregation than the other two plans, and ten schools would remain entirely segregated. But all students would at some point attend a desegregated school, because the plan did accomplish desegregation of the high schools and most of the junior high schools.[42]

Judge Johnson Jr.'s court determined that the plan proposed by the Montgomery County Board of Education should be implemented because it was the most stable for children. Judge Johnson emphasized that the schools that would remain segregated could not be desegregated in a workable manner due to residential segregation.[43] By this time, the board was guided by the desire to find a workable desegregation solution that would keep them out of court. However, white flight to the suburbs, private schools, and residential segregation made even the sincerest plans difficult. The difficulty of implementing genuine desegregation proved that the decades-long effort to keep schools and neighborhoods segregated had largely worked.

The court adopted a neighborhood proximity plan, proposed by the board, in which most children would attend the elementary school nearest to their home, even if that school was entirely segregated. Most of the junior high schools and all the high schools would be desegregated, with African American children composing more than 30 percent of the student body in every school, except McIntyre Junior High on the Westside, because it was in a deeply segregated neighborhood. Reflecting the use of highways and public housing to determine neighborhood boundaries, the court noted that school assignment did not have to be a precise mathematical distance; rather, it could be determined using "natural and man-made boundaries"[44] such as interstate highways, major roads, and large public housing developments.

The court's decision was consistent with other school integration cases throughout the South, where courts often allowed school segregation to continue if it were due to neighborhood segregation and not a racial school policy, ignoring the fact that it was often city officials who had deliberately segregated neighborhoods for decades. Judge Johnson's court cited *Hightower v. West*, from Fulton County, Georgia, where the US Fifth Circuit Court of Appeals determined that segregated schools were the product of residential segregation, and that routes of transportation, such as interstate highways, could form the boundaries of school zones, even if those school zones resulted in segregated schools.[45] The decision also relied on a 1971 US Supreme Court case from North Carolina, *Swann v. Charlotte-Mecklenburg Board of Education*, which recognized the role of neighborhood segregation in school segregation. As that court wrote, "In some circumstances certain schools may remain all or largely one race until new schools can be provided or neighborhood patterns change."[46] The decisions allowing school segregation to continue if it was the product of neighborhood segregation, however intentional, represented what city officials and the Montgomery County School Board had worked in the previous decades to achieve.

One year later, in April 1975, the *Carr* parties and the National Education Association appealed Judge Johnson's decision to the US Court of Appeals for the Fifth Circuit. The appeals court disagreed with Judge Johnson's decision and determined that a new plan for desegregation of elementary and junior high schools was needed. Recognizing the link between school segregation and neighborhood segregation, and implicating the school board for their role in both, the court ordered the school board and the lower court to come up with a plan that would include pairing white and African American schools that were across town, if no other method would work.[47]

The court was unconvinced by the school board's argument that white families would leave the city rather than send their children across town to an African American school, noting, "Nothing to achieve the constitutional mandate to desegregate can be avoided because of whimsy, white flight and fright, inconvenience, annoyance or any other actual or conjured excuse."[48] The court concluded that the school board's plans were a guise for maintaining a racially dual school system, noting, "We deal here with a school system whose roots were segregated by law. There is no indication that those roots have withered away, and that the racial separation in the present system is anything but the fruit of a tainted crop. The School Board still plans to cultivate its gardens separately; and it does not promise to integrate in any future season. Rather, its plan guarantees perennial one-race educational experiences for over a third of the black students within its elementary and junior high schools."[49] The board of education appealed to the US Supreme Court, which declined to hear the case.[50]

## CITY PLANNING AND THE 1974 NEIGHBORHOOD ANALYSIS

In 1974 the Montgomery Planning Commission adopted another neighborhood analysis using data from the 1970 census and a housing survey by the Montgomery Housing Code Department focusing on housing conditions and socioeconomic indicators. Like in previous decades, the goal of the Planning Commission was to improve economic development and neighborhood conditions. While the methodology and general format of the plan were similar to the previous two neighborhood analyses (1957 and 1965), it was strikingly different because it contained no plans for improvement in neighborhood conditions and no slum clearance plans. It also lacked some of the qualities of victim-blaming of low-income and African American residents for neighborhood conditions that the previous two plans contained. While it described disparities between African American and white neighborhoods, including a lack of indoor plumbing, it did not label residents as criminals. Nor, on the other hand, did it implicate the city's intentional infrastructure disinvestment in African American neighborhoods as the reason for neighborhood decline. Instead, the plan was more of a descriptive analysis, with no goals, objectives, or proposed actions for improving neighborhood conditions.

Despite the plan's perceived value-neutrality, the data revealed persistent socioeconomic problems among many people living in formerly segregated neighborhoods. Residents of the Westside and Centennial Hill had much lower scores in most social indicators than the east side and southeast Montgomery. Educational attainment in Cloverdale, the Garden District, and most of East Montgomery was above a 90 percent high school graduation rates, and the median number of school years completed was over thirteen. On the Westside, the median number of school years completed was around nine, and the high school graduation rate was lower than 30 percent, and in two census blocks it was just 18 percent. The historically segregated neighborhoods also had higher levels of poverty than white neighborhoods did. Centennial Hill and the Westside had median incomes under $4,660, with many residents below the poverty line. White census blocks, including the southern part of the Garden District and Cloverdale, had median incomes as high as $20,490 and poverty rates under 2 percent. Despite decades of slum clearance, housing conditions were deficient in African American neighborhoods, and 30 percent of the housing units on the Westside lacked indoor plumbing.[51]

During the period of white flight, the boundaries of African American neighborhoods grew into formerly white neighborhoods, but African American people largely remained segregated as white people moved to the suburbs and south and southeast Montgomery. The Westside remained 98.6 percent African American, and Centennial Hill was 87.4 percent African American. The African American areas initially expanded unevenly, and they began to fill in the space between Centennial Hill and the Westside, but not into East and southeast Montgomery. East Montgomery was still 100 percent white, and Cloverdale was 99.8 percent white in 1970.[52] The data revealed that the outcomes of decades of planning contributed to African American people remaining poor and disenfranchised and also that city decisionmakers of previous decades failed to realize that demolishing the homes of African American people made it more likely that they would move into predominantly white neighborhoods.[53]

# Conclusion

## People, Place, and Planning in Montgomery

The general argument presented in this book is that while city leaders in Montgomery pursued multiple planning goals, including neighborhood improvement, economic development, industrial growth, and reversal of outward development trends, white supremacy was a major part of planning throughout the mid-twentieth century. The plans and policies that were created and implemented in Montgomery reflected the pursuit of white supremacy in various ways: Sometimes white supremacy operated in the background, when policies and plans may not have had overtly racist intent but nonetheless had racially disparate outcomes, such as when city commissioners budgeted more funding for infrastructure in white neighborhoods than for infrastructure in African American neighborhoods. At other times, white supremacy was likely the central goal of plans and policies, such as when an interstate highway was rerouted through a stable middle-class African American neighborhood after a major civil rights direct action campaign by the residents. Likewise, the actors themselves—planners, elected officials, state and city staff, engineers, and others—while always motivated by multiple goals, ranged in their white supremacist beliefs, from progressives to racial extremists. While public officials pursued the multiple, sometimes conflicting goals of redevelopment of older central city neighborhoods, economic development downtown, industrial growth, riverfront development, and infrastructure investment, these goals were combined with officials' racial goals of residential segregation, school and park segregation, slum clearance, and targeting of civil rights activists.

Instead of using city planning to improve space and place for all people, city officials in Montgomery did the opposite—marginalizing people of color, keeping them segregated and poor, and disinvesting in their neighborhoods. As these public employees and elected officials advanced the economic interests of white businesspeople, African American residents were not just unintended and ignored victims; they were sometimes actively targeted. This theme isn't new or surprising, given the location and history of Montgomery. Many scholars have written about the paradox that city planning as a field was established to improve cities for the well-being of people but that city planners have actively worked to harm communities of color throughout its history.[1] Those planners relied on planning theories like the rational planning model and physical determinism to use data and analysis to justify their already desired ends.

Montgomery makes a notable case study of the use of planning to influence white supremacy, as it was the center of civil rights activism in the mid-twentieth century. While the work of activists like Rev. Dr. Martin Luther King Jr., Rev. Ralph Abernathy, Rosa Parks, Jo Ann Robinson, E. D. Nixon, and Rufus Lewis and the relationship of those activists and their activities to national politics are well known, what is often overlooked in that scholarship is a tie to home, place, space, and community. Understanding place, space, and community helps us understand critical issues of race, politics, and planning. It helps explain how people like Georgia Gilmore, a mother of six who lived at the edge of Oak Park, could fight to integrate the parks in the city and become a key fundraiser for the bus boycott, standing up to racial extremism for decades. Grounding activists like Gilmore in a physical place can give us perspectives on how they took solace in the nurturing and resilient African American communities in Montgomery, in the face of violent responses to activism from planners and other public officials.

Gilmore frequently took white children to Oak Park in her role as a nanny, but she could not take her own children to the park due to Montgomery's strict segregation laws. While her public role in desegregation is well known, what is less known is the fact that she also had to fight for basic, everyday city services in her Centennial Hill neighborhood, such as when city trash collectors refused to pick up her curbside garbage. While Rev. Dr. King adoringly gave Gilmore the nickname "tiny" and trusted her kitchen to become his unofficial meeting place, city officials declared her neighborhood a slum and built an interstate highway within blocks of her home. The white press mocked her body and her everyday struggle for basic city services. Reporter Gene Kovarik wrote, "A hefty negro woman who weighted in excess of 230 pounds was fined $25 today in city court on charges of cursing at a diminutive white garbage truck driver. R. M. Shaw, who didn't appear to weigh more than 140 pounds, testified that Georgia Gilmore, 41, called him an s.o.b. when he refused to pick up a trash can of dirt while loading garbage on a city truck at her home. . . . The truck driver stated that the defendant told him, 'you pick it up for those damn white folks, so you damn s.o.b. pick it up for me.'"[2]

Activists like Gilmore were both a product of and proof of the local context from which they emerged. Gilmore's story, and the story of other activists in Montgomery, is deeper than issues of constitutional rights, court-ordered desegregation, presidential decrees, and violent civil unrest that consumed national headlines when Montgomery emerged as the unofficial birth place of the civil rights movement. Their homes and communities were central to their activism. Activists resisted city officials' efforts to demolish their homes but also took city planning in their own hands due to the failures of government institutions. When Gilmore lost her job for testifying at the bus boycott trial, she could not depend on local government to provide small business assistance to help her open a restaurant, so MIA executive secretary Solomon Seay Sr. asked the MIA to help fund her restaurant, writing, "Miss Georgia Gilmore is demonstrating the same fighting spirit she has had since the beginning of the struggle. The project she is now sponsoring is the result of having lost her job. I recommend that a committee be appointed to see what can be done to get her better established."[3] Activists like Gilmore emerged from the resiliency and beauty of community and place in the close-knit, intimate neighborhoods of Montgomery. White supremacist planning, and activist reactions to it, was an integral part of the people and place of Montgomery.

## CITY PLANNING AS WHITE SUPREMACY IN MONTGOMERY

From the infancy of the emerging field of city planning in the 1920s, city officials in Montgomery constructed a system that was based on racial extremism, and a system in which racial objectives operated in the background and in the foreground. White supremacy was not only a byproduct or an unintentional side effect of city planning; it was sometimes a central organizing principle. From the earliest days of the establishment of institutions like the MHA, the Alabama River navigation project, the URA, the AHD, the Montgomery Planning Commission, and the Montgomery City Planning, Community Development, and Parks and Recreation Departments, white supremacy was foundational to the city's major institutions. Hired staff, including planning consultants Urban Consultant Associates, Jack Knight, Elizabeth Wright, Sam Engelhardt Jr., and hundreds of others, pursued major urban goals such as economic development, industrial growth, infrastructure improvement, and neighborhood improvement with varying degrees of racist intent—from unintended racial consequences to deliberate acts of racial extremism.

City planning that had racist intent and racial consequence, no matter the degree, was often decidedly bad planning. Not only did it arise from ill intent, but it also failed to achieve many of its major objectives—even those objectives that were not malevolent—such as economic development. City leaders' aspirations of capitalizing on the strategic position of their location on the Alabama River, hoping to grow Montgomery's industrial base, were never realized. For decades, planners hoped to make the river navigable to realize these economic goals, which never came to fruition because the geology and geography of Alabama made them impossible.[4]

When faced with the crisis of white flight to the suburbs, the physical decline of older neighborhoods, and an unrelenting housing crisis brought about by neighborhood disinvestment and residential segregation spanning several decades, city officials responded with cures that inevitably did more harm than good. What city officials failed to recognize when they demolished the homes of African American families, whether for the purposes of neighborhood improvement, public health, economic development, displaying their white supremacist power, or punishing civil rights activists, was that neighborhoods, whether healthy or depressed, are crucial for the economic stability of cities. City officials in Montgomery also failed to recognize—or simply didn't care—that a failure to provide adequate public services to segregated neighborhoods would ultimately lead to neighborhood decline. Instead, they blamed residents for issues like density, congested streets, and poor-quality infrastructure, relying on racist notions of racial difference to define neighborhood characteristics.[5]

The unfounded and racist blame that city officials placed on African American people shifted over time as their goals changed. In the 1920s public officials blamed the poor quality of African American neighborhoods on people who were in poverty and those with large families, ignoring the lack of economic opportunity and education and the fact that many of the recent rural-to-urban migrants were former sharecroppers. As the twentieth century progressed, the narrative shifted to accusing African American people of having poor morals, being unclean and lazy, or being predators of white women and girls. City officials blamed a host of urban problems like public health, crime, fires, and traffic congestion on African American people, often ignoring their own disinvestment and lack of attention to these issues in segregated neighborhoods.[6]

While pursuing their economic development goals, the conservativism of the city's white business elite, as well as civil rights activism, probably saved some of the housing and neighborhoods in the city. Montgomery's first neighborhood analysis, completed in 1957, was just a survey of neighborhood conditions—not a comprehensive plan. The city's first comprehensive plan, completed in 1963–1965, didn't include a house-by-house analysis. It was not until 1965, with adoption of the neighborhood analysis, that Montgomery had a legal basis to use eminent domain to demolish African American neighborhoods on a large scale. Planners didn't adopt the first comprehensive plan until decades after many other cities and didn't begin the first comprehensive urban renewal project until 1968, and by then urban renewal was already being criticized nationally. In contrast, Birmingham had its first comprehensive plan in 1919, and another plan published in nine volumes between 1958 and 1961, which included a comprehensive neighborhood analysis and plans for slum clearance. Those plans allowed city planners in Birmingham to begin their first urban renewal project fifteen years before Montgomery planners began their first project.[7]

Nonetheless, city officials ignored—or did not understand—the fact that the impacts of their policies would result in African American residents leaving their demolished neighborhoods for white and racially mixed neighborhoods, thereby contributing to neighborhood change. After legal segregation ended, African American people whose homes were demolished increasingly moved to formerly white neighborhoods. As other scholars have noted, slum clearance had direct and indirect spillover effects on long-term neighborhood racial composition.[8]

City officials' use of planning theories such as the neighborhood unit approach allowed them to achieve multiple urban goals, such as traffic improvement and neighborhood walkability. These approaches also provided fiscal savings by colocating parks and schools, and accomplished racist goals of maintaining and strengthening neighborhood segregation. These early planning decisions later proved useful to school board attorneys in school integration lawsuits because the practice of residential segregation, strengthened by the use of neighborhood planning principles, was also effective at keeping schools and parks segregated.

Montgomery's place as the center of persistent and effective advocacy was established long before the bus boycott. Madison Park, the City of St. Jude, and the city's segregated neighborhoods fostered activism that became well known nationally with the start of the bus boycott. It was Montgomery's place as the center of civil rights activism that delayed implementation of plans and also led white people to push for more drastic policies and plans that targeted African American neighborhoods. Montgomery mayor Gayle suggested that the Montgomery bus boycott was the reason to delay accelerating slum clearance in the 1950s, and perhaps the civil rights activities of the 1960s, including the Freedom Rides, lunch counter sit-ins, the Selma-to-Montgomery march, and school desegregation equally distracted city officials from quick action on other projects. The agenda for the Biracial Committee on Community Affairs was sidelined by the Selma-to-Montgomery march just two months after it began work. Likewise, the freeway revolt, led by middle-class civil rights activists, protracted the highway planning process for a decade.

Although comprehensive slum clearance plans for Montgomery were not fully implemented, they reveal important insights into the motivations of city officials. The city's first urban renewal project was for downtown redevelopment, and the other two had no public housing component but demolished low-income African American housing and replaced it with housing for people with moderately higher incomes. These projects reveal that economic development and white financial interests were a major motivation of planning in the city, and housing the very poor was not. At the same time, the desire to curb potential political power of African American activists and civil rights activism was another major motivation for planning. While activism delayed city planning, planning may have been a direct response to it. Some projects targeting African American neighborhoods were announced within weeks of major direct action civil rights campaigns, often targeting the leaders of those campaigns.

While public officials created Montgomery's second ghetto by strengthening residential segregation instead of abolishing it, they blamed African American people for many of the problems that city officials themselves largely caused.[9] Emblematic of that false blame is the introduction to a report from the MHA and URA, which, in poetic fashion, outlined the city's urban renewal, public housing, and slum clearance activities:

*A Tale of Two Montgomery's*
Montgomery grew without a plan.
Like most American cities it grew in a more-or-less random manner,
building by building,
street by street,
for the most part subject only to the vagaries of private speculation.
(Which proved in almost every case to be pitifully inadequate and short-sighted.)
We had no housing code, building code, electrical code, plumbing code, or permit department.
Nevertheless, for some of us Montgomery grew into a lovely city.
With paved streets, modern sewerage, comfortable homes and adequate recreational facilities.
But for many thousands of others Montgomery became an unspeakable horror.
They lived in a Second Montgomery.
Homes little more than hovels.
Drafty, twisted, leaking, unpainted shacks.
Without water, sewerage, or indoor toilets.
Rat-infested, dirty, and disease-ridden.
Most of them rented—from landlords who as businessmen would not make improvements where they could expect little or no return on their invested capital.

For most of the low-income, virtually uneducated citizens of this
Second Montgomery, there was no one to turn to for aid.
And no place to go.[10]

## RACIST PLANNING BEYOND THE MID-TWENTIETH CENTURY

The racist planning foundation that was built over decades persisted beyond the mid-twentieth century, when media attention shifted away from Montgomery and the civil rights movement. While the plans and policies changed, becoming more opaque as legal segregation ended, federal funding programs established requirements for community and citizen participation, communicative planning models replaced rational planning, and equity planning approaches replaced physical determinism. Congress passed laws such as the Civil Rights Act, but racialized planning did not end overnight. As planning practice moved toward community-centered methods and away from physical determinism, racialized planning very slowly began to give way to more equitable models in the coming decades. Planners shifted away from their deceptive reliance on the rational scientific method, which hid the fact that planning was a highly political act. However, the community-oriented planning approaches that emerged developed slowly, and sometimes community-centered approaches were equally deceptive, hiding the fact that sometimes citizen participation can be window dressing. Racialized city planning didn't stop with the end of legal segregation; it evolved.

The community centers that Lewis and Hall established when they joined the Parks and Recreation Board eventually became neighborhood service centers in the 1970s in every public housing development except Riverside Heights, which was integrated in the late 1960s but remained mostly white. The advisory committees for the community centers became neighborhood service center advisory committees for the new Montgomery Community Action Agency, part of the War on Poverty and the US Economic Opportunity Act of 1964.[11] These advisory committees operated under a system that city planners today refer to as manipulation, according to activist and planner Sherry Arnstein's classic 1969 article, *A Ladder of Citizen Participation*. In her article, Arnstein developed a typology of citizen participation ranging from citizen control, at the top of the ladder, to manipulation, at the bottom. Manipulation as a form of citizen participation came into vogue during the urban renewal era, according to Arnstein, when people of color were asked to join advisory committees, but, as Arnstein writes, it was white city officials who "educated, persuaded, and advised the citizens, not the reverse."[12] Beyond the urban renewal era these manipulation techniques were used by planners in the form of community action committees. As Arnstein continues, "This style of nonparticipation has since been applied to other programs encompassing the poor. Examples of this are seen in Community Action Committees (CAC) which have created structures called 'neighborhood councils' or 'neighborhood advisory groups.' These bodies frequently have no legitimate function or power. The CACs use them to 'prove' that 'grassroots people' are involved in the program."[13]

Although African American participation in political institutions had a major positive effect on programing, manipulation as citizen nonparticipation was sometimes used not to empower African American neighborhood people or to repair past harms from decades of racist city planning but to blame them. As coordinator of Montgomery's neighborhood service centers R. W. Pringle Jr. wrote, "The Neighborhood Service Centers Advisory Councils are being used as a base to organize the local communities to strengthen the ability of the poor to help themselves."[14] White leadership of the Montgomery CACs, a program established during the 1960s War on Poverty, blamed African American residents and communities through their advisory councils for the lack of improvements and infrastructure in their neighborhoods. For example, in a three-year plan that identified problems in various neighborhoods, the cause of the lack of play areas was determined to be a "lack of interest and coordination," and the problem of "organization of indigent groups" was caused by a "lack of concentrated effort."[15]

African American people reacted to the anti-poverty work of the CACs in a variety of ways. Some, like Rufus Lewis, Fred Gray, and Charles Langford, joined the board of directors and worked from within the system to create positive change. The committees had a lot of success and supported Head Start programs, food pantries, infrastructure improvements, summer youth employment programs, and other initiatives. However, these programs also reinforced segregation. The Head Start program had almost entirely African American children and teachers, and some activists complained that it was perpetuating school segregation. Only one-third of the board of directors of the CACs were neighborhood residents, while the other two-thirds were government agency staff, representatives of private organizations, and special interest groups. Others, such as Rev. Richard Boone, openly challenged the white leadership of the Montgomery CAC by picketing their meetings to demand an African American director, fair wages for African American janitors and staff at neighborhood service centers, and that residents to be allowed to "handle their own problems."[16]

Also reflecting citizen participation as manipulation, the Montgomery Police Department started an Operation Pride program in 1971 to encourage citizens to improve their neighborhoods. City officials remained aware that the white public was cynical of any hint that African American people were receiving more public benefits than they were, so they began the Operation Pride program to encourage residents to improve their neighborhoods themselves.

As director of public relations, R. A. Reeves told the press that Operation Pride would receive no public funds: "The purpose of the project is to instill pride in the people of the community to improve their conditions. There are no public funds involved and the people do the work themselves with the assistance of various city departments."[17] Through Operation Pride, the police department hosted clean-up events throughout the city's African American neighborhoods. Operation Pride is a classic example of planners manipulating communities and blaming residents for decades of neighborhood disinvestment, relying on unequipped citizens to tackle the major problems that stemmed from decades of neighborhood neglect. As one newspaper article described, "The rain fell heavy and wet but did not deter them [residents] from turning out in full force, from three-year-old children with homemade rakes and hoes to elderly women carrying shovels. They started to work cleaning one of the most overgrown lots in the area which was filled with tons of rusted cans, bottles, bed springs, old cars, skeletons of animals and other debris."[18] What programs such as Operation Pride obscured was that residents of neighborhoods that had been subject to disinvestment for decades were ill-equipped—using homemade rakes and shovels—to make the kind of neighborhood improvements necessary to reverse decades of decline. By using these tactics, city decisionmakers hoped to show African American residents that they were paying attention to their struggles, while demonstrating to white residents that the African American people and neighborhoods were not worthy of public investment.

Using their experience from decades of resiliency and living in disinvested and racially targeted neighborhoods, African American people found that their local organizing capacity also grew more sophisticated beyond the mid-twentieth century. In 1971 a group of African American residents formed a cooperative local development company. One of the first priorities of the company, headed by board president Joseph Dickerson, who later served on the Montgomery City Council, was development of a shopping plaza to help anchor the struggling Westside business district.[19] Members of the group also had plans to form a buying club to purchase from wholesale businesses.[20] Although low funding hindered the group's success, it represented the growing sophistication of residents and a community-led capacity.

In 1972 local economic development consultant Riley Lewis Jr. wrote a comprehensive report for the Western Hills Trade Association, an organization formed by the remaining African American business owners in the once-thriving Westside business district that was all but destroyed by interstate highway construction and urban renewal.[21] Lewis determined that Westside businesses experienced up to a 70 percent loss in sales because of the closure of thirteen streets when the interstate highway was built, eliminating foot traffic in the area and relocating 1,859 families away from the Westside. Lewis predicted that some 60 percent of the remaining businesses would soon close, and flooding, litter, dust, and noise from the interstates were constant problems. The group requested that the Westside be declared a federal economic disaster area, part of the 1969 federal Disaster Relief Act.[22] While Montgomery planning director J. Aronstein Jr. supported the federal declaration, noting that many of the pre-interstate residents did not return after the interstates were built because of "transportation problems,"[23] and Montgomery mayor Jim Robinson and Governor George Wallace wrote letters of support for the declaration to President Nixon, the effort was ultimately rejected by federal agency staff.[24] The Westside business group tried in earnest to draw customers back to the area through community festivals, raffles, construction of off-street parking, and historic preservation efforts.[25] In the coming decades, however, most of the remaining businesses closed.

Construction of I-65 severed the connection between the residents of the Westside, downtown, and the shopping districts east of the interstate. Before construction of the interstate, the residential neighborhoods of the Westside supported 280 small businesses—many of them African American-owned—along Cleveland, Holt, Oak, Jefferson Davis (now Fred D. Gray Avenue), and Mobile Streets. By 1974 there were just 186 businesses left, with 85 percent of them in financial distress. Many residents of the Westside were unable to access the shopping districts on the east side of the interstate because of a lack of transportation. One report noted, "Their customers, whose main means of transportation was shoe leather, who were not dislodged from their homes were, in many instances, isolated from the stores by the concrete moat of the interstate."[26]

Like on the Westside, the interstate highway disconnected ASU from its historic residential neighborhood and drastically altered land uses and land values along the highway. In 1978 a group of elderly homeowners who lived adjacent to I-85 in Centennial Hill requested that their homes be rezoned from residential to office and commercial because they were unable to sell their homes. The neighborhood had become less desirable because of I-85. According to a newspaper account, "Traffic generated by the interstate and Jackson Hospital has ruined the area for quiet living."[27]

As the mid-twentieth century gave way to the 1970s and 1980s, city planners continued to prioritize the needs of white neighborhoods, although the rigid boundaries of neighborhood segregation subsided. As African American residents moved into formerly white urban neighborhoods, white residents left the city altogether, moving to all-white suburbs. As schools became integrated, white flight to the suburbs increased, and they became resegregated through neighborhood segregation. City planners continued to target areas for improvement that were not the most in need. By then, planners directed

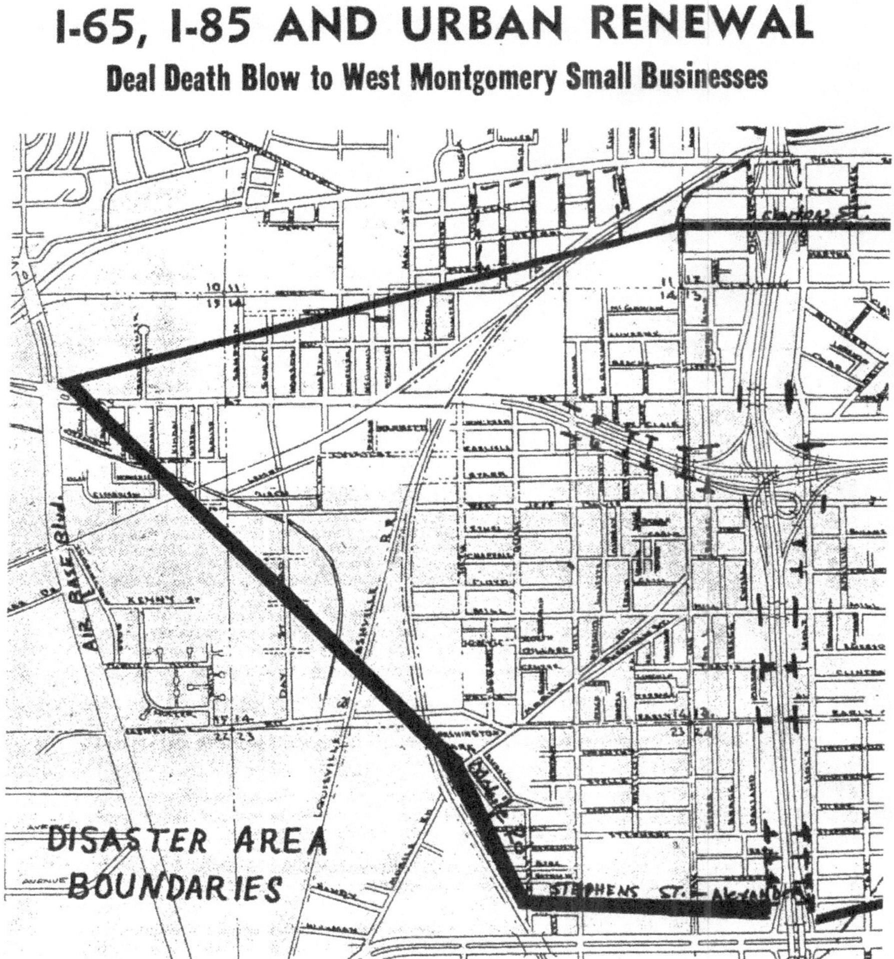


Figure C.1. This is a flyer distributed by Riley Lewis Jr. to gain support for a federal declaration of economic disaster for the Westside business district. (From: Riley Lewis, Jr., I-65, I-85 and Urban Renewal: Deal Death Blow to West Montgomery Small Businesses, October 1972, Riley Lewis, Jr., Collection, Trenholm State Community College Archives, Montgomery, Alabama.)

Figure C.2. This image shows the African American Westside residential and business district (foreground) that remained after city planners and highway engineers routed I-65 and the I-65/I-85 interchange through the neighborhood and cut off residents from downtown and the rest of the city. Downtown and the Alabama River can be seen in the background of this photograph, with the I-85/I-65 interchange at the center. (John Engelhardt Scott Collection, March 23, 1973, file Q79109, Alabama Department of Archives and History, Montgomery, Alabama.)

funding to the white neighborhoods of Cloverdale and East Montgomery and passed over African American neighborhoods for funding. In 1977, after complaints to the HUD and an unsuccessful lawsuit by African American city councilperson Joe Reed Sr., HUD advised the Montgomery Community Development Department to reallocate federal funding and put it toward low-income neighborhoods. In that case, city officials wanted to spend about $3.5 million from the 1977–78 Housing and Community Development Act on downtown development, parks in East Montgomery, and sidewalks in Cloverdale. Charles Straub, southern regional director for the HUD, pressured city officials in Montgomery to allocate the funds for infrastructure and park improvements on the Westside, sidewalks in North Montgomery, and a grant program for indoor plumbing for the elderly.[28]

In 1983 a group of citizens sued members of the Montgomery City Council for using Community Development Block Grant funds to construct sidewalks in neighborhoods that were not blighted, and a federal district court agreed. In 1985 the chairperson of the city board that recommended projects for the HUD and Community Development Block Grant funding, Bert Estes, quit the board after white members of the Montgomery City Council refused to pass a resolution encouraging the HUD to extend funding for the program.[29]

The Montgomery Parks and Recreation Department continued to increase the amount of park space in the city. In the 1970s and 1980s, the MHA, working with the Parks and Recreation Department, created new city parks in existing and new public housing developments, although the location of some of the new parks within deeply segregated neighborhoods failed to achieve integration. Nonetheless, a statewide assessment of park needs revealed that the decades-long closure of the parks had curtailed the growth of parks, which was difficult to overcome.[30]

In 1989 residents of Cleveland Court presented the MHA board with a petition to rename the development the Rosa L. Parks Complex.[31] At the same time, residents complained about crime and drug activity and urged the MHA to clean up the development. MHA staff responded by writing a letter to HUD secretary Jack Kemp to request assistance and funding for landscaping and renovations. When the HUD and MHA failed to invest significant funds in the project, the MHA supported resident clean-up campaigns and social events, persisting in their championing of citizen nonparticipation and manipulation.[32]

In 1996 activists began organizing the Montgomery portion of the Selma to Montgomery Voting Rights March National Historic Trail. In September 1997 Riley Lewis Jr., who had previously worked as a consultant for the Western Hills Trade Association, was hired to consult on the project.[33] The Alabama Department of Transportation (ALDOT) completed a master plan for the trail, and local activists were interested in planning to improve economic development along a one-mile corridor from West Jeff Davis Avenue and Oak Street to Five Points at Goldthwaite Street. Activists and Lewis eventually submitted a proposal to ALDOT that included new voting rights archives, commercial development, gift shops, heritage businesses illustrative of the community that was uprooted by the I-65/I-85 interchange, and bed-and-breakfasts in homes of civil rights activists who were active in the movement. The proposal, named *The Auspicious Prosperity Mile*, was intended to revitalize the commercial districts of the Westside, preserve and interpret the history of the community, and provide a platform for social and civil rights.[34] The Alabama National Historic Trail Foundation applied for funding from the National Endowment for the Humanities to implement the plan, but the funding was denied.[35]

Lewis and the group requested federal assistance through the federal Enterprise Zone program, and ALDOT included the proposal in their master plan. The plan was adopted in 1999, and one year later the Alabama National Historic Trail Foundation was created, with the West Montgomery Development Corporation as part of the foundation. The foundation immediately proposed a series of important projects, many of which were not completed because of a lack of funding. The first project was to stabilize Mount Zion A. M. E. Zion

Church, which had a partially collapsed roof by 2001.[36] Another project included construction of a memorial wall to honor Loveless School alumni at the Loveless School site. The foundation tried unsuccessfully to get the Alabama Historical Commission to purchase the Ben Moore Hotel, Victor Tulane Building, and the Greyhound bus station downtown, but the last was the only project to receive federal funding, after the foundation and the Alabama Historical Commission received assistance from Congressman John Lewis.[37]

Into the 1990s the Montgomery City Council pursued aggressive annexation of nearby eastern and southeastern white suburbs. Annexing white suburbs would help ensure that the racial balance continued to be tipped in favor of majority-white leadership, as white flight left the city more densely populated by African American people. By 2000, however, the rapid annexation was being met with stiff resistance from suburbanites, who preferred to remain in nearby Pike Road and other suburbs and send their children to suburban schools. In 2000, for the first time since 1900, African American residents outnumbered white residents by four thousand people in the city.[38]

Planning during the late twentieth century was a transition period from racialized and white supremacist planning to a community-oriented planning model. The projects of this period suggest a rocky transition from the 1970s to the 2000s. As city planning transitioned away from its roots in white supremacy in all its various forms and toward more authentic community planning, the city continued to struggle with the unmet goals of earlier decades, including economic and industrial growth and combating competition from the suburbs.

Despite the shift back to a majority–African American city, many problems remain, most of them stemming from planning of earlier decades. In 2015, 71 percent of the housing units in Centennial Hill were renter occupied, and the median household income was just $12,843.[39] Buildings in both Centennial Hill and the Westside were characterized by high vacancy and poorly rated structures in the city's 2040 comprehensive plan.[40] The end of legal school segregation after the *Carr* decision was not the end of school segregation as a lived experience for many children. The end of legal segregation of parks and recreation after the *Gilmore* and *Smith* decisions was not the end of racial disparities in access to parks, recreation, sports, and greenspace. The idea of constitutional equality as defined by the federal court system became characterized largely as a reaction to Jim Crow and legal segregation, and that therefore meant a corresponding blindness to neighborhood segregation. Nonetheless, despite the end of legal segregation, the Montgomery public school system remains a largely segregated experience for many children.[41]

Today, the City of St. Jude retains its campus on the Westside and all the original buildings. The hospital was converted to affordable housing in 1992, though it closed in 2023; the social center has offices and a museum; and the church and school are still in operation. The campus is listed on the National Register of Historic Places. St. Jude demonstrated what white support for civil rights could look like, at a time when such support was unheard of. St. Jude's importance to the Westside remains significant, and its growth from its aspirational principles of integration was demonstrative of the potential end of segregation decades before that dream became a reality. It also demonstrated a potential role for white clergy in the civil rights movement, subsequently taken up by figures such as Robert and Jean Graetz. Nonetheless, St. Jude is separated from the rest of the city by I-65.

In a 2018 interview with the *Montgomery Advertiser*, Montgomery resident Skip Jackson revealed the impact of the interstates next to his home, noting, "As they built the interstate we could no longer walk across, we had to get in the cars and go across the interstate. So it became a whole different lifestyle. Whereas everything we were used to going to that was convenient to us was actually cut off. And then after that, as it slowly rang into the '80s from the late '60s, early '70s, early '80s, all the businesses that were up there, other than the washerette and the butcher store, everything else began to close out. . . . We became not an identifiable neighborhood, but we became a cut off entity."[42]

## WORKING FOR ANTI-RACIST PLANNING IN MONTGOMERY

Today, little physical evidence remains of the once-thriving African American neighborhoods that were demolished by planners and public officials in Montgomery to advance the interests of white businesspeople in their pursuit of economic growth. If a tourist to the city wanted to visit the original clinic that Father Purcell established when he arrived in Montgomery (338 Holt Street); homes of the members of the Women's Political Council: Irene West (713 S. Jackson Street), Jo Ann Robinson (713 Thurman), Mary Fair Burks (1215 Tuscaloosa Street), and Thelma Glass (2784 W. Edgemont Avenue); ASU professors H. Councill Trenholm (1001 Thurman Street) and Charles Dunn (612 Thurman Street); or hundreds of other activists, they couldn't because all of their homes were demolished through slum clearance, construction of the Interstate Highway System, or other city plans or ordinances.[43]

Despite this lack of physical evidence of the neighborhoods from which the civil rights movement emerged, today's city planners, public officials, and activists in Montgomery have turned away from white supremacist city planning. City planners in Montgomery are charting a new course for community vibrancy, using planning methods that empower communities, building on the resiliency of generations of residents and neighborhoods. Together, planners and residents are working to create places of joy within all the neighborhoods of the city and overcome decades of white supremacist power and hate.

The years 2018–2020 marked a pivotal turn for city planning in Montgomery, with the election in 2019 of the city's first African American mayor, Steven Reed, who pledged to transform Montgomery into an equitable, progressive, and compassionate city. In 2020 the Montgomery Planning Commission and the Montgomery City Council adopted the Envision Montgomery 2040 comprehensive plan—the city's first post–segregation era comprehensive plan, and the result of three years of authentic public engagement and healing that began with a gathering of hundreds of community members on the ASU campus in 2018. The plan is filled with strategies to repair past harms and stop the perpetuation of harm by supporting people, investing in connections, progressing toward shared prosperity, and building great places.[44]

The construction of the National Memorial for Peace and Justice in 2018 by the Montgomery-based Equal Justice Initiative and its director, Bryan Stevenson, began to heal the history of racial injustice in the city and redefine the narrative of race in America. The memorial sits on a six-acre site just northeast of the intersection of I-85 and I-65, in a neighborhood that was formerly declared a slum, on a hill overlooking downtown. The memorial provides a sacred and contemplative space to reflect on the history of racial injustice in Montgomery and allows visitors to overlook the landscape that was built from a fusion of decades of white supremacy and African American activism and resilience. Nearby, the Freedom Monument Sculpture Park, located near the former city dump that abutted an African American neighborhood, and the Legacy Museum, located downtown, draw thousands of visitors to the city each year. Many of these visitors report having a transformational experience from visiting the spaces. The memorial, sculpture park, and the museum challenge the narrative of racial difference, an idea that gave rise to the ideology of white supremacy, which was central to city planning in Montgomery. At the same time, the memorial and museum give hope to generations that are working to build an anti-racist future.

# Notes

## *Introduction*

1. Alabama State University (ASU) was established in 1867 in Marion, Alabama, as Lincoln Normal School. When it moved to Montgomery in 1887, it was renamed Normal School for Colored Students. In 1929 the college was renamed State Teachers College. In 1948 it was renamed Alabama State College for Negroes. In 1954 it was renamed Alabama State College. In 1969 it was renamed Alabama State University, which is the name today. For clarity, this book refers to it as Alabama State University (ASU) throughout, except in quotations. See Jelani M. Favors, *Shelter in a Time of Storm: How Black Colleges Fostered Generations of Leadership and Activism* (Chapel Hill: University of North Carolina Press, 2019); Joseph Carver, *From Maron to Montgomery* (Montgomery, AL: New South Books, 2020); Karl E. Westhauser, Elaine M. Smith, and Jennifer A. Fremlin, eds., *Creating Community Life and Learning at Montgomery's Black University* (Tuscaloosa: University of Alabama Press, 2005).

2. Steven Millner, "Interview with E. D. Nixon" in *Martin Luther King, Jr. and the Civil Rights Movement*, ed. David J. Garrow (New York: Carlson Publishing, Inc., 1989), 545–51.

3. Rev. Dr. Martin Luther King Jr., "Annual Address of Dr. M. L. King, Jr., Delivered at the First Annual Institute on Non-Violence and Social Change under the Auspices of the Montgomery Improvement Association," December 3, 1956, RALC, TSCC, 1.

4. Fred Gray, *Bus Ride to Justice* (Montgomery, AL: The Black Belt Press, 1995); Belinda Robnett, *How Long? How Long? African American Women in the Struggle for Civil Rights* (New York: Oxford University Press, 1997); Kent Spriggs, ed., *Voices of Civil Rights Lawyers: Reflections from the Deep South, 1964–1980* (Gainesville: University Press of Florida, 2017); Jo Ann Robinson, *The Montgomery Bus Boycott and the Woman Who Started It: The Memoir of Jo Ann Gibson Robinson* (Knoxville: University of Tennessee Press, 1987).

5. Sharon Gay Pierson, *Laboratory of Learning: HBCU Laboratory Schools and*

*Alabama State College Lab High in the Era of Jim Crow* (Lausanne, Switzerland: Peter Lang Inc., 2013).

6. Charles Connerly, *The Most Segregated City in America: City Planning and Civil Rights in Birmingham, 1920–1980* (Charlottesville: University of Virginia Press, 2005); Bobby Wilson, *America's Johannesburg: Industrialization and Racial Transformation in Birmingham* (New York: Rowman and Littlefield Publishers Inc., 2000); Bobby Wilson, *Race and Place in Birmingham: The Civil Rights and Neighborhood Movements* (New York: Rowman and Littlefield Publishers Inc., 2000); Christopher MacGregor Scribner, *Renewing Birmingham* (Athens: University of Georgia Press, 2002); Tracy Neumann, *Remaking the Rust Belt: The Postindustrial Transformation of North America* (Philadelphia: University of Pennsylvania Press, 2016).

7. Susanna Delfino and Michele Gillespie, *Global Perspectives on Industrial Transformation in the American South* (Columbia: University of Missouri Press, 2005).

8. For information on the varying degrees of white supremacist ideologies and how those ideas were expressed in municipal politics, see J. Mills Thornton III, *Dividing Lines: Municipal Politics and the Struggle for Civil Rights in Montgomery, Birmingham, and Selma* (Tuscaloosa: University of Alabama Press, 2002).

9. Density, low-income neighborhoods, and race had long been associated with public health. See J. H. Rauch, *Public Parks: Their Effects upon the Moral, Physical, and Sanitary Condition of the Inhabitants of Large Cities, with Special Reference to the City of Chicago* (Chicago, IL: S. C. Griggs, 1869); Julie Sze, *Noxious New York: The Racial Politics of Urban Health an Environmental Justice* (Cambridge, MA: MIT Press, 2007); Natalia Mokina, *Fit to be Citizens? Public Health and Race in Los Angeles, 1879–1939* (Los Angeles: University of California Press, 2006). For information on the polio epidemic in Montgomery, see "Polio Strikes Eleven of Fourteen Family Members," *Alabama Tribune*, January 9, 1953, 1; "Rules are Set in Polio Fight, Plans Outlined," *Montgomery Advertiser*, June 29, 1953, 1.

10. Census blocks 11 and 12, US Census of Population and Housing, 1960.

11. US Census of Population and Housing, 1960.

12. Alexander von Hoffman, "Housing and Planning: A Century of Social Reform and Local Power," *Journal of the American Planning Association* 75, no. 2 (2009): 231–44; Raymond Mohl, "Race and Housing in the Postwar City: An Explosive History," *Journal of the Illinois State Historical Society* 94, no. 1 (2001): 8–30; Jeffrey Helgeson, "The State of Blame in American Cities: Race, Wealth, and the Politics of Housing," *Journal of Urban History* 37, no. 6 (2011): 992–99.

13. US Census of Population and Housing, 1960.

14. Joe Azbell, "City Limits," *Montgomery Advertiser*, October 18, 1954, 20. For another example of developers trying for many years to build African American

housing, see "Hearing Set April 7 on Negro Subdivision," *Alabama Journal*, March 17, 1964, 13.

15. Stephen Grant Meyer, *As Long as They Don't Move Next Door: Segregation and Racial Conflict in American Neighborhoods* (New York: Rowman and Littlefield, 2000); Amanda Seligman, *Block by Block: Neighborhoods and Public Policy on Chicago's West Side* (Chicago: University of Chicago Press, 2005).

16. "Exchange Club to Hear Tyson," *Montgomery Advertiser*, April 8, 1964, 17; "Montgomery Area Chamber Elects Nine Men to Board," *Montgomery Advertiser*, November 18, 1967, 8.

17. Roberta Reisig, "Family in Montgomery Forced to Move from One Temporary Home to Another," *The Southern Courier*, October 22–23, 1966, 4.

18. Roberta Reisig, "Negroes Fight a Losing Battle for Good Housing," *The Southern Courier*, October 22–23, 1966, 4.

19. Wright made this claim when federal officials tried to help African American people in the city find housing through a Federal Housing Authority veterans housing program. See Reisig, "Negroes Fight," 4.

20. Reisig, "Negroes Fight," 4.

21. For more information about the class rivalries among people living in these neighborhoods, see J. Mills Thornton, *Dividing Lines: Municipal Politics and the Struggle for Civil Rights in Montgomery, Birmingham, and Selma* (Tuscaloosa: University of Alabama Press, 2002). See also Solomon Seay Jr., *Jim Crow and Me: Stories of My Life as a Civil Rights Lawyer* (Montgomery, AL: New South Books, 2008); Belinda Robnett, *How Long? How Long? African American Women in the Struggle for Civil Rights* (New York: Oxford University Press, 1997); Morris Dees, *A Lawyers Journey: The Morris Dees Story* (Chicago, IL: American Bar Association, 2001); James Cobb, *Away Down South: A History of Southern Identity* (New York: Oxford University Press, 2005); James Cobb, *The South and America Since World War II* (New York: Oxford University Press, 2011); Vicki Crawford, Jacqueline Anne Rouse, and Barbara Woods, eds., *Women in the Civil Rights Movement: Trailblazers and Torchbearers, 1941–1965* (New York: Carson Publishing Inc., 1990); Kent Spriggs, ed., *Voices of Civil Rights Lawyers: Reflections from the Deep South, 1964–1980* (Gainesville: University Press of Florida, 2017); Richard Pride, *The Political Use of Racial Narratives: School Desegregation in Mobile, Alabama, 1954–1997* (Chicago: University of Illinois Press, 2002); Tinsley Yarbrough, *Judge Frank Johnson and Human Rights in Alabama* (Tuscaloosa: University of Alabama Press, 1981); Vivian Gunn Morris and Curtis L. Morris, *The Price They Paid: Desegregation in an African American Community* (New York: Teachers College Press, 2002); and Fred D. Gray, *Bus Ride to Justice: Changing the System by the System* (Montgomery: Black Belt Press, 1995).

22. Gray, *Bus Ride to Justice*, 7.

23. Mary Stanton, *Journey toward Justice: Juliette Hampton Morgan and the Montgomery Bus Boycott* (Athens: University of Georgia Press, 2006); Anne Permaloff and Carl Grafton, *Political Power in Alabama* (Athens: University of Georgia Press, 2008); Gene Howard, *Patterson for Alabama* (Tuscaloosa: University of Alabama Press, 2008); Carl Grafton and Anne Permaloff, *Big Mules and Branchheads: James E. Folsom and Political Power in Alabama* (Athens: University of Georgia Press, 1985); Solomon Seay Jr., *Jim Crow and Me: Stories of My Life as a Civil Rights Lawyer* (Montgomery, AL: New South Books, 2008); James Cobb, *Away Down South: A History of Southern Identity* (New York: Oxford University Press, 2005); James Cobb, *The South and America Since World War II* (New York: Oxford University Press, 2011); Vicki Crawford, Jacqueline Anne Rouse, and Barbara Woods, eds., *Women in the Civil Rights Movement: Trailblazers and Torchbearers, 1941–1965* (New York: Carson Publishing Inc., 1990); Kent Spriggs, ed., *Voices of Civil Rights Lawyers: Reflections from the Deep South, 1964–1980* (Gainesville: University Press of Florida, 2017).

24. Jo Ann Robinson, *The Montgomery Bus Boycott and the Woman Who Started It* (Knoxville: University of Tennessee Press, 1987), 7–8.

25. Major Larry Edward Kangas, "Historical Picture of Maxwell AFB," *Report No. 86-1340* (Montgomery: Air Command and Staff College Air University, 1986), 10.

26. Kangas, "Historical Picture."

27. Jeanne Theoharis, *The Rebellious Life of Mrs. Rosa Parks* (Boston, MA: Beacon Press, 2013), 28.

28. Reisig, "Negroes Fight," 4.

29. Reisig, "Negroes Fight," 4.

30. Reginald Isaacs, "The 'Neighborhood Unit' Is an Instrument for Segregation," *Journal of Housing* 5, no. 8 (1948): 215–19, 215; American Public Health Association Committee on the Hygiene of Housing, *Planning the Neighborhood* (Chicago: Public Administration Service, 1948); Reginald Isaacs, "Are Urban Neighborhoods Possible?" *Journal of Housing* 5, no. 7 (1948): 177–80; Henry Churchill, "An Open Letter to Mr. Isaacs," *Journal of the American Institute of Planners* 13, no. 3 (1948): 40–42; Charles Herrick, "Activities and Comment the Neighborhood Theory an Answer to Mr. Isaacs," *Journal of the American Institute of Planners* 14, no. 3 (1948): 38–40; Seymour Stillman, "Neighborhood Unit Planning: A Useful Method for City Planning," *Journal of the American Institute of Planners* 14, no. 3 (1948): 42–43; Max Wehrly, "Activities and Comment: Comment on the Neighborhood Theory," *Journal of the American Institute of Planners* 14, no. 3 (1948): 32–34; Joseph Allaire, *Neighborhood Boundaries*, Planning Advisory Report No. 141 (Chicago, IL: American Society of Planning Officials, 1960).

31. Reisig, "Family in Montgomery," 4. A 1974 list of voter registration officials listed a Maxine Kimbrough as a clerk working with the voter registration board, although it is not clear if it is the same Maxine Kimbrough who moved from house to house in 1966. A person named Maxine Kimbrough was listed on the voter registration rolls in 1966. See "Legal Notice," *Alabama Journal*, May 23, 1975, 10. Maxine Kimbrough's dream of continuing her education may have come true in 1967. In a newspaper article in the *Alabama Journal* in 1967, a person named Maxine Kimbrough was pictured along with other African American graduates of Carver's Evening School, an adult education program. See "Carver's Evening School Graduates," *Alabama Journal*, December 12, 1967, 17.

32. Aldon Morris, Walter Allan, David Maurrasse, and Derrick Gilbert, "White Supremacy and Higher Education: The Alabama Higher Education Desegregation Case," *National Black Law Journal* 14, no. 1 (1994): 59–91.

33. Arnold Hirsch, *Making the Second Ghetto: Race and Housing in Chicago, 1940–1960* (New York: Cambridge University Press, 1983); Simon Balto, "White Rage, White Liberals, and the Making of the Second Ghetto," *Journal of Urban History* 46, no. 3 (2020): 511–15; Roger Biles and Mark Rose, "At the Intersection of Race, Class, Gender, and Highway Politics," *Journal of Urban History* 46, no. 3 (2019): 677–84; Mark Rose and Roger Biles, "Arthur Rubloff and the Grinding Politics of Renewal in Chicago, 1947–1986," *Journal of Urban History* 46, no. 6 (2020): 1341–367; Thomas W. Hanchett, *Sorting Out the New South City: Race, Class, and Urban Development in Charlotte, 1875–1975* (Chapel Hill: University of North Carolina Press, 1998); Roger Biles, "Expressways before the Interstates: The Case of Detroit, 1945–1956," *Journal of Urban History* 40, no. 5 (2014): 843–54; Eric Avila, *The Folklore of the Freeway: Race and Revolt in the Modernist City* (Minneapolis: University of Minnesota Press, 2014); Charles Connerly, *The Most Segregated City in America: City Planning and Civil Rights in Birmingham, 1920–1980* (Charlottesville: University of Virginia Press, 2005); Bobby Wilson, *America's Johannesburg: Industrialization and Racial Transformation in Birmingham* (New York: Rowman and Littlefield Publishers Inc., 2000); Bobby Wilson, *Race and Place in Birmingham: The Civil Rights and Neighborhood Movements* (New York: Rowman and Littlefield Publishers Inc., 2000); Thornton III, *Dividing Lines*; Joseph Dimento and Cliff Ellis, *Changing Lanes: Visions and Histories of Urban Freeways* (Cambridge, MA: MIT Press, 2014); Christopher Silver, *Twentieth-Century Richmond: Planning, Politics, and Race* (Knoxville: University of Tennessee Press, 1984).

34. Bryan Stevenson often makes this point in speeches and interviews. See, for example, Emma Seslowsky, "Bryan Stevenson Says 'Slavery Didn't End in 1865, It Just Evolved,'" CNN Politics, The Axe Files, December 7, 2018, accessed April 5, 2023;

Liz Mineo, "The Need to Talk about Race," The Harvard Gazette, December 7, 2017, accessed October 11, 2023; Jamie Lowe, "Bryan Stevenson Wants the US to Face Its History," *New York Times Magazine*, January 16, 2019, accessed October 11, 2023. See also Bryan Stevenson, *Just Mercy: A Story of Justice and Redemption* (Washington, DC: Spigel and Grau, 2014).

## *Chapter 1*

1. Equal Justice Initiative, "Slavery in America: The Montgomery Slave Trade," accessed August 16, 2024.

2. An additional seventy free African American people lived in Montgomery County. US Bureau of the Census, "1860 Census of Population and Housing," US Census, accessed February 14, 2022; Equal Justice Initiative, "Slavery in America"; James Sellers, *Slavery in Alabama* (Tuscaloosa: University of Alabama Press, 1950).

3. William J. Mahoney Jr., "As I See It," *Montgomery Advertiser*, May 6, 1956, 9.

4. Mahoney Jr., "As I See It."

5. "'Partnership' at Millers Ferry," *Birmingham News*, April 14, 1960, 1; "Coosa River," n.d., PISF, ADAH.

6. For example, see Southeastern Regional Planning Commission, *Development Study of the Alabama-Coosa Basin Area: Prospectus* (Atlanta, GA: Southeastern Regional Planning Commission, 1943).

7. Andrew Wiese, "Places of Our Own: Suburban Black Towns Before 1960," *Journal of Urban History* 19, no. 3 (1993): 30–54; Thomas Healy, *Soul City: Race, Equality, and the Lost Dream of an American Utopia* (New York: Metropolitan Books, 2021); Harold Rose, *Black Suburbanization: Access to Improved Quality of Life or Maintenance of the Status Quo?* (Cambridge, MA: Ballinger Publishing Company, 1976); Carter Godwin Woodson, *The Rural Negro* (New York: Russell and Russell, 1969); Harold Rose, "The All-Negro Town: Its Evolution and Function" *Geographical Review* 55, no. 3 (1965): 362–81.

8. By the end of World War II, the city was 61 percent white and 40 percent African American. All population figures are from the US Bureau of the Census, "Census of Population and Housing," US Census, accessed February 15, 2021. See J. Mills Thornton III, *Dividing Lines: Municipal Politics and the Struggle for Civil Rights in Montgomery, Birmingham, and Selma* (Tuscaloosa: University of Alabama Press, 2002); Talitha LeFloura, *Chained in Silence: Black Women and Convict Labor in the New South* (Chapel Hill: University of North Carolina Press, 2015); Peter Levy, *The Civil Rights Movement* (Westport, CT: Greenwood Press, 1998); and Wayne Flynt, *Alabama in the Twentieth Century* (Tuscaloosa: University of Alabama Press, 2004).

9. Eric Motley, *Madison Park: A Place of Hope* (Grand Rapids, MI: Zondervan and Harper Collins, 2017).

10. "Negro Attacks Alabama System," *Southern Watchman*, January 15, 1944, 5.

11. "Chapter of Engineers Meets Monday Night," *Montgomery Advertiser*, April 9, 1922, 9.

12. There are conflicting accounts of the date the first zoning ordinance passed. Some reports place the date at 1929, and a WPA report from 1941 places it in 1928. According to a newspaper article in *The Times: Montgomery, ALA*, the first ordinance was passed on June 24, 1924, and administered by Montgomery building inspector F. A. Gillette. The ordinance was amended by the Montgomery City Commission on April 25, 1925, and August 15, 1926. See "Zoning Law Is Passed; Fruit Stands Must Go," *The Times: Montgomery, ALA*, June 24, 1924, 1; "An Ordinance," *Montgomery Advertiser*, Aug 15, 1926, 10; W. F. Day memo to Mr. Bane, February 5, 1941, RG 187, NA2; "Montgomery Will Set Up City Planning Commission," *Alabama Journal*, July 16, 1946, 1; "Ask New York Zoning Experts Aid with Montgomery Problem," *Montgomery Advertiser*, February 6, 1924, 3; "Zoning Ordinance Sweeps Sidewalks Clean of 'Stands,'" *Montgomery Advertiser*, March 21, 1924, 1; "Validity of City Zoning Ordinance Comes Under Fire," *Montgomery Advertiser*, September 2, 1924, 1. Capitol Heights, which was not then part of the city of Montgomery, established zoning in February 1924. See "Zoning Law up in Capitol Heights," *Montgomery Advertiser*, February 14, 1924, 7.

13. "City Planning Board Favored by Engineers," *Montgomery Advertiser*, April 11, 1922, 7.

14. Herbert Gans, *The Urban Villagers* (New York: Macmillian Co. Inc., 1982); Herbert Gans, *The Levittowners* (New York: Columbia University Press, 2017); Edward Goetz, Rashad A. Williams, and Anthony Damiano, "Whiteness and Urban Planning," *Journal of the American Planning Association* 86, no. 2 (2020): 142–56.

15. "On Making Dexter Avenue Beautiful and Comfortable," *Montgomery Advertiser*, May 28, 1927, 4.

16. Jon Peterson, "The City Beautiful Movement: Forgotten Origins and Lost Meanings," *Journal of Urban History* 2, no. 4 (1976): 415–34; Robert Wrigley, "The Plan of Chicago: Its Fiftieth Anniversary," *Journal of the American Institute of Planners* 26, no. 1 (1960): 31–38.

17. Raymond Mohl, "Trouble in Paradise: Race and Housing in Miami during the New Deal Era," in *The Making of Urban America*, ed. Raymond Mohl (Wilmington, DE: SR Books, 1988), 214-227; Bobby Wilson, *America's Johannesburg: Industrialization and Racial Transformation in Birmingham* (New York: Rowman and Littlefield Publishers Inc., 2000); and Christopher Silver, "The Racial Origins of Zoning: Southern Cities from 1910–40," *Planning Perspectives* 6, no. 2 (1991): 189–205.

18. Roger Biles, "The Urban South and the Great Depression," *Journal of Southern History* 56, no. 1 (1990): 71–100; Marion Clawson, *New Deal Planning* (New York: Resources for the Future Press, 2011); Gail Radford, *Modern Housing for America: Policy Struggles in the New Deal Era* (Chicago, IL: University of Chicago Press, 1996).

19. Charles Abrams, *The Future of Housing* (New York: Harper and Brothers, 1946); Radford, *Modern Housing*; Melvyn Dubofsky and Stephen Burwood, eds., *The Great Depression and the New Deal* (New York: Garland, 1990); Edward Goetz, *New Deal Ruins: Race, Economic Justice, and Public Housing Policy* (Ithaca, NY: Cornell University Press, 2013); Amanda Coleman, "Rehabilitating the Region: The New Deal, Gender, and the Remaking of the South," *Southeastern Geographer* 50, no. 2 (2010): 200–217; Kevin Fox Gotham, "Racialization and the State: The Housing Act of 1934 and the Creation of the Federal Housing Administration," *Sociological Perspectives* 43, no. 2 (2000): 291–317; Jeff Manza, "Political Sociological Models of the U.S. New Deal," *Annual Review of Sociology* 26, no. 1 (2000): 297–322; Raymond Mohl, "Trouble in Paradise: Race and Housing in Miami during the New Deal Era" in *The Making of Urban America*, ed. Raymond Mohl (Wilmington, DE: SR Books, 1988), 214–27; Bobby Wilson, *America's Johannesburg: Industrialization and Racial Transformation in Birmingham* (New York: Rowman and Littlefield, 2000); Christopher Silver, "The Racial Origins of Zoning: Southern Cities from 1910–40," *Planning Perspectives* 6, no. 2 (1991): 189–205.

20. Kenneth Jackson, "Federal Subsidy and the Suburban Dream: The First Quarter-Century of Government Involvement in the Housing Market," *Columbia Historical Society Records* 50 (1980): 421–51; "Race, Ethnicity, and Real Estate Appraisal: The Home Owners Loan Corporation and the Federal Housing Administration," *Journal of Urban History* 6, no. 4 (1980): 419–52; and *Crabgrass Frontier: The Suburbanization of the United States* (New York: Oxford University Press, 1985). See also Todd Michney and LaDale Winling, "New Perspectives on New Deal Housing Policy: Explaining and Mapping HOLC Loans to African Americans," *Journal of Urban History* 46, no. 1 (2020): 150–80; Todd Michney, "How the City Survey's Redlining Maps Were Made: A Closer Look at HOLC's Mortgage Rehabilitation Division," *Journal of Planning History* 21, no. 4 (2021): 316–44; Heather MacDonald, "City Planning and the U.S. Census: 1910–1960," *Journal of Planning History* 7, no. 4 (2008): 263–94; Amy E. Hillier, "Residential Security Maps and Neighborhood Appraisals: The Home Owners' Loan Corporation and the Case of Philadelphia," *Social Science History* 29, no. 2 (2005): 207–333; David Freund, *Colored Property: State Policy and White Racial Politics in Suburban America* (Chicago, IL: University of Chicago Press, 2007).

21. The first draft of the map was prepared by state appraiser Norman W. Gayle and revised by B. Frank Noble, an appraiser from Montgomery. The map was analyzed and approved by Arthur Mead, president of a real estate firm; Howard Copeland, owner of Copeland Insurance Agency; Theo Copeland, former secretary of the Montgomery Real Estate Exchange and then a property management field inspector for HOLC; James Holt, a real estate broker; Junaus Holt, a realtor; and Peter Nicrosi, a realtor and brother of William Nicrosi. See Morgan, "Report of Study," 25.

22. *Lucas v. South Carolina Coastal Council*, 505 U.S. 1003 (1992).

23. One B-rated block at Cleveland and Fairview was adjacent to a D-rated block. However, the B-rated block was vacant.

24. Mohl, "Whitening Miami."

25. Alec C. Morgan, "Report of Study, Montgomery Alabama, for the Division of Research and Statistics, Home Owners' Loan Corporation, Washington, D.C.," March 15, 1937, RG 195, NA2.

26. Morgan, "Report of Study," 41.

27. Morgan, "Report of Study," 30.

28. Morgan, "Report of Study," 41.

29. Compare, for example, the redlining map with a map showing the racial composition of the city in 1950: Montgomery City Planning Commission, Neighborhood Map 1950, Auburn University Archives Map Collection, Auburn, Alabama. See also Glenn Saunders, "Names of Streets Can Be Deceptive," *Montgomery Advertiser*, June 6, 1965, 16. Examples of these small enclaves are along Clay Street near Whitman Street, the alley near Mildred Avenue and Morgan Street, Cromwell Street near Perry Street, and Julia Street near McDonough Street. Morgan noted that he expected these African American "quarters" to eventually be demolished. He wrote, "the only detrimental influence affecting the F areas is the location of about four blocks of negro improved property in F-2. The buildings in this particular block are in poor condition and will undoubtedly be demolished if the areas is eventually developed into high-class residential subdivisions." See Morgan, "Report of Study," 43.

30. For example, Morgan noted that 50 percent of the homes in D-5 used surface toilets. See Morgan, "Report of Study," 42.

31. Benjamin Wilson, "It's Not Just Zoning: Environmental Justice and Land Use," *Urban Lawyer* 49, no. 4 (2017), 717–26; Patricia Salkin, "Environmental Justice and Land Use Planning and Zoning," *Real Estate Law Journal* 31 (2003), 429–48.

32. For example, see Urban Consultants Inc., *A Land Use Plan for Montgomery: Part of the Comprehensive City Plan* (Montgomery, AL: Montgomery City Planning Commission, 1965).

33. Individual letters attesting to the HOLC map and report were written by

Harry Douville, R. W. Chalker, B. Frank Noble, Theo Copeland, T. N. Steagill, Howard Copeland, Junius Smith, and Peter Nicrosi (William Nicrosi's brother). See H. E. Cox, "Letters from Personnel in the Atlanta Region regarding Montgomery, Alabama, Sent to Division of Research and Statistics by Regional Manager," September 29, 1938, RG 195, NA2.

34. Morgan, "Report of Study," 41.

35. C. B. Swope, D. Hernández, L. J. Cushing, "The Relationship of Historical Redlining with Present-Day Neighborhood Environmental and Health Outcomes: A Scoping Review and Conceptual Model," *Journal of Urban Health* 99 (2022), 959–83; Emily E. Lynch, Lorraine Halinka Malcoe, Sarah E. Laurent, Jason Richardson, Bruce C. Mitchell, Helen C. S. Meier, "The Legacy of Structural Racism: Associations between Historic Redlining, Current Mortgage Lending, and Health," *SSM—Population Health*, vol. 14 (2021), 1–10.

36. Paterson Court was named after William B. Paterson, who founded a school for African American children near the development, which eventually led to the development of ASU. The name Riverside Heights was chosen for the white project because, as Calvert noted, "the idea that its rather pretentious character would make it more attractive in the eyes of the class of people which this project is expected to house." See Louis Calvert to A. R. Clas, August 15, 1935, RG 196, NA2, 1. See also Chief of Branch 1 to Director of Housing, September 5, 1935, RG 196, NA2, 1; "Thurman Street Slum Replacements Named 'William B. Paterson Courts'" *Montgomery Advertiser*, August 31, 1935, 1; "Second PWA Slum Clearance Project Opens in Montgomery, Ala., Fix Rents," *Chicago Defender*, January 23, 1967, 6. For a list of people who were displaced and their addresses, see "Resident Parties List," October 15, 1934, RG 196, NA2.

37. The committee later changed its name to the Montgomery Advisory Committee. Nicrosi was the volunteer chairperson in the beginning. In 1936 the committee voted to recommend him for a paid part-time staff position of executive director, and he was hired to staff the committee. See Col. William Screws, R. F. Hudson, L. D. Rouse, and Charles Thigpen to Harold Ikes, April 28, 1936, RG 196, NA2, 1; Col. William Screws to Horatio Hackett, April 28, 1936, RG 196, NA2; Nicrosi remained a staff person with the housing division for about a month. During that time William Screws was the chairperson of the committee. Nicrosi was furloughed from his staff position with housing division and returned as chairperson of the Housing Committee but continued to organize the two projects. See Louis Calvert to A. R. Clas, November 29, 1935, RG 196, NA2; "The Mayors Committee for Housing Charter," September 28, 1934, RG 196, NA2. Harry E. Snow was initially the representative from the Chamber of Commerce but was replaced early on by L. D. Rouse. See "Carl Cooper Named Architect for Slum Clearance Project," *Montgomery Advertiser*,

March 13, 1934, 1; Robert B. Mitchell to Colonel Clark, March 24, 1934, RG 196, NA2; Robert Moton to Harold Ickes, March 27, 1934, RG 196, NA2; William Nicrosi to Mr. O'Brien, July 17, 1934, RG 196, NA2; ASU president H. Councill Trenholm provided a letter of recommendation for the initial application to the PWA in support of the funding for Paterson Court. See H. Councill Trenholm to William Nicrosi, January 29, 1934, RG 196, NA2.

38. Most of the resolutions referred to the project as "Negro slum clearance." See "Million-Dollar Slum Clearance Plan Endorsed by Chamber of Commerce," *Montgomery Advertiser*, March 7, 1934, 1; "Realtors to Aid in Housing Plan," *Montgomery Advertiser*, March 17, 1934, 1; "Slum Clearance in Montgomery," *Montgomery Advertiser*, April 10, 1934, 4.

39. "Noted Architect to Investigate Slums," *Montgomery Advertiser*, February 5, 1934, 8. Another person affiliated with the project was Eunice Klaber. The article likely spelled Eugene Kabor's name incorrectly, and it was not the same person.

40. A survey of the city determined that 3,500 of 11,200 white families and 9,200 of 10,000 African American families lived in substandard homes. See William Nicrosi, *Montgomery Housing* (Montgomery, AL: Montgomery Housing Authority, January 1940), PISF, ADAH. One survey found at least 1,700 white families living in unsanitary or overcrowded conditions. See "Riverside Heights Ready for First Occupant," *Montgomery Advertiser*, January 22, 1937, 16.

41. J. M. Harrison to William Nicrosi, August 13, 1934, RG 196, NA2, 1.

42. William Nicrosi to Division of Investigation, PWA, July 17, 1934, RG 196, NA2, 1.

43. Lister Hill to Heratio Hackett, August 16, 1934, RG 196, NA2, 1. Another article noted, "Social workers have discovered in recent years many white families, through necessity, living in mixed race quarters, having been attracted to such sections by low rents and simplicity of existence. The new housing program, it was pointed out, intends to correct this condition." "Locations Fixed for Government Housing Project," *Montgomery Advertiser*, July 13, 1934, 1.

44. While Ickes was the former president of the Chicago branch of the NAACP, many of the other PWA staff were segregationists. See Richard Rothstein, *The Color of Law* (New York: Liveright, 2017); Radford, *Modern Housing*; Mohl, "Whitening Miami."

45. "Changes of Mental Race Suicide," *Montgomery Advertiser*, November 8, 1934, 4.

46. For example, see "Hearing Set April 7 on Negro Subdivision," *Alabama Journal*, March 17, 1964.

47. Nicrosi used racist language and stereotypes to describe living conditions and

crime in a building on Randolph Street, writing, "There are two one-story houses, each containing 10 rooms, row on row with an alley in the center. Fifty-nine persons, all negroes, are living in these 20 rooms . . . with sanitary arrangements ordinarily sufficient for only two families. . . . Since 1927 . . . two murders have been committed by occupants of these houses and numerous petty crimes were charged against the other occupants. Three heads of families who occupied these houses are now serving terms in the penitentiary." "Progress in Local Slum Clearance Project Is Reported by Nicrosi," *Montgomery Advertiser*, November 17, 1935, 9.

48. "Low Cost Housing and Civilization," *Montgomery Advertiser*, August 11, 1937, 4; William Nicrosi to F. L. Ackerman, January 5, 1934, RG 196, NA2, 1; William Nicrosi to Robert Mitchell, April 17, 1934, RG 196, NA2, 1.

49. William Nicrosi, "Montgomery Alabama Program for Hovel Removal in Connection with Rehousing for Occupants of the Demolished Hovels," March 20, 1934, RG 196, NA2, 1.

50. Paul Mallon, "Behind the News," *Montgomery Advertiser*, February 5, 1934, 4.

51. Nicrosi, "Hovel Removal." In addition to concerns in Montgomery about white residents living among African American residents, PWA staff in Washington, DC, also viewed the problems of African American and white public housing differently. PWA division of housing technical staff Robert Mitchell wrote, "In this city the poorer class of Negroes occupy housing which the poor white population will no longer live in. Many of these buildings are densely inhabilitated [*sic*] with one family per room. There are practically no sanitary facilities." See Mitchell to Clark, March 24, 1934, RG 196, NA2, 1.

52. Little is known about the additional houses that were demolished. A *Montgomery Advertiser* editorial noted, "In order not to create a surplus of negro houses, the housing committee proposes to destroy an equal number, if not more, of occupied houses." "Carl Cooper," March 13, 1934, 1. The announcement that the initial $600,000 was awarded to Montgomery included the requirement that "for every unit of government housing erected here, a corresponding number of hovels will be destroyed." See "Slum Clearance in City Gets Federal Approval; $600,000 Is Allocated," *Montgomery Advertiser*, May 1, 1934, 1.

53. "Low-Cost Housing Survey Seeks Rent Schedule Here," *Montgomery Advertiser*, July 24, 1936, 1. See also "Slum Clearance Bids Due Soon," *Montgomery Advertiser*, March 2, 1935, 1.

54. "Slum Clearance in City Gets Federal Approval," 1; "Building Funds for Montgomery," *Prattville Progress*, May 3, 1934, 1.

55. "U.S. Housing Sites Scanned," *Montgomery Advertiser*, May 5, 1934, 1.

56. Robert Mitchell to Mr. Clas, June 28, 1934, RG 196, NA2, 2. Some people

disagreed that the site near ASU was the best location. For example, Walhon Hill, president of Union Bank and Co., wrote to PWA staff John Ritter that the site near ASU was a bad choice because there were worse housing conditions for African American people on the Westside. He wrote, "It will be occupied entirely by negroes attending the State Normal College . . . and it would be impossible to mix these educated negroes with the laboring classes of negroes." See Walton Hill to John Ritter, n.d., RG 196, NA2, 1. See also "Slum Inspection Starts This Week," *Montgomery Advertiser*, May 27, 1934, 1; "Locations Fixed for Government Housing Project," *Montgomery Advertiser*, July 13, 1934, 1; Horatio Hackett to Mr. Burlow, July 25, 1934, RG 196, NA2.

57. In Birmingham a housing project was underway in the Smithfield neighborhood, home to professionals and teachers. See Scribner, *Renewing Birmingham*; Walker Mason Beauchamp, "The Legacy of Racial Zoning in Birmingham, Alabama," *Cumberland Law Review* 48 (2017): 359–97.

58. Eunice Klaber to Robert Kohn and Horatio Hackett, June 6, 1934, RG 196, NA2, 1.

59. Walter Trevvett to Robert Mitchell, May 18, 1934, RG 196, NA2, 1.

60. Trevvett to Mitchell, May 18, 1934, RG 196, NA2, 1.

61. Trevvett to Mitchell, May 18, 1934, RG 196, NA2, 1.

62. Klaber to Kohn and Hackett, June 6, 1934, RG 196, NA2, 2.

63. A. B. Meyers to William Nicrosi, August 11, 1934, RG 196, NA2, 1. See also Rothstein, *The Color of Law*. Rothstein notes that the PWA introduced segregation to PWA housing projects.

64. H. Tudor Morsell to Colonel Hackett, June 11, 1934, RG 196, NA2. The Chappel House, a historic building that still stands on the site, was rehabilitated as a community center. See A. R. Clas to Ausfeld and Jones Architects, January 7, 1936, RG 196, NA2. An unpublished account indicates that the site was once home to American Indians and had been a cotton warehouse and an armory during the Civil War. See Peter A. Brannon, "Riverside Heights: Some Historical Associations," n.d., RG 196, NA2.

65. Klaber to Kohn and Hackett, June 6, 1934, RG 196, NA2, 2.

66. Housing Committee to Horatio Hackett, June 11, 1934, RG 196, NA2, 1.

67. Evidence that city officials were interested in demolishing more neighborhoods at a larger scale is inferred from their actions after the PWA housing was built. The MHA immediately proposed slum clearance of two more neighborhoods even after Paterson Court and Riverside Heights were complete. After the war, slum clearance accelerated.

68. See letters from representatives of the Chamber of Commerce, YMCA,

Alabama Machinery and Supply Company, Empire Laundry Co., the Montgomery County Medical Association, and the Alabama Real Estate and Insurance Exchange attached to A. B. Meker to William Nicrosi, August 11, 1934, RG 196, NA2; L. D. Rouse to William Nicrosi, August 6, 1934, RG 196, NA2; Montgomery Chamber of Commerce to William Nicrosi, August 6, 1934, RG 196, NA2; John Holman to William Nicrosi, August 5, 1934, RG 196, NA2; John Branch to William Nicrosi, August 14, 1934, RG 196, NA2.

69. Walt B. Jones to William Nicrosi, August 13, 1934, RG 196, NA2, 1.

70. Klaber to Kohn and Hackett, June 6, 1934, RG 196, NA2, 1.

71. "Preliminary Questionnaire, Public Works Emergency Housing Corporation, Washington, D.C., Montgomery, Alabama Negro Housing Questionnaire," n.d., RG 196, NA2, 5.

72. See W. P. Nelson, "Dwelling and Tenant Survey of Property Included for Proposed Project #401—Negro," n.d., RG 196, NA2, 4.

73. H. A. Gray to William Nicrosi, June 15, 1937, RG 196, NA2; H. Tudor Morsell to Colonel Hackett, August 24, 1934, RG 196, NA2; "Slum-Clearance Program Pushed," *Montgomery Advertiser*, August 21, 1934, 1. Contracts for demolition of the African American project were announced on October 19, 1934; "Razing Bids Due Today in Slum Clearance Project," *Montgomery Advertiser*, October 19, 1934, 1.

74. There were no consistent survey questions, and the data fields changed from house to house, adding to the haphazard nature of the survey. See W. P. Nelson, "Dwelling and Tenant Survey of Property Included for Proposed Project #401—Negro," n.d., RG 196, NA2; J. T. Porter, "Dwelling and Tenant Survey of Certain Properties in Montgomery, Alabama, of White Tenancy with Reference to Housing Project H-401, White Division," n.d., RG 196, NA2.

75. "Slum Clearance about to Begin," *Montgomery Advertiser*, June 27, 1935, 1; "White Slum Clearance Bid to Be Asked Soon," *Montgomery Advertiser*, July 20, 1935, 1; "Slum Clearance Bids to Be Opened Aug. 27," *Montgomery Advertiser*, July 26, 1935, 1; "Bell Housing Work Bids Slated Today," *Montgomery Advertiser*, August 27, 1935, 1; "White Slum Clearance Project Plans Received," *Montgomery Advertiser*, August 23, 1935, 1; Slum Clearance Ready to Begin," *Montgomery Advertiser*, October 1, 1935, 1; "Montgomery on Parade," *Montgomery Advertiser*, October 15, 1934, 4; "Model Housing Plans Here Are Widely Imitated," *Montgomery Advertiser*, March 14, 1935, 7; Louis Calvert to A. M. Clas, April 29, 1936, RG 196, NA2; "1934 Montgomery Zoning Ordinance," n.d., RG 196, NA2; City of Montgomery, "Code of Ordinances of the City of Montgomery, ALA" (Montgomery, AL: Montgomery City Commission, 1928), MPL.

76. A. R. Clas to William Nicrosi, June 8, 1936, RG 196, NA2, 1. Clas believed

the rezoning should be brought to Mayor Gunter from the Housing Committee—not from the PWA: "We believe that the Advisory Committee should be the agency to sell the idea to the mayor, to initiate and sponsor the rezoning." See A. R. Clas to L. L. Calvert, May 4, 1936, RG 196, NA2. While insisting on the zoning changes, PWA staff tried to avoid the appearance that they were telling municipalities how to control local land uses: "We wish to avoid any possible intimation that the Government is attempting to force or coerce the Municipality or the property owners to adopt such restrictions against their will." See A. R. Clas to L. L. Calvert, March 10, 1936, RG 196, NA2, 1.

77. Jacob Crane to H. A. Gray, June 15, 1937, RG 196, NA2, 2. For a discussion of the preservation of racial segregation under New Deal housing programs, see Roger Biles, *The South and the New Deal* (Lexington: University of Kentucky Press, 1994).

78. Crane to Gray, June 15, 1937, RG 196, NA2, 2.

79. William Nicrosi to H. A. Gray, March 8, 1937, RG 196, NA2, 3.

80. William Nicrosi to H. A. Gray, February 15, 1937, RG 196, NA2, 1; H. A. Gray to William Nicrosi, February 25, 1937, RG 196, NA2, 1; Nicrosi to Gray, March 8, 1937, RG 196, NA2.

81. Nathan Straus to William Nicrosi, November 20, 1937, RG 196, NA2; "Ordinance for Wm. B. Paterson Courts Neighborhood—Draft" October 28, 1937, RG 196, NA2; "Amendment to Zoning Ordinance," October 28, 1937, RG 196, NA2. The Alabama League of Municipalities suggested that a comprehensive rezoning of Montgomery was needed, and PWA consultant Jacob Crane agreed. See Jacob Crane to Acting Chief of Branch 1, n.d., RG 196, NA2. The American Society of Planning Officials was involved in drafting the ordinance. See H. A. Gray to Walter Blucher, October 21, 1937, RG 196, NA2.

82. Jacob Crane to Raymond Leonard, May 13, 1937, RG 196, NA2, 2.

83. Crane to Gray, June 15, 1937, RG 196, NA2, 2.

84. Crane to Gray, June 15, 1937, RG 196, NA2, 2.

85. P. W. Bourne to Acting Chief of Branch 1 and Assistant Director of Housing, March 16, 1937, RG 196, NA2.

86. Housing Authority of Montgomery, "Resolution No. 118: Resolution Establishing Rental Schedules, Policies and Standards for the Management Program of the Riverside Heights and William B. Paterson Courts Projects, H-2201, H-2202," n.d., RG 196, NA2. Riverside Heights had an on-site maintenance worker and janitor, and Paterson Court had one or two janitors. See "Meeting Minutes: Montgomery Advisory Committee on Housing," September 2, 1936, RG 196, NA2. Paterson Court cost about $125,000 less to build than Riverside Heights. See "Housing Bids Received Here: Slum Clearance Committee Discussing Management and Details of Project,"

*Alabama Journal*, April 17, 1935, 9. Some white Montgomerians claimed that amenities such as indoor plumbing were not necessary for African American people. One letter indicated, "Some have opposed the inclusion of sanitary facilities on the grounds that this is not necessary to provide for a class of tenants." See H. Wells to Horatio Hackett, October 13, 1944, RG 196, NA2, 1. Housing Committee staff indicated that African American women would not use laundry facilities, writing, "If one provided an electric washing machine to a negro washer woman, she would never use it, thinking that clothes could be better cleaned on a wash board." See Walter Trevvett to Robert Mitchell, April 12, 1934, RG 196, NA2, 1. The nursery was included in the historic building at Riverside Heights. See Horatio Hackett to William Nicrosi, February 20, 1935, RG 196, NA2; Geo. H. Wells to Horatio Hackett, October 30, 1934, RG 196, NA2; "PWA Housing Chief Arriving Today to Speed Work Here," *Montgomery Advertiser*, March 1, 1935, 1. Cleveland Court also had iceboxes instead of refrigerators. See National Housing Agency, "Federal Public Housing Authority, Project Summary Record, Cleveland Courts," February 3, 1940, RG 207, NAA.

87. ASU president H. Councill Trenholm agreed to cooperate with some activities in Paterson Court. See H. Councill Trenholm to A. R. Clas, November 8, 1935, RG 196, NA2, 1.

88. "West End Slum Clearance Project Money Is Allocated," *Montgomery Advertiser*, September 27, 1934, 1.

89. Geo. H. Wells to Horatio Hackett, January 4, 1935, RG 196, NA2; "City to Revive Housing Plan," *Montgomery Advertiser*, June 24, 1936, 3.

90. William Nicrosi to Robert Mitchell, May 4, 1934, RG 196, NA2, 2.

91. Nicrosi to Mitchell, May 4, 1934, RG 196, NA2, 2.

92. "Slum Clearance Works!" *Montgomery Advertiser*, September 29, 1940, 33.

93. Louis Calvert to A. R. Clas, July 29, 1935, RG 196, NA2, 1; Hill to Hackett, August 16, 1934, RG 196, NA2; H. A. Gray to William Nicrosi, September 12, 1936, RG 196, NA2; William Nicrosi to H. A. Gray, September 16, 1936, RG 196, NA2; "Low Cost Housing Work Progressing," *Montgomery Advertiser*, April 8, 1936, 2; "Negro Apartments Now Ready to Rent," *Montgomery Advertiser*, May 12, 1936, 11. The first tenant moved into Paterson Court in February 1937. See "Slum Clearance Works!"

94. Rental applications for Paterson Court were available to prospective tenants in April 1936, although the PWA had not released the rent rates yet. See "Low Cost Housing Work Progressing," *Montgomery Advertiser*, April 8, 1936, 2; "Negro Apartments Now Ready to Rent," *Montgomery Advertiser*, May 12, 1936, 11. The first tenant moved into Paterson Court in February 1937. See "Slum Clearance Works!," *Montgomery Advertiser*, September 29, 1940, 33.

95. Montgomery housing staff were concerned about African American employees in positions higher than white people. See Louis Calvert to A. R. Clas, January 31, 1936, RG 196, NA2; William Nicrosi, William Screws, R. D. Hudson, L. D. Rouse, and Mrs. Charles A. Thigpen to A. R. Clas, January 18, 1936, RG 196, NA2; William Nicrosi to A. R. Clas, January 6, 1936, RG 196, NA2. Paterson Court was completed just after Techwood Homes in Atlanta, making them the first two developments in the country. Riverside Heights was completed third. Paterson Court is now the oldest remaining public housing development in the country. See "Riverside Heights Ready," January 22, 1937, 16.

96. William Nicrosi to Horatio Hackett, April 30, 1935, RG 196, NA2, 2.

97. Mayor Gunter to A. R. Clas, July 10, 1936, RG 196, NA2, 2.

98. Nicrosi continued, "The negro will, however, be able to take over some of the duties at an early date and, of course, should work into complete management. . . . Several prominent negroes have approached me in regard to this, and the foregoing has been my answer. I am pleased to say that they have candidly agreed with me." See William Nicrosi to Mr. O'Brien, September 14, 1934, RG 196, NA2, 3–4.

99. A. R. Clas to Mayor Gunter, July 15, 1936, RG 196, NA2, 1.

100. William Nicrosi to H. A. Gray, November 14, 1936, RG 196, NA2.

101. Nicrosi wrote letters to Gray on September 24 and 30, and October 2, 5, and 7, 1937, complaining about these issues. On October 13 Nicrosi wrote to Gray summarizing the complaints and unanswered letters. See William Nicrosi to H. A. Gray, October 13, 1937, RG 196, NA2. See also Housing Authority of Montgomery, "Resolution No. 118, Resolution Establishing Rental Schedules, Policies and Standards for the Management Program of the Riverside Heights and William B. Paterson Courts Projects, H-2201, H-2202," n.d., RG 196, NA2; "Riverside Heights Ready," January 22, 1937, 16; "Riverside Heights All Occupied Now," *Montgomery Advertiser*, October 31, 1937, 1; William Joseph to William Nicrosi, July 21, 1936, RG 196, NA2; A. B. Meyer to William Nicrosi, n.d., RG 196, NA2; Theo Copeland to William Nicrosi, July 21, 1936, RG 196, NA2. See also Gordon Meriwether to William Nicrosi, July 23, 1936, RG 196, NA2; Eugene Heilpern to William Nicrosi, July 22, 1936, RG 196, NA2; "Meeting Minutes, Montgomery Advisory Committee," September 15, 1936, RG 196, NA2; "Loans Well Lost," *Montgomery Advertiser*, July 23, 1935, 4.

102. Louis Calvert to A. R. Clas, October 17, 1935, RG 196, NA2.

103. In Houston African American activists marched on city hall to protest the low prices paid for housing that was demolished for slum clearance projects and the high price charged for rent in the new developments. In Atlanta the average annual salary of residents at John Hope Homes was $735, while the average salary for African American employees in the city was $576. In Birmingham applicants for the

Smithfield Court development had to have a steady stream of income. See Biles, *The South and the New Deal.*

104. William Nircrosi to Robert Mitchell, May 15, 1934, RG 196, NA2, 1.

105. After rents were lowered and new income limits were applied, forty families had to move out of Riverside Heights because their incomes were too high. See "Rentals Shaved At 2 Low-Cost Housing Units," *Montgomery Advertiser*, March 15, 1940, 3; "40 Families Must Vacate Riverside," *Montgomery Advertiser*, March 16, 1940, 1.

106. William Nicrosi to H. A. Gray, quoting Daniel Henry, July 30, 1937, RG 196, NA2, 2. See also William Nicrosi to H. A. Gray, May 14, 1937, RG 196, NA2, 1.

107. William Nicrosi to H. A. Gray, quoting D. D. Williams, July 30, 1937, RG 196, NA2, 2. Such propaganda is difficult to believe. See also Edwin D. Peterman, "'Ever'body Need' Freedom' the Fourth Sunday in Lent," March 28, 1965, Flora Moore Andry Collection, TSCC. Nicrosi also noted that the playgrounds at Paterson Court were used by children from the neighborhood, writing, "Play yards draw children from the entire city. (There are no public parks or playgrounds here for colored children)." See William Nicrosi to H. A. Gray, July 30, 1937, RG 196, NA2, 2. See also Rebecca Retzlaff, "Desegregation of City Parks and the Civil Rights Movement: The Case of Oak Park in Montgomery, Alabama," *Journal of Urban History* 47, no. 4 (2019): 715–55.

108. "Slum Clearance in Montgomery," *Montgomery Advertiser*, September 11, 1935, 1.

109. Lister Hill to Horatio Hackett, September 26, 1935, RG 196, NA2; A.R. Clas to Lister Hill, October 2, 1935, RG 196, NA2. Hill wrote, "I know that you are fully aware that these projects are very small and the WHITE [emphasis in original] one particularly . . . we have ample grounds for additional development of the WHITE [emphasis in original] unit." See Lister Hill to Horatio Hackett, November 21, 1935, RG 196, NA2, 1. See also Virginia Van der Veer Hamilton, *Lister Hill: Statesman from the South* (Chapel Hill: University of North Carolina Press, 1987); Keith Finley, *Delaying the Dream: Southern Senators and the Fight against Civil Rights 1938–1965* (Baton Rouge: Louisiana State University Press, 2008); W. D. Fitzpatrick telegram to President Roosevelt, September 11, 1935, RG 196, NA2; George Schley telegram to President Roosevelt, September 11, 1935, RG 196, NA2; William Nicrosi telegram to President Roosevelt, September 11, 1935, RG 196, NA2; Lister Hill telegram to President Roosevelt, September 11, 1935, RG 196, NA2; Mayors Committee for Housing telegram to President Roosevelt, September 11, 1935, RG 196, NA2.

110. William Nicrosi to A. R. Clas, September 11, 1935, RG 196, NA2.

111. Nicrosi to Clas, September 11, 1935, RG 196, NA2; Lister Hill telegram to Franklin Roosevelt, September 11, 1935, RG 196, NA2.

112. The proposal for the African American project on Thurman Street was later expanded. See Walton Onslow to Paul Wooton, August 26, 1935, RG 196, NA2.

113. On January 1935 the US Court of Appeals for the Sixth Circuit determined that the federal government could not condemn land for housing projects, halting the use of eminent domain for a while. See Harold Ickes to Bibb Graves, August 10, 1935, RG 196, NA2.

114. William Nicrosi, "Application for Enlarging Projects No. H-2201 and H-2202, Montgomery, ALA," September 4, 1935, RG 196, NA2, 2.

115. A. R. Clas to William Nicrosi, November 1, 1935, RG 196, NA2. In 1938 the PWA approved a slum clearance project in Birmingham. See "State Gets $8,171,893," *Montgomery Advertiser*, June 24, 1938, 1. By 1939 slum clearance projects were underway in Gadsden, Mobile, Birmingham, and Phenix City. See "Hearing on Phenix City Slum Clearance Oct. 17," *Montgomery Advertiser*, October 7, 1939, 7. The MHA was established by a state charter on June 9, 1939.

116. Grover C. Hall Jr., "Home Rule for Housing Units Here," *Montgomery Advertiser*, February 22, 1939, 1. For information on Southern resistance to public housing and New Deal programs, see Biles, *The South and the New Deal*. In 1939 the US Housing Authority earmarked $1 million for the Riverside Heights expansion. See "Phoenix City Shares in Slum Clearance Fund," *Montgomery Advertiser*, October 29, 1939, 18; "City to Have $962,000 for Slum Removal," *Montgomery Advertiser*, February 6, 1940, 1. "Land Prices Balk Housing Project," *Montgomery Advertiser*, February 15, 1940, 1.

117. "Birmingham Housing Bond Issue Approved," *Montgomery Advertiser*, February 9, 1940, 2.

118. Birmingham approved for a bond issue for slum clearance in 1940. See "Legal Notice," *Montgomery Advertiser*, February 24, 1940, 9.

119. "City's Housing Project Up for State Approval," *Montgomery Advertiser*, February 24, 1940, 1; "Housing Project Bonds Approved," *Montgomery Advertiser*, March 1, 1940, 1.

120. A new defense housing project with thirty buildings was constructed near the municipal airport. Maxwell Air Force Base was out of room and began to house soldiers in a mill outside base, and the municipal airport was converted to an advanced flight training school. See "Slum Clearance Program Begins," *Montgomery Advertiser*, August 25, 1940, 28. The defense housing program constructed a housing development on Upper Wetumpka Highway. See "More Than 800 Men Busy on 3 Housing Jobs," *Montgomery Advertiser*, August 24, 1940, 8.

121. "Rogers Says Slum Clearance Will Help Not Hurt Real Estate," *Montgomery Advertiser*, March 21, 1940, 5.

122. Graves noted that the project would be for "between 250 and 300 negro families who are now living in surroundings unfit for human habitation." See "Alabama Gets $3,675,000 to Abate Its Slums," *Montgomery Advertiser*, January 30, 1941, 2. See also "Bonds Sold for Slum Clearance," *Montgomery Advertiser*, February 11, 1941, 3; "Legal Notices," *Montgomery Advertiser*, November 4, 1941, 9. Bibb Graves's nomination to the MHA board reflected white supremacist goals. Graves was elected governor with KKK support in 1926 during what was "probably the Klan's high-water mark in Alabama." See Carl Grafton and Anne Permaloff, *Big Mules and Branchheads: James E. Folsom and Political Power in Alabama* (Athens: University of Georgia Press, 1985), 50.

123. During the war the MHA completed three projects but did not initiate any new ones. See "$2,500,000 REA Steam Plant Likely to Go Up at Pinckard," *Montgomery Advertiser*, September 24, 1941, 1; Montgomery Housing Authority, *Report of the Housing Authority of the City of Montgomery Alabama* (Montgomery, AL: Montgomery Housing Authority, 1942).

124. R. Volney Riser, *Defying Disfranchisement: Black Voting Rights Activism in the Jim Crow South, 1890–1910* (Baton Rouge: Louisiana State University Press, 2010); Donald Strong, *Negroes, Ballots and Judges* (Tuscaloosa: University of Alabama Press, 1968); Robert Norrell, *The House I Live In: Race in the American Century* (New York: Oxford University Press, 2005); Stephanie Rolph, *Resisting Equality: The Citizens' Council, 1954–1989* (Baton Rouge: Louisiana State University Press, 2018).

125. Father Harold Purcell, "St. Jude's Negro Apostolate," *The Sign*, October 27, 1938, 1; "Dedication of St. Jude's Negro Apostolate, Montgomery, Alabama," October 27, 1939, PISF, ADAH.

126. Purcell, "St. Jude's," 1.

127. Alabama Historical Commission, *National Register of Historic Places Nomination for the City of St. Jude Historic District* (Montgomery: Alabama Historical Commission, 1990).

128. The nurses were Marie Meredith and Mary Brelsford. See Purcell, "St. Jude's." See also Fulton Ouster, "The Beggar of St. Jude," *Reader's Digest*, October 1946, 47–51.

129. B. S. Thompson, ed., *A Century of Progress in Montgomery City and County* (Montgomery, AL: Centennial Celebration Steering Committee, 1963).

130. Toolen had a colorful history with desegregation during his time as bishop of the Roman Catholic Diocese of Mobile from 1927 to 1969. See Keith Robert Claridy, *Bring God to the Negro, Bring the Negro to God: Thomas Joseph Toolen, Archbishop of Mobile (1927–1969), His Culture, His Religion, and His Mission*, unpublished thesis (2006), Auburn University, accessed March 4, 2022. See also Rebecca Retzlaff,

"Catholics v. the Interstates: The Fight to Protect Catholic Institutions from Interstate Highways in Birmingham, Alabama," *Journal of Transport History* 41, no. 3 (2020): 402–33. It was Toolen's decision to desegregate Catholic schools that led to Alabama's first desegregated private school in 1963 in Huntsville. St. Jude's in Montgomery unofficially admitted white students years earlier. See Rev. T. J. Toolen to Priests, April 22, 1964, AMA, 1. See also Mark Newman, *Desegregating Dixie: The Catholic Church in the South and Integration, 1945–1992* (Jackson: University Press of Mississippi, 2018); Andrew Moore, "Practicing What We Preach: White Catholics and the Civil Rights Movement in Atlanta," *Georgia Historical Quarterly* 89, no. 3 (2005): 334–67; Mark Newman, "Desegregation in the Catholic Diocese of Richmond, 1945–1973," *Virginia Magazine of History and Biography* 117, no. 4 (2009), 356–71; John McGreevy, *Catholicism and American Freedom: A History* (New York: W. W. Norton and Company, 2004); Andrew S. Moore, *The South's Tolerable Alien: Roman Catholics in Alabama and Georgia, 1945–1970* (Baton Rouge: Louisiana State University Press, 2007).

131. Grafton Scott Jr., "Pennsylvanian Is Credited with Founding of St. Jude," *Montgomery Advertiser-Journal*, June 22, 1969, 38; Grafton Scott Jr., "City of St. Jude Founded in 1934 by Father Purcell," *Alabama Journal*, June 21, 1969, 11; Tony Walker, "Purcell Sees Another Dream Come True—School Finished," *Montgomery Advertiser*, March 14, 1948, 1.

132. Danielle McGuire, *At the Dark End of the Street: Black Women, Rape, and Resistance: A New History of the Civil Rights Movement from Rosa Parks to the Rise of Black Power* (New York: Doubleday, 2010), 39.

133. Eric Motley, *Madison Park: A Place of Hope* (Grand Rapids, MI: Zondervan and Harper Collins, 2017).

134. The identity the first African American attorney in Alabama is unclear. See John G. Browning, "Blazing the Trail: Alabama's First Black Lawyers," *Alabama Lawyer*, December 27, 2021.

135. Gwen Patton, "Rufus Lewis Papers Biography," n.d., RALC, TSCC; Gwen Patton, "Interview with Rufus Lewis," November 6, 1996, RALC, TSCC.

## *Chapter 2*

1. African American people were experiencing a similar housing crisis throughout the country. See Jo Ann E. Argersinger, *Toward a New Deal in Baltimore: People and Government in the Great Depression* (Chapel Hill: University of North Carolina Press, 1988); James Loewen, *Sundown Towns: A Hidden Dimension of American Racism* (New York: The New Press, 2005). For information about wartime rent control in Montgomery, see Carroll T. McConnell to Tom Tippett, October 31, 1943, RG 252, NAA.

2. J. Mills Thornton III, *Dividing Lines: Municipal Politics and the Struggle for Civil Rights in Montgomery, Birmingham, and Selma* (Tuscaloosa: University of Alabama Press, 2002). This section on the political and demographic changes in Montgomery was greatly informed by Thornton's book. Between 1920 and 1930, the city of Montgomery annexed land in Cloverdale and Capitol Heights, increasing the amount of land in the city by about 300 percent. See Alec C. Morgan, "Report of Study, Montgomery Alabama, for the Division of Research and Statistics, Home Owners' Loan Corporation, Washington, D.C.," March 15, 1937, RG 195, NA2.

3. Thornton III, *Dividing Lines.*

4. Joe Asbell, "City Limits," *Montgomery Advertiser*, Sept 18, 1952, 2; Joe Azbell, "Montgomery Builds for the Future," *Montgomery Advertiser*, December 7, 1952, 20.

5. For evidence of minimal expansion of African American neighborhoods, compare a map from 1929 and 1933 (Montgomery City Commission Map, 1929, corrected 1933, RG 196, NA2) with a hand-drawn map from 1950 identifying the race of all households in the city (Montgomery City Planning Commission, 1950, Auburn University Archives Map Collection, Auburn, Alabama). The comparison shows almost no expansion of African American neighborhoods.

Arnold Hirsch and Raymond Mohl, eds., *Urban Policy in Twentieth-Century America* (New Brunswick, NJ: Rutgers University Press, 1993); Arnold Hirsch, *Making the Second Ghetto* (New York: Cambridge University Press, 1983); Raymond Mohl, "Making the Second Ghetto in Metropolitan Miami, 1940–1960" in *The New African American Urban History*, eds. Kenneth Goings and Raymond Mohl (Thousand Oaks, CA: Sage, 1996), 266–89.

6. Urban Consultant Associates, *Land Use Plan (2nd Draft), Montgomery, Alabama* (Montgomery, AL: Montgomery City Planning Commission, 1957). It was not uncommon for African American neighborhoods to lack basic infrastructure in American cities. Biles notes that one-fourth of African American residents in New Orleans had no running water. In Birmingham, about 30 percent of African American homes had no sewer connection, one in twenty homes had a bathtub, and the city never collected trash in African American neighborhoods. See Roger Biles, *The South and the New Deal* (Lexington: University of Kentucky Press, 1994).

7. For more information about municipal politics in Montgomery, see Thornton III, *Dividing Lines.*

8. "2 Negroes Sue for Franchise in Circuit Court," *Montgomery Advertiser*, December 31, 1943, 18. The goal of registering fifty thousand African American voters was announced in A. M. Wendell Malliet, "Fight to Vote Includes Registration of 50,000 Qualified Voters at Polls," *New York Amsterdam News*, July 15, 1944, n.p. An article in the *Montgomery Advertiser* reported on Madison's goal of five thousand

voters. It is unclear if Madison changed his goal or if the newspapers reported the number incorrectly. See "Negro Lawyer Is Fined $2,500 in Vote Appeals," *Montgomery Advertiser*, April 15, 1944, Madison Family Collection, TSCC, 2.

9. Brian Lyman, "The Believer: Arthur Madison Launched a Montgomery Voter Registration Drive in 1944—and Paid a Price," *Montgomery Advertiser*, February 25, 2021, updated February 2, 2022, accessed February 17, 2022.

10. The individuals claiming that Madison did not legally represent them were Ola Galloway, Sarah Madison, Annie Banks, Mildred Hardy, John Winston, and Frankie Lee Winston. Frankie Lee Winston told the court that he was acting on behalf of Emma Madison and Nicholas Madison, who did not request representation from Arthur Madison. See "Negroes Drop Appeals, Deny the Authorized Action," *Montgomery Advertiser*, February 9, 1944, 1. See Eric Motley, *Madison Park: A Place of Hope* (Grand Rapids, MI: Zondervan and Harper Collins, 2017).

11. *Smith v. Allwright*, 321 U.S. 649 (1944).

12. "Negro Attacks Alabama System," *Southern Watchman*, January 15, 1944, 5.

13. Lyman, "The Believer." Lyman notes that Madison's former roommate, Herman Dreer, accused police of beating Madison. See also "Negro Vote Lawyer Put in Jail Here," *Montgomery Advertiser*, April 9, 1944, 1. Madison asked the court for a continuation, but the request was denied by Judge Walter B. Jones. See "Court Convicts Negro Lawyer," *Alabama Journal*, April 14, 1944, 1; "Negro Lawyer is Fined $2,500 in Vote Appeals," *Montgomery Advertiser*, April 15, 1944, 2. The eight African American activists who continued with their case were Willie L. Madison, General P. Madison, William F. Madison, James T. Emery, Sallie B. Madison, Henry G. Payne, Alfonso Felder, and Edgar D. Nixon. Arthur Madison appealed his disbarment and the fine and lost. See "Negro Appeals Disbarment to Circuit Court," *Montgomery Advertiser*, April 20, 1944, Madison Family Collection, TSCC.

14. By 1949 the population of Madison Park was 261 adults and 425 children, and the total acreage of the town had grown to 2,718. See Centennial Celebration Committee, *A Century of Negro Progress in Montgomery City and County* (Montgomery, AL: Centennial Celebration Committee, 1963). Thornton also notes that the first voter registration efforts had positive results for African American organizing because it was the failure of the Montgomery branch of the NAACP to fully embrace Madison's voter registration drive that led Nixon to take over the organization. See Thornton III, *Dividing Lines*. The reaction from white people led to passage of the Boswell Amendment, which Alabama legislature passed in 1945 and Alabama voters ratified in 1946. The amendment required voter registration applicants to be able to understand any article of the US Constitution. The amendment was declared unconstitutional in 1949 by the US Supreme Court. See Juliette Morgan, letter to Citizens of

Montgomery, 1946, Juliette Hampton Morgan Collection, TSCC; "Leaflet from Citizen's Committee against Amendment No. 4, Facts: Vote No on Amendment Number 4," Juliette Hampton Morgan Collection, TSCC.

15. E. D. Nixon was a well-loved and effective activist, and people went to him with a wide variety of problems. In one instance, he received complaints about the segregated women's restroom at Union Station and wrote a letter to J. B. Hill, president of Louisville and Nashville (L&N) Railroad in Louisville, Kentucky, describing deplorable conditions of the bathroom: a mop bucket was used as a sink and there were broken toilets and rude staff. See E. D. Nixon to J. B. Hill, February 7, 1944, E. D. Nixon Collection, LWLC.

16. Burns Bennett, "$1,500,000 Negro Hospital to Rise Here; Father Purcell to Realize Another Dream," *Montgomery Advertiser*, May 1, 1949, 17.

17. Jorden later worked at the AHD.

18. "Economy Boost Seen in River Program," *Alabama Journal*, Nov. 12, 1957, 1.

19. "Economy Boost Seen," 1.

20. Tom Johnson, "Protest Hearing Ended on Coosa River Project," *Montgomery Advertiser*, Feb 2, 1956, 1.

21. Eventually the Leesburg Dam, built by Alabama Power, flooded some twenty-seven thousand acres of farmland and displaced approximately six thousand families. The landowners were mostly poor farmers, and appraisers valued the land at just fifty dollars an acre. Some newspapers reported that the number of persons to be displaced by the dam was only 1,500. The actual number is unknown. See "Coosa Valley Unit Opposes Leesburg Dam," *Montgomery Advertiser*, May 23, 1957, 1.

22. Southeastern Regional Planning Commission, *Development Study of the Alabama-Coosa Basin Area: Prospectus* (Atlanta, GA: Southeastern Regional Planning Commission, 1943).

23. Part of the impetus for establishing the Planning Commission was a zoning dispute. See "Montgomery Will Set Up City Planning Commission," *Alabama Journal*, July 16, 1946, 1. See also G. C. Long Jr., "City Planning Body Evolves Master Plan," *Montgomery Advertiser*, September 21, 1947, 13; "Jefferson Planning Commission Filled," *Montgomery Advertiser*, March 11, 1942, 3; "Planning Commission Named for Jefferson," *Montgomery Advertiser*, March 11, 1942, 5; Jack Knight had an engineering degree from Auburn University and worked for the Allis-Chalmers Manufacturing Company in Wisconsin after graduating from Auburn. He returned to Alabama to work on federal New Deal programs and enlisted in the army during World War II before he worked with the Planning and Industrial Development Board. See Gene Kovarik, "Jack Knight," *Alabama Journal*, June 12, 1963, 13.

24. In 1961 Judge Marks found eleven activists, including Rev. Ralph Abernathy,

Bernard Lee, and Fred Shuttlesworth, guilty of breaching the peace and unlawful assembly in connection with the freedom rides. See "Mob Wins Again in Alabama," *Southern Christian Leadership Conference Newsletter* 1, no. 3 (September 1961).

25. See "Zoning Map," *Montgomery Advertiser*, February 3, 4, 5, and 6, 1948; Montgomery City Planning Commission and Alabama State Planning Board, *Montgomery Zoning Ordinance*, July 1948.

26. See "Zoning Map," *Montgomery Advertiser*, February 3, 4, 5, and 6, 1948; Montgomery City Planning Commission and Alabama State Planning Board, *Montgomery Zoning Ordinance*, July 1948.

27. G. C. Long Jr., "Coosa-Alabama River Project" *Montgomery Advertiser*, Dec 22, 1946, 27.

28. Montgomery City Planning Commission and the Alabama State Planning Board, *Master Plan for Public Recreation* (Montgomery, AL: City Planning Commission, 1949).

29. "City Takes Steps to Form Water and Sewerage Board," *Montgomery Advertiser*, July 16, 1952, 1; "Moving Out of the Slums" *Alabama Journal*, February 12, 1954, 4; "Tell It to Old Grandma," *Montgomery Advertiser*, June 26, 1963, 4; Virginia Gibson, "Carver Area White Exodus Continues," *Alabama Journal*, December 24, 1970, 9.

30. See Montgomery City Code, 21–57, June 4, 1957. See also *Gilmore v. City of Montgomery, Alabama*, 94 S. Ct. 2416 (1974). Parks were used as barriers between white and African American neighborhoods in other cities, such as Atlanta, where a parkway with a park in the middle of two roads was proposed as a racial barrier, with a fence on both sides of the park to prevent anyone from using it on an integrated basis. The parkway was designed to prevent African American encroachment into the white neighborhoods. See Ronald Bayor, *Race and the Shaping of Twentieth-Century Atlanta* (Chapel Hill: University of North Carolina Press, 1996).

31. Carl Poteat, "Park Has Hosted Fun for 85 Years," *Alabama Journal*, September 14, 1973, PISF, ADAH, n.p.; Victoria W. Wolcott, *Race, Riots, and Roller Coasters* (Philadelphia: University of Pennsylvania Press, 2012); Jason Byrne and Jennifer Wolch, "Nature, Race, and Parks: Past Research and Future Directions for Geographic Research," *Progress in Human Geography* 33, no. 6 (2009): 743–65. See also Glenda Elizabeth Gilmore, *Defying Dixie: The Radical Roots of Civil Rights* (New York: W. W. Norton and Company, 2008); James W. Loewen, *Sundown Towns: A Hidden Dimension of American Racism* (New York: The New Press, 2005); Marsha Dean Phelts, *An American Beach for African Americans* (Gainesville: University Press of Florida, 1997); J. Austin Burkhart, "Yonder Sits the Rocking-Chair," *The Crisis* 59, no. 10 (1952): 619–52; William O'Brien, "The Strange Career of a Florida State Park:

Uncovering a Jim Crow Past," *Historical Geography* 35 (2007): 160–84. See also "State Parks," *National Municipal Review Supplement* (November 1921): 583–600; Robert D. Bullard, *Dumping in Dixie: Race, Class and Environmental Quality* (San Francisco: Westview Press, 1990); Ney C. Landrum, *The State Park Movement in America* (Columbia: University of Missouri Press, 2004); William E. O'Brien, *Landscapes of Exclusion* (Amherst: University of Massachusetts Press, 2016); Robert McKay, "Segregation and Public Recreation," *Virginia Law Review* 40, no. 6 (1954): 697–731.

32. Jessie MacGuire, "Beautiful Flowers Transform Oak Park into Color Paradise," *Montgomery Advertiser*, April 7, 1946, PISF, ADAH.

33. Maylon Nicholson, "A Pall of Desolation Hangs Over Oak Park," *Alabama Journal*, December 31, 1958, PISF, ADAH; Anny Lyle, "Big Round-Up Begins at Oak Park Zoo," *Alabama Journal*, December 14, 1959, PISF, ADAH.

34. Montgomery City Planning Commission and the Alabama State Planning Board, *Master Plan for Public Recreation*, 52.

35. *Gilmore v. City of Montgomery, Alabama*, 94 S. Ct. 2416 (1974); Ronald Bayor, *Race and the Shaping of Twentieth-Century Atlanta* (Chapel Hill: University of North Carolina Press, 1996).

36. Montgomery City Planning Commission and Alabama State Planning Board, *Master Plan for Public Recreation.*

37. After publication of the plan, there was attention to parks for African American people driven by the desire of white public officials to try to prove that the concept of "separate but equal" was working. By 1955 there were nineteen parks in Montgomery, four of which were available to African American people, including Washington Park, which had a small community center with a concrete basketball court, a wading pool, and playground equipment; King Hill Park, a ten-acre forested park with playground equipment and a community center that housed a shop and a craft room; George Washington Carver High School Playground, a playground and sports field next to the only African American high school in the city; and Trenholm Court Park, which included a basketball court, tennis court, softball field, and playground equipment in a public housing development. By 1958 two more African American parks were added, including a five-acre park with playground equipment in Mobile Heights, a new African American subdivision built in 1950, and Houston Hill Park, part of the North Montgomery slum clearance project. See "No Intention of Integrating Parks Say Officials," *Montgomery Advertiser*, August 26, 1958, PISF, ADAH; "Citywide Play Program Set," *Montgomery Advertiser*, June 15, 1955, 1.

38. "Slum Clearance on Major Scale Seen for City," *Montgomery Advertiser*, June 23, 1948, 1.

39. Joe Azbell, "City Limits," *Montgomery Advertiser*, March 18, 1956, 11.

40. "City Commission Told Slums Being Created," *Alabama Journal*, January 4, 1949, 1. Tight housing markets after slum clearance is not unique to Montgomery. See Thomas Sugrue, *The Origins of the Urban Crisis* (Princeton, NJ: Princeton University Press, 1996).

41. Alexander von Hoffman, "A Study in Contradictions: The Origins and Legacy of the Housing Act of 1949," *Housing Policy Debate* 11, no. 2 (2000) 299–326; and Edward Goetz, *Fair Housing and the Pursuit of Racial Justice in American Cities* (Ithaca, NY: Cornell University Press, 2018). While the compromise allowed the bill to pass, its effect on improving lives is doubtful. As Rothstein explains, "Whether such segregation was in anyone's best interests is doubtful. True, without public housing, tens of thousands of African Americans would have to remain in tenement houses that were out of compliance with the most minimal municipal building and health codes. But with the segregated projects, African Americans became more removed from mainstream society than ever, packed into high-rise ghettos where community life was impossible, where access to jobs and social services was more difficult, and where supervision of adolescents and even a semblance of community policing was impractical." See Richard Rothstein, *The Color of Law* (New York: Liveright, 2017), 31–32.

42. von Hoffman, "A Study in Contradictions," 312. See also Arnold R. Hirsch, "Searching for a 'Sound Negro Policy': A Racial Agenda for the Housing Acts of 1949 and 1954," *Housing Policy Debate* 11, no. 2 (2010): 393–411; Robert Beauregard, *Voices of Decline: The Postwar Fate of U.S. Cities, 2nd ed.* (New York: Routledge, 2003).

43. President Dwight D. Eisenhower, "Annual Message to the Congress on the State of the Union," Eisenhower Library, January 6, 1955, accessed December 6, 2021.

## *Chapter 3*

1. Four African American police officers began active duty in Montgomery in May 1954. See J. Mills Thornton III, *Dividing Lines: Municipal Politics and the Struggle for Civil Rights in Montgomery, Birmingham, and Selma* (Tuscaloosa: University of Alabama Press, 2002), 27. Levy explains that the growing number of African American voters reshaped voting patterns throughout the South. See Peter Levy, *The Civil Rights Movement* (Westport, CT: Greenwood Press, 1998).

2. Lewis suggested that "Operation 10,000" could one day become a reality. See Rufus Lewis to Fellow Citizens, November 3, 1955, RALC, TSCC, 1.

3. Some of the questions were the following: "Are you a qualified voter?" "In what election did you last vote?" "Have you paid the poll tax for 1953–54?" "If you are not a qualified voter, will you briefly state your reasons for not qualifying?" "Do you think it is important to vote?" "In what way can your committee on Social and Political Action assist you in becoming a qualified voter?" Members of the committee were

Mary Fair Burks, Jo Ann Robinson (co-chairs), W. D. Petus, R. T. Adair, Frank Taylor Sr., and Rufus Lewis. See "Political and Social Action Committee of Dexter Avenue Baptist Church Questionnaire," October 17, 1954, RALC, TSCC.

4. In 1952 Lewis filed for incorporation of the Citizens' Club at 1903 Myles Street (another address listed for the club was 101 Myles Street) with Montgomery County Probate Court, stating that membership was open to "all interested citizens who are voters or potential voters and are concerned with the social and civic development of our community and who comply with the requirements of the by-laws for membership." Officers of the club were Lewis (president), C. E. Anderson (vice president), W. Ivey (second vice president), James Kendrick (secretary), and Bruce Rollins (treasurer). See R. A. Lewis, "Constitution and By-Laws of the Citizens' Club, Exhibit A," August 29, 1952, RALC, TSCC. Lewis applied for a business license in 1956 for the club, and in 1957 he hired Donald Luther Horton to design the club, which included a dining room, garden, ballroom, and offices. See Donald Horton letter to Rufus A. Lewis, September 24, 1962, RALC, TSCC. In 1960 the officers were Lewis (president), Joseph Marshall (vice president), Charles Langford (secretary), and Edward McCall (no title). In a 1996 interview Lewis reflected on the Citizens' Club: "The Citizens Club was an effort to get people to vote. That's what it was all about. You are a citizen! If you are a citizen, you've got to vote." See Gwen Patton, "Interview with Rufus Lewis Transcript," November 6, 1996, RALC, TSCC, 5.

5. Robert Graetz, *A White Preacher's Message on Race and Reconciliation* (Montgomery, AL: New South Books, 2006); Thornton, *Dividing Lines*; R. Volney Riser, *Defying Disfranchisement: Black Voting Rights Activism in the Jim Crow South, 1890–1910* (Baton Rouge: Louisiana State University Press, 2010); Margaret Price, *The Negro and the Ballot in the South* (Atlanta, GA: Southern Regional Council, 1959); Virginia Foster Durr, *Outside the Magic Circle* (Tuscaloosa: University of Alabama Press, 1985); Glenn Eskew, ed., *Labor in the Modern South* (Athens: University of Georgia Press, 2001); James Cobb, *The South and America Since World War II* (Oxford: Oxford University Press, 2011); and David Goldfield, *Black, White, and Southern: Race Relations and Southern Culture 1940 to the Present* (Baton Rouge: Louisiana State University Press, 1990). The author has come across many instances of Lewis and Nixon working together in their collections at TSCC and LWLC and notes that most of the letters are friendly. Perhaps the narrative of their rivalry has been overblown and is the result of people's tenancy to focus on difference and conflict. See, for example, a letter in which Nixon asked Lewis if he could borrow his typewriter: E. D. Nixon to Rufus Lewis, February 22, 1966, RALC, TSCC.

6. Belinda Robnett, *How Long? How Long?* (New York: Oxford University Press, 1997), 56, quoting Mary Fair Burks in an interview with the author; Patricia Sullivan,

"Virginia Foster Durr: The Liberation of Pure White Southern Womanhood," in *Alabama Women: Their Lives and Times*, eds. Susan Youngblood Ashmore and Lisa Lindquist Dorr (Athens: University of Georgia Press, 2017), 270–86.

7. Rosa Parks was asked why African American men were not arrested on buses and noted, "In the white south, it would usually be fatal or so near fatal, in most cases, if they take a stand." See Belinda Robnett, *How Long? How Long?* (New York: Oxford University Press, 1997), 67, quoting Rosa Parks in an interview from the Civil Rights Documentation Project at the Moorland-Spingarn Center at Howard University. Similarly, Johnnie Carr recalled in an interview with Stephen Millner, "Black men have a rough time now. They have a much rougher time than women have. That's a fact." See David Garrow, *The Walking City: The Montgomery Bus Boycott* (Brooklyn, NY: Carlton, 1989), 43, quoting Johnnie Carr. The first presidents of the Women's Political Council were Mary Fair Burks, an ASU English professor; Jule Clayton Lewis, Rufus Lewis's wife; and Jo Ann Robinson, an ASU English professor. Thelma Glass, ASU geography professor, and Irene West, the wife of a dentist, were also active members. See Mary Fair Burks, "Trailblazers: Women in the Montgomery Bus Boycott," in *Black Women in United States History*, ed. Darlene Clark Hine (Brooklyn, NY: Carlson, 1990), 71–83; Glenn Eskew, *Labor in the Modern South*. Wilson notes that middle-class African American leaders were much more conservative about civil rights than working class individuals were. See Bobby Wilson, *Race and Place in Birmingham: The Civil Rights and Neighborhood Movements* (New York: Rowman and Littlefield, 2000). See also Jonathan Eig, *King: A Life* (New York: Farrar, Strauss, and Grioux, 2023).

8. Nigel Taylor, *Urban Planning Theory since 1945* (London: Sage, 1998); Christine Boyer, *Dreaming the Rational City: The Myth of American City Planning* (Boston, MA: MIT Press, 1983); Peter Hall, *Cities of Tomorrow: An Intellectual History of Urban Planning and Design Since 1880, 4th ed.* (Hoboken, NJ: Wiley-Blackwell, 2014).

9. The number of substandard dwelling units was 13,403. See "Slum-Clearance Fund Requested By Montgomery," *Alabama Journal*, January 25, 1950, 1; "$938,210 Sought to Clear Slums," *Montgomery Advertiser*, January 26, 1950, 2; "Slum Clearance Fund Reserved," *Alabama Journal*, February 3, 1950, 1; "Slum Clearance Fund Allotted," *Montgomery Advertiser*, July 3, 1950, 2; "Sites to Be Surveyed For Slum Clearance," *Alabama Journal*, May 24, 1951, 1; "Slum Clearance Survey Slated," *Montgomery Advertiser*, May 25, 1951, 33; "City Creates New Position," *Montgomery Advertiser*, March 13, 1952, 15. In 1942 the members of the MHA board were all white businesspeople, including chairperson Frank Seeger, Seeger Packing Company; Paul Fuller, Montgomery Chamber of Commerce; John DeMotte, Montgomery Broadcasting Company; Thomas Edwards, engineer; Joseph W. Wells, J. W. Wells Lumber

Company; Charles P. Rogers, MHA executive director; and Thomas E. Martin, MHA attorney. See Montgomery Housing Authority, *Report of the Housing Authority of the City of Montgomery, Alabama* (Montgomery, AL: Montgomery Housing Authority, 1942). By 1978 the city had added just one African American member to the MHA board and declined to add a second one. See Lenore Reese, "Council Declines to Name Black Woman to Board," *Alabama Journal*, June 21, 1978, 41. One reporter noted that the North Montgomery urban renewal area was home to 222 African American families and ten white families. See Bob Ingram, "A Long Overdue Cleaning," *Montgomery Advertiser*, February 21, 1954, PISF, ADAH, 23. See also "Slum Area to Be Cleared," *Montgomery Advertiser*, n.d., PISF, ADAH; "U.S. Loan Okayed for Redevelopment Project," *Montgomery Advertiser*, July 10, 1953, PISF, ADAH.

10. "City Planning Group Approves Plans for Clearance of Slums," *Montgomery Advertiser*, April 10, 1953, 1.

11. For an example of the more sophisticated planning methods, compare Montgomery Board of City Commissioners, *North Montgomery Slum Clearance Plan* (Montgomery, AL: Montgomery City Commission, 1951), with the surveys for Paterson Court and Riverside Heights: W. P. Nelson, "Dwelling and Tenant Survey of Property Included for Proposed Project #401—Negro," n.d., RG 196, NA2, 4; J. T. Porter, "Dwelling and Tenant Survey of Certain Properties in Montgomery, Alabama of White Tenancy with Reference to Housing Project H-401, White Division," n.d., RG 196, NA2. The survey for the North Montgomery slum clearance project included a more systematic assessment of blight, housing conditions, zoning, streets, and public utilities, while the earlier PWA surveys were much more haphazard, with inconsistent survey questions and no apparent systematic survey methodology.

12. One newspaper reported, "At least one of the Negroes at the hearing was opposed to this plan. He would have to give up his chickens and rabbits if he moved into an apartment." See "Planning Committee Okehs Slum Redevelopment Plan," *Alabama Journal*, April 10, 1953, 9. See also Bob Ingram, "51-Acre Project to Cost Total of $1,396,000," *Montgomery Advertiser*, December 5, 1953, 1; Lawrence Vale, "The Future of Planned Poverty: Redeveloping America's Most Distressed Public Housing Projects," *Netherlands Journal of Housing and the Built Environment* 14, no. 1 (1999): 13–31.

13. US Census of Population and Housing, 1950.

14. Allan Rankin, "Rankin File" *Montgomery Advertiser*, May 9, 1954, 17.

15. The area is the present-day site of Whitfield Foods. See "Notice of Public Hearing City Planning Commission," *Montgomery Advertiser*, April 2, 1953, 24; "City Gives Okeh on Initial Phase of Slum Clearance," *Montgomery Advertiser*, June 13, 1951, 13; "Housing Authority Given Green Light by City to Ask Loan, Grant for Redevelopment Project," *Montgomery Advertiser*, April 15, 1953, 5. A new fire station

was later added to the project. See "Youthful 1954 Glows Brightly in Montgomery," *Montgomery Advertiser*, January 1, 1954, 1.

16. In 1965 the Whitfield Pickle Company expanded on the last vacant lot. See Gene Kovarik, "Renewal Adds Dollars to City's Treasury," *Alabama Journal*, December 6, 1963, 6; Joe McFadden, "Intended Alterations for Montgomery Listed," *Alabama Journal*, May 21, 1965, 1.

17. The Tulane Court property was purchased before the war. See Fields Varner, "Slum Clearance Survey Ordered," *Montgomery Advertiser*, September 28, 1949, 1; "Housing Project Dedication Slated," *Montgomery Advertiser*, March 4, 1951, PISF, ADAH.

18. The Alabama Supreme Court upheld the law in October 1950. See "Slum Clearance Law Is Upheld," *Montgomery Advertiser*, October 26, 1950, 10; Opinion of the Justices, 254 Ala. 343, Supreme Court of Alabama, No. 119, Oct. 25, 1950. See also Themis Chronopoulos, "Robert Moses and the Visual Dimension of Physical Disorder: Efforts to Demonstrate Urban Blight in the Age of Slum Clearance," *Journal of Planning History* 13, no. 3 (2014): 207–33.

19. An FHA statement noted, "The proposed new regulations will not mean an end to racial segregation in private developments. It means that FHA insurance assistance cannot be given to projects which have written agreements—either on tenants or landlords—that are discriminatory." See "Racially Restricted Properties," *Montgomery Advertiser*, December 7, 1949, 4. See also "Race Housing Order Held Up for 60 Days," *Montgomery Advertiser*, December 4, 1949, 1; "Equitable Treatment Required in Public Housing Program," *Montgomery Advertiser*, December 22, 1949, 1; James Lanham, "New Orleans Firm Receives Contract for Negro Project," *Montgomery Advertiser*, July 16, 1952, PISF, ADAH.

20. The annual income limits were a minimum of $2,100 for a family with fewer than three children and $2,400 for a family with more than three children. See "New Orleans Firm Receives Contract for Negro Project," *Montgomery Advertiser*, July 16, 1952, 1.

21. "Minimum Housing Code Fights Sub-Standard Living," *Montgomery Advertiser*, October 21, 1962, 63.

22. "Big Development Program Shaped Near Cramton Bowl," *Alabama Journal*, June 13, 1952, 1; "Houston Hill Project Here Will Be Developed with U.S. Aid," *Montgomery Advertiser*, January 4, 1953, 27; "Street, Utility Bids Sought on Houston Hill Area Work," *Montgomery Advertiser*, December 22, 1961, 1. Rothstein notes that public housing authorities throughout the country also built segregated public housing in formerly integrated neighborhoods. See Richard Rothstein, *The Color of Law* (New York: Liveright Publishing Corporation, 2017).

23. "Let's Keep in Step," *Montgomery Advertiser*, September 27, 1937, 5.

24. "Houston Hill Funds Ok'd," *Montgomery Advertiser*, April 27, 1956, 1; "Houston Hill Project Okayed," *Alabama Journal*, January 13, 1956, 1.

25. "Houston Hills, Former Slum, Gets New Look," *Alabama Journal*, June 27, 1963, 27.

26. "Houston Hill Funds Ok'd," 1; "Houston Hill Project Okayed."

27. "Houston Hill Request Awarded Board's OK," *Montgomery Advertiser*, January 13, 1956, 1.

28. "City Seeks Negro Housing," *Montgomery Advertiser*, November 13, 1954, 1.

29. A survey by the First Federal Savings and Loan Association determined that there were 386 families that needed to be relocated and were unable to find housing. See "Negro Building Project Aired by City Commission," *Montgomery Advertiser*, November 12, 1954, 34.

30. "301 Homes for Negroes to Be Built at Chisholm," *Alabama Journal*, April 7, 1955, 9.

31. Quoting Senator Humphrey from Minnesota, who also supported the bill. See "Housing Unit Hike Is Seen," *Alabama Journal*, December 27, 1954, 1.

32. "City Seeks Negro Housing," *Montgomery Advertiser*, November 13, 1954, 1; "301 Homes."

33. Joe Azbell, "City Limits," *Montgomery Advertiser*, July 3, 1955, 11.

34. "Realtors Take Firm Stand on Use of Public Housing," *Alabama Journal*, April 29, 1955, 8; "Public Housing Plans for City Given Approval," *Alabama Journal*, May 3, 1955, 1; "Mayor Announces Receipt of Housing Plan Approval," *Montgomery Advertiser*, May 4, 1955, 10; "Federal Group Eyes Housing in Capital City," *Montgomery Advertiser*, May 6, 1955, 14.

35. "City Planning to Continue Negotiating for 184-Unit Jackson Heights Project," *Montgomery Advertiser*, May 12, 1955, 1.

36. Jackson Heights was purchased for $811,032. See "Plan for Buying Housing Talked," *Alabama Journal*, May 19, 1955, 1; "Detailed Review of Improvement Reported For City's 5-Year Plan," *Montgomery Advertiser*, August 13, 1956, 1–3. Jackson Heights was demolished in 1978. See Lenore Reese, "HUD Nays More Funds for Razing," *Alabama Journal*, December 1, 1978, PISF, ADAH.

37. For an example of the increasing sophistication of planning methods, compare the PWA surveys for Riverside Heights and Paterson Court, W. P. Nelson, "Dwelling and Tenant Survey of Property Included for Proposed Project #401—Negro," n.d., RG 196, NA2, 4; J. T. Porter, "Dwelling and Tenant Survey of Certain Properties in Montgomery, Alabama of White Tenancy with Reference to Housing Project H-401, White Division," n.d., RG 196, NA2; with Montgomery Board of

City Commissioners, *North Montgomery Slum Clearance Plan* (Montgomery, AL: Montgomery City Commission, 1951); and City Planning Commission, *A Transportation Plan for Montgomery: A Part of the Comprehensive City Plan* (Montgomery, AL: City Planning Commission, 1966); demonstrating the evolution of planning methods.

## *Chapter 4*

1. The advertisement also accused politicians of allowing city employees to live in Riverside Heights to create a voting bloc. See "Is It Fair?," *Montgomery Advertiser*, March 11, 1951, 13. On the other side of the discussion were those who equated slums with tuberculosis, fires, and crime. See "Slum Arguments," *Alabama Journal*, July 14, 1945, 4; "Report Reveals 33 Diseases Suitable for Germ Warfare," *Montgomery Advertiser*, May 19, 1947, 2. See also "Home Building," *Alabama Journal*, September 17, 1945, 4.

2. Although incremental planning was not a stated goal of planning, much of the earlier planning in Montgomery was on a case-by-case basis. See Charles Lindblom, "The Science of 'Muddling Through,'" *Public Administration Review* 19, no. 2 (1959): 79–88.

3. "Cities' Decay Seen without New Highways," *Montgomery Advertiser*, September 29, 1947, 7.

4. *Brown v. Board of Education of Topeka*, 347 U.S. 483 (1954).

5. "Tuskegee Honors Advertiser Scribe," *The Huntsville Times*, January 14, 1954; "Thurgood Marshall to Speak in Anniston, Ala.," *Alabama Tribune*, January 15, 1954, 1.

6. "Negroes to Abide by Court's Ruling," *The Huntsville Times*, January 24, 1954, 3. At the time of Marshall's speeches in Alabama, the US Supreme Court had not yet released its decision in the *Brown* case.

7. "School Bars 23 Negroes in Alabama," *Hartford Courant* (Hartford, Connecticut), September 3, 1954, 35. Horace Bell was murdered in 1959 while fishing outside Montgomery. His son, William Bell, applied for admission to Auburn University in 1948 but withdrew his application because of the threats and bullying.

8. Abraham's Vineyard was labeled "totally dilapidated" in the 1965 neighborhood analysis.

9. Joseph Bagley, *The Politics of White Rights* (Athens: University of Georgia Press, 2018). The parents asked for a lunchroom for the school, but the school board told them that it was not practical to have dining facilities at a school for just eighty children. The relocation of the school situated it closer to the students' homes so they could walk home for lunch. It was also convenient for segregationists because it was

farther away from the new white school. See "What Makes One School Better Than Another?," *Montgomery Advertiser*, September 6, 1954, 4.

10. Fred Gray wrote that students in Abraham's Vineyard needed to travel to Booker T. Washington Elementary School across town, passing by Harrison Elementary School. However, other accounts indicate that students attended Vineyard School when the integration attempt occurred. See Fred Gray, *Bus Ride to Justice* (Montgomery, AL: Black Belt Press, 1995); "What Makes One School Better Than Another?," *Montgomery Advertiser*, September 6, 1954, 4.

11. Most of the signatories of the petition were the parents who sought to enroll their children in the school. See Walt Harrington, "A Person Who Wanted to Be Free," *The Washington Post*, October 8, 1995, accessed April 15, 2021; "Negro Parents Blame Registration Effort on 'Broken Promises,'" *The Dothan Eagle*, September 7, 1954, 2.

12. Joe Azbell, "Montgomery NAACP Requests Hearing to Discuss End of School Segregation," *Montgomery Advertiser*, September 17, 1954, 1, 9.

13. Ironically, editors of the *Montgomery Advertiser* and *Alabama Journal* published stories about cancelation of the meeting because of unwanted publicity. See Jack Freeman, "School Parley Out to Avoid Any Publicity," *Montgomery Advertiser*, September 10, 1954, 1; "School Parley Is Canceled," *Alabama Journal*, September 10, 1954, 13.

14. "NAACP to Skip Board Meeting," *Alabama Journal*, October 8, 1954, 1.

15. "Pupil's Parents Split on Ending Segregation in Public Schools," *Alabama Citizen*, October 9, 1954, 1.

16. Joe Azbell, "Montgomery NAACP Requests Hearing to Discuss End of School Segregation," *Montgomery Advertiser*, September 17, 1954, 1, 9.

17. Carl Grafton and Anne Permaloff, *Big Mules and Branchheads: James E. Folsom and Political Power in Alabama* (Athens: University of Georgia Press, 1985), 186.

18. Alabama Citizens' Committee for Schools, "Questions and Answers," October 3, 1955, RALC, TSCC.

19. Rex Thomas, "Private School Bill Proposed by Legislator," *Montgomery Advertiser*, December 7, 1952; Gene Wortsman, "'Workable' School Segregation Plan Given to Persons," *Birmingham Post-Herald*, September 9, 1954; "Kennedy Will Have to Clear Up Engelhardt Backing, Says Powell," *Alabama Journal*, July 16, 1960.

20. Randolph Hohle, "The Color of Neoliberalism: The 'Modern Southern Businessman' and Postwar Alabama's Challenge to Racial Segregation," *Sociological Forum* 27, no. 1 (March 2012): 142–62; Lewis W. Jones, "Desegregation of Public Education in Alabama," *Journal of Negro Education* 24, no 3 (1955): 165–71; Charles Cooper, "Memorandum Prepared for Hon. Sam Engelhardt, Jr.: Segregation in Public Schools," November 26, 1952, SEC, ADAH; "Segregation Solution Talked,"

*Birmingham News*, September 9, 1954; "Jefferson's Legislatures Favor Special Session on Segregation," *Birmingham News*, October 11, 1954.

21. Joseph Bagley, *The Politics of White Rights* (Athens: University of Georgia Press, 2018); Hugh Sparrow, "Segregation Legislation Speedup Is Indicated," *Birmingham News*, January 10, 1955.

22. Hugh Sparrow, "Segregation Legislation Speedup Is Indicated," *Birmingham News*, January 10, 1955; Gordon Harvey, *A Question of Justice, New South Governors and Education, 1968–1976* (Tuscaloosa: University of Alabama Press, 2002).

23. "Negro Park Board Member to Get City Consideration," *Montgomery Advertiser*, January 19, 1955, 1.

24. "Negro Park Hearing Set This Afternoon," *Alabama Journal*, September 13, 1955, 1.

25. Alabama Council on Human Relations, "New Stroke in the South's Cold War," November 1955, RALC, TSCC.

26. Cleere's brother was the bus driver involved in the arrest of Claudette Colvin. See Patricia Sullivan, ed., *Freedom Writer: Virginia Foster Durr, Letters from the Civil Rights Years* (New York: Routledge, 2003); Thornton, *Dividing Lines*.

27. See Thornton, *Dividing Lines*, 48. See also Evan Faulkenbury, *Poll Power: The Voter Education Project and the Movement for the Ballot in the American South* (Chapel Hill: University of North Carolina Press, 2019).

28. Before the election, Clyde Sellers gave "the most blatantly and insistently racist addresses heard in Montgomery since disfranchisement in 1901." Thornton, *Dividing Lines*, 50. See also "Win with Sellers," *Montgomery Advertiser*, March 20, 1955, 28; "Reelect W. A. Gayle, Mayor," *Montgomery Advertiser*, February 1, 1955, 7.

29. For more information on municipal politics in Montgomery, see Thornton, *Dividing Lines*.

30. In Birmingham, I-65, I-59, and I-20 were routed through the heart of the city, and I-459 was located to the south. However, plans for interstates in small and mid-size cities such as Anniston-Oxford, Gadsden-Attalla, Huntsville, Tuscaloosa, and Montgomery had interstate highways located outside of town, with spur connectors into downtown. See "Interstate Highway Locations, revised 11/12/76," November 12, 1976, RG 406, NA2. Federal highway engineer B. P. McWhorter wrote to B. A. Scott that the interstate in Birmingham should justifiably be located through town: "Alabama does not have the traffic and other data needed to fully justify these requests [in other Alabama cities], but we feel that the need in the Birmingham area is sufficiently apparent to justify." See B. P. McWhorter to B. A. Scott, July 14, 1955, RG 406, NA2, 1. See also "Original Submissions of Urban Additions in Reply to Memo of January 5, 1955," n.d., RG 406, NA2; Ryan Reft, Amanda K. Phillips De Lucas, and Rebecca C.

Retzlaff, eds., *Justice and the Interstates: The Racist Truth about Urban Highways* (Washington, DC: Island Press, 2023); Sarah Jo Peterson, *The Transportation Research Board: Everyone Interested Is Invited* (Washington, DC: National Academies Press, 2020); A. C. Clark letter to Division and District Engineers, July 9, 1955, RG 406, NA2.

31. Helen Leavitt, *Superhighway—Superhoax* (Garden City, NY: Doubleday and Company, Inc., 1970); Mark Rose, *Interstate: Express Highway Politics, 1941–1956* (Lawrence: Regents Press of Kansas, 1979); Bruce Seely, *Building the American Highway System: Engineers as Policy Makers* (Philadelphia, PA: Temple University Press, 1987), 214; Richard Weingroff, "Federal-Aid Highway Act of 1956: Creating the Interstate System," Federal Highway Administration, accessed December 4, 2019; Richard Weingroff, "From 1916 to 1939: The Federal-State Partnership at Work," Federal Highway Administration, accessed December 4, 2019; Mark Rose and Raymond Mohl, *Interstate: Highway Politics and Policy Since 1939, 3rd ed.* (Knoxville: University of Tennessee Press, 2012); Matthew Roth, "Whittier Boulevard, Sixth Street Bridge, and the Origins of Transportation Exploitation in East Los Angeles," *Journal of Urban History* 30, no. 5 (2004): 729–48; Mark Rose, "Reframing American Highway Politics, 1956–1995," *Journal of Planning History* 2, no. 3 (2003): 212–36; Henry Moon, *The Interstate Highway System* (Washington, DC: Association of American Geographers, 1994).

32. B. P. McWhorter to B. A. Scott, July 14, 1955, RG 406, NA2. The proposed bypass routes would closely follow the system of at-grade bypasses around Montgomery that began construction in the early 1950s. The system, when fully constructed, would allow motorists to bypass the city entirely, with the exception of a small part of the northwest section of the city. Once constructed, the southern bypass immediately posed access management problems because they were designed as surface roads.

33. Mark Rose and Raymond Mohl, *Interstate: Highway Politics and Policy Since 1939, 3rd ed.* (Knoxville: University of Tennessee Press, 2012); Thomas Karnes, *Asphalt and Politics: A History of the American Highway System* (Jefferson, NC: McFarland, 2009).

34. Colvin was arrested on March 2, her trial was on March 18, and the election was on March 21. The charge was dropped on appeal and her juvenile record was expunged in 2021.

35. Colvin's charges of violating the bus segregation ordinance were dropped on appeal, and the circuit court found her guilty of assault and battery of a police officer. In October Mary Louise Smith was also arrested for violating the Montgomery bus segregation ordinance, but she pled guilty, and the issue did not become public

knowledge. Smith was later a party in the YMCA desegregation cases. See Jonathan Eig, *King: A Life* (New York: Farrar, Strauss, and Grioux, 2023).

36. Patricia Sullivan, ed., *Freedom Writer: Virginia Foster Durr, Letters from the Civil Rights Years* (New York: Routledge, 2003), 90. Lister Hill authored the federal Hospital Construction and Survey Act of 1946, which funded segregated hospital facilities and later gave hospitals priority for locating in an urban renewal area. See Christopher MacGregor Scribner, *Renewing Birmingham: Federal Funding and the Promise of Change, 1929–1979* (Athens: University of Georgia Press, 2002); Rebecca Retzlaff, "Catholics v. the Interstates: The Fight to Protect Catholic Institutions from Interstate Highways in Birmingham, Alabama," *Journal of Transport History* 41, no. 3 (2020): 402–33.

37. Carl Grafton and Anne Permaloff, *Big Mules and Branchheads: James E. Folsom and Political Power in Alabama* (Athens: University of Georgia Press, 1985); Stephanie Rolph, *Resisting Equality: The Citizens' Council, 1954–1989* (Baton Rouge: Louisiana State University Press, 2018); Mark Newman, *Desegregating Dixie* (Jackson: University of Mississippi Press, 2008); Alabama Council on Human Relations Newsletter, "White Citizens Council Moves to the City," October 1955, RALC, TSCC; Alabama Council on Human Relations Newsletter, "Ku Klux Klan Revival," October 1955, RALC, TSCC.

38. Rufus Lewis letter to community members, December 1954, RALC, TSCC.

39. "Realtors, Home Builders Plan Rehabilitation Drive," *Alabama Journal*, August 26, 1955, 9; "Building Plans Will Be Talked," *Alabama Journal*, October 26, 1955, 1; "Operation Home Improvement Takes Strong Hold in Program Starting This Week, Lasting for a Year," *Montgomery Advertiser*, April 1, 1955, 54.

40. The new group established four subcommittees: administrative, legal, financing, and public relations. See "Move Launched to Clear City of Slum Sections," *Alabama Journal*, October 28, 1955, 5.

41. "City's Sub-Standard Property Called Second Worse in U.S.," *Montgomery Advertiser*, March 7, 1956, 9.

42. Fred Gray, Willy Leventhal, Frank Sikora, J. Mills Thornton III, *The Children Coming On . . . A Retrospective of the Montgomery Bus Boycott* (Montgomery, AL: Black Belt Press, 2007); Fred Gray, *Bus Ride to Justice* (Montgomery, AL: Black Belt Press, 1995); Fred Gray, "The Making of a Lawyer," in *Voices of Civil Rights Lawyers*, ed. Kent Springs (Tallahassee: University Press of Florida, 2017), 9–16; Clippings File, E. D. Nixon, MPL.

43. Sullivan, *Freedom Writer*.

44. The boycott had largely been led by women to that point, but WPC members believed that large-scale mobilization of the boycott needed the assistance and

leadership of male ministers. While ministers were the formal head of the boycott, women did much of the legwork, and they were most affected by bus segregation. As Robnett explains, "Most of the cars owned by African Americans were owned and driven by men. The ministers had cars. It was African American women who suffered the indignities of segregated busses daily." See Belinda Robnett, *How Long? How Long?* (New York: Oxford University Press, 1997); Mary Fair Burks, "Trailblazers: Women in the Montgomery Bus Boycott," in *Black Women in United States History*, ed. Darlene Clark Hine (Brooklyn, NY: Carlson, 1990), 71–83; Robert Gratz, *A White Preacher's Message on Race and Reconciliation* (Montgomery, AL: New South Books, 2006); Jo Ann Robinson, *The Montgomery Bus Boycott and the Woman Who Started It* (Knoxville: University of Tennessee Press, 1987); Edward Cashin and Glenn Eskew, eds., *Paternalism in a Southern City* (Athens: University of Georgia Press, 2001); Robert Norrell, *The House I Live In: Race in the American Century* (New York: Oxford University Press, 2005); "Programs: Mass Meeting Programs," n.d., Montgomery Improvement Association Collection, LWLC.

45. "City's Sub-Standard Property Called Second Worse in U.S.," *Montgomery Advertiser*, March 7, 1956, 9.

46. Joe Azbell, "City Limits," *Montgomery Advertiser*, March 18, 1956, 11.

47. Rebecca Retzlaff, "Desegregation of City Parks and the Civil Rights Movement: The Case of Oak Park in Montgomery, Alabama," *Journal of Urban History* 47, no. 4 (2021): 715–52.

48. Joseph Bagley, *The Politics of White Rights: Race, Justice, and Integrating Alabama's Schools* (Athens: University of Georgia Press, 2018), 13; Sullivan *Freedom Writer*; Clippings File, E. D. Nixon, MPL; Centennial Celebration Committee, *A Century of Negro Progress in Montgomery City and County* (Montgomery, AL: Centennial Celebration Committee, 1963).

49. Jack Freeman, "White School Turns Down 23 Negro Children in City," *Montgomery Advertiser*, September 3, 1954, 1. Aubrey Williams Jr., one of the white people who accompanied the group, received death threats that evening. See "Aubrey Williams Jr. Reports 2 Threats Made against Life," *Montgomery Advertiser*, September 3, 1954, 1.

50. Joe Azbell, "City Limits," *Montgomery Advertiser*, March 18, 1956, 11.

51. Thornton points out that white supremacy—not just segregation—was the overall objective of white public officials, after they rejected proposals from African American people that would preserve segregation, such as a plan for bus seating that maintained segregation but did not allow bus drivers to unseat African American passengers, and a proposal for a African American jitney service. As Thornton writes, "The initiative of blacks and under black control was unacceptable because

authorities' genuine motive, whether consciously or unconsciously, was not the separation of the races but the subordination of blacks to whites." See J. Mills Thornton III, *Dividing Lines: Municipal Politics and the Struggle for Civil Rights in Montgomery, Birmingham, and Selma* (Tuscaloosa: University of Alabama Press, 2002), 73, 78.

52. Robinson, *The Montgomery Bus Boycott and the Woman Who Started It*, 112; Graetz, *A White Preacher's Message on Race and Reconciliation.*

53. Congressional Research Service, *A Chronology of Housing Legislation and Selected Executive Actions, 1892–1992* (Washington, DC: US Government Printing Office, 1993).

54. Lillian Deloach, "Citizens Group Declares War on City Slum Areas," *Montgomery Advertiser*, December 5, 1956, 1.

## *Chapter 5*

1. "Qualified Voters in Montgomery County, Alabama," *Montgomery Advertiser*, March 31, 1958; "Official List of Voters" *Montgomery Examiner*, March 23, 1949. See also Montgomery County Board of Registers, "Alphabetical List of the Qualified Electors in Montgomery County, Alabama, 1928," ADAH; "Alphabetical List of Qualified Electors in Montgomery County, Alabama," *Montgomery Advertiser*, March 12, 1938.

2. Committee on Countywide Registration and Voting to Montgomery Improvement Association Executive Committee, March 8, 1956, RALC, TSCC.

3. Rufus Lewis to Block Leader, November 18, 1957, RALC, TSCC.

4. Women's Political Council, "Voter's Education Handbook on Voting in City, County, State, National Elections," n.d., RALC, TSCC.

5. Lillian Deloach, "Citizens Group Declares War on City Slum Areas," *Montgomery Advertiser*, December 5, 1956, 1, 6; "Mayor Gayle Denies Shunning Private Housing Improvements," *Montgomery Advertiser*, January 18, 1957, 7.

6. The group proposed the following housing code language: "The dwellings that are worth repairing would be made to comply with the new city housing code. Only those which are not worth repairing would be torn down. The vacant lots can be sold by the owners or used by them as sites for new dwellings. The owner of the property may decide whether to repair or remove the substandard dwelling but he must do one or the other." See "Montgomery, Second in Substandard Housing," *Montgomery Advertiser*, December 7, 1956, 4; "Mayor Answers Critics About Slum Clearance," *Alabama Journal*, December 6, 1956, 48.

7. John Bitter, "Insurance Firm's Premium Writing Exceeds $5 Million," *Montgomery Advertiser*, March 15, 1970; Vernon Guidry, "City Acts Thursday on Garbage Fees," *Montgomery Advertiser*, January 11, 1967; "Engineers Tour Plant at Prattville," *Montgomery Advertiser*, July 16, 1966; Gene Kovarik, "Closeup . . . Gene Brock,"

*Montgomery Advertiser*, November 1, 1964. The firm worked on plans in Illinois, Florida, Georgia, Mississippi, and Alabama. Other staff included Tom Bulloch, Jerry Mitchell, Mike Mandelbaum, and James Turner.

8. The only copy that this author has been able to locate is marked "draft," from the Montgomery Public Library.

9. The consultant who prepared the land use plan, Urban Consultants Associates, based in Montgomery, also authored the 1966 Montgomery transportation plan and many other plans in the city. Very little information about the consultant or its staff has been uncovered by this author. See City Planning Commission, *A Transportation Plan for Montgomery: A Part of the Comprehensive City Plan* (Montgomery, AL: City Planning Commission, 1966); Urban Consultant Associates, *Land Use Plan (2nd Draft), Montgomery, Alabama* (Montgomery: City Planning Commission, 1957).

10. Nicholas N. Patricios, "The Neighborhood Concept: A Retrospective of Physical Design and Social Interaction," *Journal of Architectural and Planning Research*, 19, no. 1 (2002): 70–90; Henry Churchill, "Henry Wright," in Don Krueckeberg, ed., *The American Planner: Biographies and Recollections, 2nd ed.* (New Brunswick, NJ: Center for Urban Policy Research, 1983), 243–64; Jon Paterson, *The Birth of City Planning in the United States, 1840–1917* (Baltimore, MD: Johns Hopkins University Press, 2003). The neighborhood unit concept borrowed from earlier neighborhood planning ideas, including the plan for Sunnyside Gardens in New York. See Daniel Pearlstein, "Sweeping Six Percent Philanthropy Away: The New Deal in Sunnyside Gardens," *Journal of Planning History* 9, no. 3 (2010): 170–82.

11. Cities throughout Alabama and the South used the neighborhood unit theory to keep schools segregated. In Opelika the *Southern Courier* reported that the neighborhood unit theory was being used to keep schools segregated: "The city officials are using urban renewal to move Negroes from one part of town to another . . . when they have the town divided into Negro and white sections, they'll try to set up school zones along these lines. That way they'll have segregated housing and segregated schools." See Mary Ellen Gale, "Is Opelika Keeping Segregation?," *Southern Courier* 1, no. 8 (1965), 5. In Union Springs the NAACP opposed the city housing authority's plans to build white public housing in white neighborhoods and African American public housing in African American neighborhoods, on the grounds that it would perpetuate segregation. See Mary Ellen Gale, "Public Housing Fight Is Settled in Bullock," *Southern Courier* 3 no. 23 (1967), 2. In Birmingham planning consultant Harland Bartholomew used the neighborhood unit theory in the 1961 comprehensive plan and recommended that an elementary school be at the center of every neighborhood. The plan was an attempt to maintain school segregation by keeping neighborhoods segregated. See Harland Bartholomew and Associates, *The*

*Comprehensive Plan, Birmingham, Alabama* (Birmingham, AL: Birmingham Planning Commission 1961); Charles Connerly, *The Most Segregated City in America: City Planning and Civil Rights in Birmingham, 1920–1980* (Charlottesville: University of Virginia Press, 2005); Rebecca Retzlaff, "Connecting Public School Segregation with Urban Renewal and Interstate Highway Planning: The Case of Birmingham, Alabama," *Journal of Planning History* 19, no. 4 (2020): 256–80; Christopher Silver, *Twentieth-Century Richmond: Planning, Politics, and Race* (Knoxville: University of Tennessee Press, 1984); Harland Bartholomew, "City Planning and Housing," *Planning and Civic Comment* 1, no. 2 (April-June 1935), 12–13; Harland Bartholomew, "Neighborhood Rehabilitation and the Taxpayer," *The American City* (February 1938), 57; Harland Bartholomew, "The Neighborhood—Key to Urban Redemption," *American Planning and Civic Annual* (1941), 243–47; Thomas Hanchett, *Sorting out the New South City* (Chapel Hill: University of North Carolina Press, 1998); Nicholas N. Patricios, "The Neighborhood Concept: A Retrospective of Physical Design and Social Interaction," *Journal of Architectural and Planning Research* 19, no. 1 (2002): 70–90; Henry Churchill, "Henry Wright," in *The American Planner: Biographies and Recollections, 2nd ed.*, ed. Don Krueckeberg (New Brunswick, NJ: Center for Urban Policy Research, 1983), 243–64; Jon Paterson, *The Birth of City Planning in the United States, 1840–1917* (Baltimore, MD: Johns Hopkins University Press, 2003).

12. Just ten of the thirty-eight white neighborhoods contained any blight. See Urban Consultant Associates, *Land Use Plan (2nd Draft)*, 42.

13. Three African American neighborhoods located far from downtown were not declared blighted. All had very low populations (populations of 386, 70, and 175, respectively). The only African American neighborhood that contained no blight was a newly built subdivision.

14. The proposed population increase for neighborhood 49 was from 70 people to 4,000, neighborhood 50 from 175 people to 4,600 people, and neighborhood 51 from 170 people to 5,000 people. See Urban Consultant Associates, *Land Use Plan (2nd Draft)*.

15. Urban Consultant Associates, *Land Use Plan (2nd Draft)*, 42.

16. Rosalind McClellan, "New Homes Hard to Find; Decent One Costs $12,000," *Southern Courier* 2, no. 35 (1966), 4. The Fifth Amendment of the US Constitution limits the government's power of eminent domain through the Takings Clause, which stipulates "nor shall private property be taken for public use, without just compensation." Accordingly, property owners were paid for their land, but renters were not compensated because they did not own the property.

17. McClellan, "New Homes Hard to Find," 4.

18. McClellan, "New Homes Hard to Find," 4.

19. In the 1800s the neighborhood was home to wealthy white residents, but by 1920 it transitioned to an African American neighborhood. E. D. Nixon, Dr. Alfred Colman Dungee, Rosa Parks, and Lucille Times also lived in the neighborhood. See City of Montgomery Planning Commission, *Rosa Parks Combined Communities and Five Points Neighborhood Plan* (Montgomery, AL: Montgomery Planning Commission, 2008); Gratz, *A White Preacher's Message on Race and Reconciliation.*

20. The interchange was eventually shifted a few blocks southwest and the two churches were not demolished.

21. The plan had the goal of modernizing shopping areas. Planners noted, "Many of the older small shopping areas were not designed for modern living and do not provide adequate automobile parking. In some of these areas, there is a history of business failure." Planners dismissed African American–owned businesses as less legitimate than white-owned businesses, writing, "In a number of places in the older parts of the city the pattern of existing businesses is such that the term, Local Shopping, could not describe the business area. This is particularly true of the two largest Negro areas. The businesses in these cases are indicated on the plan as 'Business' and have in a very minor way the characteristics of a central business area." See Urban Consultant Associates, *Land Use Plan (2nd Draft)*, 50.

22. For other research supporting the idea that midcentury urban policy could not counteract the forces of suburbanization, see Kevin Kruse and Thomas Sugrue, eds., *The New Suburban History* (Chicago: University of Chicago Press, 2006); Kevin Kruse, *White Flight: Atlanta and the Making of Modern Conservatism* (Princeton, NJ: Princeton University Press, 2005).

23. The FHA required approval of housing plans and codes as a condition of receiving federal urban renewal assistance. See "Home Code Held Likely after Talks," *Montgomery Advertiser*, September 28, 1957, 1; "City Commission Okays Housing Code Ordinance," *Alabama Journal*, October 15, 1957, 1–2; "Toned-Down House Code Awaits Commission's OK," *Montgomery Advertiser*, October 15, 1957, 10; "More Changes Aimed at Proposed Housing Code," *Alabama Journal*, October 4, 1957, 1; and Gordon Cavanaugh, "Public Housing: From Archaic to Dynamic to Endangered," *Journal of Affordable Housing and Community Development Law* 14, no. 3 (2005): 228–47.

24. Rosalind McClellan, "New Homes Hard to Find; Decent One Costs $12,000," *Southern Courier* 2, no. 35 (1966): 4.

25. These numbers were reported in newspapers, but the author was unable to find a comprehensive list of the number homes that were demolished. See "Minimum Housing Code Fights Sub-Standard Living," *Montgomery Advertiser*, October 21, 1962, 63; "Housing Code Fights Decay," *Montgomery Advertiser*, December 28,

1958, 65; Gene Kovarik, "City to Build 1,000 Public Low Rent Units," *Alabama Journal*, November 3, 1964, PISF, ADAH. In December 1960 sewerage infrastructure was provided along Mary, Houser, Auburn, Bellview, Broadview, Council, and Dorothy Streets, which were among the last in the city to get sewerage lines. See "Council Okays Sewers for Streets," *Alabama Journal*, December 9, 1960, 19.

26. "Engelhardt Is Dubbed 'Leading Segregationist,'" *Alabama Journal*, June 22, 1960, SECS, ADAH.

27. "Emergency Announcement to White Voters," *Montgomery Advertiser*, March 21, 1959, 11.

28. Gene Howard, *Patterson for Alabama: The Life and Career of John Patterson* (Tuscaloosa: University of Alabama Press, 2008); Warren Trest, *Nobody but the People: The Life and Times of Alabama's Youngest Governor* (Montgomery, AL: New South Books, 2008). "The City Election," *Montgomery Improvement Association Newsletter* 1, no. 2 (April 30, 1959), RALC, TSCC, 1. Rufus Lewis sent letters to African American residents urging them to vote for Earl James, and L. B. Sullivan. See Rufus Lewis to Fellow citizens, n.d., RALC, TSCC.

29. "The City Election," *Montgomery Improvement Association Newsletter* 1, no. 2 (April 30, 1959), The Honorable Rufus A. Lewis Collection, MIA and ACAH box 3, TSCC, 1.

30. After route B (the downtown route) was ruled out, route C (the bypass route) was sometimes referred to as route B or route 2. The author uses the terms "peninsula route," "downtown route," and "bypass route" for clarity.

31. Charles Connerly, "From Racial Zoning to Community Empowerment: The Interstate Highway System and the African American Community in Birmingham, Alabama," *Journal of Planning Education and Research* 22, no. 2 (2002): 99–114; Ronald Bayor, "Roads to Racial Segregation: Atlanta in the Twentieth Century," *Journal of Urban History* 15, no. 1 (1988): 3–21; Charles Connerly and Bobby Wilson, "The Roots and Origins of African-American Planning in Birmingham, Alabama," in *Urban Planning and the African American Community: In the Shadows*, ed. June Manning Thomas (New York: Sage, 1997): 201–19.

32. The AHD limited the scope of the USGS analysis, only requesting analysis based on one issue: if there would be enough space between the interstate bridge and an exit for Highway 152. The USGS analysis noted that the AHD specifically asked them not to study the hydraulic properties of the entire interstate crossing and concluded that there would be sufficient room for the exit. See B. A. Scott to H. L. Nelson, September 23, 1958, RG 30, NAA, 1.

33. Murrel Wilburn to B. A. Scott, November 13, 1958, RG 30, NAA, 2; B. E. Huggins to Reese Harvey, November 4, NAA; M. R. Steward, "Alabama River At

Montgomery, Alabama, Hydraulic Factors at Bridge Site on Interstate Route Montgomery County," October 1958, RG 30, United States Geologic Survey Report no. I-202–2, RG 30, NAA; B. A. Scott to Rex Anderson, May 6, 1960, RG 30, NAA.

34. B. A. Scott to Rex Anderson, February 28, 1957, RG 30, NAA; Alabama Highway Department to employees, March 21, 1958, RG 30, NAA; City of Montgomery Resolution, March 24, 1958, RG 30, NAA; Montgomery City Commission, "City of Montgomery Resolution Exhibit A," March 24, 1958, RG 30, NAA.

35. The amount budgeted for the two proposed new parks was $633,000. See "2 Negro Parks For $633,000 Agency's Aim," *Montgomery Advertiser*, February 14, 1957, PISF—General, SG6978/1, ADAH.

36. "Facts Relating to Recent Violence Inflicted Upon Negro Citizens of Montgomery, Alabama," May 28, 1959, Montgomery Improvement Association Collection, LWLC. See also Martin Luther King Jr., Ralph D. Abernathy, and S. S. Seay Sr. to Governor Patterson, May 28, 1959, Gwen Patton Collection, TSCC; Martin Luther King Jr., Ralph D. Abernathy, and S. S. Seay Sr. to William P. Rogers, n.d., Gwen Patton Collection, TSCC.

37. Parks was charged with disorderly conduct for refusing to obey the orders of a bus driver to give up her seat to a white man. See "Police Report of Rosa Parks Arrest," Dec. 1, 1955, RG 21, NAA.

38. Judy Wagnon, "Negro to Appeal Oak Park Fine," *Montgomery Advertiser*, October 15, 1957, 1.

39. Eugene Kavorik, "City Commission Orders Parks to Close Jan 1," *Montgomery Advertiser*, 2.

40. Emily Blejwas, "Georgia Gilmore," Encyclopedia of Alabama, September 24, 2019, accessed April 6, 2021.

41. "Negro Leaders to Meet Ike," *Alabama Journal*, June 20, 1958; "Judge Upholds Ruling," *Alabama Journal*, June 23, 1958, 2.

42. Dan Dowe, "Integration Drive Faces Stiff Fight," *Alabama Journal*, December 31, 1958, PISF, ADAH (quoting Rev. Dr. Martin Luther King Jr.), 1.

43. "Council Head Sees Integration Failure," *Selma Times-Journal*, December 31, 1958, 2.

44. David Pearson, "School Integration Aimed at Capital," *Birmingham Post-Herald*, December 31, 1958, 3; George Prentice, "King Avows Push Slated Early in '59," *Montgomery Advertiser*, December 31, 1958, 1.

45. Dan Dowe, "Integration Drive Faces Stiff Fight," *Alabama Journal*, December 31, 1958, 1.

46. "Warning Issued by Klan on Race Mixing," *Alabama Journal*, January 3, 1959, 11.

47. "Judges Silent on Jury Plea," *Alabama Journal*, January 7, 1959, 1.

48. "King Back; Vows Fight to Continue," *Alabama Journal*, March 24, 1959, 11; "Doings of the Dexterites . . ." *The Dexter Echo: The Official Publication of Dexter Avenue Baptist Church*, March 11, 1959, RALC, TSCC.

49. "No Intention of Mixing Parks Say Officials," *Montgomery Advertiser*, August 26, 1958, PISF, ADAH, 1.

50. "No Intention of Mixing Parks Say Officials," *Montgomery Advertiser*, August 26, 1958, PISF, ADAH, 1; "Citizens Find Barriers at Local Parks," *Montgomery Advertiser*, January 2, 1959, PISF, ADAH, 1.

51. "Abernathy Assaulted—King Arrested," *Montgomery Improvement Association Newsletter* 1, no. 10 (September 27, 1958), RALC, TSCC.

52. "Parks Fight Has Been Continuing New Story," *Montgomery Advertiser*, December 31, 1958, 2.

53. Taking a cue from the Montgomery committees on community affairs, Shuttlesworth suggested the creation of a biracial committee in Birmingham to open up communication over desegregation issues, including parks.

54. "Court Action Could Outlaw Segregation in City Parks," *Montgomery Advertiser*, September 8, 1959, PISF, ADAH, 1.

55. Dick Hines, "U.S. Judge Rules Out Segregated City Parks," *Montgomery Advertiser*, September 9, 1959, 1–2; Dan Dowe, "City Must Close or Mix Parks; Segregation Out, Court Asserts," *Alabama Journal*, September 8, 1959, 1–2.

56. "Georgia Theresa Gilmore v. City of Montgomery," *Race Relations Law Reporter* 5, no. 2 (Summer 1960): 455–59; "Georgia Theresa Gilmore v. City of Montgomery," *Race Relations Law Reporter* 4, no. 2 (Spring 1959): 977–88; "Board of Commissioners Resolution, December 1958," *Race Relations Law Reporter* 4, no. 1 (Spring 1959): 206.

57. Dick Hines, "Hospital Group Eyes Oak Park Site," *Montgomery Advertiser*, September 11, 1959, PISF, ADAH, 1.

58. Hines, "Hospital Group Eyes Oak Park Site," 1.

59. Dick Hines, "Decision Tightens Lock on Recreation Facilities," *Montgomery Advertiser*, September 9, 1959, 1.

60. Hines, "Decision Tightens Lock on Recreation Facilities," 2.

61. "All Animals at Zoo Offered for Sale," *Alabama Journal*, December 11, 1959, PISF, ADAH, 1.

62. Dick Hines, "Before-After Views of Oak Park Show Carefree Life, Quiet Death," *Montgomery Advertiser*, January 14, 1960, 9.

63. "Idle Oak Park," *Montgomery Advertiser*, June 21, 1960, 4.

64. Eugene Kovarik, "City Commission Orders Parks to Close Jan 1," *Montgomery Advertiser*, Dec 30, 1958, 1–2.

65. "It Is Not to Be in Oak Park," *Montgomery Advertiser*, August 27, 1958, 4.

66. Rex Thomas, "Integration Drive Bared," *Montgomery Advertiser*, August 30, 1959, 1.

67. Thomas, "Integration Drive Bared," 1.

68. "No Special Meet on Integration Says McKee," *Alabama Journal*, August 31, 1959, 19.

69. $46,500 in 1913 (the earliest year available) would be $137,602 in 1959. See "Private School Corporation Buys Old Governor's Mansion," *Alabama Journal*, April 9, 1959, 1.

70. "Patterson Hopes New School Terms Open without Racial Disturbances," *Montgomery Advertiser*, August 30, 1959, 2.

71. "Governor Makes Plea to Negroes," *Montgomery Advertiser*, September 6, 1959, 1.

72. Rev. Dr. Martin Luther King Jr., Annual Address by President Martin Luther King Jr. on the Fourth Anniversary of the Montgomery Improvement Association, December 3, 1959, RALC, TSCC, 7.

73. "Negro Says Governor 'Sounds Desperate,'" *Alabama Journal*, September 7, 1959, 23.

74. "King Says Integration Try off This Week," *Alabama Journal*, August 31, 1959, 19; Art Osgoode, "Negroes Will Omit School Bid Thursday," *Montgomery Advertiser*, August 31, 1959, 1.

75. "No Integration Tried," *Alabama Journal*, September 3, 1959, 37.

76. King decided to leave Montgomery for many reasons, and school integration was just one of them. As fall approached, teachers and parents pressured Rev. Dr. King and the MIA to hold off on their school desegregation plans due to fears that the schools could be closed as the parks were. As Thornton notes, "During the fall, Paterson's admonitions began more and more to take hold among black schoolteachers, who formed a very large part of the city's black middle class—and an even larger part of King's own Dexter Avenue congregation—and who stood to pay with their jobs, of course, if the public schools were abolished. King and the MIA thereupon fell under quiet but urgent and rapidly mounting importunity from the black teachers not to turn to the courts. The parks suit seemed to prove that, though blacks would certainly win the order from Judge Johnson that they wanted, the actual result would only be private schools for well-to-do whites and none at all for poorer whites and blacks." Thornton, *Dividing Lines*, 105. See also Eig, *King: A Life*.

77. "School Integration Suit to Be Filed, King Asserts," *Alabama Journal*, December 4, 1959, 6.

78. The Montgomery Council on Human Relations urged African American

activists to resist splintering into class divisions, focus on big issues, and avoid divisive rumors and gossip. See "Yes, We Can, Too!" Montgomery Council on Human Relations Newsletter, April 21, 1960, RALC, TSCC; Rev. Martin Luther King Jr. to Rufus Lewis, January 12, 1959, RALC, TSCC. King recognized the potential problems with unity when he announced his departure, noting, "The important thing is that you get behind the person who is elected president, and be as loyal to him as you have been to me." See Rev. Dr. Martin Luther King Jr., *Annual Address by President Martin Luther King, Jr., on the Fourth Anniversary of the Montgomery Improvement Association*, December 3, 1959, RALC, TSCC, 15.

79. In the weeks prior to Rev. Dr. King's departure from Montgomery, Governor Patterson told the press that teachers and parents did not want schools integrated, announcing, "I am reliably informed that a number of Negro school teachers in this community have told Martin Lither King that . . . they weren't behind him on his school integration efforts, and that they were satisfied with the state's school program." See "King, Teachers Disagreed, Says Gov. Patterson," *Alabama Journal*, December 30, 1959, 1–2.

## *Chapter 6*

1. "Engelhardt Is Dubbed 'Leading Segregationist,'" *Alabama Journal*, June 22, 1960, 2.

2. "Negro Demand for Candidacy Court Hearing Opens Today," *Daily Times-Democrat*, March 22, 1962, SECS, ADAH; Sam Engelhardt to A. E. Johnson, "Biography" March 3, 1961, SEC, ADAH; Neil R. McMillen, *The Citizens' Council: Organized Resistance to the Second Reconstruction, 1954–64* (Chicago: University of Illinois Press, 1971); Carl Grafton and Anne Permaloff, *Big Mules and Branchheads: James E. Folsom and Political Power in Alabama*, (Athens: University of Georgia Press, 1985). In 1955 Engelhardt organized the Central Alabama Citizens' Council. He later became president of the Citizens' Council of Alabama, executive secretary for the National Association of Citizens' Councils, and chairman of the Citizens' Councils of America. The Citizens' Council also provided the core of his political support throughout his career. Although the Citizens' Council was established as a "respectable" segregationist organization and an alternative to the violence of the KKK, they were a serious threat because they used economic sanctions against African American people who favored integration. See "Citizens Council: The South's Only Answer," leaflet from the Citizens' Councils of Alabama, n.d., SEC, ADAH; "Constitution of the Wilcox County Citizens' Council," n.d., SEC, ADAH; Edward Pilley, "Council Leaders Exchange Blasts" *Birmingham Post-Herald*, SECS, ADAH; Sam Engelhardt speech, n.d., SEC, ADAH; "Sam Engelhardt's Tasks Ahead" *Centerville Press*, August 31, 1961,

SECS, ADAH, 73; "What Others Are Saying . . ." *The Wilcox Progressive Era*, SEC, ADAH, April 20, 1961; "Alabama Knights of the Ku Klux Klan Newsletter," n.d., SEC, ADAH; Sam Engelhardt speech to the Sylacauga Citizens' Council, n.d., SEC, ADAH.

3. Gene Howard, *Patterson for Alabama* (Tuscaloosa: University of Alabama Press, 2008). The $60 million bond for the highway program was quickly promoted as a political accomplishment, along with increased highway building. See Alabama Highway Department, *Forty-Ninth Annual Report of the Alabama Highway Department, October 1, 1959, to September 30, 1960* (Montgomery: Alabama Highway Department, 1960). Although the Alabama legislature established a gas tax in 1923, Patterson wanted to accelerate the highway program early in his term. The bond would be funded by a one-cent-per-gallon gas tax that was enacted during the Folsom administration. See Anne Permaloff and Carl Grafton, *Political Power in Alabama: The More Things Change . . .* (Athens: University of Georgia Press, 1995); Bob Ingram, "Patterson Confident on Bond Issue," *Montgomery Advertiser*, January 29, 1959, SEC, ADAH.

4. The memo from BPR engineer G. M. Williams noted, "The state has not sufficiently proved that its formal choice, line A . . . is the best location for Interstate 65 . . . line C passing just west of the city is less costly than line A by $14 million . . . benefit cost ratios, annual rates of return and solvency quotients for the three alternative locations are indecisive. . . . Line C is definitely superior from the hydraulic point of view inasmuch as lines A and B through 'the peninsula' involve a stretch of the Alabama River that is undergoing a long-time meander." G. M. Williams to R. S. Anderson, July 15, 1960, RG 30, NA2, 1. For a discussion of the BPR engineer's environmental concerns about route A, see B. A. Scott to Rex Anderson, March 10, 1959, RG 30, NAA, 4.

5. As B. A. Scott wrote, "It might be noted here that two major factors in Montgomery's economy are military installations . . . and a concentration of State and Federal Government activities in this State Capital, none of which are in or dependent on the C.B.D." See B. A. Scott to Rex Anderson, March 10, 1959, RG 30, NAA, 2.

6. B. A. Scott to B. P. McWhorter, August 28, 1956, RG 30, NAA; Bruce Maulden, "W. Bypass 'Treacherous,'" *Montgomery Advertiser*, July 7, 1976, 13; Lenore Reese, "Hearing Tonight to Focus on Maxwell-Interstate Link," *Alabama Journal*, September 7, 1978, 7.

7. Mark Rose and Raymond Mohl, *Interstate: Highway Politics Since 1939, 3rd ed.* (Knoxville: University of Tennessee Press, 2012).

8. B. A. Scott to Rex Anderson, March 10, 1959, RG 30, NAA, 3.

9. BPR engineers expressed serious concerns about the peninsula route, writing, "[The peninsula route] requires the construction of a high embankment along the

peninsula to the north of the Alabama River. The embankment will be a minimum of 30' in height and will rise to much greater heights at the interchange . . . the peninsula is low and is less than a mile wide. Obviously there will be serious problems of fill protection, hydraulic gradients through relief structures, space for an interchange between the bridge structures, etc." B. A. Scott to Rex Anderson, March 10, 1959, RG 30, NAA, 2. For an analysis of parking, see Alabama Highway Department, *1965 Parking Study, Montgomery, Alabama* (Montgomery: Alabama Highway Department, 1967).

10. B. A. Scott to Rex Anderson, February 28, 1957, RG 30, NAA, 1–2. Scott concluded that the I-65 route bypassing Montgomery was preferable because it was a midsize city and was not growing very fast: "It appears to this office that the expenditure of some 12 million dollars or more . . . to carry FAI 65 [I-65] through the city rather than on a bypass is hardly justified. It is also questionable as to whether such a location is in the best interest of a city of this size. Certainly the traffic needs can be met with at grade improvements." See B. A. Scott to Rex Anderson, March 10, 1959, RG 30, NAA, 4.

11. R. D. Jordan to B. A. Scott, April 2, 1959, March 10, 1959, RG 30, NAA, 1.

12. B. A. Scott to Sam Engelhardt, May 5, 1959, RG 30, NAA; Wilbur Smith to Reese Harvey, April 17, 1959, RG 30, NAA; Joseph W. Hurt to B. A. Scott, January 6 1960, RG 30, NAA; Rex Anderson to B. A. Scott, November 14, 1960, RG 30, NAA; B. A. Scott to Rex Anderson, July 1, 1959, RG 30, NAA; B. A. Scott to Sam Engelhardt, July 6, 1959, RG 30, NAA; Wilbur Smith and Associates, *Major Route Plan: Montgomery Metropolitan Area: Volume 2—Street and Highway Plan* (Montgomery: Alabama Highway Department, 1960); Wilbur Smith and Associates, *Major Route Plan: Montgomery Metropolitan Area: Volume 1—Highway and Travel Facts* (Montgomery: Alabama Highway Department, 1960); Montgomery City Planning Commission, *A Transportation Plan for Montgomery: A Part of the Comprehensive City Plan* (Montgomery, AL: Montgomery Planning Commission, 1962). The 1962 transportation plan roughly followed the Wilbur Smith plan. See G. M. Williams to Rex Anderson, August 24, 1961, RG 30, NA2.

13. Rex Anderson to B. A. Scott, July 7, 1960, RG 30, NA2, 1; B. A. Scot to Rex Anderson, July 18, 1960, RG 30, NA2.

14. C. A. Bowles to B. A. Scott, June 22, 1960, RG 30, NA2; "Agreement with Messner Engineers, Inc. for a Detailed Cost Estimate," May 18, 1960, RG 30, NA2.

15. B. A. Scott to Rex Anderson, May 27, 1960, RG 30, NAA, 1; B. A. Scott to Sam Engelhardt, March 22, 1960, RG 30, NAA; Henry Parrish to B. A. Scott, April 1, 1960, RG 30, NAA; M. K. Ferguson to B. A. Scott, November 14, 1960, RG 30, NAA. BPR engineer's analysis of the cost estimates uncovered errors of over $8 million for the bypass route and $300,000 for the peninsula route. See R. H. Talley to Rex Anderson,

November 4, 1960, RG 30, NAA; B. A. Scott to Sam Engelhardt, April 12, 1960, RG 30, NAA; B. A. Scott to Rex Anderson, May 6, 1960, RG 30, NAA, 1.

16. R. H. Talley to Rex Anderson, November 4, 1960, RG 30, NA2.

17. Raymond Mohl, "The Interstates and the Cities: Highways, Housing, and the Freeway Revolt," *Poverty and Race Research Action Council*, 2002, 23.

18. Raymond Mohl, "The Interstates and the Cities: Highways, Housing, and the Freeway Revolt," *Poverty and Race Research Action Council*, 2002, 24. Mohl quotes James Hutchinson to John Sparkman, November 3, 1963, RG 406, NA2; Rex M. Whitton to John Sparkman, November 20, 1963, RG 406, NA2. The letter was copied word-for-word many times in response to protests from homeowners, including in many letters concerning the interstates in Montgomery that used the same "based on a thorough evaluation of all engineering, economic, and sociological factors involved" wording.

19. B. A. Scott to Sam Engelhardt, August 2, 1960, RG 30, NAA; "Proposed Route of East-West Expressway through City," *Montgomery Advertiser*, April 16, 1960, 8; Sam Engelhardt to Governor Patterson, October 9, 1961, GPC, ADAH.

20. BPR assistant commissioner O. M. Williams told Rex Anderson that land use plans and the route of I-65 were inconsistent. The land use plan proposed an increase in commercial and industrial space north of downtown, without any new connections to major state highways. See O. M. Williams to Rex Anderson, August 24, 1961, RG 30, NA2.

21. Urban Consultant Associates, *Land Use Plan, 2nd Draft* (Montgomery, AL: Montgomery Planning Commission, 1957), 17.

22. Frank Bruer, "Expert Says Freeway Will Hurt Some," *Mobile Register*, June 21, 1957, 1, quoting R. D. Jordan. Jordan was discussing the highway in Mobile.

23. Urban Consultant Associates, *Land Use Plan, 2nd Draft* (Montgomery, AL: Montgomery Planning Commission, 1957), 17; Wilbur Smith and Associates, *Major Route Plan: Montgomery Metropolitan Area* (Montgomery: Alabama Highway Department, 1960), 15. In 1960 the AHD and the Montgomery City Commission authorized funding for the northern bypass, connecting the southern bypass with Court Street, north of downtown, to the proposed I-65 as it crossed into the Alabama River peninsula, including a large interchange at US 31. Like the southern bypass, which had been constructed five years earlier, most of the northern bypass was built without service roads and quickly developed access management problems. See "Montgomery Bypass," *Birmingham News*, September 23, 1955, PISF, ADAH; R. G. James to W. H. White, June 15, 1967, RG 406, NA2; "Bypass Proposal Draws Fire, Praise," *Montgomery Advertiser*, May 15, 1975, PISF, ADAH.

24. Sam Engelhardt Memo to Governor John Patterson, August 1, 1960, SEC, ADAH, 1.

25. "Route Hearing Set on Interstate Highway," *Montgomery Advertiser*, April 14, 1960, SECS, ADAH, 13; Forest Castleberry, "East-West Highway's Hearing Set Tuesday," *Alabama Journal*, April 13, 1960, 8.

26. Forrest Castleberry, "Planned Federal Route Stirs Strong Opposition," *Alabama Journal*, April 20, 1960, PISF, ADAH, 1.

27. Castleberry, "Planned Federal Route," 1. Another article estimated that seven hundred people attended the meeting, with most opposed to the route. See Max York, "Engineers Explain Route of Highway Across City," *Montgomery Advertiser*, April 20, 1960, PISF, ADAH, 1.

28. Cost estimates varied significantly over the planning process, but all the estimates were that the south route was more expensive than the north route. Along the south route, the Hutchinson Missionary Baptist Church would be demolished, with a land price of $70,000. See Lamar Smith to B. A. Scott, March 18, 1960, RG 30, NAA. Another estimate was $2,118,500 for the south route and $1,519,500 for the north route. See Gene Kovarik, "Interstate 85 Hits Route Snag," *Alabama Journal*, June 22, 1963, PISF, ADAH.

29. "Controversial Highway Is Routed According to the Original Plan," *Southern Star*, November 2, 1961, SECS, ADAH, 2; "Gov. Patterson Blasts Politics; White House Beats Quick Retreat," *Demopolis Times*, November 2, 1961, SECS, ADAH, 1; Sam Engelhardt to Governor Patterson, October 9, 1961, GPC, ADAH.

30. Sam Engelhardt to Governor Patterson, October 9, 1961, GPC, SG14022/6, ADAH, 8; B. A. Scott letter to Sam Engelhardt, November 22, 1960, RG 30, NAA; Sam Engelhardt letter to Governor Patterson, October 9, 1961, GPC, ADAH; Stark to B. A. Scott, November 22, 1960, RG 30, NAA; Rex Whitton to U.S. Representative Leonor K. Sullivan, July 3, 1960, RG 30, NA2. For the approval of the route of I-85 through Alabama, including the Oak Park area, see B. A. Scott to Sam Engelhardt, December 6, 1961, RG 30, NAA.

31. Ralph Abernathy Telegram to Department of Commerce and President Kennedy, October 3, 1961, RG 30, NA2; "Highway Department Lacks Confirmation of Re-Route," *Montgomery Advertiser*, October 24, 1961, SECS, ADAH, 2; Rex Whitten to Ralph Abernathy, October 3, 1961, RG 30, NA2. See also "East-West Highway Possible," *DeKalb County News*, July 27, 1961, noting that Highway 35 was relocated away from a white high school. See also Chester Hartman, "The Housing of Relocated Families," *Journal of the American Institute of Planners*, 1964, 30(4): 266–86.

32. Sam Engelhardt to Governor Patterson, October 9, 1961, GPC, ADAH; F. C. Turner to Senator Lister Hill, August 26, 1960, RG 30, NAA; E. A. Knox to Senator Lister Hill, August 8, 1960, RG 30, NAA.

33. As the petitioners wrote, the highway would demolish "the most choice residential areas occupied by Negro citizens of Montgomery." See Property Owners Committee, "Petition Appeal," April 28, 1960, RG 30, NA2. See also Ralph David Abernathy, *And the Walls Came Tumbling Down* (New York: Harper and Row, 1989). Rev. George Curry was a civil rights activist and pastor, John Garrick Hardy was a professor and administrator at ASU and a civil rights activist, and C. R. Williams was the president of the Emancipation Proclamation Committee of Montgomery. See C. L. Williams to M. L. King, Jr., November 25, 1955, Martin Luther King, Jr., Papers, 1954–1968, Howard Gotlieb Archival Research Center, Boston University, Boston, Massachusetts, accessed March 22, 2018.

34. Dara Byrne, *The Unfinished Agenda of the Selma-Montgomery Voting Rights March* (Hoboken, NJ: John Wiley and Sons, 2005); Robert Pratt, *Selma's Bloody Sunday* (Baltimore, MD: Johns Hopkins University Press, 2017). Alabama Code Sections 1111–136 (1886) created the poll tax. The tax maintained public schools and tied the race of the individual voter to the race of the school. If African American people from were prevented from voting, African American schools would also be unfunded. See David Martin, "The Birth of Jim Crow in Alabama, 1865–1896," *National Black Law Journal* 13, no. 1 (1993): 184–97.

35. Property Owners Committee, "Petition Appeal," April 28, 1960, RG30, NA2.

36. Property Owners Committee, "Petition Appeal," April 28, 1960, RG 30, NA2, 4. Less than a decade later, AHD highway engineer B. L. Bray told the *Montgomery Advertiser* that the southern bypass should have been an interstate highway. See Raymond Massey, "U.S. Road Engineer Helps Smooth Bumpy City-State Bypass Issue," *Montgomery Advertiser*, June 28, 1967, 20.

37. Rev. Ralph D. Abernathy statement for Montgomery Improvement Association, released by Rev. S. S. Seay Sr., n.d., RALC, TSCC.

38. Sam Engelhardt to R. G. Underwood, March 29, 1960, SEC, ADAH.

39. "City Enjoys Slight Drop in Tensions," *Montgomery Advertiser*, March 2, 1960, 1.

40. Robinson left Montgomery for a job at Grambling State College in Louisiana, and Burks moved to Maryland. See Belinda Robnett, *How Long? How Long?* (New York: Oxford University Press, 1997).

41. R. D. Jordan to George Curry, February 2, 1961, RG 30, NA2.

42. R. D. Jordan to George Curry, February 2, 1961, RG 30, NA2.

43. Jordan wrote, "As we explained to the committee, the tentative selection of the route south of the park was made in order to get the interchange with Hall Street as far southward as practical in order to draw off traffic from the traffic corridor moving in and out from the southwest generally along the Carter Hill Road." This is ironic

because the Hall Street exit was not constructed. See R. D. Jordan to George Curry, February 2, 1961, RG 30, NA2.

44. R. D. Jordan to George Curry, February 2, 1961, RG 30, NA2; Sam Engelhardt to Governor John Patterson, August 1, 1960, SEC, ADAH; Governor Patterson to Sam Engelhardt, August 2, 1960, SEC, ADAH.

45. John Roxborough Memorandum for Record, June 23, 1961, RG 30, NA2. Bookbinder was perhaps skeptical of Engelhardt's intentions. He wrote, "You may rest assured that I will maintain an 'open mind' on this subject and do my utmost to bring about a solution that will benefit all of the people involved in this dispute." See Hyman Bookbinder to Rex Whitten, July 19, 1961, RG 30, NA2.

46. The memo mentions Rev. Abernathy's church, which is not near an interstate. Perhaps the letter was supposed to refer to his house because other letters referenced Rev. Abernathy's house. See John Roxborough, "Memorandum for Record," June 23, 1961, RG30, NA2; Hyman Bookbinder to Rex Whitton, July 12, 1961, RG30, NA2; Berl Bernhard to Hyman Bookbinder, June 29, 1961, RG30, NA2.

47. Two months after the meeting with US Civil Rights Commission, the BPR approved preparation of the final cost estimates for the south route. See B. A. Scott to Sam Engelhardt, August 2, 1960, RG 30, NAA.

48. Curry and the property owners were initially represented by Roy M. Ellis, an attorney from Washington, DC. Marjorie Lawson and Belford Lawson replaced Ellis after he died. See Rex Whitton to Marjorie Lawson, July 26, 1961, RG 30, NA2.

49. Engelhardt told Governor Patterson that Rex Whitton told him not to attend the meeting, likely because he wanted to maintain the perception that it was engineers—not politicians—making highway routing decisions. See Sam Engelhardt to Governor Patterson, August 28, 1961, SEC, ADAH, 1.

50. R. D. Jordan to Sam Engelhardt, September 26, 1961, GPC, ADAH, 3. For information on Belford Lawson, see Gregory Parks, "Belford Vance Lawson, Jr.: Life of a Civil Rights Litigator," *University of Maryland Law Journal of Race, Religion, Gender, and Class* 12, no. 320 (2012): 103–37.

51. Roger Biles and Mark Rose, "At the Intersection of Race, Class, Gender, and Highway Politics," *Journal of Urban History* 46, no. 3 (2019): 677–84.

52. "Highway Department Lacks Confirmation of Re-Route," *Montgomery Advertiser*, October 24, 1961, SECS, ADAH, 1; "Governor Raps Road Politics: Threatens to Abandon Project," *Birmingham Post-Herald*, October 25, 1961, SECS, ADAH.

53. R. D. Jordan to Sam Engelhardt, September 26, 1961, SEC, ADAH, 4. Two days later, Whitton called Engelhardt and told him that he was still in agreement with the south route. As Engelhardt wrote to Governor Patterson, "He [Whitton] assured me that he was still on our side and if he was forced to make a statement contrary

to that, I would know that he was lying." See Sam Engelhardt to Governor Patterson, September 28, 1961, SEC, ADAH, 1.

54. "Alabama Highway Ordered Rerouted," *Birmingham Post-Herald*, October 23, 1961, SECS, ADAH.

55. "Highway Change Story Unverified," *Alabama Journal*, October 23, 1961, SEC, ADAH.

56. "New Highway Faces Delay," *Birmingham Post-Herald*, October 24, 1961, SECS, ADAH.

57. "New Highway Faces Delay," *Birmingham Post-Herald*, October 24, 1961, SECS, ADAH.

58. "Highway Department Lacks Confirmation of Re-Route," *Montgomery Advertiser*, October 24, 1961, SECS, ADAH; "Highway Change Story Unverified," *Alabama Journal*, October 23, 1961, SECS, ADAH; "Finagling Charged In Federal Road Route Revision," *Selma Times-Journal*, October 24, 1961, SECS, ADAH; "State Officials Seek Data on Road Change," *Mobile Register*, October 24, 1961, SECS, ADAH; "Eleanor Started It, Says Road Official," *Alabama Journal*, October 24, 1961, SECS, ADAH.

59. "Governor Raps Road Politics: Threatens to Abandon Project," *Birmingham Post-Herald*, October 25, 1961, SECS, ADAH; "Minutes of the Executive Committee of the Montgomery Improvement Association," October 18, 1956, RALC, TSCC.

60. William Taylor, a US Civil Rights Commission employee, attended the meeting. See "Denial Issued by White House on Road Deal," *Florence Times*, October 25, 1961, SECS, ADAH.

61. "Governor Raps Road Politics: Threatens to Abandon Project," *Birmingham Post-Herald*, October 25, 1961, SECS, ADAH. See also "Finagling Charged In Federal Road Route Revision," *Selma Times-Journal*, October 24, 1961, SECS, ADAH. Governor Patterson asserted, "If the project is re-routed the state will drop that portion of the highway entirely." See "Roosevelts, JFK Linked to Dispute Over Road Routing," *Birmingham News*, October 25, 1961, SECS, ADAH.

62. "Roosevelts, JFK Linked to Dispute Over Road Routing," *Birmingham News*, October 25, 1961, SECS, ADAH; "Denial Issued by White House on Road Deal," *Florence Times*, October 25, 1961, SECS, ADAH; "JFK Aides Spike Story of Reroute," *Alabama Journal*, October 25, 1961, SECS, ADAH; "JFK Denies Patterson's Road Charge," *Montgomery Advertiser-Journal*, October 26, 1961, SECS, ADAH. Patterson told newspapers, "The situation was 'serious' and that the President himself was 'concerned' about it," and that the Civil Rights Commission complained that the route would "disturb some of the most able and educated people of the Negro race . . . important to the North as well as the South." Governor Patterson also claimed, ironically,

to be concerned with discrimination against the low-income African American residents living north of Oak Park. As he told newspapers, "The only other possible route through Montgomery would adversely affect more residents and several hundred 'poor negroes.'" And he accused the Civil Rights Commission of discrimination: "He [Governor Patterson] accused the White House and the Civil Rights Commission of discrimination against those negroes in favor of members of that race who are better off financially and more influential politically." See "Finagling Charged In Federal Road Route Revision," *Selma Times-Journal*, October 24, 1961, SECS, ADAH.

63. Jim Lowrey, "Patterson Blasts Action in Highway Intervention," *Anniston Star*, October 25, 1961, SECS, ADAH, 1.

64. Jim Lowrey, "Patterson Blasts Action," 1.

65. Governor John Patterson Statement, July 25, 1961, GPC, ADAH.

66. Sam Engelhardt to Governor Patterson, October 9, 1961, GPC, ADAH, 10. In the meantime, the AHD completed construction of the expressway at both the east and west ends while waiting for approval from the BPR to connect the two sides together. Plans for I-65 through the Westside were also quickly progressing, making the route through the Oak Park area inevitable because building both ends of the interstate meant that a bypass route was no longer a possibility. See MacDonald Gallion to Frank Mizell, July 28, 1959, SEC, ADAH; "Oak Park Routing Still up in Air," *Alabama Journal*, March 20, 1964, PISF, ADAH. BPR engineers approved the route of I-85 from the east of the state to Mount Meigs Road in 1957. See Rex Anderson to B. A. Scott, February 28, 1957, RG 30, NAA; Rex Anderson to B. A. Scott, April 9, 1957, RG 30, NAA; B. A. Scott to H. L. Nelson, June 1, 1957, RG 30, NAA; B. A. Scott to H. L. Nelson, April 1, 1958, RG 30, NAA.

67. Bob Duke, "Controversy Punctuates Interstate 65 Hearing," *Montgomery Advertiser*, November 22, 1961, 1.

68. "Montgomery Downtown Business Association: Resolution," November 20, 1961, RG 30, NA2; Rex Whitton to Senator John Sparkman, December 7, 1961, RG 30 NAA; Rex Whitton to Senator Lister Hill, December 4, 1961, RG 30, NAA.

69. In at least one instance, an individual white business owner had a role in interstate re-routing. When the exit to Highway 152 from I-65 was supposed to run directly though the Whitfield Pickle and Alaga Syrup Company in North Montgomery, L. B. Whitfield Jr., owner of the company, wrote to Governor Patterson to request rerouting the exit. It took AHD engineers less than a week to relocate the exit away from Mr. Whitfield's property. See L. B. Whitfield to Governor Patterson, August 14, 1962, GPC, ADAH; Sam Engelhardt to Governor Patterson, August 23, 1962, GPC, ADAH; Rex Whitton to Senator Sparkman, December 7, 1961, RG 30, NAA; Rex Whitton to Lister Hill, December 4, 1961, RG 30, NAA.

70. Uriah Fields sent a letter to Engelhardt to protest the segregated seating arrangements. See U. J. Fields to Sam Engelhardt, November 23, 1961, SEC, ADAH. See Uriah J. Fields, *The Montgomery Story: The Unhappy Effects of the Montgomery Bus Boycott* (New York: Exposition Press, 1959); Uriah Fields, "Negroes Hit by Hwy 65," *Montgomery Status Quo Challenger Newsletter* 1, no. 2 (1961), RALC, TSCC, 1; C. A. Bowles to B. A. Scott, December 6, 1961, RG 30, NAA. The public hearing was scheduled one day after the Downtown Business Association adopted the resolution recommending the peninsula route. See Rex Anderson to B. A. Scott, November 14, 1961, RG 30, NAA; "Freeway Hearing Tonight," *Alabama Journal*, November 21, 1961, 13; Forrest Castleberry, "State, Federal Authorities to Decide Interstate Route," *Alabama Journal*, November 22, 1961, 9. Researchers have noted that many public hearings for interstate highways were not well attended because by the time the public hearings occurred, the routes were already finalized and there was no opportunity for meaningful input. See Ryan Reft, Amanda Phillips De Lucas, and Rebecca Retzlaff, *Justice and the Interstates: The Racist Truth about Interstate Highways* (Washington, DC: Island Press, 2023).

71. L. C. Pinson to Bureau of Public Roads, November 29, 1961, RG 30, NA2, 1. See also Rex Whitton to Mr. Pinson, December 11, 1961, RG 30, NA2.

72. Bob Duke, "Controversy Punctuates Interstate 65 Hearing," *Montgomery Advertiser*, Nov. 22, 1961, 1.

73. One resident wrote to the BPR, saying, "Route A would have several miles of fill 30′0″ high to reach the river and all in a flood area, move 2400 families on city owned property, build overpasses for city streets, etc. This against building on thinly populated land that now has one bridge over the river to be used, will move 900 families and Route 'A' will only cost $5,000,000 more than Route 'C'? . . . I cannot see the State and Federal Governments building a highway contrary to all 'good judgement' and reason, solely to benefit a Highway Department head and a few other individuals." See L. C. Pinson to Bureau of Public Roads, November 29, 1961, RG 30, NA2, 2. The BPR did not require state highway departments to respond to criticism at public hearings—it only required that a public hearing be held. Even poorly run public hearings met basic federal requirements. See the example of I-40 in Nashville, Tennessee: Raymond Mohl, "Citizen Activism and Freeway Revolts in Memphis and Nashville: The Road to Litigation," *Journal of Urban History* 40, no. 5 (2014), 870–93.

74. For the approval letter for of the peninsula route, see B. A. Scott to Sam Engelhardt, December 6, 1961, RG 30, NAA.

75. Sam Engelhardt to Governor John Patterson, November 29, 1961, SEC, ADAH.

76. "Highway Department Lacks Confirmation of Re-Route," *The Montgomery Advertiser*, October 24, 1961, SECS, ADAH.

77. "Controversial Highway Is Routed According to the Original Plan," *Southern Star*, November 2, 1961, SECS, ADAH, 2.

78. "Appraisals Due on Interstate," *Alabama Journal*, February 18, 1961, SECS, ADAH, 9. By December 1962, a few appraisals were complete and property acquired. The appraisal for 747 South Court Street was for $15,300. The appraisal for the house across the street was $15,600. See John Dallhouse to E. H. Swick, December 12, 1962, RG 406, NA2. The property at 335 Forest Avenue appraised for $10,200. See Mrs. William Harris Jr. to Senator John Sparkman, March 1, 1966, RG 406, NA2. 702 S. Lawrence Street appraised for $28,000, but the initial offer to purchase was for $16,500, and the second offer was $21,700. See Edna Pickett Dismukes to Senator Lister Hill, November 1, 1961, RG 406, NA2. The appraisal for 601 Pleasant Avenue was $10,000. See Mr. and Mrs. Walden to President Kennedy, September 22, 1961, RG 30, NA2.

79. "Urban-Interstate Road Projects Nearing Construction Stage," *Montgomery Advertiser-Journal*, October 20, 1961, SECS, ADAH.

80. J. Arnold Feldman to Ellis Armstrong, August 23, 1960, RG 30, NA2; J. Francis Pohlhaus to Bertran Tallamy, July 27, 1960, RG 30, NA2; Edwin Lukas to Luther Hodges, August 28, 1961, RG 30, NA2.

81. Forrest Castleberry, "U.S. Bureau Asks Removal of KKK Signs," *Montgomery Advertiser*, August 31, 1960, 1.

82. 23 U.S.C. §§123, 127, approved August 27, 1958, effective May 11, 1960.

83. Rex Anderson to Governor Patterson, September 15, 1960, RG 30, NA2.

84. BPR attorney C. W. Enfield believed that regulation for KKK signs civic organization signs should be similar, writing, "Assuming that the Klu [*sic*] Klux Klan is an organization permitted under the laws of the United States and the State of Alabama, it is felt that the same determination should be made with respect to that sign as with respect to the signs erected by the Presbyterian Church, the Lions Club, etc." See C. W. Enfield to G. M. Williams, June 14, 1960, RG 30, NA2, 1.

85. Bureau of Public Roads, "Instructional Memorandum 21-1-61," April 13, 1961, RG 30, NA2; Charles Wittenstein to Roy Millenson, November 3, 1961, RG 30, NA2.

86. The KKK of Alabama and the KKK of Montgomery were not on the list (from Executive Order No. 10450). See Sam Engelhardt to Governor Patterson, October 9, 1961, RG 30, NA2.

87. "KKK Signs Thrown Out Over Alabama," *Montgomery Advertiser*, November 15, 1961, 6; "Five Wooden Crosses Burned in Three Sections of City," *Montgomery Advertiser*, December 24, 1961, 16; Roy Millenson to Hyman Bookbinder, November 6, 1961, RG 30, NA2.

88. Walter Craig to Roy Deason, May 21, 1962, RG 30, NA2, 1. Craig was responding to a letter from Roy Deason, from Marion, Alabama, speculating that he had to remove the signs because of disagreements within KKK leadership. See Roy Deason to Walter Craig, May 15, 1962, RG 30, NA2, 1. The local press also speculated that removal of the signs was due to disagreements within the KKK leadership. See "Two Klan Signs Come Down," *Montgomery Advertiser*, November 21, 1960, 23.

89. Privatizing parks was a crucial part of preserving segregation. As an editorial in the *Montgomery Advertiser* noted, "If and when negroes gain admission to white parks under the Supreme Court ruling [referring to *Brown v. Board of Education*], these amendments are vital to the preservation of segregation in our state . . . they offer us the surest legal means by which we may insure segregat[ion]." See "Amendment No. 3," *Montgomery Advertiser*, August 26, 1956, 24.

90. "It Is Not to Be in Oak Park," *Montgomery Advertiser*, August 27, 1958, PISF, ADAH; State Voters to Get Chance to Decide Fate of School Choice," *Montgomery Advertiser*, August 26, 1956, 1.

91. "Park Facilities Up for Sale," *Montgomery Advertiser*, December 28, 1960, PISF, ADAH; Joe Azbell, "Chasing a 10-Year Lag in Building of Parks," *The Montgomery Independent*, May 14, 1970, 3. An Atomedic Children's Hospital, constructed in the southeast corner of Oak Park, continued to operate after the park reopened, but one year later it was demolished for a parking lot. I-85 was constructed through the southwest corner of the park. Tom Mackin, "City Parks Scheduled to Reopen," *Montgomery Advertiser*, February 25, 1965, PISF, ADAH; Dee Bryant, "Work Gets Underway on Oak Park Project," *Alabama Journal*, June 21, 1966, PISF, ADAH. A fire station was later built on the site. See Tom Mackin, "City Parks Scheduled to Reopen," *Montgomery Advertiser*, February 25, 1965, PISF—Parks and Zoos—Oak Park, SG6914/20, ADAH.

92. "Preserve Oak Park to the End!," *Alabama Journal*, September 12, 1959, PISF, ADAH, 4; "Negro Group Asks Parks Opening," *Alabama Journal*, April 28, 1959, PISF, ADAH, 11.

93. Proposed land swaps included a new Baptist hospital and a new trade school, but the proposals were rejected. See "Park Ruled Out As Hospital Site," *Alabama Journal*, September 14, 1959, PISF, ADAH; Carl Poteat, "Park Has Hosted Fun for 85 Years," *Alabama Journal*, September 14, 1973, PISF, ADAH; Dick Hines, "Gayle Pleased with Hospital Plans," *Montgomery Advertiser*, September 12, 1959, PISF, ADAH.

94. The agreement would "co-ordinate their various athletic programs so that both agencies would not be offering similar programs for the same age bracket . . . to co-ordinate their club programs and informal education classes with those of the city

community centers in their neighborhood areas." See *Smith v. Young Men's Christian Association of Montgomery*, 316 F. Supp 899 (US District Court, 1970), *903.

## *Chapter 7*

1. Robert Francis Kennedy Jr., *Judge Frank M. Johnson, Jr.: A Biography* (New York: G. P. Putman's Sons, 1978); J. Mills Thornton III, *Dividing Lines: Municipal Politics and the Struggle for Civil Rights in Montgomery, Birmingham, and Selma* (Tuscaloosa: University of Alabama Press, 2002); Charles V. Hamilton, *The Bench and the Ballot* (New York: Oxford University Press, 1973).

2. Less than one percent of the housing in the United States was covered under the order. See Mittie Olion Chandler, "Public Housing Desegregation: What Are the Options?," *Housing Policy Debate* 3, no. 2: 509–33.

3. James R. Wood to W. T. Walker, October 26, 1961, RALC, TSCC.

4. George Wallace was elected in November 1962 and inaugurated in January 1963.

5. Gene Kovarik, "Interstate 85 Hits Route Snag," *Alabama Journal*, June 22, 1963, PISF, ADAH. In November 1968 Robert Kendall Jr. became the state highway director after H. L. Nelson died. See A. R. Rankin to Directors, November 4, 1968, RG 406, NA2.

6. Judge Johnson Jr. ordered desegregation of the bus station after the assault on the freedom riders, the city airport in January 1961, and libraries and museums in August 1962. After the libraries were desegregated, the City Commission ordered removal of the chairs and tables so African American people and white people could not sit together, a tactic they later used when they removed the benches and seating and banned picnicking in the parks. St. Margaret's Hospital allowed African American doctors to practice in 1965, when Dr. Hagalyn Seay Wilson, the city's first female African American doctor, began working in the basement of the hospital in the African American ward.

7. Gene Kovarik, "Houston Hill Urban Renewal Protest Aired," *Alabama Journal*, January 9, 1962, 11.

8. Gene Kovarik, "Houston Hill Program Not Housing Program," *Alabama Journal*, January 9, 1962, RALC, TSCC.

9. "Mayor Tries to Clear Up Houston Hill Confusion," *Montgomery Advertiser*, January 9, 1962, 11.

10. "Houston Hill Priority Given," *Alabama Journal*, January 17, 1962, 13.

11. Gene Kovarik, "Houston Hill Bids Rejected," *Alabama Journal*, June 29, 1962, 17.

12. The two lots that were not sold to the developer were sold to African American families. See Gene Kovarik, "Renewal Adds Dollars to City's Treasury," *Alabama Journal*, December 6, 1963, 6.

13. Tom Mackin, "Houston Hills Complete," *Montgomery Advertiser*, May 29, 1966, 35. The city initially proposed a new park and swimming pool for African American residents, but those did not make it into the final plan. See "Houston Hill," *Montgomery Advertiser*, February 29, 1956, 4; "Joint Plan for Financing Approved for Houston Hill," *Montgomery Advertiser*, February 29, 1956, 4; Irwin Rosen, "Houston Hills Project Stymied by Appeals," *Alabama Journal*, May 27, 1958, 1; Joe McFadden, "Intended Alterations for Montgomery Listed," *Alabama Journal*, May 21, 1965, 1; Tom Mackin, "Houston Hills Complete," *Montgomery Advertiser*, May 29, 1966, 35; Gene Kovarik, "Renewal Adds Dollars to City's Treasury," *Alabama Journal*, December 6, 1963, 6.

14. Gene Kovarik, "Renewal Imperative, DU Fears," *Alabama Journal*, February 27, 1964, 35; "City Seeks Funds for Downtown Renewal Studies," *Alabama Journal*, September 27, 1963, 31. The Planning Commission did not adopt a new comprehensive plan until 2020, although it did create neighborhood plans in the interim period.

15. Thornton, *Dividing Lines*.

16. US Census of Population and Housing.

17. Office space includes general and professional centers, legal services, financial, medical services, government, industrial, transportation, and utilities. Retail includes shopping, convenience, and miscellaneous goods. Downtown Montgomery had 358,856 square feet of vacant space. See Urban Consultants Inc., *An Economic Analysis of the Montgomery C.B.D.: A Part of the Comprehensive City Plan* (Montgomery, AL: Montgomery City Planning Commission, 1965), 75–76.

18. Urban Consultants Inc., *A Land Use Plan for Montgomery: Part of the Comprehensive City Plan* (Montgomery, AL: Montgomery City Planning Commission, 1965), 103.

19. Jane Holtz Kay, *Asphalt Nation: How the Automobile Took Over America and How We Can Take It Back* (Oakland: University of California Press, 1998); Catherine Lutz, *Carjacked: The Culture of the Automobile and Its Effect on Our Lives* (New York: St. Martin's Press, 2010).

20. The consultants wrote about the desirability of strip commercial development: "Most of Montgomery's older neighborhoods have a strip of unrelated stores extending along one of their most used streets; all of these strips consist of various types of commercial land uses. In planning of new neighborhoods, this type of land use has been replaced by neighborhood shopping centers in most cases." Urban Consultants Inc., *Land Use Plan*, 103.

21. Urban Consultants Inc., *Land Use Plan*, 106.

22. The proposed increase in industrial land consisted of 2,600 acres of new industrial land, plus 25 percent for new streets, rail connections, and associated land

use, totaling 3,450 acres of new industrial land in the city and 4,250 in Montgomery County. Planners wrote that they wanted to provide more industrial land than is needed because new industries were attracted by larger tracts and wanted choices when locating new industries, so they included 7,900 new acres of industrial land in the county and city combined. In Centennial Hill, planners hoped to replace homes with industry along S. Decatur Street north of I-85, Adams Avenue, Chestnut Street, and S. Decatur Street across from Paterson Court. See Urban Consultants Inc., *Land Use Plan*, 98.

23. The consultants projected a need for an additional 22,250 acres of land to support the new neighborhoods, such as roads, churches, parks, and playgrounds. Urban Consultants Inc., *Land Use Plan*, 95–96.

24. Urban Consultants Inc., *People and Economy: A Part of the Comprehensive City Plan* (Montgomery, AL: Montgomery City Planning Commission, 1965).

25. Bob Duke, "Series of Hearings Slated on Streamlined Rezoning," *Montgomery Advertiser*, June 2, 1963, 44; "Zoning Hearings Start Monday Night," *Montgomery Advertiser*, June 10, 1963, 6; "Second Hearing Set Wednesday Night," *Montgomery Advertiser*, June 12, 1963, 6. "Street, Utility Bids Sought on Houston Hill Area Work," *Montgomery Advertiser*, December 22, 1961, 1. Zoning is path dependent, with updates based on past ordinances, not on changing community character significantly. See Jill Grant, Pierre Filion, and Scott Low, "Path Dependencies Affecting Suburban Density, Mix, and Diversity in Halifax," *The Canadian Geographer* 63, no. 2 (2018): 240–53; Anthony Woodlief, "The Path-Dependent City," *Urban Affairs Review* 33, no. 3 (1998): 405–37.

26. Steve Ball, "Zoning on Southern Bypass Protested During Hearing," *Montgomery Advertiser*, June 13, 1963, 14; Bob Duke, "Change in Proposed Zoning Plan Requested for L&M Land at Selma, Mobile Highways," *Montgomery Advertiser*, June 21, 1963, 16.

27. Urban Consultants Inc., *A Community Facilities Plan for Montgomery* (Montgomery, AL: Montgomery City Planning Commission, 1965), 137.

28. Urban Consultants Inc., *Community Facilities Plan*, 137.

29. Urban Consultants Inc., *Community Facilities*, 109.

30. Joseph Bagley, *The Politics of White Rights* (Athens: University of Georgia Press, 2018), 137; Robert Gratz, *A White Preacher's Message on Race and Reconciliation* (Montgomery: New South Books, 2006); Fred Gray, Willey Leventhal, Frank Sikora, J. Mills Thornton III, *The Children Coming On . . . A Retrospective of the Montgomery Bus Boycott* (Montgomery, AL: Black Belt Press, 1998).

31. Fred Gray, *Bus Ride to Justice* (Montgomery, AL: Black Belt Press, 1995).

32. One report indicates that two white children attended St. Jude's School in

1940. See Ashley Creek, "Montgomery Catholic Mission Finally Celebrates Its Role in the Selma Marches," *WBHM: News for the Heart of Alabama*, March 22, 2015, accessed February 8, 2023. Integration of public schools in Huntsville involved disputes over segregation at schools that received funding from the US military due to base expansion. In 1960 the US Justice Department ordered four schools to desegregate outside Alabama due to the presence of military bases. Although Huntsville was not on the initial list, Governor Patterson announced that the order was "the opening of an all-out war" and spent years fighting the eventual desegregation. See "Satellites and Segregation," *Alabama Council on Human Relations Newsletter*, February 1960, RALC, TSCC, 1.

33. See Hasan Kwame Jeffries, *Bloody Lowndes: Civil Rights and Black Power in Alabama's Black Belt* (New York: New York University Press, 2009).

34. "Outline Map," *Montgomery Advertiser*, December 30, 1964, PISF, ADAH.

35. Gene Kovark, "Oak Park South Route Still No. 1 Selection," *Alabama Journal*, January 6, 1965, PISF, ADAH.

36. Kovark, "Oak Park South Route."

37. See *State of Alabama v. Fannie Turner, et al.*, Probate Court of Montgomery County, Alabama, Case no. 6549, April 25, 1967, RALC, TSCC.

38. Felicia McGhee, "The Montgomery Bus Boycott and the Fall of the Montgomery City Lines," *Alabama Review* 68, no. 3 (2015): 251–68; Urban Consultant Associates, *A Transportation Plan for Montgomery* (Montgomery, AL: City Planning Commission, 1962).

39. J. M. O'Connor to Dowell Anders, November 13, 1968, RG 406, NA2; Albert Brewer to Lowell Bridwell, October 22, 1968, RG 406, NA2; Albert Brewer, "Interim State Assurance with Regard to Equal Employment Opportunity as Required by the Federal-Aid Highway Act of 1968," n.d., RG 406, NA2.

40. "Coosa-Alabama Funds Approved by House Committee," *Birmingham News*, June 20, 1965, 1; "Alabama-Coosa to get $13 Million," *Birmingham News*, August 18, 1964, 1.

41. Milo Dakin, "$39.4 Million Sought in Budget for Coosa-Alabama River System," *Montgomery Advertiser*, January 27, 1972, 1. The National Environmental Policy Act of 1970 presented a formidable barrier to finishing the project. Coosa-Alabama River Improvement Association, "The Waterway Forward," Coosa-Alabama River Improvement Association, accessed December 6, 2021.

## *Chapter 8*

1. Mittie Olin Chandler, "Public Housing Desegregation: What Are the Options?," *Housing Policy Debate* 3, no. 2 (1992): 509–33.

2. Michael Uschan, *The March from Selma to Montgomery* (San Diego, CA: Lucent Books, 2011); Barbara Harris Combs, *From Selma to Montgomery* (New York: Routledge, 2013).

3. Dick Hines, "City Appoints Two Committees to Advise on Racial Matters," *Montgomery Advertiser*, January 16, 1964, 1.

4. Dick Hines, "City Appoints Two Committees to Advise on Racial Matters," *Montgomery Advertiser*, January 16, 1964, 1, 11. African American members of the committee included many civil rights activists, including Solomon Seay Sr., Rufus Lewis, R. D. Nesbitt, E. D. Nixon, Henry Spears, Levi Watkins, and C. R. Williams. White people on the committee included at least two members of the White Citizens' Council. The committees were established on January 15, 1964. See "The Committees," *Montgomery Advertiser*, January 16, 1964, 4. A similar committee formed in Birmingham a decade earlier. See Mary Stanton, *Journey toward Justice: Juliette Hampton Morgan and the Montgomery Bus Boycott* (Athens: University of Georgia Press, 2006). New Orleans had a similar committee. See Arnold Hirsch, "Simply a Matter of Black and White: The Transformation of Race and Politics in Twentieth-Century New Orleans," in *Creole New Orleans: Race and Americanization*, eds. Arnold Hirsch and Joseph Logsdon (Baton Rouge: Louisiana State University Press, 1992), 262–319.

5. Victoria Wolcott, *Race, Riots, and Roller Coasters: The Struggle Over Segregated Recreation in America* (Philadelphia: University of Pennsylvania Press, 2012).

6. J. Mills Thornton III, *Dividing Lines: Municipal Politics and the Struggle for Civil Rights in Montgomery, Birmingham, and Selma* (Tuscaloosa: University of Alabama Press, 2002), 135. Thornton was quoting *Selma Times-Journal* March 4 and 5, 1963.

7. "Oak Park Apparently Reopened," *Montgomery Advertiser*, July 7, 1968, 2; "Blount and Nesbitt Outline Community Group's Plans," *Alabama Journal*, February 25, 1965, 31; L. B. Sullivan to E. D. Nixon, May 27, 1966, E. D. Nixon Collection, LWLC.

8. Michael Wilson, "Man Remembers Fight to Attend School," *Montgomery Advertiser*, May 14, 1993, 1.

9. The *Carr* case was filed on May 11, 1964, on behalf of Bathsheba, John, James, and Phillip Thompson, by their parents, Rev. Bishop and Lois Thompson. Bishop Thompson was a Methodist minister, and the regional Methodist Bishop church immediately transferred Thompson to a church in Mississippi after he filed the lawsuit. See Arthur Osgoode, "Judge Denies Dismissal, Sets Hearings on 'Mix,'" *Montgomery Advertiser*, July 2, 1964, 1; Steven Millner, "Interview with Johnnie Carr, July 17, 1977," in *Martin Luther King, Jr., and the Civil Rights Movement*, ed. David J. Carrow

(New York: Carlson Publishing, 1989), 527–32. Seay stepped down from leadership of the MIA a month after the lawsuit was filed. The new leader of the MIA, Rev. Jesse Douglass, was initially much more interested in the kind of direct action proposed by SCLC.

10. Myrna Oliver, "Winton Blount, 81; U.S. Postal System Chief, Philanthropist," *Los Angeles Times*, October 28, 2002, accessed September 18, 2020; Lewis W. Jones, "Two Years of Desegregation in Alabama," *Journal of Negro Education* 25, no. 3 (1956): 205–11.

11. Robert Sauer to Rufus Lewis, June 29, 1966, RALC, TSCC. After Governor Albert Brewer was elected in 1968, Rufus Lewis, chairperson of the Alabama Democratic Council; Joe Reed, executive director of the Alabama State Teachers Association; and Rev. K. L. Buford, field director for the Alabama NAACP wrote to Governor Brewer, complaining about the lack of African American state employees. African American people were not employed above the laborer level within state government. They requested there be more African American representatives on policy-making and administrative boards and an increase in African American civil service employees. They urged Governor Brewer to avoid "'hand-picked' Negro representation." See Rufus Lewis, "Items for discussion with Albert P. Brewer by Rufus Lewis, Chairperson of the Alabama Democratic Council, Joe Reed, Executive Director of the Alabama State Teachers Association, and Rev. K. L. Buford, Field Director for the Alabama NAACP," n.d., RALC, TSCC.

12. *Carr v. Montgomery County Board of Education*, 232 F. Supp 705 (US District Court, n.d., 1964).

13. Rex Thomas, "U.S. Court in Veiled Mix Order," *Montgomery Advertiser*, July 15, 1964, 1.

14. Angela Kuper, "Carr Remembers School Integration," *Montgomery Advertiser*, January 16, 1994, 116. "Capital Schools Admit Negroes without Fuss," *Selma Times-Journal*, September 8, 1964, 1; "Schools Here Integrate Calmly," *Alabama Journal*, September 8, 1964, 1.

15. "Oak Park Apparently Reopened," *Montgomery Advertiser*, July 7, 1968, 2.

16. Thornton, *Dividing Lines*.

17. "Our Leaders Speak," *Montgomery Advertiser*, March 25, 1965, 15.

18. The article included letters signed by different groups. This section was signed by Bishop D. C. Rice, Rev. E. I. Marlow, Rev. S. S. Seay Sr., and Rev. A. W. Wilson. The letter from the Committee on Community Affairs, urging schoolchildren to stay in school, was signed by African American and white members of the committee. Mayor Earl James wrote a letter urging people to remain calm. See "Our Leaders Speak," *Montgomery Advertiser*, March 25, 1965, 14–15.

19. Martin Luther King Jr., "Address at the Conclusion of the Selma to Montgomery March," *Martin Luther King, Jr. Papers (Series I-IV)*, Martin Luther King Jr., Center for Nonviolent Social Change Inc., Atlanta, Georgia, accessed March 8, 2021.

20. Ashley Cleek, "Montgomery Catholic Mission Finally Celebrates Its Role in the Selma Marches" *WBHM: NPR News From the Heart of Alabama*, March 22, 2015, accessed April 5, 2023; Carol McPhail, "Meet the Catholic Parish That Dared Take in Civil Rights Marchers 50 Years Ago," Al.com, March 25, 2015, accessed April 5, 2023. Rev. Dr. King wrote about white moderates' calls to "wait" and criticism of "outside agitators" in his 1963 *Letter from Birmingham Jail*. See Rev. Martin Luther King Jr., *Letter from Birmingham Jail*, August 1963; Scott Clark, "When 'Wait' Means 'Never': American Tolerance of Racial Injustice," *National Black Law Journal* 13, no. 1 (1993): 123–33. St. Jude leased the hospital to a group of African American doctors in 1975. It was renamed Fairview Medical Center and closed in 1985. See Mark McIntyre, "St. Jude Hospital to be Sold, Renamed," *Alabama Journal*, October 22, 1975, 1.

21. Urban Consultants Inc., *Neighborhood Analysis*, 40. The term *blight* remains a racialized and politically contrived term. See Mark Rose and Roger Biles, "Arthur Rubloff and the Grinding Politics of Renewal in Chicago, 1947–1986," *Journal of Urban History* 46, no. 6 (2020): 1341–367.

22. Urban Consultants Inc., *Neighborhood Analysis*, 3.

23. Thornton, *Dividing Lines*.

24. Urban Consultants Inc., *Neighborhood Analysis*, 3.

25. Urban Consultants Inc., *Neighborhood Analysis*, 8. There were 3,956 families that lived in areas that were 25 percent or more dilapidated, 5,088 families that lived in areas that were 30 percent or more deteriorating or dilapidated, and 1,872 families that lived in areas that were 10 to 30 percent blighted. The analysis indicated that neighborhoods that had 25 percent or more dilapidated buildings were slums. See Urban Consultants, *Neighborhood Analysis*, 10.

26. Urban Consultants Inc., *Neighborhood Analysis*.

27. Gloria German and Pat Pranditi, "Poor People Struggle to Improve Homes," *The Southern Courier* 2 no. 28 (1966): 4.

28. Superintendent of Mail, Montgomery, Alabama to Postal Carriers, January 31, 1967, E. D. Nixon Collection, LWLC.

29. David Dunn to E. D. Nixon, February 6, 1967, E. D. Nixon Collection, LWLC.

30. Gloria German and Pat Pranditi, "Poor People Struggle to Improve Homes," *The Southern Courier* 2 no. 28 (1966): 4, 4.

31. By the late 1960s the City Commission was funding water and sewer infrastructure in many African American neighborhoods, although it did not in earlier years. For example, in 1968 the City Commission approved funding for some streets

on the Westside (Banks, Center, Dillard, Hill, Hugh, North, and Palma Streets). See Raymond Massey, "City Oks Grant on Water Line," *Alabama Journal*, July 9, 1968, 11. For descriptions of life in Montgomery's African American neighborhoods before sewer and water infrastructure, see various authors "Newtown Oral History Project," interviews in winter 2019 with Montgomery residents at the Newtown Community Center, ADAH. For assessments of infrastructure, see Urban Consultant Associates, *A Public Improvements Program for Montgomery* (Montgomery, AL: Montgomery Planning Commission, 1962). The Parks and Recreation Board feared that restoring Oak Park to its original design would lead to interaction between the races. See Camile Wallace, "Planetarium Will Show 'the Heavens,'" *Alabama Journal*, August 21, 1968, 13; Franklin Skinner, "Women's Group Want 'Old' Park Back," *Montgomery Advertiser*, May 22, 1969, 11, Dee Bryant, "Work Gets Underway on Oak Park Project" *Alabama Journal*, July 21, 1966, 33.

32. Urban Consultants Inc., *Neighborhood Analysis*, 41–42.

33. Urban Consultants Inc., *Neighborhood Analysis*, 47.

34. Planners also proposed two small industrial areas in the neighborhood, one on either side of Houston Hill Junior High School, which conflicted with the goal of keeping industrial land use separate from houses and schools. See Urban Consultants Inc., *Neighborhood Analysis*. The land use plan proposed industrial development for the neighborhood. See Montgomery City Planning Commission, *A Land Use Plan for Montgomery* (Montgomery, AL: Montgomery Planning Commission, 1965), 107. The homes of Georgia Theresa Gilmore, Johnnie Rebecca Carr, and Dr. Richard Harris, and Rev. Martin Luther King's former home (he had already moved to Atlanta), were declared blighted. The Ben Moore Hotel, an important meeting place for civil rights activists, was designated slightly blighted. A sixteen-block area on what is now the ASU campus, which was home to many ASU faculty, was declared blighted. The neighborhood was home to ASU president H. Councill Trenholm, dean and basketball coach Charles Dunn, geography professor Thelma Glass, and the childhood home of jazz musician Nat King Cole. Nat King Cole's house was originally located at 1524 St. John and was moved next to Ralph Abernathy's house on Hall Street, where it still stands. King Cole did not live in the home at the time. H. Councill Trenholm's home was at 611 Thurman, and Charles Dunn's home was at 612 Thurman.

35. For example, the neighborhood between the Westside and Centennial Hill, south of downtown. See Urban Consultants Inc., *Neighborhood Analysis*.

36. Planners wrote, "Expansion of the CBD will eventually include much of this residential area." See Urban Consultants Inc., *Neighborhood Analysis*, 29.

37. Mark Rose and Raymond Mohl, *Interstate: Highway Politics and Policy Since*

*1939, 3rd ed.* (Knoxville: University of Tennessee Press, 2012); Ronald Bayor, *Race and the Shaping of Twentieth-Century Atlanta* (Chapel Hill: University of North Carolina Press, 1996).

38. Mausiki Scales, "Interview with Earnest A. Grant," *Behind the Veil: Documenting African American Life in the Jim Crow South* (Charlotte, NC: Duke University Center for Documentary Studies, 2005); Peter Levy, *The Civil Rights Movement* (Westport, CT: Greenwood Press, 1998).

39. William Nettles to Honorable James N. Beck, October 17, 1967, Alabama Governor Administrative Files, ADAH.

40. Mary Ann Johnson, "Slum Clearance Is Mrs. Wright's Aim," *Montgomery Advertiser*, March 28, 1965, 22; Gene Kovarik, "Rosy Future Predicted," *Alabama Journal*, September 29, 1964, 9; Gene Kovarik, "Bill Would End Merit Status for Two Posts," *Alabama Journal*, August 12, 1964, 21.

## *Chapter 9*

1. The elementary schools ordered closed were Abraham's Vineyard, Phillips, Cecil, Arthur Cook, Battle, McCant's, Katie Brown, Lillian Dungee, Waugh, Woodley, Zion Hill, McLean, McLemore, and Mt. Zion Road. See *Carr v. Montgomery County Board of Education*, 253 F. Supp. 306 (US District Court, 1966).

2. Bob Valder, "Rights Commissions Sponsors School Desegregation Meet," *Alabama Council Bulletin*, May 31, 1966, RALC, TSCC.

3. Brian Ponder, "Curiosity, Not Stares, Greets Carr," *Alabama Journal*, November 15, 1989, 1; Bob Johnson "School Wish Became Reality," *Birmingham Post-Herald*, February 17, 1997, 1; Robbie Jean Walker, "Youths Help Battle Struggle," *Montgomery Advertiser*, March 7, 1993, 6G.

4. Joseph Bagley, *The Politics of White Rights* (Athens: University of Georgia Press, 2018). In 1969 the Montgomery Community Action Committee created a new pony football program for low-income boys in seventh grade who were too young to play football for schools or the parks and recreation football program. See Lattimore Martin, "Montgomery Community Action Committee Football Program Report," September–October 1969, RALC, TSCC.

5. Sandra Colvin and Franklin Howard, "'For the People of Prattville' Arrests, Beating," *Southern Courier* 3, no. 25 (1967).

6. One of the marches was in Cleveland Court. See Patricia Gorence, "Goals No Closer for Marchers in Capital," *Southern Courier* 3, no. 26 (1967): 1.

7. Even before the 1965 neighborhood analysis was complete, planners began working on expanding demolition of African American neighborhoods. Tom Mackin, "Downtown Plan Gets Federal Okay," *Montgomery Advertiser*, June 25, 1964,

1. Gene Kovarik, "Urban Renewal Plans on View All Day Tuesday," *Alabama Journal*, September 28, 1964, 11; "Offices Open at Ceremony," *Montgomery Advertiser*, September 29, 1964, 13. Urban Consultants Inc. was also involved in planning the new redevelopment areas, and executive Eugene Brock spoke at the open house.

8. Theda Skopol, *Housing Soldiers and Mothers: The Political Origins of Social Policy in the United States* (Cambridge, MA: Belknap Press, 1995); Mary E. Triece, *Urban Renewal and Resistance: Race, Space, and the City in the Late to Early Twenty-First Century* (Lanham, MD: Lexington Books, 2016); Roger Biles and Mark Rose, *A Good Place to Do Business: Then Politics of Downtown Renewal Since 1945* (Philadelphia, PA: Temple University Press, 2022).

9. Lawrence Vale, *Purging the Poorest: Public Housing and the Design Politics of Twice-Cleared Communities* (Chicago: University of Chicago Press, 2013), 3.

10. "Know the Facts," *Montgomery Advertiser*, April 26, 1954, 5; "Jaycees Okay Plan to Study Slums in City," *Montgomery Advertiser*, March 25, 1956, 4; "Housing Bill Goes through Senate, 60-28," *Montgomery Advertiser*, February 6, 1959, 1. Although Sparkman opposed civil rights legislation, he believed that slum clearance was good for business. See "Urban Renewal 'Boon' Advocated by Sparkman," *Alabama Journal*, February 9, 1960, 11. Sparkman, Rains, and other members of Congress from Alabama supported slum clearance bills and funding increases, including a billion-dollar funding increase for slum clearance introduced by Sparkman in 1957 and a $2.5 billion housing bill introduced by Sparkman in 1959. By 1962 Alabama ranked third in the nation for urban renewal funds. See "Group Boosts Slum Program," *Montgomery Advertiser*, May 1, 1957, 17; "Senate Vote Scales Down Housing Bill" *Montgomery Advertiser*, May 30, 1957, 32; "Alabama Near Top in Public Housing" *Montgomery Advertiser*, October 21, 1962, 164.

11. Tom Mackin, "Urban Renewal Study Board Sought by Citizens Forum," *Montgomery Advertiser*, April 13, 1965, 2.

12. Elizabeth Wright to Businessmen, n.d., RALC, TSCC.

13. Gene Kovarik, "Supporters See Renewal as City's Rebirth," *Alabama Journal*, December 5, 1963, 6.

14. Tom Mackin, "Downtown Plan Gets Federal Okay," *Montgomery Advertiser*, June 25, 1964, 1.

15. Gene Kovarik, "Urban Renewal Stirs Words," *Alabama Journal*, December 2, 1964, 11.

16. For example, a developer proposed a seventy-five-acre African American subdivision in southwest Montgomery, but development was not approved by the Montgomery Planning Commission. See "Controversial Petition Before Planning Group," *Alabama Journal*, December 2, 1964, 11. For another example, see the

proposed Westwood subdivision, next to the white Westgate neighborhood, "Hearing Set April 7 on Negro Subdivision," *Alabama Journal*, March 17, 1964, 13.

17. Elizabeth Wright conceded that it was difficult to find public housing for large families. She noted, "'We need five rooms for somebody like her, but they're full because there are so many like her,' Mrs. Wright said. 'I don't know what to do.' She added. 'It's real pathetic. . . . We have 100 cases on our books now, and we can't do any better.'" See Roberta Reisig, "Negroes Fight a Losing Battle for Good Housing," *Southern Courier* 2, no. 43 (1966), 4.

18. "Virtually Two City Blocks to Be Bought and Razed," *The Montgomery Independent*, February 1, 1968, PISF, ADAH.

19. Tom Makin, "UR Agency Urges Closing Sections of Court Street," *Montgomery Advertiser*, November 11, 1964, 1; Gene Kovarik, "Downtown Program Contract Signed," *Alabama Journal*, July 7, 1964, 1; Gene Kovarik, "Downtown Core First Urban Renewal Project," *Alabama Journal*, July 8, 1964, 20; Gene Kavorik, "3 Downtown Renewal Proposals Announced," *Alabama Journal*, November 12, 1964, 1. Less than ten years after the pedestrian mall was created, businesses petitioned City Council to open it up to cars again. See Louis Berney, "Is Court a Street? Or, a Plaza? Or, Could it Be a Blocked Street?," *Montgomery Advertiser*, December 13, 1973.

20. "Authority O.K.s Plan for Renewal," *Montgomery Advertiser*, April 21, 1965, 1. The land that was transferred to private developers was used for an expansion of the Belk department store, an addition to Union Bank and Trust Co., and a new parking structure for the Montgomery Shriners. See Sid Thomas, "$7.8-Million Project OKd," *Montgomery Advertiser*, January 13, 1968.

21. Urban Consultant Associates, *An Economic Analysis of the Montgomery C.B.D.* (Montgomery, AL: City Planning Commission, 1993).

22. It is unknown if MIA representatives replied to Wright's letter. See Elizabeth Wright to Montgomery Improvement Association, August 29, 1967, Montgomery Improvement Association Files, LWLC; Tom Mackin, "Urban Renewal Reality; Three Programs in Plan," *Alabama Journal*, December 31, 1964, 22; Raymond Massey, "Court Square Is Approved, City Ready," *Alabama Journal*, August 8, 1968, 1. The original plan, which was eventually scaled back, called for displacing 695 white families, 82 African American families, and 868 commercial buildings. See Gene Kovarik, "Downtown Core First Urban Renewal Project," *Alabama Journal*, July 8, 1964. The Montgomery URA was careful to save the historic Confederate buildings on the site, such as the Confederate Post Office and the office of Confederate successionist William Yancey. Historical buildings that were important to the civil rights movement, such as the building where Rosa Parks worked as a seamstress and where she got on the bus the day of the 1955 Montgomery bus boycott, were not on the list of historic

buildings (the façade of the building was saved in 2018, and it is now a pocket park). See Sid Thomas, "Renewal Plan to Spare Historic Buildings," *Montgomery Advertiser*, January 25, 1968, PISF, ADAH; Gene Kovarik, "Downtown Renewal to Be a 10-Year Program," *Alabama Journal*, October 2, 1963. Along with the Court Street project, the URA also announced the next two phases of the downtown urban renewal plan. The first was near the proposed I-65/I-85 interchange in the Five Points/Peacock Tract neighborhood, on forty-eight acres of land. That plan would demolish most of the neighborhood to make way for a large multilane road along Mobile Street. Two hundred sixty-two buildings would be demolished, and only thirty-four buildings would be saved. The project was never completed. The third phase, which was never constructed, was in the warehouse district, north of Madison Avenue, next to the Alabama River. That project would construct large overpasses along two streets and close other streets to create a pedestrian mall. The overpasses would be from Goldthwaite to Tallapoosa Streets and from Coosa to Lafayette Streets. The pedestrian mall would be near Goldthwaite and Bibb Streets. See Gene Kovarik, "3 Projects in Urban Renewal's Plan," *Alabama Journal*, November 13, 1964, 13; Gene Kavorik, "New Maxwell AFB Traffic Artery Considered by City," *Alabama Journal*, March 1, 1965, 13. The fourth phase would convert fifty-three acres around Clayton Street into a hotel and auto center, demolishing twenty-one of 127 buildings. The fifth phase would extend Stone Street and demolish twenty of 254 buildings. The sixth phase would demolish some of the 299 buildings along Herron Street near the highway interchange. The seventh phase would demolish some of the 246 buildings in the northeast corner of downtown. The eighth phase would be to rehabilitate 131 buildings along Dexter Avenue near the Alabama capitol building. The ninth phase would convert about 262 buildings from residential to commercial use downtown. See Joe McFadden, "Intended Alterations for Montgomery Listed," *Alabama Journal*, May 21, 1965, 1–2.

23. "City Commission Approves Historic Development Unit," *Montgomery Advertiser*, June 7, 1967, PISF, ADAH.

24. Ned Kaufman, *Place, Race, Story: Essays on the Past and Future of Historic Preservation* (New York: Routledge, 2009).

25. Sid Thumas, "Renewal Plan to Spare Historic Buildings," *Montgomery Advertiser*, January 25, 1968, PISF, ADAH.

26. Not all these historic sites were demolished, but they were not protected from the possibility of demolition. See Sid Thumas, "Renewal Plan to Spare Historic Buildings," *Montgomery Advertiser*, January 25, 1968, PISF, ADAH.

27. Herbert Gans, *The War against the Poor: The Underclass and Antipoverty Policy* (New York: Basic Books, 1996).

28. The press reported different figures for the acreage for the plan. One estimate was as high as eight hundred to one thousand acres. See Gene Kovarik, "Two Neighborhood Studies Authorized," *Alabama Journal*, July 31, 1964, 13; Gene Kovarik, "West End Renewal Mostly Clearance," *Alabama Journal*, August 26, 1964, 11; Ann Lyle, "City Asks Federal Funds for Western Hills Project," *Alabama Journal*, June 22, 1965, 9.

29. Wright asked the FHA for $1.5 million to finance the project. See "City Will Ask $1.5 Million to Finance Slum Clearance," *Montgomery Advertiser*, August 27, 1964, 6; Gene Kovarik, "Link Between Slums, Crime Pictured," *Alabama Journal*, August 27, 1964, 29. Ironically, Elizabeth Wright credited her meagre upbringing during the Depression as her qualification for her job: "'I remember well the feed sack dresses . . . I wore to school and the sacks our bed sheets were made of. . . . I also remember the kerosene lights, open fire places, wood stoves, pan baths, the outdoor well and privy and the Sears-Roebuck catalogue. . . . My heart is made very sad when I go into areas of poverty and filth in our great city; therefore, I thank God that I will have a part in trying to help lift the standards of living of our people. . . . I know exactly how they feel.'" See Gene Kovarik, "Mrs. Elizabeth Wright," *Montgomery Advertiser*, October 4, 1964, 3; "FHA Gives Tentative GNRP O.K.," *Montgomery Advertiser*, May 18, 1965, 12. The boundaries of the project were Hill, Carlisle, and Mill Streets, and the Atlantic Coast Line Railroad, adjacent to McIntyre School. See "Sale Date Set on Renewal Lots," *Alabama Journal*, August 6, 1971, 21; Tom Mackin, "Town House Project Set," *Montgomery Advertiser*, April 9, 1965, 1; "FHA Gives Tentative GNRP O.K.," *Montgomery Advertiser*, May 18, 1965, 12.

30. Roberta Reisig, "Family in Montgomery Forced to Move from One Temporary Home to Another," *The Southern Courier*, October 22–23, 1966, 4.

31. Two hundred homes in the ASU urban renewal area were demolished by 1971. See Betty Vereen, "Sale Date Set on Renewal Lots," *Alabama Journal*, August 6, 1971, 21; Joe McFadden, "Intended Alterations for Montgomery Listed," *Alabama Journal*, May 21, 1965, 1; Joe McFadden, "Contract Let on Renewal Project Here," *Alabama Journal*, May 31, 1965, 13.

32. Urban Consultant Associates, State College Urban Renewal Area Map, November 3, 1965, GPC, ADAH.

33. "Third Renewal Area," *Alabama Journal*, August 6, 1964, PISF, ADAH; Raymond Massey, "Court Square Is Approved, City Ready," *Alabama Journal*, August 8, 1968, 1; Franklin Skinner, "South Montgomery Project of Urban Renewal Growing," *Montgomery Advertiser*, August 15, 1968, 2; Gene Kovarik, "Renewal to Provide ASC Expansion," *Alabama Journal*, September 4, 1964, 11.

34. "Renewing Montgomery Downtown . . .," *Montgomery Advertiser*, August 12,

1969, 4. See also Urban Consultant Associates, "Montgomery, Alabama State College Urban Renewal Area," November 3, 1965, Alabama Governor Administrative Files, ADAH; Raymond Massey, "ASU Urban Renewal Increases $500,000," *Alabama Journal*, February 19, 1971, 15.

35. It is unknown if the meeting occurred. See Rev. R. C. Boone and J. L. Carr to Governor Wallace and Urban Renewal Agency, n.d., Montgomery Improvement Association Files, LWLC. See an earlier draft of the letter in RALC, TSCC.

36. Elizabeth Wright, "Remarks," n.d., RALC, TSCC. See also "Public Hearing: State College Urban Renewal Project Area, ALA R-65," October 11, 1967, RALC, TSCC; "Informational Statement to Families and Individuals," 1967, RALC, TSCC.

37. The *Alabama Journal* reported that the number of families needing relocation was 1,443 from urban renewal, 1,248 from highway construction, and 275 from housing code enforcement. Gene Kovarik, "City to Build 1,000 Public Low Rent Units," *Alabama Journal*, November 3, 1964, 1; Gene Kovarik, "Loan Approved, Housing Sites Sought in City," *Alabama Journal*, February 18, 1965, 31. The boundaries of the project were west of Mobile Street between the railroad and Old Hayneville Road, and the boundaries of the project near Maxwell were along Air Base Boulevard and Old Hayneville Road. See "$6 Million Housing Loan Approved for Montgomery," *Montgomery Advertiser*, October 9, 1965, 20.

38. Raymond Massey, "Low-Rent Housing Land Is Sought," *Alabama Journal*, May 13, 1967, RALC, TSCC; "Housing Unit Seeks New Site for Project," *Montgomery Advertiser*, May 14, 1967.

39. "$2.49 Million Loan OKd for Housing Development," *Montgomery Advertiser*, March 29, 1969.

40. "Negro Physician Appointed to City's Housing Board," *Montgomery Advertiser*, July 17, 1968, 1.

41. Elizabeth Wright, "Remarks," n.d.; Betty Vereen, "2 Blacks on New Board," *Alabama Journal*, November 16, 1971, 11; "Minutes of Meeting: Parks and Recreation Board and Center Directors," August 21, 1972, RALC, TSCC.

42. Mayor Earl James to E. D. Nixon, March 6, 1967, E. D. Nixon Papers, LWLC; M. Y. Forte letter to Mayor James, March 27, 1967, E. D. Nixon Papers, LWLC.

43. W. H. Edgar, "Minutes of the City Commissioners' Committee on Community Affairs, Joint Meeting of the General Committees," February 28, 1968, RALC, TSCC.

44. Developers leased housing to the MHA for ten years or more on Cleveland Avenue and Watts and Jefferson Street, Mobile Boulevard, Air Base Boulevard, West Jefferson Davis Avenue, and Mill, Day, Flood, Malvern, and Mobile Streets. See Raymond Massey, "Uniform City Codes Planning Shapes Up," *Alabama Journal*, October 16, 1968, 13.

45. The zoning district in West Montgomery was R-60a. The building was located at Cleveland Avenue and Watts and Jefferson Streets. See Franklin Skinner, "Planning Group Denies Amendment on Housing until Further Study," *Montgomery Advertiser*, October 25, 1968, 2; Raymond Massey, "Low-Rent Zone Category Urged," *Alabama Journal*, October 25, 1968, 13.

46. Franklin Skinner, "City Commission to Face Zoning, 'Instant Housing' Issues Today," *Montgomery Advertiser*, October 22, 1968, 1.

47. Skinner, "City Commission to Face Zoning," 1.

48. "Save Us from Instant Slums," *Montgomery Advertiser*, October 25, 1968, 4.

49. "Save Us from Instant Slums," 4.

50. Raymond Massey, "Uniform City Codes Planning Shapes Up," *Alabama Journal*, October 16, 1968, 13. The archival record of where these private developments leased to the MHA were located is sparse. One MHA resident newsletter lists Northgate Manor and Dixie Courts as two such developments. See "Rover's Findings: A Monthly Newsletter to the Tenants of the Montgomery Housing Authority," March 1971, RALC, TSCC. During this time the Central Alabama Planning and Development Commission got involved in housing issues for the first time with the publication of a regional housing strategy. See Sheldon Schaffer to Don Horton, September 18, 1969, RALC, TSCC.

51. National Commission on Urban Problems, *Building the American City: Report of the National Commission on Urban Problems to the Congress and to the President of the United States* (Washington, DC: US Government Printing Office, 1968); Mark Gelfand, *A Nation of Cities: The Federal Government and Urban America, 1933–1965* (New York: Oxford University Press, 1975); Urbanism Committee, National Resources Committee, *Our Cities: Their Role in the National Economy* (Washington, DC: US Government Printing Office, 1973); Daniel P. Moynihan, "Toward a National Urban Policy," *Public Interest* 17 (Fall 1969): 3–20; Stuart Meck and Rebecca Retzlaff, "President Jimmy Carter's Urban Policy: A Reconstruction and an Appraisal," *Journal of Planning History* 11, no. 3 (2012): 242–80.

52. See "Oak Park Tables Back," *Alabama Journal*, July 6, 1968; Carol-Faye Bruchac, "Oak Park Attractions Disappear," *Montgomery Advertiser*, August 28, 1968.

53. Glenn Saunders, "City's Longest Fence Now Encloses Oak Park," *Montgomery Advertiser*, May 28, 1965, 28; "Oak Park Set to Stay Open until Sundown," *Alabama Journal*, March 12, 1969, 25.

54. Morris Dees with Steve Fiffer, *A Lawyer's Journey: The Morris Dees Story* (Chicago, IL: American Bar Association, 2001).

55. "City Board Recommends Oak Park Be Restored," *Montgomery Advertiser*, February 13, 1969; "Bird Sanctuary," *Montgomery Advertiser*, February 21, 1969.

56. Franklin Skinner, "HUD Denies Funds for Dannelly Park," *Montgomery Advertiser*, May 20, 1969.

57. "City's Application for Parks Funds May Be Filed Too Late," *Montgomery Advertiser*, January 14, 1970, PISF, ADAH.

58. Raymond Massey, "City's Chisholm Park to Open Gate in May," *Alabama Journal*, February 24, 1971, PISF, ADAH; Franklin Skinner, "2 U.S. Officials to Survey Park Needs in Montgomery," *Montgomery Advertiser*, January 16, 1970, 15; "Some Extras for Oak Park," *Alabama Journal*, February 3, 1969, PISF, ADAH; "Montgomery's Zoo Gets Tall, Skinny, Boarder," *Alabama Journal*, October 5, 1971, 9.

59. "We Favor Public Parks . . . and Public Swimming Pools Too," WSFA-TV editorial, September 3, 1970, 1. See also "Oak Park Tables Back," *Alabama Journal*, July 6, 1968, 9.

60. Raymond Massey, "State Turned Down on River Land Bid," *Alabama Journal*, March 7, 1968, 35.

61. Massey, "State Turned Down," 35. See also "State Sues to Take River Peninsula Strip," *The Montgomery Independent*, February 29, 1968, PISF; ADAH, Raymond Massey, "State Fails to Appeal I-65 Land Refusal," *Alabama Journal*, November 7, 1969, PISF, ADAH.

62. Massey, "State Turned Down," 35.

63. "State Sues To Take River Peninsula Strip," *Montgomery Independent*, February 29, 1968.

64. "State Sues to Take, " 2. See also Harry Stark to Lowell Bridwell, July 5, 1968, RG 406, NA2; Raymond Massey, "River Land Use Opposed," *Alabama Journal*, September 17, 1969, 17.

65. Raymond Massey, "State Fails to Appeal I-65 Land Refusal," *Alabama Journal*, November 7, 1969, PISF, ADAH.

66. AHD paid $9,000 for 32.77 acres of land. See *State of Alabama v. Mrs. Beryl Palitz et al.*, Montgomery County Probate Court Case 7251, August 23, 1968, MCPCA; *State of Alabama v. Mrs. Beryl Palitz et al.*, Notice of Lis Pendens June 18, 1968, MCPCA; Raymond Massey, "Appeal Deadline Past on Property for Road," *Montgomery Advertiser*, November 8, 1969, 18.

67. Wm. L. Dickinson letter to Director of BPR, May 16, 1969, RG 406, NA2; "Central Alabama Regional Planning Commission, Resolution," May 1, 1969, RG 406, NA2; "Montgomery County Board of Revenue Resolution," May 5, 1969, RG 406, NA2.

68. Randy Durden, "I-65 Prepares to Leap Montgomery's River," *Alabama Journal*, September 19, 1969, PISF, ADAH. The cost of the bridge was $3 to $4 million. See "State to Open Bids Oct. 23 On Big Bell Street Bridge," *Alabama Journal*, October 4, 1970. In a

separate court action in 1970, ALDOT acquired an easement along I-65 to prohibit filling, excavation, removal of soil, erection of billboards or signs, junkyards, and dumping of trash. In 1978 the FHA approved a southbound interchange on the peninsula at State Highway 143 because the Tyler Goodwin Bridge was in poor condition and needed to be removed. Approval of the interchange was conditional on protecting the floodplain. See Karl Bowers to J. D. Lacy, June 14, 1978, RG 406, NA2; *State of Alabama v. Mrs. Beryl Palitz et al.*, Montgomery County Probate Court, October 21, 1970, MCPCA; Montgomery Planning and Development Department, *Montgomery Riverfront Plan* (Montgomery, AL: Montgomery Planning and Development Department, 1975); G. M. Williams to William Dickinson, May 21, 1969, RG 406, NA2; William L. Dickinson to Director of the Bureau of Public Roads, May 16, 1969, RG 406, NA2; G. M. Williams to William Dickinson, May 21, 1969, RG 406, NA2; Frank Johnson to C. R. Green, May 19, 1978, RG 406, NA2; J. D. Lacy to H. A. Lindberg, April 21, 1978, RG 406, NA2.

69. *Carr v. Montgomery County Board of Education*, 289 F. Supp 647 (US District Court, n.d., 1968).

70. *Carr v. Montgomery County Board of Education*, 289 F. Supp 647 (US District Court, n.d., 1968).

71. *Carr v. Montgomery County Board of Education*, 289 F. Supp 647 (US District Court, n.d., 1968), *651.

72. By the mid 1960s developers had managed to get some new African American subdivisions built, despite several decades of white pressure on the City Commission to not build African American subdivisions. One editorial noted that these new subdivisions would help maintain school segregation because they were entirely segregated and more affordable than homes in formerly white neighborhoods. The article noted, "If future school desegregation is governed by developing housing patterns, very little will occur. In Montgomery, what was called a 'desperate need for better Negro housing' early this year is being met now by several all-Negro subdivisions. With the primary pressure being relieved by the growing subdivisions, most young Negro families have found the new houses a better buy than the ones in older white border neighborhoods." See Joe McFadden, "Negroes Gain Education, Opportunities for Jobs," *Montgomery Advertiser*, October 16, 1966, 5.

73. *Carr v. Montgomery County Board of Education*, 289 F. Supp 647 (US District Court, n.d., 1968).

74. *Montgomery County Board of Education v. Carr*, 400 F.2d 1 (US Court of Appeals, 5th Circuit 1968), *1. In an evenly split decision, the court denied the board of education's petition for rehearing, leaving the modification from "substantially" to "approximately" in place. See *Montgomery County Board of Education v. Carr v. Montgomery County Board of Education* 402 F.2d.782 (US Court of Appeals, 5th Circuit 1968).

75. *United States v. Montgomery County Board of Education*, 395 U.S. 225 (1969).

76. *Carr v. Montgomery County Board of Education*, 429 F.2d 382 (US Court of Appeals, 5th Circuit 1970).

77. *Carr v. Montgomery County Board of Education*, 429 F.2d 382 (US Court of Appeals, 5th Circuit 1970).

78. Aldon Morris, Walter Allan, David Maurrasse, and Derrick Gilbert, "White Supremacy and Higher Education: The Alabama Higher Education Desegregation Case," *National Black Law Journal* 14, no. 1 (1994): 59–91.

## *Chapter 10*

1. *Vincent Leonard Smith, et al. v. Young Men's Christian Association of Montgomery*, 316 F. Supp 899, July 20, 1970.

2. Morris Dees, *A Lawyer's Journey: The Morris Dees Story* (Montgomery, AL: Southern Poverty Law Center, 2001); *Browder v. Gale*, 142 F. Supp. 707 (1956); Belinda Robnett, *How Long: African American Women in the Struggle for Civil Rights* (New York: Oxford University Press, 1997).

3. Morris Dees with Steve Fiffer, *A Lawyer's Journey: The Morris Dees Story* (Chicago, IL: American Bar Association, 2001), 103.

4. Dees with Fiffer, *A Lawyer's Journey*, 105.

5. *Smith v. Young Men's Christian Association of Montgomery*, 316 F. Supp 899 (US District Court, n.d., 1970), *903.

6. Morris Dees, *A Lawyers Journey: The Morris Dees Story* (Montgomery, AL: Southern Poverty Law Center, 2001), 116.

7. An African American YMCA branch had long been a dream of activists. The MIA donated $20,000 to construct the Cleveland Avenue branch of the YMCA. See Rev. Dr. Martin Luther King Jr., "Annual Address by President Martin Luther King, Jr., on the Fourth Anniversary of the Montgomery Improvement Association," December 3, 1959, RALC, TSCC.

8. In March 1971 there were forty-four African American boys at the camp. See Affidavit of Charles Shelton, March 1971, RALC, TSCC.

9. *Smith v. Young Men's Christian Association of Montgomery*, 316 F. Supp 899 (US District Court, n.d. 1970), *904.

10. The YMCA Board of Directors considered building an African American camp for the Cleveland Avenue branch or allowing children from that branch to use the white camps exclusively one week every summer. Morris Dees recounted how he found the coordinating committee agreement by accident in his book *A Lawyers Journey: The Morris Dees Story*: "I had subpoenaed YMCA records for the last ten years. . . . When it was time to break for lunch, I was more interested

in looking at the documents than going out to eat. 'Mind if I stay here and look through the minutes?' I asked Oakley [YMCA's attorney]. 'No problem.' Oakley and everyone else departed. . . . I came upon a bunch of unfiled papers, three inches thick, sitting at the back of one of the boxes. . . . Mimeograph paper, stencils, more mimeograph paper, and then—Bang! The smoking gun: a 1958 document describing the 'City Recreation—YMCA Coordinating Committee,' a committee no one outside a few trusted YMCA and city officials had ever heard of. . . . I shivered. It was as clear as the Confederate flag still flying over Alabama's capitol: At the same time that the city had responded to the *Gilmore* suit by shutting down the swimming pools and parks, it had surreptitiously drafted an agreement with the YMCA for the Y to provide those terminated recreational activities. Why? Because the YMCA, a supposedly private organization, could continue to operate those activities in a segregated fashion out of the reach of the federal courts." See Morris Dees, *A Lawyers Journey: The Morris Dees Story* (Montgomery, AL: Southern Poverty Law Center, 2001), 116.

11. *Smith v. Young Men's Christian Association of Montgomery*, 316 F. Supp 899 (US District Court, n.d., 1970).

12. *Vincent Leonard Smith et al. v. the Young Men's Christian Association of Montgomery*, 462 F.2d 634 (US District Court, n.d., 1972).

13. Judith Helms, "For Not Ending Park Segregation," *Alabama Journal*, August 13, 1970, PISF, ADAH.

14. The plan for the softball complex at Chisholm Park was modified in 1974 after years of complaints that it promoted racial segregation, but the Parks and Recreation Board kept the golf course in the plan. See "Parks and Recreation Board Drops Softball Complex Plan," *Alabama Journal*, June 12, 1974, PISF, ADAH; "Park Sites Withdrawn from U.S. Court Suit," *Alabama Journal*, October 21, 1970, PISF, ADAH.

15. *Georgia Theresa Gilmore, et al., v. City of Montgomery, Alabama, et al.*, 94 S. Ct. 2416 (1974); *Gilmore v. Montgomery*, 417 U.S. 556, 94 S. Ct. 2416, 41 L. Ed. 2d 304; *Gilmore v. Montgomery*, 176 F. Supp. 776 (US District Court, n.d., 1959); *Gilmore v. Montgomery*, 473 F.2d 832 (US Court of Appeals 5th Circuit 1973); *Gilmore v. Montgomery*, 337 F. Supp. 22 (US District Court, n.d., 1972).

16. As Brown wrote, "Supervisors in the department are primarily supervisors of activities rather than personnel." Brown recommended eliminating the guards at Oak Park who were hired to keep African American people out of the park. See Roger K. Brown, *An Organizational Report of the Montgomery, Alabama, Park and Recreation Department* (Montgomery, AL: Montgomery Parks and Recreation Department, August 1971), RALC, TSCC, 4, 6.

17. See Roger K. Brown, *An Organizational Report of the Montgomery, Alabama, Park and Recreation Department* (Montgomery, AL: Montgomery Parks and Recreation Department, August 1971), RALC, TSCC.

18. The Parks and Recreation Department paid $57,752.50 to the schools for athletics staff during the 1970–71 fiscal year. See Brown, *An Organizational Report*.

19. Joseph Bagley, *The Politics of White Rights* (Athens: University of Georgia Press, 2018).

20. *Gilmore v. Montgomery*, 337 F. Supp. 22 (US District Court, n.d., 1972). After the order, the athletics director for the Parks and Recreation Department, Lynn Bozeman, requested to meet every potential new employee in the sports program. See Lynn Bozeman to Jim Vice, August 1, 1972, RALC, TSCC.

21. In 1972 attorneys for the Gilmore case filed a motion to compel the city to spend $2.8 million on recreation facilities for African American residents. City attorneys responded that the Parks and Recreation Board had substantially complied with the court order, which was set to expire in 1974, because it had built recreation centers at Goode Street, Washington Park, and Hayneville Road. See Marcia Kunstel, "Board Says Parks Order Followed," *Montgomery Advertiser*, December 13, 1972, PISF, ADAH. In another action, attorneys for the city argued that Georgia Gilmore should pay attorney and court fees because the city constructed a track at Carver High School that was substantially equal to the one at Jefferson Davis High School. See *Georgia Theresa Gilmore, et al., v. City of Montgomery, Alabama, et al.*, Civil Action No. 1490-N (US District Court, n.d., 1972), RALC, TSCC. The court denied the request because the track at Carver High School would wear out more rapidly and require more maintenance than the track at Jefferson Davis High School would because they used different construction materials. See *Georgia Theresa Gilmore, et al., v. City of Montgomery, Alabama, et al.*, Civil Action No. 1490-N (U.S. District Court, n.d., 1972), RALC, TSCC.

22. William Chandler to Jim Vice, March 3, 1972, RALC, TSCC.

23. William Brannon to Henry Andrews, "Monthly Report," February 8, 1972, RALC, TSCC; Montgomery Parks and Recreation Department, "Recreation Newsletter for Montgomery Seniors," January 1972, RALC, TSCC.

24. William Brannon to Henry Andrews, January 10, 1972, RALC, TSCC. Lewis and Hall established advisory councils only at African American parks.

25. Willie Harris, "Monthly Report: Newton Recreational Center," December 1971, RALC, TSCC; Richard Moncrief, "Monthly Report: Kiwanis Park," December 1971, RALC, TSCC; Willie Harris to whom it may concern, n.d., RALC, TSCC; Montgomery Parks and Recreation Board, Minutes of Meeting, February 8, 1972, RALC, TSCC.

26. *Gilmore v. City of Montgomery*, 94 S. Ct. 2416 (1974), *2423.

27. *Gilmore v. City of Montgomery*, 94 S. Ct. 2416 (1974), *569.

28. The court did not intervene in the question of whether such facilities could be used nonexclusively by segregated schools. *Gilmore v. City of Montgomery*, 94 S. Ct. 2416 (1974).

29. Randall Williams, "U.S. Court Will Be Asked to Drop Order Pertaining to Development of Parks," *Montgomery Advertiser*, November 19, 1975, PISF, ADAH.

30. "Reopening Oak Park Pool," *Montgomery Advertiser*, August 5, 1976, PISF, ADAH.

31. Morris Dees, *A Lawyers Journey: The Morris Dees Story* (Montgomery, AL: Southern Poverty Law Center, 2001), 126.

32. Alexander von Hoffman, "A Study in Contradictions: The Origins and Legacy of the Housing Act of 1949," *Housing Policy Debate* 11, no. 2 (2000): 299–326; Jon Teaford, "Urban Renewal and Its Aftermath," *Housing Policy Debate* 11, no. 2 (2000): 443–65.

33. Central Alabama Regional Planning and Development Commission, *Regional Housing Program* (Montgomery, AL: Central Alabama Regional Planning and Development Commission, 1976).

34. Department of Housing and Urban Development, *Analysis of the Montgomery, Alabama Housing Market* (Washington, DC: Department of Housing and Urban Development, 1971).

35. Stefanie DeLuca, Philip Garboden, and Peter Rosenblatt, "Segregating Shelter: How Housing Policies Shape the Residential Locations of Low-Income Minority Families," *The Annals of the American Academy of Political and Social Science* 647 (2013): 268–99.

36. Arnold Hirsch, *Making the Second Ghetto* (New York: Cambridge University Press, 1983); Wendell Pritchett, "Which Urban Crisis? Regionalism, Race, and Urban Policy, 1960–1974," *Journal of Urban History* 34, no. 2 (2008): 266–86; Angela Simms, "The 'Veil' of Racial Segregation in the 21st Century: The Suburban Black Middle Class, Public Schools, and Pursuit of Racial Equality," *Phylon* 56, no. 1 (2019): 81–110.

37. Mary Glass, "Montgomery Mayor's Committee has been Separated for over a Year," *Alabama Journal*, November 12, 1971, 21. W. E. Thompson was the principal of George Washington Carver High School. See "City's Biracial Committee Is Inactive," *Montgomery Advertiser*, November 13, 1971, 13.

38. Mary Glass, "Montgomery Mayor's Committee has been Separated for over a Year," *Alabama Journal*, November 12, 1971.

39. Montgomery Planning and Development Department, *Montgomery Riverfront Plan* (Montgomery, AL: Montgomery Planning and Development Department, 1975).

40. Montgomery Planning and Development Department, *Montgomery Riverfront Plan*, 1975.

41. As the court's decision notes, "The evidence reflects that the pairing or clustering of schools would require extensive cross-city busing from beyond the westernmost part of the city to beyond the easternmost part of the city. . . . Elementary children at all grade levels, one through six, would be involved in this cross-city busing." See *Carr v. Montgomery County Board of Education*, 377 F. Supp. 1123 (US District Court, n.d., 1974), *1129.

42. Daisy Lawrence, Booker T. Washington, Carver, Fews, Loveless, Hayneville Road, Paterson, Pintlala, Davis, and Bellinger Hill elementary schools and McIntyre Junior High would remain entirely segregated.

43. According to the decision, "The schools that remain predominantly black in the Montgomery school system are the result of the concentrations of blacks in the western area of Montgomery." See *Carr v. Montgomery County Board of Education*, 377 F.Supp. 1123 (US District Court, n.d., 1974), *1135.

44. *Carr v. Montgomery County Board of Education*, 377 F. Supp. 1123 (US District Court, n.d., 1974), *1135.

45. *Hightower v. West*, 430 F.2d 552 (US Court of Appeals, 5th Circuit, 1970).

46. *Carr v. Montgomery County Board of Education*, 377 F. Supp. 1123 (US District Court, n.d., 1974), *1134. In the North Carolina decision, the court determined that school desegregation does not mean that every school must reflect the racial composition of that school system. See *Swan v. Charlotte-Mecklenburg Bd. Of Educ.*, 402 U.S. 1, 24, 91 S. Ct. 1267, 28 L.Ed.2d 554 (1971).

47. *Carr v. Montgomery County Board of Education*, 511 F.2d 1374 (US Court of Appeals, 5th Circuit 1975).

48. *Carr v. Montgomery County Board of Education*, 511 F.2d 1374 (US Court of Appeals, 5th Circuit, 1975), *1385. As late as 1982 the schools that the board of education said would remain African American continued to be so. Loveless and Fews elementary were entirely African American, according to one article, and high school students had to be bused across town to avoid segregated high schools. See Joe Simmons, "Has Busing Run Course in State?," *Montgomery Advertiser*, September 19, 1982.

49. The appeals court decision in this case is particularly colorful in its condemnations of the school board: "Desegregation is not impossible in Montgomery. It might be uncomfortable, expensive, disturbing, or even disconcerting. But these words are not amendments to the Fourteenth Amendment's commands." See *Carr v. Montgomery County Board of Education*, 511 F2d 1374 (US Court of Appeals, 5th Circuit 1975), *1387.

50. *Carr v. Montgomery County Board of Education*, 423 U.S. 986 (1975). Multiple other cases involved school desegregation, including desegregating the school board itself. See, for example, *Arlam Carr, Jr., et al. v. Montgomery County Board of Education*, Civil Action 2072-N, (US Court of Appeals, n.d., 1978), RALC, TSCC.

51. All the data in this section comes from Montgomery Department of Planning and Development, *Neighborhood Analysis for Montgomery, Alabama* (Montgomery, AL: Montgomery Department of Planning and Development, 1974).

52. Montgomery Department of Planning and Development, *Neighborhood Analysis for Montgomery, Alabama*, 1974.

53. Charles Connerly, *The Most Segregated City in America: City Planning and Civil Rights in Birmingham, 1920–1980* (Charlottesville: University of Virginia Press, 2005); Christopher Silver, *Twentieth-Century Richmond: Planning, Politics, and Race* (Knoxville: University of Tennessee Press, 1984).

## *Conclusion*

1. Melissa Heil, Lou Turner, and David Wilson, "People of Color: Confronting White Supremacy in Planning," in *Alternative Planning History and Theory*, ed. Dorina Pojani (New York: Routledge, 2023), 125–44.

2. Gene Kovarik, "Huge Negro Woman Draws Cursing Fine," *Alabama Journal*, November 3, 1961, 13. See also Georgia Gilmore to Gwen Patton, December 10, 2003, Gwen Patton Collection, TSCC.

3. Solomon S. Seay to MIA Executive Committee, November 10, 1958, RALC, TSCC.

4. Charles Connerly, *The Most Segregated City in America: City Planning and Civil Rights in Birmingham, 1920–1980* (Charlottesville: University of Virginia Press, 2005).

5. Silver reached a similar conclusion in Richmond, writing, "The planner's cure for neighborhood ills sometimes proved more deadly than the disease." See Christopher Silver, *Twentieth-Century Richmond: Planning, Politics, and Race* (Knoxville: University of Tennessee Press, 1984), 99. See also Thomas Hanchett, *Sorting out the New South City: Race, Class, and Urban Development in Charlotte, 1875–1975* (Chapel Hill: University of North Carolina Press, 1998); Francesca Russello Ammon, "Commemoration Amid Criticism: The Mixed Legacy of Urban Renewal in Southwest Washington, D.C.," *Journal of Planning History* 8, no. 3 (2009): 175–220.

6. Joe Azbell, "City Limits," *Montgomery Advertiser*, March 18, 1956, 11.

7. Warren H. Manning, *City Plan of Birmingham* (Birmingham, AL: Birmingham Planning Commission, 1919).

8. Laura Tach and Allison Dwyer Emory, "Public Housing Redevelopment,

Neighborhood Change, and the Restructuring of Urban Inequality," *American Journal of Sociology* 123, no. 3 (2017): 686–739; Amanda Seligman, *Block by Block: Neighborhoods and Public Policy on Chicago's West Side* (Chicago, IL: University of Chicago Press, 2005); Richard Casey Sadler, "Racist Housing Practices as a Precursor to Uneven Neighborhood Change in a Post-Industrial City," *Housing Studies* 32, no. 2 (2016): 186–208; Karl Taeuber and Alma Taeuber, *Residential Segregation and Neighborhood Change* (New York: Routledge, 2009).

9. Arnold Hirsch, *Making the Second Ghetto: Race and Housing in Chicago, 1940–1960* (New York: Cambridge University Press, 1983).

10. Housing Authority and Urban Renewal Agency of Montgomery, *1939–1969: 30 Years of Progress* (Montgomery, AL: Housing Authority and Urban Renewal Agency of Montgomery, 1969), RALC, TSCC.

11. US Economic Opportunity Act, P.L. 88–452 (1964).

12. Sherry Arnstein, "A Ladder of Citizen Participation," *Journal of the American Institute of Planners* 35, no. 4 (1969): 216–24, 218.

13. Arnstein, "A Ladder," 218. Planners established four Neighborhood Service Centers in the city and three in the county: Mount Meigs, Pine Level, Macedonia, Ramer, Trenholm, Gibbs Village, Bell Street, Chisholm, Cleveland Avenue, plus one vocational center at St. Jude. See also R. W. Pringle Jr., "Neighborhood Service Center Program Monthly Report," March 1971, RALC, TSCC. Governor George Wallace appointed an all-white committee, so Rufus Lewis, J. T. Alexander, and S. S. Seay Sr. petitioned for more African American representation. See Rufus Lewis, J. T. Alexander, and S. S. Seay Sr. to George Wallace, n.d., RALC, TSCC, Rufus Lewis to Orzell Billingsley Jr., n.d., RALC, TSCC.

14. R. W. Pringle Jr. memo to MCAC Board Members, April 26, 1971, RALC, TSCC, 1.

15. R. W. Pringle Jr., "3-Year Plan Development Major Problem Identification and Section Gap," April 19, 1971, RALC, TSCC.

16. Boone posted signs outside CAC meetings that read "That Alabama Action Committee wants a Black Director for MCAC to be Chosen either from Mr. Sims Williams, Mr. Franz Wilson, or Mr. John Tolbert." See "Montgomery Community Action Committee Meeting Minutes," September 8, 1969, RALC, TSCC, 2. Sheldon was replaced by J. A. Gannon. See J. A. Gannon to MCAC Board Members, March 31, 1970, RALC, TSCC. Lewis was on the CAC board from the beginning. Fred Gray joined later. Langford replaced Gray in May 1970. See "Montgomery Community Action Committee Meeting Minutes," May 11, 1970, RALC, TSCC. In 1972 Lewis suggested half the board represent the poor and moving meetings to 7:00 p.m. so they could attend. See "Montgomery Community Action Committee, Meeting Minutes,"

February 24, 1972, RALC, TSCC; Community Action Strategy Team, "Dear CAST Constituent," *The Advocate* 1, no. 8 (August 1971), RALC, TSCC; "Articles of Incorporation of Montgomery Community Action Committee, Inc., A Non-Profit Corporation, draft," n.d., RALC, TSCC. Lewis allowed the Citizens' Club to be used for a Head Start program on the Westside, but it was closed because the building needed improvement. See A. T. Sullivan to Lillie Jones, July 14, 1966, RALC, TSCC; John Tolbert letter to Rufus Lewis, August 23, 1968, RALC, TSCC. In April 1970 Barbara Whitaker, assistant regional director for child development for the Montgomery CAC, wrote to CAC director Joe Cannon that the Head Start program was almost entirely segregated, including teachers, staff, and children. See Barbara Whitaker to Joe Cannon, April 7, 1970, RALC, TSCC. In 1971 H. W. Suddath, administrator for the Montgomery County Commission, wrote to W. E. Thompson, chairperson of the Montgomery CAA, to complain that county officials were left out of decision making on CAA issues. See H. W. Suddath letter to W. E. Thompson, March 2, 1971, The Honorable Rufus A. Lewis Collection, Letters Box, TSCC.

17. Virginia Gibson, "Operation Pride Spreading to City's King Hill Area," *Alabama Journal*, January 22, 1971.

18. Jerry Tillotson, "King Hill Citizens Wage War on Filth," *Montgomery Advertiser*, February 2, 1971.

19. "Montgomery Local Development Company Meeting Minutes," March 14, 1973, Riley Lewis Collection, TSCC.

20. Brenda Login to Board Members, August 17, 1972, Riley Lewis Collection, TSCC.

21. Riley Lewis Jr., "I-65, I-85 and Urban Renewal: Deal Death Blow to West Montgomery Small Businesses," October 1972, Riley Lewis Collection, TSCC.

22. The group cited the 1969 Federal Disaster Relief Act and Executive Order 11495.

23. J. Aronstein Jr. to Mayor Jim Robinson, October 24, 1972, Riley Lewis Collection, TSCC.

24. George Wallace to President Nixon, November 22, 1972, Riley Lewis Collection, TSCC; Jim Robinson to George Wallace, October 25, 1972, Riley Lewis Collection, TSCC.

25. John Vaughn to Mayor Jim Robinson, September 13, 1974, Riley Lewis Collection, TSCC; Marcia Kunstel, "Improvements Set for Western Hills," *Montgomery Advertiser*, December 19, 1972, 15; Dennis Baily, "Hundreds Attend Festival," *Montgomery Advertiser*, June 12, 1972, 16; "Plans for Black Preservation Project Taking Shape," *Landmarks Foundation Quarterly* 1, no. 2 (Fall 1975), Riley Lewis Collection, TSCC.

26. "Misplaced Optimism," *Montgomery Advertiser*, October 28, 1974, 4.

27. Lenore Reese, "Council Okays Rezoning For Oak Park Neighborhood," *Alabama Journal*, September 20, 1978.

28. The case likely involved Urban Development Action Grants.

29. *Martin v. United States Department of Housing and Urban Development*, 82–252-N (US District Court, n.d., 1983) (unpublished opinion); Virginia Martin, "City Board Chairman Quits in Protest," *Montgomery Advertiser*, December 18, 1985; "Four Couples Fighting Carter Hill Project," *Montgomery Advertiser*, April 8, 1982; Roy Summerfield, "Grant Money Must Go for Low-Income Areas," *Montgomery Advertiser*, October 28, 1977.

30. Urban Consultants Inc., *Recreation and Culture Report for the State of Alabama* (Montgomery: Alabama Development Office, 1973).

31. J. C. Miller to Wiley Thomas, Jr., April 4, 1989, Gwen Patton Collection, TSCC; Willie Lofton to Riley Lewis, February 25, 1989, Gwen Patton Collection, TSCC. The group proposed historical markers at 634 Cleveland Court, Rosa Parks's apartment, and 654 Mill Street, E. D. Nixon's apartment at one time.

32. Riley Lewis, Jr. to Debra Dumas, January 9, 1990, Gwen Patton Collection, TSCC. The MHA received funds to revitalize Cleveland Court in 1978. See Lenore Reese, "Cleveland Court to be Model Project," *Alabama Journal*, September 20, 1978. The HUD denied a request from the MHA for $10 million to upgrade Trenholm Court. See Lenore Reese, "Housing Authority Fails to Receive $10 Million Grant," *Alabama Journal*, October 5, 1978.

33. "Chronology: Activity Involved in Organizing the One Mile Enterprise Periphery on the Selma to Montgomery Voting Rights Trail," Riley Lewis, Jr. Collection, LWLC.

34. Alabama National Historic Trail Foundation, "The Auspicious Prosperity Mile," n.d., Riley Lewis, Jr. Collection, LWLC.

35. National Endowment for the Humanities letter to Herschel Mann, November 30, 2001, Riles Lewis, Jr. Collection, LWLC.

36. "Chronology: Activity." See also Rev. Claude Shuford and Dr. Gwendolyn Patton, "Memorandum of Agreement," July 11, 2000, Riley Lewis, Jr. Collection, LWLC; Bobby Bright to Alabama National Historic Trail Foundation, February 15, 2001, Riley Lewis, Jr. Collection, LWLC; Rev. Vaughncile C. Fitzpatrick and Rev. Claude A. Shuford to Bobby Bright, March 28, 2001, Riley Lewis, Jr. Collection, LWLC; Catherine Farmer to Samuel Kaufman, August 10, 2001, Riley Lewis, Jr. Collection, LWLC.

37. "Civil Rights Coordinating Committee Meeting Minutes," September 10, 2001, Riley Lewis Collection, LWLC.

38. US Census of Housing and Population, 1990, 2000.

39. Dover, Kole, and Partners, *The Plan for Oak Park and Centennial Hill* (Montgomery, AL: Montgomery Planning Commission, 2011).

40. Montgomery Planning Department, "Housing and Community Development Data," Montgomery Planning Department, accessed March 15, 2021.

41. Mark Golub, "Remembering Massive Resistance to School Desegregation," *Law and History Review* 31, no. 3 (2013): 491–530; Twala Grant, "The Missed Mandate of *Brown v. Board of Education*: Educationally Effective Schools with All Deliberate Speed," *National Black Law Journal* 13, no. 1 (1993): 134–46.

42. Andrew Yawn, "Cleaved by Concrete: The Legacy of Montgomery's Interstates and the Neighborhoods They Destroyed," *Montgomery Advertiser*, March 7, 2018, accessed February 4, 2020, quoting Montgomery resident Skip Jackson.

43. Some residents moved so these addresses reflect just one point.

44. Montgomery Planning Department, *Envision Montgomery 2040 Comprehensive Plan* (Montgomery, AL: Montgomery Planning Department, 2020).

# Bibliography

## ARCHIVES


### Alabama Department of Archives and History, Montgomery, Alabama (ADAH)

Alabama Governor (1959–1963: Patterson) (GPC)
Alabama Industrial Development Board
Housing Authority
Industrial Development Board
John Engelhardt Scott Negative Collection
Public Information Subject Files (PISF)
Sam Engelhardt Collection (SEC)
Sam Engelhardt Collection, Scrapbooks (SECS)

### Alabama State University Archives, Levi Watkins Learning Center, Montgomery, Alabama (LWLC)

E. D. Nixon Collection
Montgomery Improvement Association Collection
Ralph Abernathy Collection
Riley Lewis Jr. Collection
Vertical Files

### Archdiocese of Mobile, Alabama, Archives (AMA)

Records of the City of St. Jude, Montgomery, Alabama

### Auburn University Special Collections, Ralph Brown Draughon Library, Auburn, Alabama

Alabama Collection
Map Collection
Rare Books Collection

### Birmingham Public Library Department of Archives and Manuscripts, Central Branch, Birmingham, Alabama (BPL)

J. W. Morgan Papers

### Martin Luther King Jr. Institute, Center for Nonviolent Social Change, Atlanta, Georgia

Martin Luther King Jr. Papers

### Montgomery County Probate Court Archives, Montgomery, Alabama

Montgomery County Circuit Court, Chancery, and City Courts Records
Montgomery County Probate Court Records

### Montgomery Public Library Archives, Juliette Hampton Morgan Branch, Montgomery, Alabama (MPL)

Alabama-Southeastern Rare Book Collection
E. D. Nixon Files
Vertical Files

### National Archives and Records Administration II, College Park, Maryland (NA2)

RG 30: Bureau of Public Roads
RG 187: National Resource Planning Board
RG 195: Federal Home Loan Bank Board
RG 196: Public Housing Administration
RG 207: Department of Housing and Urban Development
RG 252: Office of the Housing Expediter
RG 406: Federal Highway Administration

### National Archives and Records Administration Southeast Branch, Atlanta, Georgia (NAA)

RG 1: War Labor Policies Board
RG 21: District Courts of the United States
RG 30: Bureau of Public Roads
RG 207: General Records of the Department of Housing and Urban Development
RG 252: Office of the Housing Expediter

### Trenholm State Community College Archives, Montgomery, Alabama (TSCC)

Flora Moore Andry Collection

Gwen Patton Collection
Honorable Rufus A. Lewis Collection (RALC)
Idessa Redden Collection
Juliette Hampton Morgan Collection
Lucille Times Collection
Madison Family Collection

## FEDERAL, STATE, AND MUNICIPAL PLANS AND REPORTS

Alabama Highway Department. *1965 Parking Study: Montgomery, Alabama*. Montgomery: State of Alabama Highway Department Bureau of Urban Planning, 1967.

Alabama Highway Department. *Forty-Ninth Annual Report of the Alabama Highway Department: October 1, 1959 to September 30, 1960*. Montgomery: Alabama Highway Department, 1960.

Alabama Historical Commission. *National Register of Historic Places Nomination for the City of St. Jude Historic District*. Montgomery: Alabama Historical Commission, 1990.

Alabama State Planning Board. *Public Recreation in Alabama*. Montgomery: Alabama State Planning Board, 1948.

Bureau of Public Roads. *Toll Roads and Free Roads*. Washington, DC: US Bureau of Public Roads, 1939.

Centennial Celebration Committee. *A Century of Negro Progress in Montgomery City and County*. Montgomery, AL: Centennial Celebration Committee, 1963.

Central Alabama Regional Planning and Development Commission. *Regional Housing Program*. Montgomery: Central Alabama Regional Planning and Development Commission, 1976.

Department of Housing and Urban Development. *Analysis of the Montgomery, Alabama Housing Market*. Washington, DC: Department of Housing and Urban Development, 1971.

Dobbins, W. O., Jr. *Alabama's Planning Program, 1943–1947: Report to the Governor*. Montgomery: Alabama State Planning Board, 1946.

Dover, Kole, and Partners. *The Plan for Oak Park and Centennial Hill*. Montgomery, AL: Montgomery Planning Commission, 2011.

Harland Bartholomew and Associates. *The Comprehensive Plan: Birmingham, Alabama*. Birmingham, AL: Birmingham Planning Commission 1961.

Manning, Warren H. *City Plan of Birmingham*. Birmingham, AL: City of Birmingham, 1919.

McIntosh, Henry, Earle Draper, and Raymond Leonard. *Status and Future of State and Regional Planning*. Atlanta, GA: National Resources Committee, 1938.

Montgomery Department of Planning and Development. *Neighborhood Analysis for Montgomery, Alabama*. Montgomery, AL: Montgomery Department of Planning and Development, 1974.

Montgomery Housing Authority. *Report of the Housing Authority of the City of Montgomery Alabama*. Montgomery, AL: Montgomery Housing Authority, 1942.

Montgomery Planning and Development Department. *Montgomery Riverfront Plan*. Montgomery, AL: Montgomery Planning and Development Department, 1975.

Montgomery Planning Commission. *Rosa Parks Combined Communities and Five Points Neighborhood Plan*. Montgomery, AL: Montgomery Planning Commission, 2008.

Montgomery Planning Commission and the Alabama State Planning Board. *Master Plan for Public Recreation*. Montgomery, AL: City Planning Commission, 1949.

Montgomery Planning Department. "Envision Montgomery 2040 Comprehensive Plan." Montgomery Planning Department, accessed March 15, 2021.

Montgomery Planning Department. "Housing and Community Development Data." Montgomery Planning Department, accessed March 15, 2021.

Montgomery Public School System. *A Study of Montgomery City and County*. Montgomery, AL: Montgomery Public Schools City and County, 1938.

National Commission on Urban Problems. *Building and American City: Report of the National Commission on Urban Problems to the Congress and to the President of the United States*. Washington, DC: US Government Printing Office, 1968.

National Resources Planning Board, Atlanta Field Office. *Elements of Action within a Program of Regional Development*. Atlanta, GA: National Resources Planning Board, 1940.

Nicrosi, William. *Montgomery Housing*. Montgomery, AL: Montgomery Housing Authority, 1940.

Southeastern Regional Planning Commission. *Development Study of the Alabama-Coosa Basin Area: Prospectus*. Atlanta, GA: Southeastern Regional Planning Commission, 1943.

Urban Consultant Associates. *A Public Improvements Program for Montgomery*. Montgomery, AL: Montgomery Planning Commission, 1962.

Urban Consultant Associates. *A Transportation Plan for Montgomery: A Part of the Comprehensive City Plan*. Montgomery, AL: City Planning Commission, 1966.

Urban Consultant Associates. *Land Use Plan (2nd Draft): Montgomery, Alabama*. Montgomery: Montgomery Planning Commission, 1957.

Urban Consultants Inc. *An Economic Analysis of the Montgomery C. B. D.: A Part of the Comprehensive City Plan*. Montgomery, AL: Montgomery Planning Commission, 1965.

Urban Consultants Inc. *A Land Use Plan for Montgomery: Part of the Comprehensive City Plan*. Montgomery, AL: Montgomery City Planning Commission, 1965.

Urban Consultants Inc. *Neighborhood Analysis for Montgomery, Alabama*. Montgomery: Montgomery Planning Commission, January 1965.

Urban Consultants Inc. *People and Economy: A Part of the Comprehensive City Plan*. Montgomery, AL: Montgomery Planning Commission, 1965.

Urban Consultants Inc. *Recreation and Culture Report for the State of Alabama*. Montgomery: Alabama Development Office, 1973.

Wilbur Smith and Associates. *Major Route Plan: Montgomery Metropolitan Area: Volume 1—Highway and Travel Facts*. Montgomery: Alabama Highway Department, 1960.

Wilbur Smith and Associates. *Major Route Plan: Montgomery Metropolitan Area: Volume 2—Street and Highway Plan*. Montgomery: Alabama Highway Department, 1960.

## CASES AND LAWS

23 U.S. Code, Section 123 (August 27, 1958).

23 U.S. Code, Section 127 (August 27, 1958).

Alabama Pupil Placement Act, Article 52, Section 61(4) (1955).

*Arlam Carr Jr., et al. v. Montgomery County Board of Education,* Civil Action 2072-N, US Court of Appeals (1978).

*Browder v. Gale,* 142 F. Supp. 707 (1956).

*Brown v. Board of Education of Topeka,* 347 U.S. 483 (1954).

*Buchanan v. Warley,* 245 U.S. 60 (1917).

*Carr v. Montgomery County Board of Education,* 289 F. Supp. 647 (1968).

*Carr v. Montgomery County Board of Education,* 377 F. Supp. 1123 (1974).

*Carr v. Montgomery County Board of Education,* 511 F.2d 1374 (1975).

*Carr v. Montgomery County Board of Education,* 423 U.S. 986 (1975).

City of Montgomery, *Code of Ordinances of the City of Montgomery, ALA* (Montgomery, AL: Montgomery City Commission, 1928).

City of Montgomery, *Ala v. Gilmore*, 277 F.2d 364 (1960).

Code of Alabama, Article 11, Section 1121 (1935).

Code of Alabama, Article 11, Section 1126 (1935).

Code of Alabama, Article 11, Section 1978 (1923).

Disaster Relief Act of 1969, P.L. 91–80 (1969).

*Georgia Theresa Gilmore, et al., v. City of Montgomery, Alabama, et al.*, 94 S. Ct. 2416 (1974).

*Gilmore v. Montgomery*, 176 F. Supp. 776 (1959).

*Gilmore v. Montgomery*, 337 F. Supp. 22 (1972).

*Gilmore v. Montgomery*, 417 U.S. 556 (1974).

*Gilmore v. Montgomery*, 473 F.2d 832 (1973).

*Gomillion v. Lightfoot*, 364 U.S. 339 (1960).

*Hightower v. West*, 430 F.2d. 552 (1970).

*Lucas v. South Carolina Coastal Council*, 505 U.S. 1003 (1992).

*Martin v. United States Department of Housing and Urban Development*, unpublished opinion no. 82–252-N (1983).

Montgomery City Planning Commission and Alabama State Planning Board, *Montgomery Zoning Ordinance*, July 1948.

*Montgomery County Board of Education v. Carr*, 400 F.2d 1 (1968).

*Montgomery County Board of Education v. Carr v. Montgomery County Board of Education*, 402 F.2d.782 (1968).

President Richard Nixon, Executive Order 11495, Providing for the Administration of the Disaster Relief Act of 1969 (November 18, 1969).

*Smith v. Young Men's Christian Association of Montgomery*, 316 F. Supp 899 (1970).

*Smith v. Young Men's Christian Association of Montgomery*, 462 F.2d 634 (1972).

*State of Alabama v. Fannie Turner, et al.*, Montgomery County Probate Court, Case no. 6549, April 25, 1967.

*State of Alabama v. Fannie Turner, et al.*, Probate Court of Montgomery County, Alabama, unpublished opinion no. 6549 (April 25, 1967).

*State of Alabama v. Mrs. Beryl Palitz et al.*, Montgomery County Probate Court (August 23, 1968).

*State of Alabama v. Mrs. Beryl Palitz et al.*, Montgomery County Probate Court, October 21, 1970.

*State of Alabama v. Mrs. Beryl Palitz et al.*, Notice of Lis Pendens, June 18, 1968.

*Swan v. Charlotte-Mecklenburg Bd. of Educ.*, 402 U.S. 1 (1971).

*United States v. Montgomery County Board of Education*, 395 U.S. 225 (1969).

*United States v. Montgomery County Board of Education*, 429 F.2d 382 (1970).

US Civil Rights Act of 1964, P.L. 88-352 (1964).

US Economic Opportunity Act of 1964, P.L. 88-452 (1964).

US Fair Housing Act of 1968, P.L. 90-284 (1968).

US Federal-Aid Highway Act of 1956, P.L 84-627 (1956).

US Hospital Construction and Survey Act of 1946, 79-725 (1946).

US Housing Act of 1949, P.L. 171-81 (1949).

US Housing Act of 1956, P.L. 84-1020 (1956).

US Housing and Community Development Act of 1977, P.L. 95-128 (1977).

US Housing and Urban Development Act of 1965, P.L. 89-117 (1965).

US National Environmental Policy Act of 1970, P.L. 91-190 (1970).

US National Industrial Recovery Act, P.L. 73-67 (1933).

US Rivers and Harbors Act of 1945, P.L. 79-14 (1945).

US Voting Rights Act of 1965, P.L. 89-110 (1965).

*Vincent Leonard Smith et al. v. the Young Men's Christian Association of Montgomery*, 316 F. Supp 899 (1970).

*Vincent Leonard Smith et al. v. the Young Men's Christian Association of Montgomery*, 462 F.2d 634 (1972).

Wagner-Steagall Housing Act of 1934, P.L. 73-479 (1934).

## NEWSPAPERS AND MAGAZINES

*Alabama Citizen*

*Alabama Conservation*

*Alabama Council Bulletin*

*Alabama Forest News*

*Alabama Journal*

*Alabama Roadbuilder*

*Alabama Tribune*

*Anniston Star*

*Atlanta Journal-Constitution*

*Birmingham News*

*Birmingham Post-Herald*

*Centerville Press*

*Chicago Defender*

*Chilton County News*

*Daily Times-Democrat* (Cullman, Alabama)

*Decatur Daily*
*Dothan Eagle*
*Florence Herald*
*Florence Times*
*Hartford Courant*
*Huntsville Times*
*Los Angeles Times*
*Mobile Register*
*Montgomery Advertiser*
*Montgomery Examiner*
*Montgomery Independent*
*Montgomery Times*
*New York Amsterdam News*
*Philadelphia Inquirer*
*Prattville Progress*
*Selma Times-Journal*
*The Sign*
*South: The New Magazine of Dixie*
*Southern Courier*
*Southern Watchman*
*Talladega Daily Home*
*The Times: Montgomery ALA*
*The Wall Street Journal*

## BOOKS, ARTICLES, AND CHAPTERS

"1860 Census of Population and Housing." US Census, accessed February 14, 2022.

Abernathy, Ralph David. *And the Walls Came Tumbling Down*. New York: Harper and Row, Publishers, 1989.

Abrams, Charles. *The Future of Housing*. New York: Harper and Brothers, 1946.

Advisory Committee on City Planning and Zoning of the US Department of Commerce. *A Standard City Planning Enabling Act*. Washington, DC: US Department of Commerce, 1928.

Advisory Committee on Zoning. *A Standard State Zoning Enabling Act*. Washington, DC: US Department of Commerce, 1926.

Alabama Department of Education. "Education Report Card: 2018." Alabama State Department of Education, accessed May 21, 2019.

Allaire, Joseph. *Neighborhood Boundaries*. Planning Advisory Report No. 141 (Chicago, IL: American Society of Planning Officials, 1960).

American Public Health Association Committee on the Hygiene of Housing. *Planning the Neighborhood*. Chicago, IL: Public Administration Service, 1948.

Ammon, Francesca Russello. "Commemoration Amid Criticism: The Mixed Legacy of Urban Renewal in Southwest Washington, DC." *Journal of Planning History* 8, no. 3 (2009): 175–220.

Argersinger, Jo Ann E. *Toward a New Deal in Baltimore: People and Government in the Great Depression*. Chapel Hill: University of North Carolina Press, 1988.

Arnstein, Sherry. "A Ladder of Citizen Participation." *Journal of the American Institute of Planners* 35, no. 4 (1969): 216–24.

Ashmore, Susan Youngblood. *Carry It On: The War on Poverty and the Civil Rights Movement in Alabama: 1964–1972*. Athens: University of Georgia Press, 2008.

Ashmore, Susan Youngblood and Lisa Lindquist Dorr, eds. *Alabama Women: Their Lives and Times*. Athens: University of Georgia Press, 2017.

Avila, Eric. *The Folklore of the Freeway: Race and Revolt in the Modernist City*. Minneapolis: University of Minnesota Press, 2014.

Bagley, Joseph. *The Politics of White Rights: Race, Justice, and Integrating Alabama's Schools*. Athens: University of Georgia Press, 2018.

Balto, Simon. "White Rage, White Liberals and the Making of the Second Ghetto." *Journal of Urban History* 46, no. 3 (2020): 511–15.

Barske, Carolyn. "Civilian Conservation Corps in Alabama." Encyclopedia of Alabama, May 21, 2019, accessed October 25, 2022.

Bartholomew, Harland. "City Planning and Housing." *Planning and Civic Comment* 1, no. 2 (April–June 1935), 12–13.

———. "The Neighborhood—Key to Urban Redemption." American Planning and Civic Annual (1941), 243–47.

———. "Neighborhood Rehabilitation and the Taxpayer." *The American City* (February 1938), 57.

———. *"What Is Comprehensive Planning?" Planning Problems of Town, City, and Region, Papers and Discussions at the National Conference on City Planning*. Washington, DC: National Conference on City Planning, 1928.

Bass, Jack. *Taming the Storm*. New York: Doubleday, 1992.

Bauman, John Bauman. "Visions of a Post-War City." In *Introduction to Planning History in the United States*, edited by Don Krueckeberg, 170–89. New Brunswick, NJ: Center for Urban Policy Research, 1993.

Bayor, Ronald. *Race and the Shaping of Twentieth-Century Atlanta.* Chapel Hill: University of North Carolina Press, 1996.

———. "Roads to Racial Segregation: Atlanta in the Twentieth Century." *Journal of Urban History* 15, no. 1 (1988): 3–21.

Beauchamp, Walker Mason. "The Legacy of Racial Zoning in Birmingham, Alabama." *Cumberland Law Review* 48 (2017): 359–97.

Beauregard, Robert. *Voices of Decline: The Postwar Fate of US Cities, 2nd ed.* New York: Routledge, 2003.

Biles, Roger. "Expressways before the Interstates: The Case of Detroit, 1945–1956." *Journal of Urban History* 40, no. 5 (2014): 843–54.

———. *The South and the New Deal.* Lexington: University of Kentucky Press, 1994.

———. "The Urban South and the Great Depression" *Journal of Southern History* 56, no. 1 (1990): 71–100.

Biles, Roger and Mark Rose. *A Good Place to Do Business: Then Politics of Downtown Renewal Since 1945.* Philadelphia, PA: Temple University Press, 2022.

Biles, Roger, and Mark Rose. "At the Intersection of Race, Class, Gender, and Highway Politics." *Journal of Urban History* 46, no. 3 (2019): 677–84.

Blejwas, Emily. "Georgia Gilmore." Encyclopedia of Alabama, September 24, 2019, accessed April 6, 2021.

"Board of Commissioners Resolution, December 1958." *Race Relations Law Reporter* 4, no. 1 (Spring 1959): 206.

Boyer, Christine. *Dreaming the Rational City: The Myth of American City Planning.* Boston, MA: MIT Press, 1983.

Brown, Roger K. *An Organizational Report of the Montgomery, Alabama, Park and Recreation Department.* Montgomery, AL: Montgomery Parks and Recreation Department, August 1971.

Browning, John G. "Blazing the Trail: Alabama's First Black Lawyers." *Alabama Lawyer* 83, no. 1 (2022): 20–27.

Bullard, Robert D. *Dumping in Dixie: Race, Class and Environmental Quality.* San Francisco: Westview Press, 1990.

Burgess, Patricia. "Of Swimming Pools and 'Slums.'" In *Planning the Twentieth-Century American City*, edited by Mary Corbin Sies and Christopher Silver, 213–39. Baltimore, MA: Johns Hopkins University Press, 1996.

Burkhart, J. Austin. "Yonder Sits the Rocking-Chair," *The Crisis* 59, no. 10 (1952): 619–52.

Burks, Mary Fair. "Trailblazers: Women in the Montgomery Bus Boycott." In *Black Women in United States History*, edited by Darlene Clark Hine, 71–83. Brooklyn, NY: Carlson, 1990.

Byrne, Dara. *The Unfinished Agenda of the Selma-Montgomery Voting Rights March*. Hoboken, NJ: John Wiley and Sons Inc., 2005.

Byrne, Jason, and Jennifer Wolch. "Nature, Race, and Parks: Past Research and Future Directions for Geographic Research." *Progress in Human Geography* 33, no. 6 (2009): 743–65.

Callow, Alexander, Jr., ed. *American Urban History, 3rd ed.* New York: Oxford University Press, 1982.

Carroll, Fred. "The Racial Politics of Place: Jim Crow, the New Deal, and Suburban Housing on the Virginia Peninsula." *Journal of Urban History* 40, no. 3 (2014): 514–35.

Carver, Joseph. *From Maron to Montgomery*. Montgomery, AL: New South Books, 2020.

Cashin, Edward, and Glenn Eskew, eds. *Paternalism in a Southern City*. Athens: University of Georgia Press, 2001.

Catlin, Robert. *Racial Politics and Urban Planning: Gary, Indiana, 1980–1989*. Lexington: University Press of Kentucky, 1993.

Cavanaugh, Gordon. "Public Housing: From Archaic to Dynamic to Endangered." *Journal of Affordable Housing and Community Development Law* 14, no. 3 (2005): 228–47.

Chandler, Mittie Olion. "Public Housing Desegregation: What Are the Options?" *Housing Policy Debate* 3, no. 2: 509–33.

Chronopoulos, Themis. "Robert Moses and the Visual Dimension of Physical Disorder: Efforts to Demonstrate Urban Blight in the Age of Slum Clearance." *Journal of Planning History* 13, no. 3 (2014): 207–33.

Churchill, Henry. "Henry Wright." In *The American Planner: Biographies and Recollections, 2nd ed.*, edited by Don Krueckeberg, 243–64. New Brunswick: Center for Urban Policy Research, 1983.

———. "An Open Letter to Mr. Isaacs." *Journal of the American Institute of Planners* 13, no. 3 (1948): 40–42.

Claridy, Keith Robert. "Bring God to the Negro, Bring the Negro to God: Thomas Joseph Toolen, Archbishop of Mobile (1927–1969), His Culture, His Religion, and His Mission." Unpublished thesis, Auburn University, 2006.

Clark, Scott. "When 'Wait' Means 'Never': American Tolerance of Racial Injustice." *National Black Law Journal* 13, no. 1 (1993): 123–33.

Clawson, Marion. *New Deal Planning: The National Resources Planning Board*. Baltimore, MD: Resources for the Future, 1981.

Cobb, James. *Away Down South: A History of Southern Identity*. New York: Oxford University Press, 2005.

———. *The South and America Since World War II*. Oxford: Oxford University Press, 2011.

Coffman, Sister Mary Ruth. *Build Me a City: The Life of Father Harold Purcell*. Montgomery, AL: Pioneer Press, 1984.

Coleman, Amanda. "Rehabilitating the Region: The New Deal, Gender, and the Remaking of the South." *Southeastern Geographer* 50, no. 2 (2010): 200–217.

Combs, Barbara Harris. *From Selma to Montgomery*. New York: Routledge, 2013.

Congressional Research Service. *A Chronology of Housing Legislation and Selected Executive Actions, 1892–1992*. Washington, DC: US Government Printing Office, 1993.

Connerly, Charles. *The Most Segregated City in America: City Planning and Civil Rights in Birmingham, 1920–1980*. Charlottesville: University of Virginia Press, 2005.

———. "From Racial Zoning to Community Empowerment: The Interstate Highway System and the African American Community in Birmingham, Alabama." *Journal of Planning Education and Research* 22, no. 2 (2002): 99–114.

Connerly, Charles, and Bobby Wilson, "The Roots and Origins of African-American Planning in Birmingham, Alabama." In *Urban Planning and the African American Community: In the Shadows*, edited by June Manning Thomas, 201–19. New York: Sage, 1997.

Cook, Royrickers, and Ralph Foster. "Alabama Department of Commerce." Encyclopedia of Alabama, updated March 19, 2013, accessed October 3, 2022.

Coosa-Alabama River Improvement Association. "The Waterway Forward." Coosa-Alabama River Improvement Association, accessed December 6, 2021.

Cowie, Jefferson, and Nick Salvatore. "The Long-Exception: Rethinking the Place of the New Deal in American History." *International Labor and Working-Class History* 74, no. 1 (2008): 3–32.

Crawford, Vicki, Jacqueline Anne Rouse, and Barbara Woods, eds. *Women in the Civil Rights Movement: Trailblazers and Torchbearers, 1941–1965*. New York: Carson Publishing Inc., 1990.

Creek, Ashley. "Montgomery Catholic Mission Finally Celebrates Its Role in the Selma Marches." WBHM: News for the Heart of Alabama, March 22, 2015, accessed February 8, 2023.

Dees, Morris. *A Lawyer's Journey: The Morris Dees Story*. Chicago, IL: American Bar Association, 2001.

Delfino, Susanna, and Michele Gillespie, eds. *Global Perspectives on Industrial*

*Transformation in the American South*. Columbia: University of Missouri Press, 2005.

DeLuca, Stefanie, Philip Garboden, and Peter Rosenblatt. "Segregating Shelter: How Housing Policies Shape the Residential Locations of Low-Income Minority Families." *The Annals of the American Academy of Political and Social Science* 647 (2013): 268–99.

Dimento, Joseph, and Cliff Ellis. *Changing Lanes: Visions and Histories of Urban Freeways*. Cambridge, MA: MIT Press, 2014.

Dobbins, W. O., Jr. "Community Planning in North Alabama." *Public Administration Review* 4, no. 3 (1944): 220–25.

Dubofsky, Melvyn, and Stephen Burwood, eds. *The Great Depression and the New Deal*. New York: Garland Publishing Inc., 1990.

Durr, Virginia Foster. *Outside the Magic Circle*. Tuscaloosa: University of Alabama Press, 1985.

Eig, Jonathan. *King: A Life*. New York: Farrar, Strauss, and Grioux, 2023.

Eisenhower, President Dwight D. "Annual Message to the Congress on the State of the Union." Eisenhower Library, January 6, 1955, accessed December 6, 2021.

Equal Justice Initiative, "Slavery in America: The Montgomery Slave Trade" Equal Justice Initiative, accessed March 2, 2021.

Eskew, Glenn. *But for Birmingham: The Local and National Movements in the Civil Rights Struggle*. Chapel Hill: University of North Carolina Press, 1997.

———, ed. *Labor in the Modern South*. Athens: University of Georgia Press, 2001.

Fairbanks, Robert. "Planning, Public Works, and Politics: The Trinity River Reclamation Project in Dallas." In *Planning the Twentieth-Century American City*, edited by Mary Corbin Sies and Christopher Silver, 185–212. Baltimore, MD: Johns Hopkins University Press, 1996.

Faulkenbury, Evan. *Poll Power: The Voter Education Project and the Movement for the Ballot in the American South*. Chapel Hill: University of North Carolina Press, 2019.

Favors, Jelani M. *Shelter in a Time of Storm: How Black Colleges Fostered Generations of Leadership and Activism*. Chapel Hill: University of North Carolina Press, 2019.

Feldman, Glenn. "Southern Disillusionment with the Democratic Party: Cultural Conformity and 'The Great Melding' of Racial and Economic Conservatism in Alabama during World War II." *Journal of American Studies* 43, no. 2 (2009): 199–230.

Fields, Uriah J. *The Montgomery Story: The Unhappy Effects of the Montgomery Bus Boycott*. New York: Exposition Press, 1959.

Finley, Keith. *Delaying the Dream: Southern Senators and the Fight Against Civil Rights 1938–1965*. Baton Rouge: Louisiana State University Press, 2008.

Fishman, Robert, ed. *The American Planning Tradition: Culture and Policy*. Washington, DC: Woodrow Wilson Center Press, 2000.

Flynt, Wayne. *Alabama in the Twentieth Century*. Tuscaloosa: University of Alabama Press, 2004.

Freund, David. *Colored Property: State Policy and White Racial Politics in Suburban America*. Chicago, IL: University of Chicago Press, 2007.

Gafton, Carl, and Anne Permaloff. *Big Mules and Branchheads: James E. Folsom and Political Power in Alabama*. Athens: University of Georgia Press, 1985.

Gans, Herbert. *People and Plans: Essays on Urban Problems and Solutions*. New York: Basic Books, 1968.

———. *The Levittowners*. New York: Columbia University Press, 2017.

———. *The Urban Villagers*. New York: Macmillan Co. Inc., 1982.

———. *The War against the Poor: The Underclass and Antipoverty Policy*. New York: Basic Books, 1996.

Garrow, David. *The Walking City: The Montgomery Bus Boycott*. Brooklyn, NY: Carlton, 1989.

Gelfand, Mark. *A Nation of Cities: The Federal Government and Urban America, 1933–1965*. New York: Oxford University Press, 1975.

"Georgia Theresa Gilmore v. City of Montgomery." *Race Relations Law Reporter* 4, no. 2 (Spring 1959): 977–88.

"Georgia Theresa Gilmore v. City of Montgomery." *Race Relations Law Reporter* 5, no. 2 (Summer 1960): 455–59.

Gilmore, Glenda Elizabeth. *Defying Dixie: The Radical Roots of Civil Rights*. New York: W. W. Norton and Company, 2008.

Goetz, Edward. *Fair Housing and the Pursuit of Racial Justice in American Cities*. Ithaca, NY: Cornell University Press, 2018.

———. *New Deal Ruins: Race, Economic Justice, and Public Housing Policy*. Ithaca, NY: Cornell University Press, 2013.

———. *The One-Way Street of Integration*. Ithaca, NY: Cornell University Press, 2018.

Goetz, Edward, Rashad A. Williams, and Anthony Damiano. "Whiteness and Urban Planning." *Journal of the American Planning Association* 86, no. 2 (2020): 142–56.

Goldfield, David. *Black, White, and Southern: Race Relations and Southern Culture 1940 to the Present*. Baton Rouge: Louisiana State University Press, 1990.

Golub, Mark. "Remembering Massive Resistance to School Desegregation." *Law and History Review* 31, no. 3 (2013): 491–530.

Gotham, Kevin Fox. "Racialization and the State: The Housing Act of 1934 and the Creation of the Federal Housing Administration." *Sociological Perspectives* 43, no. 2 (2000): 291–317.

Grant, Jill, Pierre Filion, and Scott Low. "Path Dependencies Affecting Suburban Density, Mix, and Diversity in Halifax." *The Canadian Geographer* 63, no. 2 (2018): 240–53.

Gratz, Robert. *A White Preacher's Message on Race and Reconciliation*. Montgomery, AL: New South Books, 2006.

Grant, Twala. "The Missed Mandate of *Brown v. Board of Education*: Educationally Effective Schools with All Deliberate Speed." *National Black Law Journal* 13, no. 1 (1993): 134–46.

Gray, Fred. *Bus Ride to Justice*. Montgomery, AL: The Black Belt Press, 1995.

———. "The Making of a Lawyer." In *Voices of Civil Rights Lawyers*, edited by Kent Springs, 9–16. Tallahassee University Press of Florida, 2017.

Gray, Fred, Willy Leventhal, Frank Sikora, and J. Mills Thornton III. *The Children Coming On . . . A Retrospective of the Montgomery Bus Boycott*. Montgomery, AL: Black Belt Press, 2007.

Haar, Charles, and Jerald Kayden, eds. *Zoning and the American Dream: Promises Still to Keep*. Washington, DC: Planners Press, 1989.

Hall, Peter. *Cities of Tomorrow: An Intellectual History of Urban Planning and Design since 1880, 4th ed.* Hoboken, NJ: Wiley-Blackwell, 2014.

Hamilton, Charles V. *The Bench and the Ballot*. New York: Oxford University Press, 1973.

Hamilton, Virginia Van der Veer. *Lister Hill: Statesman from the South*. Chapel Hill: University of North Carolina Press, 1987.

Hanchett, Thomas. *Sorting Out the New South City: Race, Class, and Urban Development in Charlotte, 1875–1975*. Chapel Hill: University of North Carolina Press, 1998.

Hartman, Chester Hartman. "The Housing of Relocated Families." *Journal of the American Institute of Planners*, 30, no. 4 (1964) 266–86.

Harvey, Gordon. *A Question of Justice, New South Governors and Education, 1968–1976*. Tuscaloosa: University of Alabama Press, 2002.

Healy, Thomas. *Soul City: Race, Equality and the Lost Dream of an American Utopia*. New York: Metropolitan Books, 2021.

Heathcott, Joseph. "The City Quietly Remade: National Programs and Local Agendas in the Movement to Clear Slums, 1942–1952." *Journal of Urban History* 34, no. 2 (2008): 221–42.

Heil, Melissa, Lou Turner, and David Wilson. "People of Color: Confronting White Supremacy in Planning." In *Alternative Planning History and Theory*, edited by Dorina Pojani, 125–44. New York: Routledge, 2023.

Helgeson, Jeffrey. "The State of Blame in American Cities: Race, Wealth, and the Politics of Housing." *Journal of Urban History* 37, no. 6 (2011): 992–99.

Herrick, Charles. "Activities and Comment the Neighborhood Theory an Answer to Mr. Isaacs." *Journal of the American Institute of Planners* 14, no. 3 (1948): 38–40.

Hillier, Amy E. "Residential Security Maps and Neighborhood Appraisals: The Home Owners' Loan Corporation and the Case of Philadelphia." *Social Science History* 29, vol. 2 (2005): 207–33.

Hirsch, Arnold. *Making the Second Ghetto: Race and Housing in Chicago, 1940–1960*. New York: Cambridge University Press, 1983.

———. "Simply a Matter of Black and White: The Transformation of Race and Politics in Twentieth-Century New Orleans." In *Creole New Orleans: Race and Americanization* edited by Arnold Hirsch and Joseph Logsdon, 262–319. Baton Rouge: Louisiana State University Press, 1992.

———. "'Containment' on the Home Front: Race and Federal Housing Policy from the New Deal to the Cold War." *Journal of Urban History* 26, no. 2 (2000): 158–89.

———. "Searching for a 'Sound Negro Policy': A Racial Agenda for the Housing Acts of 1949 and 1954." *Housing Policy Debate* 11, no. 2 (2000): 393–411.

Hirsch, Arnold, and Joseph Logsdon, eds. *Creole New Orleans: Race and Americanization*. Baton Rouge: Louisiana State University Press, 1992.

Hirsch, Arnold, and Raymond Mohl, eds. *Urban Policy in Twentieth-Century America*. New Brunswick, NJ: Rutgers University Press, 1993.

"History of MHA." Montgomery Housing Authority, accessed October 5, 2020.

Hohle, Randolph. "The Color of Neoliberalism: The 'Modern Southern Businessman' and Postwar Alabama's Challenge to Racial Segregation." *Sociological Forum* 27, no. 1 (March 2012): 142–62.

Howard, Gene. *Patterson for Alabama: The Life and Career of John Patterson*. Tuscaloosa: University of Alabama Press, 2008.

Hunt, D. Bradford. "Was the 1937 Housing Act a Pyrrhic Victory?" *Journal of Planning History* 4, no. 3 (2005): 195–221.

Isaacs, Reginald. "The 'Neighborhood Unit' Is an Instrument for Segregation." *Journal of Housing* 5, no. 8 (1948): 215–19, 215.

———. "Are Urban Neighborhoods Possible?" *Journal of Housing* 5, no. 7 (1948): 177–80.

Jackson, Kenneth. *Crabgrass Frontier: The Suburbanization of the United States.* New York: Oxford University Press, 1985.

———. "Federal Subsidy and the Suburban Dream: The First Quarter-Century of Government Involvement in the Housing Market." *Columbia Historical Society Records* 50 (1980): 421–51.

———. "Race, Ethnicity, and Real Estate Appraisal: The Home Owners Loan Corporation and the Federal Housing Administration." *Journal of Urban History* 6, no. 4 (1980): 419–52.

Jeffries, Hasan Kwame. *Bloody Lowndes: Civil Rights and Black Power in Alabama's Black Belt.* New York: New York University Press, 2009.

Jones, Lewis W. "Desegregation of Public Education in Alabama" *Journal of Negro Education* 24, no. 3 (1955): 165–71.

———. "Two Years of Desegregation in Alabama." *Journal of Negro Education* 25, no. 3 (1956): 205–11.

Kangas, Larry Edward. "Historical Picture of Maxwell AFB" *Report No. 86-1340.* Montgomery, AL: Air Command and Staff College Air University, 1986.

Karnes, Thomas. *Asphalt and Politics: A History of the American Highway System.* Jefferson, NC: McFarland, 2009.

Kay, Jane Holtz. *Asphalt Nation: How the Automobile Took Over America and How We Can Take It Back.* Oakland: University of California Press, 1998.

Kaufman, Ned. *Place, Race, Story: Essays on the Past and Future of Historic Preservation.* New York: Routledge, 2009.

Kennedy, Robert Francis, Jr. *Judge Frank M. Johnson Jr.: A Biography.* New York: G. P. Putman's Sons, 1978.

King, Rev. Martin Luther, Jr. *Letter from Birmingham Jail.* August 1963.

Knack, Ruth, Stuart Meck, and Isreal Stollman. "The Real Story Behind the Standard Planning and Zoning Enabling Acts of the 1920s." *Land Use Law and Zoning Digest* 48, no. 2 (1996): 3–9.

Kotval, Zenia. "Opportunity Lost: A Clash between Politics, Planning, and Design in Defense Housing for Pittsfield, Massachusetts." *Journal of Planning History* 2, no. 1 (2003): 25–46.

Kruse, Kevin. *White Flight: Atlanta and the Making of Modern Conservatism.* Princeton, NJ: Princeton University Press, 2005.

Kruse Kevin and Thomas Sugrue, eds., *The New Suburban History.* Chicago: University of Chicago Press, 2006.

Landrum, Ney C. *The State Park Movement in America.* Columbia: University of Missouri Press, 2004.

Leavitt, Helen. *Superhighway—Superhoax.* Garden City, NY: Doubleday and Company Inc., 1970.

LeFloura, Talitha. *Chained in Silence: Black Women and Convict Labor in the New South.* Chapel Hill: University of North Carolina Press, 2015.

Levy, Peter. *The Civil Rights Movement.* Westport, CT: Greenwood Press, 1998.

Light, Jennifer. "The City as Natural Resource: New Deal Conservation and the Quest for Urban Improvement." *Journal of Urban History* 35, no. 4 (2009): 531–60.

Lindblom, Charles. "The Science of 'Muddling Through.'" *Public Administration Review* 19, no. 2 (1959): 79–88.

Loewen, James. *Sundown Towns: A Hidden Dimension of American Racism.* New York: The New Press, 2005.

Lowe, Jamie. "Bryan Stevenson Wants the US to Face Its History," *New York Times Magazine,* January 16, 2019, accessed October 11, 2023.

Lutz, Catherine. *Carjacked: The Culture of the Automobile and Its Effect on Our Lives.* New York: St. Martin's Press, 2010.

Lynch, Emily, Lorraine Halinka Malcoe, Sarah E. Laurent, Jason Richardson, Bruce C. Mitchell, and Helen C. S. Meier. "The Legacy of Structural Racism: Associations between Historic Redlining, Current Mortgage Lending, and Health." *SSM—Population Health* vol. 14 (2021), 1–10.

MacDonald, Heather. "City Planning and the US Census: 1910–1960." *Journal of Planning History* 7, no. 4 (2008): 263–94.

Manza, Jeff. "Political Sociological Models of the US New Deal." *Annual Review of Sociology* 26, no. 1 (2000): 297–322.

Martin, David. "The Birth of Jim Crow in Alabama, 1865–1896." *National Black Law Journal* 13, no. 1 (1993): 184–97.

McGhee, Felicia. "The Montgomery Bus Boycott and the Fall of the Montgomery City Lines." *Alabama Review* 68, no. 3 (2015): 251–68.

McGreevy, John. *Catholicism and American Freedom: A History.* New York: W. W. Norton and Company, 2004.

McGuire, Danielle. *At the Dark End of the Street: Black Women, Rape, and Resistance: A New History of the Civil Rights Movement from Rosa Parks to the Rise of Black Power.* New York: Doubleday Publishing Group, 2010.

McKay, Robert. "Segregation and Public Recreation," *Virginia Law Review* 40, no. 6 (1954): 697–731.

McMillen, Neil R. *The Citizens' Council: Organized Resistance to the Second Reconstruction, 1954–64*. Chicago: University of Illinois Press, 1971.

McPhail, Carol. "Meet the Catholic Parish that Dared Take in Civil Rights Marchers 50 Years Ago." Al.com, March 25, 2015, accessed April 5, 2023.

Meck, Stuart, ed. *Growing Smart Legislative Guidebook: Model Statutes for Planning and the Management of Change*. Chicago: American Planning Association, 2002.

Meck, Stuart, and Rebecca Retzlaff. "President Jimmy Carter's Urban Policy: A Reconstruction and an Appraisal." *Journal of Planning History* 11, no. 3 (2012): 242–80.

Meyer, Stephen Grant. *As Long as They Don't Move Next Door: Segregation and Racial Conflict in American Neighborhoods*. New York: Rowman and Littlefield, 2000.

Michney, Todd. "How the City Survey's Redlining Maps Were Made: A Closer Look at HOLC's Mortgage Rehabilitation Division." *Journal of Planning History* 21, vol. 4 (2021): 316–44.

Michney, Todd, and LaDale Winling. "New Perspectives on New Deal Housing Policy: Explaining and Mapping HOLC Loans to African Americans." *Journal of Urban History* 46, no. 1 (2020): 150–80.

Millner, Steven. "Interview with E. D. Nixon." In *Martin Luther King, Jr. and the Civil Rights Movement*, edited by David J. Garrow, 545–51. New York Carlson Publishing Inc., 1989.

———. "Interview with Erna Dungee Allen, August 6, 1977." In *Martin Luther King, Jr. and the Civil Rights Movement*, edited by David Garrow, 521–25. New York: Carlson Publishing Inc., 1989.

———. "Interview with Johnnie Carr, July 17, 1977." In *Martin Luther King, Jr., and the Civil Rights Movement*, edited by David Garrow, 527–32. New York: Carlson Publishing Series, 1989.

———. "Interview with Rufus Lewis, July 18, 1977." In *Martin Luther King, Jr. and the Civil Rights Movement*, edited by David Garrow, 536–43. New York: Carlson Publishing, Inc.

Mineo, Liz. "The Need to Talk about Race." *The Harvard Gazette*, December 7, 2017, accessed October 11, 2023.

"Mob Wins Again in Alabama." *Southern Christian Leadership Conference Newsletter* 1, no. 3 (September 1961).

Mohl, Raymond. "Citizen Activism and Freeway Revolts in Memphis and Nashville: The Road to Litigation." *Journal of Urban History* 40, no. 5 (2014), 870–93.

———. "The Interstates and the Cities: Highways, Housing, and the Freeway Revolt." Poverty and Race Research Action Council, 2002.

———. "Making the Second Ghetto in Metropolitan Miami, 1940–1960." In *The New African American Urban History*, edited by Kenneth Goings and Raymond Mohl, 266–89. Thousand Oaks, CA: Sage Publications, 1996.

———. "Race and Housing in the Postwar City: An Explosive History." *Journal of the Illinois State Historical Society* 94, no. 1 (2001): 8–30.

———. "Trouble in Paradise: Race and Housing in Miami during the New Deal Era." In *The Making of Urban America*, edited by Raymond Mohl, 214–27. Wilmington, DE: SR Books, 1988.

———. "Whitening Miami: Race, Housing, and Government Policy in Twentieth-Century Dade County." *Florida Historical Quarterly* 79 no. 3 (2001): 319–45.

Mohl, Raymond, Robert Fisher, Carl Abbott, Roger Lotchin, Robert Fairbanks, and Zane Miller. *Essays on Sunbelt Cities and Recent Urban America*. College Station: Texas A&M University Press, 1990.

Mokina, Natalia. *Fit to Be Citizens? Public Health and Race in Los Angeles, 1879–1939*. Los Angeles: University of California Press, 2006.

Moon, Henry. *The Interstate Highway System*. Washington, DC: Association of American Geographers, 1994.

Moore, Andrew. "Practicing What We Preach: White Catholics and the Civil Rights Movement in Atlanta." *Georgia Historical Quarterly* 89, no. 3 (2005): 334–67.

———. *The South's Tolerable Alien*. Baton Rouge: Louisiana State University Press, 2007.

Morris, Aldon, Walter Allan, David Maurrasse, and Derrick Gilbert. "White Supremacy and Higher Education: The Alabama Higher Education Desegregation Case." *National Black Law Journal* 14, no. 1 (1994): 59–91.

Morris, Vivian Gunn, and Curtis L. Morris. *The Price They Paid*. New York: Teachers College Press, 2002.

Motley, Eric. *Madison Park: A Place of Hope*. Grand Rapids, MI: Zondervan and Harper Collins Publishers, 2017.

Moynihan, Daniel P. "Toward a National Urban Policy." *Public Interest* 17 (Fall 1969): 3–20.

Neumann, Tracy. *Remaking the Rust Belt: The Postindustrial Transformation of North America*. Philadelphia: University of Pennsylvania Press, 2016.

Newman, Mark. *Desegregating Dixie*. Jackson: University of Mississippi Press, 2008.

———. "Desegregation in the Catholic Diocese of Richmond, 1945–1973." *Virginia Magazine of History and Biography* 117, no. 4 (2009), 356–71.

Norrell, Robert. *The House I Live In: Race in the American Century*. New York: Oxford University Press, 2005.

O'Brien, William. "The Strange Career of a Florida State Park: Uncovering a Jim Crow Past." *Historical Geography* 35 (2007): 160–84.

O'Brien William E. *Landscapes of Exclusion*. Amherst: University of Massachusetts Press, 2016.

Ouster, Fulton. "The Beggar of St. Jude," *Reader's Digest*, October 1946, 47–51.

Parks, Gregory. "Belford Vance Lawson, Jr.: Life of a Civil Rights Litigator." *University of Maryland Law Journal of Race, Religion, Gender and Class* 12, no. 320 (2012): 103–37.

Pasquill, Robert. *The Civilian Conservation Corps in Alabama, 1933–1942: A Great and Lasting Good*. Tuscaloosa: University of Alabama Press, 2008.

Patricios, Nicholas N. "The Neighborhood Concept: A Retrospective of Physical Design and Social Interaction." *Journal of Architectural and Planning Research*, 19, no. 1 (2002): 70–90.

Pearlstein, Daniel. "Sweeping Six Percent Philanthropy Away: The New Deal in Sunnyside Gardens." *Journal of Planning History* 9, no. 3 (2010): 170–82.

Permaloff, Anne, and Carl Grafton. *Political Power in Alabama: The More Things Change . . .* Athens: University of Georgia Press, 1995.

Peterson, Jon. *The Birth of City Planning in the United States, 1840–1917*. Baltimore, MD: Johns Hopkins University Press, 2003.

———. "The City Beautiful Movement: Forgotten Origins and Lost Meanings." *Journal of Urban History* 2, no. 4 (1976): 415–34.

Peterson, Sarah Jo. *The Transportation Research Board: Everyone Interested Is Invited*. Washington, DC: National Academies Press, 2020.

Phelts, Marsha Dean. *An American Beach for African Americans*. Gainesville: University Press of Florida, 1997.

Pierson, Sharon Gay. *Laboratory of Learning: HBCU Laboratory Schools and Alabama State College Lab High in the Era of Jim Crow*. Lausanne, Switzerland: Peter Lang Inc., 2013.

"Postwar Plans." *Alabama: The New Magazine of the Deep South*, December 3, 1943.

Pratt, Robert. *Selma's Bloody Sunday*. Baltimore, MD: Johns Hopkins University Press, 2017.

Price, Margaret. *The Negro and the Ballot in the South*. Atlanta, GA: Southern Regional Council, 1959.

Pride, Richard. *The Political Use of Racial Narratives: Desegregation in Mobile, Alabama, 1954–1997*. Chicago: University of Illinois Press, 2002.

Pritchett, Wendell. "Which Urban Crisis? Regionalism, Race, and Urban Policy, 1960–1974." *Journal of Urban History* 34, no. 2 (2008): 266–86.

"Public Housing Timeline, 1933–1993." *Journal of the American Planning Association* 78, no. 4 (2012): 359.

Radford, Gail. *Modern Housing for America: Policy Struggles in the New Deal Era*. Chicago, IL: University of Chicago Press, 1996.

Rauch, J. H. *Public Parks: Their Effects upon the Moral, Physical, and Sanitary Condition of the Inhabitants of Large Cities, with Special Reference to the City of Chicago*. Chicago, IL: S. C. Griggs, 1869.

"Rectory to Be Built as City of St. Jude, Montgomery." Catholic Week, July 25, 1953.

Reft, Ryan, Amanda K. Philips De Lucas, and Rebecca C Retzlaff, eds. *Justice and the Interstates: The Racist Truth About Urban Highways*. Washington, DC: Island Press, 2023.

Ress, Thomas. "State Parks of Alabama." Encyclopedia of Alabama, February 28, 2019, accessed April 6, 2021.

Retzlaff, Rebecca. "Catholics v. the Interstates: The Fight to Protect Catholic Institutions from Interstate Highways in Birmingham, Alabama." *Journal of Transport History* 41, no. 3 (2020): 402–33.

———. "Connecting Public School Segregation with Urban Renewal and Interstate Highway Planning: The Case of Birmingham, Alabama." *Journal of Planning History* 19, no. 4 (2020): 256–80.

———. "Desegregation of City Parks and the Civil Rights Movement: The Case of Oak Park in Montgomery, Alabama." *Journal of Urban History* 47, no. 4 (2019).

Riser, R. Volney. *Defying Disfranchisement: Black Voting Rights Activism in the Jim Crow South, 1890–1910*. Baton Rouge: Louisiana State University Press, 2010.

"Riverside Heights, Montgomery County." The historical marker database, accessed August 14, 2020.

Roberts, Charles. "New Deal Community-Building in the South: The Subsidence Homesteads around Birmingham, Alabama." *The Alabama Review* 66, no. 2 (2013): 83–121.

Robinson, Jo Ann. *The Montgomery Bus Boycott and the Woman Who Started It*. Knoxville: University of Tennessee Press, 1987.

Robnett, Belinda. *How Long? How Long?* New York: Oxford University Press, 1997.

Rockwell, Landon G. "The Planning Function of the National Resources Planning Board." *Journal of Politics* 7, no. 2 (1945): 169–78.

Rodriguez, Joseph. *City Against Suburb: The Culture Wars in an American Metropolis*. Westport, CT: Praeger, 1999.

Rolph, Stephanie. *Resisting Equality: The Citizens' Council, 1954–1989*. Baton Rouge: Louisiana State University Press, 2018.

Rose, Harold. "The All-Negro Town: Its Evolution and Function." *Geographical Review* 55, no. 3 (1965): 362–81.

———. *Black Suburbanization: Access to Improved Quality of Life or Maintenance of the Status Quo?* Cambridge, MA: Ballinger Publishing Company, 1976.

Rose, Mark, and Roger Biles. "Arthur Rubloff and the Grinding Politics of Renewal in Chicago, 1947–1986." *Journal of Urban History* 46, no. 6 (2019): 1341–367.

———. *Interstate: Express Highway Politics, 1941–1956*. Lawrence: Regents Press of Kansas, 1979.

———. "Reframing American Highway Politics, 1956–1995." *Journal of Planning History* 2, no. 3 (2003): 212–36.

Rose, Mark, and Raymond Mohl. *Interstate: Highway Politics and Policy Since 1939, 3rd ed*. Knoxville: University of Tennessee Press, 2012.

Roth, Matthew. "Whittier Boulevard, Sixth Street Bridge, and the Origins of Transportation Exploitation in East Los Angeles." *Journal of Urban History* 30, no. 5 (2004): 729–48.

Rothstein, Richard. *The Color of Law*. New York: Liveright Publishing Corporation, 2017.

Sadler, Richard Casey. "Racist Housing Practices as a Precursor to Uneven Neighborhood Change in a Post-Industrial City." *Housing Studies* 32, no. 2 (2016): 186–208.

Salkin, Patricia. "Environmental Justice and Land Use Planning and Zoning." *Real Estate Law Journal* 31 (2003): 429–48.

Scales, Mausiki. *"Interview with Ernest A. Grant" behind the Veil: Documenting African American Life in the Jim Crow South*. Charlotte: Duke University Center for Documentary Studies, 2005.

Scribner, Christopher MacGregor. *Renewing Birmingham*. Athens: University of Georgia Press, 2002.

Seay, Solomon, Jr. *Jim Crow and Me: Stories of My Life as a Civil Rights Lawyer*. Montgomery, AL: New South Books, 2008.

Seely, Bruce. *Building the American Highway System: Engineers as Policy Makers*. Philadelphia, PA: Temple University Press, 1987.

Seligman, Amanda. *Block by Block: Neighborhoods and Public Policy on Chicago's West Side*. Chicago, IL: University of Chicago Press, 2005.

Sellers, James. *Slavery in Alabama*. Tuscaloosa: University of Alabama Press, 1950.

Seslowsky, Emma. "Bryan Stevenson Says 'Slavery Didn't End in 1865, It Just Evolved.'" CNN Politics, The Axe Files, December 7, 2018, accessed April 5, 2023.

Shugart, William. "The New Deal and Modern Memory." *Southern Economic Journal* 77, no. 3 (2011): 515–42.

Sies, Mary Corbin, and Christopher Silver, eds. *Planning the Twentieth-Century American City*. Baltimore, MA: Johns Hopkins University Press, 1996.

Silver, Christopher. "The Racial Origins of Zoning: Southern Cities from 1910–40." *Planning Perspectives* 6, No. 2 (1991): 189–205.

———. *Twentieth-Century Richmond: Planning, Politics, and Race*. Knoxville: University of Tennessee Press, 1984.

Simms, Angela. "The 'Veil' of Racial Segregation in the 21st Century: The Suburban Black Middle Class, Public Schools, and Pursuit of Racial Equality." *Phylon* 56, no. 1 (2019): 81–110.

Skopol, Theda. *Housing Soldiers and Mothers: The Political Origins of Social Policy in the United States*. Cambridge, MA: Belknap Press, 1995.

Smith, Douglas. *The New Deal in the Urban South*. Baton Rouge: Louisiana State University Press, 1988.

Spriggs, Kent, ed. *Voices of Civil Rights Lawyers: Reflections from the Deep South, 1964–1980*. Gainesville: University Press of Florida, 2017.

Stanton, Mary. *Journey toward Justice: Juliette Hampton Morgan and the Montgomery Bus Boycott*. Athens: University of Georgia Press, 2006.

"State Parks," *National Municipal Review Supplement* (November 1921): 583–600.

Stevenson, Bryan. *Just Mercy: A Story of Justice and Redemption*. Washington, DC: Spigel and Grau, 2014.

Stillman, Seymour. "Neighborhood Unit Planning: A Useful Method for City Planning." *Journal of the American Institute of Planners* 14, no. 3 (1948): 42–43.

Strong, Donald. *Negroes, Ballots and Judges*. Tuscaloosa: University of Alabama Press, 1968.

Sugrue, Thomas. *The Origins of the Urban Crisis*. Princeton, NJ: Princeton University Press, 1996.

Sullivan, Patricia, ed. *Freedom Writer: Virginia Foster Durr, Letters from the Civil Rights Years*. New York: Routledge, 2003.

Swope, C. B., D. Hernández, L. J. Cushing. "The Relationship of Historical Redlining with Present-Day Neighborhood Environmental and Health Outcomes: A Scoping Review and Conceptual Model." *Journal of Urban Health* 99 (2022): 959–83.

Sze, Julie. *Noxious New York: The Racial Politics of Urban Health an Environmental Justice.* Cambridge, MA: MIT Press, 2007.

Szylvian, Kristin. *The Mutual Housing Experiment.* Philadelphia, PA: Temple University Press, 2015.

Tach, Laura, and Allison Dwyer Emory. "Public Housing Redevelopment, Neighborhood Change, and the Restructuring of Urban Inequality." *American Journal of Sociology* 123, no. 3 (2017): 686–739.

Taeuber, Karl, and Alma Taeuber. *Residential Segregation and Neighborhood Change.* New York: Routledge, 2009.

Talen, Emily. "Zoning and Diversity in Historical Perspective." *Journal of Planning History* 11, vol. 4 (2012): 330–47.

Taper, Bernard. *Gomillion versus Lightfoot: The Tuskegee Gerrymander Case.* New York: McGraw-Hill Book Company, Inc., 1960.

Taylor, Nigel. *Urban Planning Theory since 1945.* London: Sage, 1998.

Teaford, Jon. "Urban Renewal and Its Aftermath." *Housing Policy Debate* 11, no. 2 (2000): 443–65.

Theoharis, Jeanne. *The Rebellious Life of Mrs. Rosa Parks.* Boston, MA: Beacon Press, 2013.

Thompson, B. S., ed. *A Century of Progress in Montgomery City and County.* Montgomery, AL: Steering Committee of the Centennial Celebration, 1963.

Thornton, J. Mills, III. *Archipelagoes of My South: Episodes in the Shaping of a Region, 1830–1965.* Tuscaloosa: University of Alabama Press, 2016.

———. *Dividing Lines: Municipal Politics and the Struggle for Civil Rights in Montgomery, Birmingham, and Selma.* Tuscaloosa: University of Alabama Press, 2002.

Trest, Warren. *Nobody but the People: The Life and Times of Alabama's Youngest Governor.* Montgomery, AL: New South Books, 2008.

Triece, Mary E. *Urban Renewal and Resistance: Race, Space, and the City in the Late to Early Twenty-First Century.* Lanham, MD: Lexington Books, 2016.

Urbanism Committee, National Resources Committee. *Our Cities: Their Role in the National Economy.* Washington, DC: US Government Printing Office, 1973.

Uschan, Michael. *The March from Selma to Montgomery.* San Diego, CA: Lucent Books, 2011.

Vale, Lawrence. "The Future of Planned Poverty: Redeveloping America's Most Distressed Public Housing Projects." *Netherlands Journal of Housing and the Built Environment* 14, no. 1 (1999): 13–31.

———. *Purging the Poorest: Public Housing and the Design Politics of*

*Twice-Cleared Communities*. Chicago, IL: University of Chicago Press, 2013.

von Hoffman, Alexander. "The End of the Dream: The Political Struggle of America's Public Housers" *Journal of Planning History* 4, no. 3 (2005): 222–53.

———. "Housing and Planning: A Century of Social Reform and Local Power" *Journal of the American Planning Association* 75, no. 2 (2009): 231–44.

———. "A Study in Contradictions: The Origins and Legacy of the Housing Act of 1949" *Housing Policy Debate 11*, no. 2 (2000): 299–326.

Walt Harrington. "A Person Who Wanted to be Free." *Washington Post*, October 8, 1995, accessed April 15, 2021.

Ward, Stephen. *Planning the Twentieth-Century City*. New York: John Wiley and Sons Inc., 2002.

Wehrly, Max. "Activities and Comment: Comment on the Neighborhood Theory." *Journal of the American Institute of Planners* 14, no. 3 (1948): 32–34.

Weingroff, Richard. "Federal-Aid Highway Act of 1956: Creating the Interstate System." *Federal Highway Administration* 60, no. 1 (1996): 10.

———. "From 1916 to 1939: The Federal-State Partnership at Work." *Federal Highway Administration* 60, no.1 (1996): 7.

Westhauser, Karl E., Elaine M. Smith, and Jennifer A. Fremlin, eds. *Creating Community Life and Learning at Montgomery's Black University*. Tuscaloosa: University of Alabama Press, 2005.

Wiese, Andrew. "Places of Our Own: Suburban Black Towns before 1960." *Journal of Urban History* 19, no. 3 (1933): 30–54.

Williams, Norman, Jr., and John M. Taylor. *American Land Planning Law, 2009 ed*. Washington, DC: Thomson-West, 2009.

Wilson, Barbara Brown. "Before the 'Triple Bottom Line': New Deal Defense Housing as Proto-Sustainability." *Journal of Planning History* 14, no. 1 (2014): 4–18.

Wilson, Benjamin. "It's Not Just Zoning: Environmental Justice and Land Use." *Urban Lawyer* 49, no. 4 (2017), 717–26.

Wilson, Bobby. *America's Johannesburg: Industrialization and Racial Transformation in Birmingham*. New York: Rowman and Littlefield Publishers Inc., 2000.

———. *Race and Place in Birmingham: The Civil Rights and Neighborhood Movements*. New York: Rowman and Littlefield Publishers Inc., 2000.

Wolcott, Victoria. *Race, Riots, and Roller Coasters: The Struggle Over Segregated Recreation in America*. Philadelphia: University of Pennsylvania Press, 2012.

Wolfinger, James. "The Limits of Black Activism: Philadelphia's Public Housing in the Depression and World War II." *Journal of Urban History* 35 no. 6 (2009): 787–814.

Woodlief, Anthony. "The Path-Dependent City." *Urban Affairs Review* 33, no. 3 (1998): 405–37.

Woodson, Carter Godwin. *The Rural Negro*. New York: Russel and Russel, 1969.

Wrigley, Robert. "The Plan of Chicago: Its Fiftieth Anniversary." *Journal of the American Institute of Planners* 26, vol. 1 (1960): 31–38.

Yarbough, Tinsley E. *Judge Frank Johnson and Human Rights in Alabama*. Tuscaloosa: University of Alabama Press, 1981.

Zarembka, Arlene. *The Urban Housing Crisis: Social, Economic, and Legal Issues and Proposals*. New York: Greenwood Press, 1990.

# Index

*Page numbers in italics refer to figures.*